FAMILIES IN WAR

FAMILIES IN WAR AND PEACE

Chile from Colony to Nation

Sarah C. Chambers Duke University Press Durham and London 2015

Typeset in Quadraat

by Westchester Publishing Services

Library of Congress Cataloging-
in-Publication Data

Chambers, Sarah C., 1963–

Families in war and peace : Chile from colony
to nation / Sarah C. Chambers.

pages cm

Includes bibliographical references and index.

ISBN 978-0-8223-5898-5 (hardcover :
alk. paper)

ISBN 978-0-8223-5883-1 (pbk. : alk. paper)

ISBN 978-0-8223-7556-2 (e-book)

1. Families—Chile—History—18th century.
2. Chile—History—18th century. 3. Chile—
Social conditions—18th century.
4. Families—Political aspects—Chile—18th
century. I. Title.

HQ595.C436 2015

306.850983—dc23

2014043466

Cover credit: (*top row, left to right*) José Gregorio Argomedo; Bernardo O'Higgins; (*second
row*) Agustín de Eyzaguirre; Javiera Carrera;
José Miguel Carrera; (*third row*) Ana María
Cotapos; Juan Egaña; Juan José Carrera;
(*bottom row*) Luis Carrera; Mercedes Fontecilla.

Permissions/Subventions:

For my family
across three generations

CONTENTS

ACKNOWLEDGMENTS

In letters penned during the wars of independence, Chileans asked the recipients to share their news and greetings with many others identified by name. I similarly offer this book to a broad network of family, friends, and colleagues. Although it is the product of many solitary hours of research and writing, it would never have seen the light of day without the support and advice of many. In Chile, I was welcomed by scholars with whom I shared coffee, meals, and, most important, engaging conversations on history. I wish to thank (in no particular order) Eduardo Cavieres, Ana María Stuven, Julio Retamal, Sol Serrano, Margarita Iglesias, Rafael Sagredo, Claudia Arraya, and Celia Cussen, as well as Peruvian scholar Carmen McEvoy, who was researching in Chile at the same time. All the staff at the National Archive were helpful and consummate professionals. I had the opportunity to teach a summer seminar on the Atlantic Revolutions for the graduate program in gender studies at the University of Chile, and I valued the discussions with those students. Three of them went on to work on the project as assistants—Carolina González, José Tomás Cornejo, and María Eugenia Albornoz—and their contributions were invaluable. Tania Mella Lizana also assisted during a second phase of research. Back in the United States, I thank graduate assistants Karen Carmody-McIntosh and Marianne Samayoa who helped to review congressional minutes and transcribe letters.

I would not have been able to travel to Chile and had time off for research and writing without the generous support of a Fulbright fellowship from the Department of Education and the Fulbright Commission in Chile, funding from the Grant-in-Aid and Imagine Fund programs at the University of Minnesota, as well as funding for a sabbatical and single semester leave.

I spent a wonderful year in Santiago with my family in 2002–2003 and I also wish to thank those who made us all feel welcome: the staff, students, and parents at Santiago College and the Las Lilas Preschool, María Elizabeth Ríos, as well as Heidi Tinsman, Erik Kongshaug, and their son Arlo.

My ideas and analysis benefited from the opportunity to present various aspects of this project at conferences and in the supportive workshops at the University of Minnesota: the Workshop in the Comparative History of Gender, Women and Sexuality and the Legal History Workshop. Those who made comments at conferences are too numerous to acknowledge by name, but I would like to thank the organizers and discussants, including Catherine Davies, Heidi Tinsman, Peter Blanchard, Eric Van Young, Carolina González, Jose Tomás Cornejo, Pablo Piccato, Erika Pani, José Moya, Karen Hagemann, Judith Miller, Natalia Sobrevilla, Rebecca Earle, Sueann Caulfield, Linda Lewin, Miguel Centeno, Agustín Ferraro, Alejandro Gómez and Clément Thibaud. I am particularly grateful to colleagues who have read and commented on drafts of various chapters, including Julio Pinto, Sueann Caulfield, Bianca Premo, Karin Rosemblatt, Mary Jo Maynes, Lisa Norling, Nara Milanich, Barbara Welke, Susanna Blumenthal, Ruth Karras, and of course the anonymous reviewers for Duke University Press. Some of the material in the book appeared in an earlier formulation in "The Paternal Obligation to Provide: Political Familialism in Early Nineteenth-Century Chile," *American Historical Review* (October 2012); the comments of the anonymous readers of that manuscript helped me clarify the analysis and comparative context. Thanks as well to Gisela Fosado, Lorien Olive, Christine Riggio, and other staff at Duke University Press for all their help in getting the manuscript into print.

This is a book about family, and three generations of my own extended family have shaped my ideas and provided constant support and encouragement. On the eve of my first research trip to Chile, my sister Katy Easton passed away. Katy was a leader and motivator, the Javiera Carrera of our family. Being with her during her final days strengthened the already deep bonds with my other siblings, Jenny Willow and Robert Chambers. I thought of them often as I perused the correspondence of the Carrera clan. I thank Robert, our family historian, for designing the Carrera genealogy that appears in the book. Our patriarch, Clarke Chambers, is a historian, and so he has always had a great professional as well as personal influence upon me. My mother, Florence Wood Chambers, passed away as I was writing the book; a source of unconditional support but also one of my best copyeditors, she was on my mind during final revisions. My husband, Gene Ozasky, has been a constant and supportive companion. I never had to face the familial separations suffered by Javiera Carrera, because he has always been game to journey with me, including to Chile. Like the Chileans in this book, I feel linked to ancestors but place my great hopes upon future generations. Our sons were children in Chile; already Alex is an adult and Easton well on the way. They are my inspiration.

INTRODUCTION

On March 1, 1781, some of Santiago's most distinguished residents entered the Cathedral to witness the baptism of a newborn girl, who was anointed not only with holy water but also a long string of Christian names: Francisca Xaviera Eudocia Rudecinda Carmen de los Dolores. She was the daughter of Lieutenant Colonel of the Cavalry Señor don Ignacio de la Carrera Cuevas and doña Francisca de Paula Verdugo y Valdivieso, who would later rejoice at their first child to survive into adulthood. Her grandfathers were Field Master don Ignacio de la Carrera Ureta and Señor Doctor don Juan Verdugo, royal counselor and judge of the Royal Audiencia of Santiago.[1] Were one to trace Javiera (henceforth the modern spelling of her name will be used) only through the ecclesiastical records of Santiago, the outlines would emerge of a life typical for an elite woman during the period of "traditional Chile" (a term used for the eighteenth to the mid-nineteenth centuries). The parish records reveal her marriage at age fifteen to an eligible young man from the cream of Santiago society, Manuel José de la Lastra, followed by the baptisms of their two children Manuel and Dolores. A sad, but not all that unusual, widowhood at age seventeen was followed within two years by a second marriage to a recently arrived royal official of noble Spanish descent, Pedro Díaz de Valdés, and five more baptisms over the ensuing decade. Widowed again at the more respectable age of forty-five, Javiera retired from the bustle of Santiago to tend the gardens at her family estate, where she delighted in visits from children, grandchildren, nieces, and nephews along with more formal receptions for senators and government officials. At the ripe old age of eighty-one, having survived most of her own children, she was buried in the Franciscan monastery. Benjamín Vicuña Mackenna, one of Chile's rising statesmen and historians, eulogized her virtues. Having perused Javiera Carrera's correspondence, he pronounced, "She wrote only of consolation, of Christian beliefs, of intense love for all her family members [*por cuanto llevaba su nombre*], and above all of a limitless capacity for abnegation based on a disregard for herself."[2]

At one level, then, Javiera Carrera appears as a model domestic matron. Visitors to the Cathedral where she had been baptized, however, would find a clue to the more public dimension of her life that reveals the way in which family and politics were intertwined in nineteenth-century Chile. In 1952, Javiera's remains were reinterred there alongside those of her three brothers: Juan José, José Miguel, and Luis. A commemorative plaque proclaimed: "The Fatherland to the Carreras: grateful for their services, sympathetic with their misfortunes." The dates, moreover, showed that her brothers, though younger, had considerably shorter lifespans than Javiera, having died between 1818 and 1821. Vicuña Mackenna's eulogy reveals those services and misfortunes had taken place during the Chilean movement for independence from Spain. "This woman," he declared, "was at the summit of the revolution and the irresistible advisor to its promoters."[3] Javiera's father and brothers served in the local provisional government that began to take steps toward independence between 1810 and 1814, roles for which they were pursued by imperial authorities. Although Javiera neither held office nor took up arms, she had assisted her brothers' plans and served as official hostess in what came to be called the *Patria Vieja* (the old, or first, fatherland). Therefore, she too feared reprisals from royal officials and decided in 1814 to accompany her three brothers into exile in the United Provinces of the Río de la Plata (the territory that would later become the nation of Argentina). She brought her youngest son on the difficult journey over the Andes, but left behind in Santiago her husband and other children. For seven years she continued to assist her brothers in their unsuccessful efforts to return to power. When she returned to Chile in 1824, the construction of an independent nation-state was underway. Although she was no longer as politically active, Javiera did go to court to recuperate property that had been seized by first royal and then patriot officials, advocated for the repatriation of her brothers' remains, and stayed in contact with prominent figures across the continent. The Carrera story, in the twists and turns that will unfold in this book, makes for compelling drama. But their experiences were paralleled by those of countless other Chilean families, some famous but most ordinary, caught up in a turbulent period of war followed by nation-state formation.

The case of the Carreras invites us to analyze the connections between family and politics too often left out of accounts of independence and state building in Latin America during the first half of the nineteenth century.

Although historians have noted the familial language of revolution, such as metaphors about coming of age and overthrowing the tyranny of the father king, this book goes farther by using these rhetorical clues to uncover the place of family first in power struggles and subsequently in the formation of policies on property, pensions, and child support that were critical for the stability of the new nation. Chile underwent significant turmoil, especially between 1810 and 1830, and contemporaries experienced and interpreted this disorder in terms of threats to familial integrity and survival. Elites mobilized their kin to advance political agendas and ambitions, and their relations often bore the consequences of imprisonment, property confiscation, and banishment. Poor households also experienced the war in terms of family disruption as members were displaced and providers pressed into military service. The various partisan blocs that came to power during and after the independence war all saw family reintegration as one of the keys to forming a stable government and society. Notions of paternal authority and responsibility, therefore, became central to the Chilean process of state building. At the elite level, these leaders attempted to promote reconciliation and national identity by pardoning the relations of their former enemies. More broadly, policies to support vulnerable dependents with state funds or to force fathers to provide for all family members benefited more humble Chileans, tying their fate to that of the emerging nation-state.

Chile from Colony to Nation

On September 4, 1811, troops led by Juan José and Luis Carrera surrounded the building where the two-month-old Chilean Congress was meeting, while inside their brother José Miguel Carrera demanded the ejection of representatives suspected of loyalty to the old regime. José Miguel had recently arrived from war-torn Spain and his siblings had informed him of dissatisfaction with the conservative majority in Congress among Chileans who had hoped that the opportunity created by Napoleon's capture of King Fernando VII would lead to greater change and reform. Although the Carreras were the public face of the September coup, another prominent family had taken the lead in laying the plans and expected to reap the rewards. José Miguel recorded in his diary a fateful conversation with the chief instigator, Friar Joaquín Larraín, who allegedly said: " 'My family holds all the presidencies: I, President of the Congress; my brother-in-law of the Executive; my nephew of the High Court. What more could we desire?' " "Upset by his pride," wrote Carrera, "I had the urge to reply imprudently by asking him who had the presidency of the bayonets?"[4] The answer was clear. José Miguel, Juan José, and Luis, all military officers, controlled the bayonets, and having used them in September to purge Congress at the behest of Fray Joaquín, they would in November turn them against the Larraín clan and dissolve Congress entirely.

The politics of family analyzed in this book unfolded during a turbulent period in Chilean history. The colony had been relatively calm during the eighteenth century, in comparison to other regions of Spanish America, but its inhabitants experienced a similar pattern of first anti-imperial struggle and then civil warfare between 1810 and 1830. Political order was reestablished in the form of an authoritarian if formally representative state in 1830. In terms of paternalist social policy and family law, however, efforts to promote reconciliation and stability occurred under various post-independence administrations from 1817 to 1860. Chapters in this book are organized both thematically and chronologically, so the narrative circles back to key moments more than once. An overview of this period provides general historical context for the subsequent exploration of the place of families in that process of war and state formation. Readers may also consult the chronology of events in the appendix.

Chile during the eighteenth century provides an exemplary case of an early modern elite held together by kinship. In particular, a multigenerational pattern of Chilean-born daughters marrying recent immigrants from Spain reduced the potential for colonial conflict. The family networks created by these marriages were critical to the success of commercial enterprises.[5] Although Chile was not Spain's wealthiest colony, on the whole the elite prospered from the late eighteenth-century loosening of trade restrictions within the empire and improvements in transportation infrastructure carried out by the governors of Chile between 1788 and 1808.[6] The mining and export of copper in the north and the raising of wheat and cattle in the center and south formed the basis of the Chilean economy. As they married into the local elite, many merchants or their offspring used the profits from commerce to purchase the rural estates that provided status as well as additional wealth. Finally, access to income from royal service supplemented elite livelihoods, especially in families with numerous children who would divide the patrimony they inherited.

Throughout the empire, the Spanish Bourbon monarchs attempted to limit the integration of royal officials into local elite family networks. In 1776, for example, the Crown replaced the judges on the high court (*audiencia*) of Santiago; all had been born in the colonies, and most had ties through marriage to Chilean elites. Nonetheless, within twenty years Chilean relatives of the transferred judges were again sitting on the court.[7] The ability to reconstruct such local, kin-based networks of influence reinforced strategies before 1810 to work within the imperial system rather than to openly resist colonial exactions, even during the Bourbon efforts to increase fiscal and administrative oversight from Madrid. Some of those born in Chile did resent that aspirants from Spain were favored in royal service, but competition for posts pitted them as frequently against their local peers. Members of the Larraín Salas family, one of the largest and most powerful clans, held positions in municipal government, the royal bureaucracy, the colonial militia, and ecclesiastical administration, but occasionally faced charges of nepotism from rivals.[8] Although particular individuals might resent their failure to secure appointments, overall the Chilean elite recognized the Crown as the ultimate arbiter. Rather than channel their ambitions into efforts to separate Chile from Spain, therefore, most were sincere in their professions of loyalty and hopeful that fidelity would be rewarded. As late as 1817, a Spanish colonel reported that many Chileans were royalists and that the kingdom would remain part of the empire if the authorities knew how to maintain peace with and among the principal families.[9]

Given significant social inequality, the absence of coordinated rebellion from below is more difficult to explain than the loyalism of elites. The population of Chile north of the Biobío River and south of the Atacama Desert was about 750,000 in 1800. The majority inhabited the rural areas of the central valley, while approximately 35,000 lived in Santiago and 6,000 in the southern city of Concepción. There may have been up to another half million indigenous inhabitants of the region south of the Biobío.[10] Although conflict between the Mapuche and settlers in southern Chile was endemic, during periodic negotiations colonial officials provided gifts to indigenous leaders in exchange for peace. Although the Mapuche formally recognized Spanish sovereignty, therefore, in practice they controlled the territory south of the Biobío, except for a few forts such as Valdivia.[11] In contrast both to this far southern zone and to Andean regions farther north, fewer indigenous villages with their own ethnic authorities and communal structures remained in central Chile by the eighteenth century. Nor were there plantations with large numbers of African slaves as in Brazil and the Caribbean region. Most of the rural poor, of mixed Spanish and indigenous descent, worked on estates through a variety of tenancy arrangements, especially in the central valley, or eked out subsistence on smallholdings, more commonly in the south.[12] Just as elites appealed to the king to mediate their disputes, those who worked for them likely negotiated their place within a society dominated by

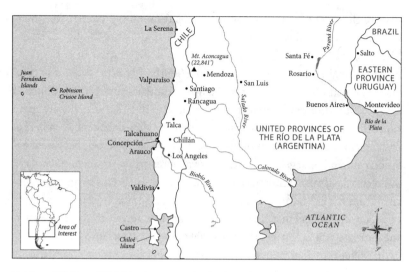

I.1. Map of Chile and Neighboring Countries in the Independence Era, c. 1810s.

an ethos of paternalism or challenged authority through smaller-scale acts of resistance.[13]

In 1808, the death of the governor captain general of Chile in February followed in May by the capture of King Fernando VII in Spain by Napoleon interrupted the relative calm that had characterized colonial society.[14] As in many cities throughout the empire, the notables of Santiago held a public assembly on September 18, 1810, at which they established an interim governing body, which swore allegiance to the king but not to assemblies in Spain nor to the viceroy in Lima. Some members of this junta hoped to preserve the existing order, others saw an opportunity for greater local autonomy within an imperial framework, and a few imagined an independent nation.[15] During the subsequent four years, a period called the Patria Vieja, Chileans took initiatives toward ever greater autonomy, though without openly declaring independence. On July 4, 1811, a Congress with representatives elected from municipalities across Chile, convened in Santiago. Although the date symbolically linked the assembly to the revolution in British America, many of its members were loyalist and conservative. From this situation arose the brief alliance and then enduring rivalry between factions of Chilean patriots led by the Larraín and Carrera families respectively. Friar Joaquín Larraín, president of the Congress, recruited the Carreras to help purge the assembly of the more conservative members in September, but two months later the Carreras led a coup that dissolved Congress and reconfigured the governing junta. José Miguel Carrera, who had more military experience than his brothers, as well as reportedly greater charisma, rose to lead the movement. Although he did not openly repudiate the sovereignty of the Spanish Crown, he began to lay the foundation for an independent nation with its own flag, purportedly sewn by his sister Javiera, and a provisional constitution in 1812. He also imported the first printing press to Chile, and the newspapers issued under official auspices promoted republican views. Viceroy José Fernando de Abascal in Lima, therefore, sent a military expedition that landed in Talcahuano, the port for Concepción, in March 1813, with orders that Chileans recognize his authority. Many residents of the southern region did join the royal forces.

Over the next eighteen months, Chileans battled among themselves as well as against royal troops. The internal opposition to Carrera, led by the Larraín family and their allies, did not put forward alternative policies so much as criticize Carrera's personal control of the evolving government. By early 1814, they managed to dominate the junta and replaced Carrera as commander-in-chief with Bernardo O'Higgins. Until that point O'Higgins, unlike either the Larraíns or the Carreras, had been marginal to elite power struggles. His father, Ambrosio O'Higgins, an Irishman who offered his services to Catholic Spain, was appointed intendant governor of Concepción in 1776. In that position, he met young Isabel Riquelme, member of a family prominent in the southern town of Chillán. She bore his child, Bernardo, in 1778, but by then Ambrosio O'Higgins had been promoted to the position of captain general in Santiago and within eight years was viceroy of Peru in Lima. The Carreras, scornful of Bernardo's illegitimate status and provincial origins, referred to their rival as the *huaso*, or cowboy. Although Bernardo Riquelme (only later did he take his paternal surname) grew up far from Santiago society, his father did send him as a young man to England to be educated. Upon his return to Chile, he struck up a friendship with one of his father's associates, Juan Mackenna. Mackenna, married to Josefa Vicuña Larraín, brought him into that family's political circle. Although O'Higgins and Carrera belatedly and briefly agreed to join forces in 1814, they were unable to prevent the advance of royal troops. On October 2, the patriots suffered a severe defeat at Rancagua, after which many survivors fled over the Andes to Mendoza. Within a week, General Mariano Osorio took control of Santiago and initiated a period known as the royalist reconquest.

Later patriot accounts depict the period from 1814 to 1817 as one of dire repression, with royal soldiers patrolling the streets of Santiago and entering households to harass patriot families. Most notably, over fifty prominent members of the local elite, including those with connections to either the Carreras or the Larraíns, were detained on a remote prison island in the Juan Fernández Archipelago.[16] Patriot propaganda attempted to discredit the restored royalist authorities in part by depicting them as coldhearted toward the families of prisoners. Although such depictions may be exaggerated, treating moderate supporters of home rule as if they were radical separatists likely pushed them into supporting full independence.[17] Meanwhile, over the Andes in the United Provinces of the Río de la Plata, which were free from Spanish rule, Bernardo O'Higgins teamed up in Mendoza with the local governor of Cuyo Province, General José de San Martín, to plan a joint overland expedition to reclaim Chile. O'Higgins tried to prepare the way by encouraging Chilean-born officers in the royal forces to switch sides, in part by accusing Spanish officials of "dividing our great family and forcing brothers to destroy one another."[18] Nonetheless rivalries among Chilean exiles also continued, prompting José Miguel Carrera to travel to the United States in an attempt to raise support for his own planned naval campaign to Chile. By the time Carrera returned to Buenos Aires with a ship full of recruits, the joint Army of the Andes under the command of San Martín and O'Higgins had already crossed the mountain passes and, on February 12, 1817, defeated royal troops at the Battle of Chacabuco.

The drama of that daring trek followed by rapid victory can easily make Chacabuco stand out as a definitive transition to independence. Within a year, however, forces led by the Spanish were on the verge of retaking Santiago. Even after the declaration of independence issued by O'Higgins and the patriot victory at the Battle of Maipú on April 5, 1818, the war continued in the south. The last Spanish troops were ejected from Chiloé Island in 1826, but irregular royalist forces made up mostly of Chileans, labeled bandits by the new government, were defeated only in the 1830s. Chilean troops also accompanied San Martín's expedition against royal forces in Peru in 1820. Meanwhile, disagreements over the direction of the new state continued to divide Chileans. Although there were no formal parties in Chile at that time, there were coalitions that clustered around liberal and conservative ideas, referred to by the nicknames respectively of *pipiolos* (novices) and *pelucones* (big wigs). Liberals tended to favor greater freedom of speech and the press, elected assemblies at both the national and local levels, and varying degrees of federalism. Conservatives believed that a more centralized state with a strong executive and the ability to limit individual liberties were keys to social and political order.

Although O'Higgins began the process of constructing an independent state in Chile, he did so while warfare continued. He ordered the seizure of property belonging to suspected royalists and émigrés as part of a strategy to weaken the enemy and provide critical funds for the new government, some of which were used to provide for those affected by the war: refugees, widows, and orphans. These goals, however, sometimes came into conflict as O'Higgins did not want to undermine the legitimacy of the new regime by seeming to persecute the families of royalists, and so he also pardoned Spaniards who agreed to recognize the independence of Chile. Indeed, various initiatives taken by O'Higgins created injured parties without sufficiently winning over potential supporters. He tried to abolish the practice of entailing estates and to bring the Church under greater state regulation, issues that were unpopular with conservatives. Santiago elites regarded O'Higgins as a provincial outsider, but residents of the north and south did not feel represented by his central administration. Aristocrats and republicans alike resented his authoritarian tendencies: he put forward a constitution with little consultation and when he did call elections, he tried to control the outcome.[19] Facing growing opposition, championed in the south by military commander and provincial governor Ramón Freire, O'Higgins abdicated in April 1823, and went into exile in Peru. Freire served as the new supreme director until 1826, when he successfully defeated the last of the official royal troops in the garrison of Chiloé far to the south, and remained politically influential until 1830.

When Freire addressed the new Congress in August 1823 he defended his use of force during the rebellion against the administration of O'Higgins but also called for reconciliation. "I have looked upon all Chileans as a great family united by the noble bond of love for the Fatherland and interested in not debasing its dignity with disturbances among themselves," he pronounced. "All the justice of the cause that I have embraced," he continued, "cannot erase from my soul the terrible image of the blood of Chileans spilled by their brothers."[20] Therefore, Freire favored returning confiscated property to former royalists as long as it had not been awarded or sold to patriots. Freire, like O'Higgins, did not come from the highest elite. Although he was born in Santiago, his parents died when he was young and he was raised on the country estate of an uncle. At age sixteen, he moved to Concepción to work as clerk to a merchant, and at twenty-three he joined the movement for independence and began to rise through the ranks of the patriot army. As head of state, Freire particularly championed reforms to extend pensions to the widows and orphans of his comrades-in-arms. In most policy matters, however, Freire gave greater leeway to the legislative branch than O'Higgins.

Generations of historians, beginning with opponents to the liberal government Freire established, depicted the years from 1823 to 1830 as a period of "anarchy." Two constitutions were enacted in 1823 and 1828, each in force for only one year, the provinces established their own assemblies in opposition to the central government in 1825, and four different individuals held the executive from July 1826 to May 1827. More recent accounts, however, have depicted this period in a more positive light as one when freedom of speech allowed a burgeoning of the press, and elections were held under conditions as fair as any in the hemisphere for that time.[21] Such liberal reforms were embodied in the Constitution of 1828 that enumerated civic guarantees, such as the privacy of personal correspondence and property rights, and eliminated confiscation as a criminal penalty. It also abolished slavery and entailed estates, the latter a measure unpopular with the country's aristocratic landowning families. In the first elections under the new constitution, Francisco Antonio Pinto, Freire's widely respected former vice-president, received a clear majority for president. Rather than allow the conservative who had come in second to serve in the vice-presidency, however, Congress declared another liberal the winner of that post.

Opposition to this partisan decision and to the liberal charter galvanized conservative forces. On April 17, 1830, at the Battle of Lircay, General José Joaquín Prieto defeated Freire, who was sent into exile in Peru. The conservative constitution promulgated in 1833 established stability at the expense of liberty. This charter authorized the government to declare states of siege, which suspended normal constitutional protections, in response to either foreign invasion or domestic instability. Rather than representative government at the local level, presidents gained the power to appoint provincial intendants who were charged explicitly with carrying out executive decrees and implicitly with getting out the vote in favor of the sitting government. Legislators drafted the constitution, but interior minister Diego Portales is credited with deploying its powers to establish a durable, authoritarian regime. "Social order in Chile," as he famously wrote to an associate, "is maintained through the weight of the night . . ."[22] Under his influence, the executive repeatedly invoked emergency powers in order to repress the opposition and manipulated elections to maintain the status quo.[23] A merchant by profession, Portales was never elected to office but exercised influence as a cabinet minister until his assassination in 1837 during a troop mutiny; thereafter, conservatives continued the legacy of this martyr to their cause.

Provisions in the 1833 constitution allowing two consecutive, five-year executive terms resulted in the election of only three presidents between 1831 and 1861: José Joaquín Prieto, Manuel Bulnes, and Manuel Montt. The administrations of Prieto and Bulnes were marked by fluctuations between repressive and reconciliatory policies in an ongoing attempt to unify and stabilize the nation symbolized as "the greater Chilean family." Prieto urged Congress to compensate property owners for wartime confiscations, for example, and Bulnes pardoned officers who had fought under Freire at Lircay. Montt, by contrast, took a tougher line even though he was the country's first civilian president. When allegations of fraud during Montt's election led to renewed civil war in 1851, Bulnes returned to military service and achieved a major victory at the Battle of Loncomilla. Although he advised Montt to declare an amnesty, the new president refused and governed with an iron fist through frequent declarations of states of siege. With almost no liberal representation, the Congress in the 1850s codified conservative policies on the family: the recognition of sequestered assets from independence as part of the national debt, tighter regulations on pensions for military widows and orphans, and a Civil Code that reinforced patriarchal authority.

Attention to family both reveals specific characteristics of the Chilean process of independence and state building and suggests ways in which we might rethink the transition to nationhood throughout Spanish America. In comparative accounts of Latin American nation-state construction, the Chilean case is often left out as exceptional because of its political stability after 1830 relative to other countries in the region. Only further research will demonstrate whether the Chilean state was distinctive or simply more successful than other governments in implementing policies that refashioned paternal governance from royal to republican terms. Given the centrality of family to social organization throughout the region, however, national differences were likely more a matter of degree than of kind.

Rethinking Politics through the Family

That Chileans would interpret in familial terms the political turmoil that accompanied their transition from subjects of the Spanish king to members of a republican nation resonates with language used by their contemporaries elsewhere. These common tropes arose in part because elites throughout the Americas read European political philosophy and followed events throughout the Atlantic world, but also were rooted in shared understandings of society and governance. Historians have amply demonstrated the centrality of family metaphors to justifying both early modern monarchies and the revolutions against them. British Americans rebelling against King George had envisioned themselves as sons justly opposing the authority of a tyrannical patriarch rather than a caring father.[24] French revolutionaries went a step farther, killing off their symbolic father in order to begin anew as a band of brothers.[25]

Although scholars have thoroughly analyzed the consequences of Atlantic revolutions for the legal and political status of women, less frequently have they explored the broader implications of republican rhetoric for state policy related to the family.[26] Notably, scholarship on the French Revolution has demonstrated how successive regimes repeatedly reformed family law. Initially, revolutionaries passed radical measures to promote individualism and equality: legalizing divorce, ending paternal authority over adult offspring, abolishing primogeniture, and requiring equal inheritance among all recognized offspring.[27] Support (a *pension alimentaire*) was promised to widows lacking a patrimony whose husbands died in the course of service to the Revolution.[28] During this period, the state even pressured wives to divorce émigré husbands and briefly experimented with adopting the orphans of counterrevolutionaries as children of the nation.[29] After 1793, French policies took a socially conservative turn toward reinforcing patriarchal authority over the supposedly private household.[30] In particular, on the grounds that forcing a man to recognize a child violated his individual liberty, French laws abolished investigations into paternity, a prohibition subsequently enshrined in Article 340 of the 1804 (Napoleonic) Civil Code.[31] Policies toward émigrés and laws on naturalization also increasingly followed patriarchal principles, allowing for lenience toward the wives of exiles but making the nationality of women dependent upon their husbands.[32] Finally, regulations increasingly limited eligibility for and amounts of pensions to widows.[33] The French case, by revealing multiple ways in which state and family were mutually constituted, invites comparison.[34]

Although references to family in Chilean political discourse of the late eighteenth to mid-nineteenth centuries were ubiquitous, they are surprisingly absent from historical analyses of the transition from colonialism to independence. Chilean historians have studied various aspects of family life, such as marital conflict, fertility, and illegitimacy, but for the period of approximately 1700 to 1850, termed "traditional Chile," they tend to focus on dynamics internal to the household and emphasize continuity over change.[35] "The importance of family in Latin American life goes unquestioned," Mary Lowenthal Felstiner noted in 1976, "Yet the political history of Latin America has often been written as if great events happened outside the home, while families stayed within it."[36] Felstiner mapped the kin ties of the wealthy Larraín family onto the politics of independence in Chile and analyzed family metaphors in revolutionary rhetoric.[37] Despite a burgeoning of family and gender history since the 1980s, especially for the modern period, Felstiner's observation is still largely true for the historiography of Spanish-American independence.[38] This book will trace the influence of family politics both at and beyond the elite level to demonstrate how the state in Chile garnered legitimacy by enacting policies aimed at providing for families across the society.

For almost three centuries, Spanish hegemony over American colonies rested in great part on the philosophy and practice of paternal governance, which promised beneficence toward all the king's subjects, who were figured as children, and mediated the competing interests among varied ethnic and socioeconomic groups.[39] Long before the modern welfare state, the eighteenth-century Bourbon dynasty increasingly extended its jurisdiction over the family and public welfare, areas that previously had been primarily the domain of the Catholic Church. Monarchs sponsored the construction of public institutions to both contain and maintain orphans and other "worthy" poor, established pension funds for the widows and orphans of high-ranking civil and military officials, exercised their prerogative to legitimate those born out of wedlock, and passed decrees increasing royal jurisdiction over marriage.[40] Strengthening imperial control over distant colonies also hinged upon preventing other sources of patrimonial influence from becoming too powerful. Bourbon monarchs, therefore, increased the enforcement of rules that prohibited administrators from holding office in districts where they had family connections in order to limit opportunities for placing the pursuit of personal interests above service to the king. Such restrictions interfered with the custom of local patricians marrying their daughters to Spanish bureaucrats. The rise in Bourbon regulation, moreover, may have led to a decline in the less formal largesse dispensed by prior kings in response to individual petitioning, thereby creating an opening for independence leaders to deploy their own paternalistic credentials in a bid for hegemony.[41]

When Napoleon invaded Spain and captured King Fernando VII in 1808, some elite Chileans saw an opportunity to exercise greater authority in their homeland. Over generations, they had used marital alliances to facilitate the consolidation and transmission of property and the transaction of commerce. With the crisis in the Spanish monarchy, they mobilized these kin networks in order to pursue their political ambitions, recruiting siblings, in-laws, and cousins as allies and rewarding them with appointments if they came to power. The resulting military conflict lasted over a decade and divided the population. In addition to fighting royalists, rival factions of patriots, often led by different patrician families, fought amongst themselves. For patriot leaders attempting to end these civil wars and establish a stable state, the family offered a powerful model of the passionate ties that bound together members of a presumed natural community.[42] As the military conflict declined in the 1820s, therefore, the victorious patriot officials embraced their role as founding fathers and addressed their compatriots as members of "*la gran familia chilena*" (the greater Chilean family).

Rhetorically configuring the new nation in familial terms had different meanings for distinct strata in the society. National identity appealed particularly to elites, who came to identify themselves as Chileans, first in opposition to Spanish subjects and increasingly in distinction from citizens of neighboring republics. After the independence war, victors invoked the symbolic ties of family when issuing pardons in an attempt to reconcile rival clans and to integrate those royalist émigrés who returned seeking amnesty and naturalization. Some soldiers from the lower classes, who had been mobilized to fight against the royal army, may have also begun to see themselves as citizens of the new Chilean nation. For the majority of the ethnically mixed population, however, local identities would remain more meaningful than the abstraction of nation well into the nineteenth and even twentieth centuries.[43] Although nationality may not have been the foremost identity for nonelites, many did respond to official rhetoric about "the greater Chilean family" by making claims upon the new state to come to the aid of their households and families.

When Chilean patricians referred to family, they usually highlighted blood relations or in-laws and emphasized their distinguished lineage, but the term was flexible enough to encompass other members of households as well as godparents and courtesy kin.[44] Although the politicized kin networks mobilized during independence had been made up predominantly of the Hispanic elite, the subsequent process of state formation extended membership in the "greater Chilean family" to at least some sectors of the broader society. New public institutions and policies emerged from a dynamic engagement between state agents and the populace they claimed to represent.[45] During and after the war, Chileans appealed to patriots to act as good fathers by taking care of those who had been displaced or who had lost providers. Many residents of Chile had migrated, some choosing to flee to the United Provinces, Peru, or the southern frontier, and others forcibly relocated by either the royal or patriot armies to prevent local populations from aiding their enemies. In the process, members of households were separated and survivors struggled to support themselves after the loss of loved ones and breadwinners. Displaced refugees pleaded for assistance and widows requested pensions. Both armies had seized the assets of those they suspected as enemies, and wives and children of the original owners petitioned for restitution.

Gender is an essential category for understanding familial relations of power within as well as beyond the household. A small but growing literature on gender during the transition from colonialism to nationhood has made critical contributions, but tends to concentrate on wartime discourse or on longer-term legal trends and, with a few exceptions, focuses either on women or on men.[46] This book builds upon this scholarly literature by uncovering how gender influenced the actions and experiences of families during and after war, familial metaphors in colonial and nationalist rhetoric, and evolving state policies that regarded family as a key underpinning of social order. Although Chilean society was patriarchal, lived experience presented challenges to these conventions, particularly in an era of conflict and transition. Women could exercise influence as sisters and mothers, while some men felt frustrated by their inability to fulfill their breadwinning responsibilities or even found themselves dependent upon others. Expectations of gender roles within families varied by class, but during the crisis of household survival brought on by war even some relatively poor Chileans were able to press claims for support from either their wealthier relations or the state.

National policies on pensions and the enforcement of laws on family maintenance correlated paternalism in the home and the state, reinforcing male roles as providers and authority figures. Patriotic speeches praised the heroism of those who risked their lives for the homeland, proving their honor and acquiring citizenship in the new nation.[47] Thus officers, even at the lowest ranks, earned recognition as responsible husbands, fathers, or sons who could call upon the government to care for their families should they make the ultimate sacrifice. Other areas of state policy, however, did not always affirm popular notions of masculine honor and feminine virtue. In wartime, patriot officials seized enemy property and rewarded wives who repudiated their royalist husbands. Judges, moreover, often overruled men's protests of the damage to their reputations when required to maintain alleged children even when the conduct of the mothers might cast doubt on paternity. Although dependents entitled to support were most often women and children, there were also adult men who were unable to fulfill expectations as breadwinners. Within a process of nation-state formation modeled on the family, claims based on the entitlement to basic welfare may have been more successful than those articulating a right to political participation.[48] By providing for diverse Chileans, paternalist policies contributed to state hegemony, but they also prioritized patrician responsibilities over citizen rights.

Thus Chile offers an important case where independence leaders recast the terms of paternal authority and responsibility in an effort to unify diverse populations and stabilize society in the wake of divisive wars. Although ultimately there were winners as well as losers, when the dust settled on the battlefield almost all families—whether elite, middling, or poor—had suffered losses in terms of both loved ones and patrimony. Civil conflict among Chileans continued past the defeat of the royal army well into the nineteenth century, and reconciliation became critical to reestablishing social stability and building new state institutions. Social scientists Brian Loveman and Elizabeth Lira have identified frequent metaphorical references to the nation as family within a Chilean political culture characterized by repeated efforts at political reconciliation throughout the modern period.[49] This book digs beneath such official proclamations to the petitions and lawsuits in which Chileans and various state authorities negotiated paternalism within both the home and the homeland. Rather than acting as rebellious sons, Chilean political elites constructed a state that "refashioned notions of male familial responsibility."[50] Once in power, postindependence leaders asserted their legitimacy by acting as father figures who could ensure both the welfare and unity of the national family.

Political leaders repeatedly used family metaphors to promote national reconciliation: Chileans were called upon to demonstrate their solidarity as brothers and show their loyalty to a republican government that would treat them like a benevolent father. Families left without providers held officials literally to their words, expecting them to step in and fulfill that duty. Specifically, archival research reveals that a central yet understudied principle of Spanish family law—the paternal obligation to provide for dependents— was key to both national reconciliation and public welfare. Widows and orphans of military officers who had given their lives for the nation petitioned for pensions, and their efforts resulted in a significant expansion of eligibility. More surprising were the arguments successfully advanced by those in opposing political camps. Wives and heirs of royalists, whose belongings had been confiscated, not only claimed their own share of such properties but also requested that the state pay child support from those assets that had belonged to their husbands or fathers. Providing for the dependents of defeated rivals, moreover, served as an opportunity to reunite the "greater Chilean family." Finally, both adult legitimate offspring and out-of-wedlock children increasingly and successfully sued their fathers in court for financial support.

The new government consciously used the opportunity to dispense paternalistic benefits to Chileans across a relatively wide socioeconomic spectrum, as well as toward the families of their defeated adversaries, in order to garner support and gain legitimacy. The first head of state, Bernardo O'Higgins, enacted these measures in an ad hoc manner from 1817 to 1823, but later governments shifted from informal patronage to more enduring policies that helped maintain social and political stability. This book will demonstrate how various branches of the emerging Chilean state institutionalized paternalism from the 1820s to the 1850s by passing legislation, establishing policies, and enforcing laws on property restitution, military pensions, and family maintenance allowances, initiatives that identified family welfare as a key foundation of national order and a stable state.

Organization of the Book

This book is organized into two parts, corresponding to the periods during and after the independence movement. Part I, "Families at War," covers the military struggle between royalists and patriots, as well as among the latter, from 1810 to 1823 as families both forged political alliances and were torn apart by conflict. Chapter 1 uses the case of the Carrera family, based principally upon their voluminous correspondence, to demonstrate how both men and women worked through extended family networks to carry out political plans. From 1810 to 1814, they were among the principal leaders of the movement to push beyond expanded local authority within an imperial framework to full independence for Chile. After 1814, as most of the Carreras went into exile in the Río de la Plata, their efforts increasingly focused on opposition to the government established in Santiago by their rival O'Higgins. This chapter also analyzes contemporary expectations of one's political affiliation and activism based upon both gender and specific familial roles as spouses, siblings, parents, and offspring. Although particularly dramatic, the story of the Carreras was not exceptional, and they will reappear at the beginning of each chapter as experiences of particular members of that family highlight the themes explored throughout the book.

Chapter 2 draws upon letters, military communiqués, and courts martial to explore how other families, famous and obscure, mobilized politically and experienced the impact of war from 1814 to 1823. While some patriot leaders, like the Carreras, escaped over the Andes, others remained in Chile to face the restoration of Spanish rule in 1814. The wives of those imprisoned on suspicion of having participated in the Patria Vieja denounced the tyranny of the royal governor in terms of failed paternalism. But patriot forces, upon their return to Chile in 1817, carried out similar tactics that targeted not only known royalist activists but also their relatives. Particularly in southern Chile, where the conflict became as much a civil war as an anti-imperial struggle, those who tried to stay in touch with their loved ones, separated by voluntary or forced migrations, could face trial for espionage and corresponding with the enemy.

Chapter 3 analyzes in depth one of the primary reprisals that affected all members of a family during this period: the seizure by royalists and patriots alike of property belonging to those suspected of aiding the enemy. Faced with a flood of petitions from wives and heirs who painted themselves as innocent bystanders rather than compromised partisans, officials often decided that it was ultimately less costly to pay some dependents a maintenance allowance, or even return some assets, than to have a population of destitute refugees that could serve as an ongoing political challenge. In turn, those for whom the new state provided were expected to shift their fidelity from biological to political fathers. This chapter, then, serves as a transition to the next part of the book: in the heat of war, patriot as well as royalist forces recognized few individuals as politically neutral, but in the wake of hostilities political leaders believed that pardoning the relations of former enemies could help reestablish civil order.

Part II, "Reconciling the National Family," focuses on the period of state formation from 1823 to the 1850s, specifically the development and enforcement of laws and policies that leaders of independent Chile hoped would facilitate national reconciliation on the basis of family reconstitution. The application of the legal principle of a paternal obligation to provide, dating back to medieval Spanish codes, constitutes a unifying thread as different state agencies responded to claims regarding property confiscation, military pensions for widows and orphans, and family maintenance disputes. Applicants for pensions and plaintiffs in lawsuits over sequestered property and family maintenance allowances came from some of the country's wealthiest families but also from those of more humble origins.

Chapter 4 continues the analysis of policies regarding the properties that had been seized, the patrimony of Chilean families, as these evolved after the war. Ultimately, most returning émigrés were allowed to join the nation configured as the "greater Chilean family," but the process was slow and uneven because requests for the return of sequestered assets clashed with the interests of those who had been renting or had even purchased those properties.

For families of military officers, a salary was often their only patrimony, and chapter 5 traces how the petitions filed by widows and orphans of those who had given their lives for the nation resulted in a significant expansion of the pension system. Treasury officials, facing chronic budget shortfalls and strictly applying the restrictive requirements of existing Spanish laws, rejected many applications, but the impression that the state was abandoning the widows and children of national heroes was politically untenable for presidents and legislators. Providing for the dependents of defeated rivals as well as patriot families, whether by returning seized assets or granting pensions, further served as an opportunity to reunite the "greater Chilean family."

Finally, chapter 6 analyzes the political implications of the adjudication of family law after independence. As political leaders used the state treasury to support families who had lost their providers, Chilean judges required patriarchs to support the dependents for whom they were responsible. Faced with a growing number of suits for maintenance, courts enforced paternal responsibilities even toward those living outside their households: to wives who were suing for or had won ecclesiastical separations, to children born out of wedlock, and to adult legitimate offspring who were not self-supporting at a level befitting their status in society. Sentencing in lawsuits over custody was more complicated, however, and signaled a shift in emphasis from paternal responsibility to patriarchal authority by the middle of the nineteenth century.

During the first decade of the nineteenth century, Peruvian artist José Gil de Castro moved to Chile to find a less saturated market for his services. Over the next fifteen years or so, including the period of the independence wars and Spanish reconquest, he painted richly colored portraits of the Chilean elites and military leaders of the new nation. Among the numerous uniformed officers standing at attention and seated ladies and gentlemen, one painting particularly captures the role of family in the politics and

Within the painting, the inscription reads:

Hijos mios queridos,
èsta memoria.espera de
buestro cariño,los sufrajios,
p.ᵣ q.ᵉ tanto suspira.el alma
de un P.ᵉ,que vien supo
amaros.

S.D.ʳ Ramon Martinez de Luco
...Su hijo D.ⁿ Jose Favian.

I.2. Don Ramón Martínez de Luco y Caldera with his son don José Fabián. Oil painting by José Gil de Castro, 1816.

state building of that period. Don Ramón Martínez de Luco y Caldera chose not to be depicted as a solitary figure, but rather with one arm draped protectively around his first-born son, José Fabián, standing at his side. Don Ramón, the father, looks out at the viewer and points with his other hand to the inscription he requested Gil de Castro paint centrally on the canvas: "My beloved children, this memento awaits of your loving care, the good works and prayers so longed for by the soul of a Father who knew well how to love thee." The young boy looks and points in a different direction, perhaps to the future when he will be called upon to advocate for his father's soul in purgatory and to carry on the family name and fortune. Captured on canvas in 1816, this pair stood at the crossroads of Chilean history, tied to past colonial generations and poised to carry longstanding values of mutual care into a new era of republicanism. Although the painting lacks a female figure, also so central to familial relations within both the home and homeland, it otherwise represents well a core theme of this book. Parents and children in the Spanish empire had long been expected to care for each other, but with the crisis precipitated by independence the obligation to provide was challenged by war and then reinforced by a new paternalist nation-state.

PART I
FAMILIES AT WAR

CHAPTER 1

Kin Mobilized for War: The Carrera Family Drama, 1810–1824

On Christmas Day, 1800, Bishop Pedro of Barcelona wrote to congratulate his nephew, Pedro Díaz de Valdés Galán, on his marriage in Chile to Javiera Carrera y Verdugo. After observing that he had made a good match, the bishop went on to impart some advice, which would have resonated with contemporaries throughout the Spanish empire, on his new role as father as well as husband:

> Congratulations and may God grant you happiness. You will achieve it if you mutually love each other and forgive the inevitable follies of humanity. Regard the children of your wife as your own, in order to please her and so that one day they recognize and are grateful for the fatherly role that you played. You will avoid disagreements in the future if you clarify their rights and shares now, so that you will know what you can count on for your family and so that no one can ever say that you took advantage of the assets of your wards.[1]

Such matches, between merchants or imperial officials from Spain and young ladies from prominent Chilean families, were quite common in this period. Indeed, ten years later, when Díaz de Valdés had embarked on a return visit to the Spanish royal court, his wife wrote to inform him of her cousin's upcoming marriage to Manuel de Figueroa, the son of a Spanish military officer, who had lived in Chile since the age of fifteen. Although she approved of the engagement, she asked Valdés (as she always called him) not to talk openly about the upcoming nuptials. As someone closely following the rising unpopularity of the current governor of Chile, and the accompanying "inevitable follies of humanity," she may have sensed that 1810 was a less auspicious year than 1800 to marry a Spaniard. Javiera nonetheless assured her husband that fortunately the groom was very different from his father don Tomás.[2] Tomás de Figueroa certainly adhered to the formalities of his class and generation, writing to Damiana de la Carrera to ask permission for his son to marry her daughter Dolores Aráoz Carrera. The union, he wrote, would bring him even greater pleasure than his impending promotion to colonel and battalion commander.[3] Son Manuel was more familiar in his correspondence, referring to his mother-in-law not as *señora doña* Damiana, but simply *mamita* when writing her with the good news of the birth of a child and the health of the mother "Lolo."[4]

Family letters were soon to take on a more serious tone. Within a year of formally asking the hand of Dolores for his son Manuel, Lieutenant Colonel Tomás de Figueroa was dead. On April 1, 1811, he had put himself at the head of royal troops protesting the establishment in Santiago of a junta that recognized the captive King Fernando VII but not the government in Spain acting during his imprisonment by Napoleon. Javiera's brother, Sergeant Major Juan José Carrera, captured Figueroa, and her father, Ignacio de la Carrera, reluctantly signed the execution orders along with other members of the junta. Sometime in 1812, Manuel de Figueroa left for Lima. As a merchant, he used the trip to attend to business, but wrote to his wife that in Peru he was not persecuted as a Spaniard, as he had been in Chile:

> even though I have not opposed the ideas of the patriot cause, I am not therefore free, because anyone could go to the Government [in Chile] and ask that I be arrested or punished according to their whims; this is the general situation and what is happening to many honorable men, and the worst of it is that the Government cannot ignore requests made in the name of the *patria*.[5]

Nonetheless, as a devoted husband and father, he swore to Dolores that he would willingly give up his security to be with her and their young son José Raimundo in Chile and to live quietly "in any corner of that beautiful realm." "When will God grant us a general Peace," he asked at the end of his letter, "and that all of us regard each other with the love and charity with which we were raised?"[6] He received his wish to return to his family in Chile, but the hoped for day of general peace was still years away. In February 1815, his uncle Pedro de Valencia, a royal naval commander, wrote Figueroa a letter of recommendation to the new captain general of Chile, Mariano Osorio, who had led a military expedition that successfully reestablished Spanish control over Chile. Valencia reminded Osorio that his nephew was the son of the unfortunate Figueroa "assassinated by the insurgents" and advocated that "Sons are deserving of being rewarded for the merits of their Fathers: I believe he has inherited, along with his blood, his virtues."[7] Back in Santiago,

Figueroa served on the Board of Public Health until sometime late in 1816 when Osorio's successor, Casimiro Marcó del Pont, sent him to Spain with official government correspondence. Figueroa decided to take along José Raimundo, the oldest son but still just a boy, and having taken ill, both died at sea. The death of three generations of Figueroa men within five years left Dolores Aráoz Carrera alone to face the sanctions imposed by patriot forces against their reputed enemies upon retaking Santiago in 1817.[8]

Neither Javiera Carrera in 1800 nor even Dolores Aráoz early in 1810 could have imagined how much their world, and their families' place within it, was about to change. From 1810 to 1814, José Miguel Carrera, with the support of his brothers, alternated in power with Bernardo O'Higgins, who joined the Larraín coalition. This rivalry continued in the period of exile in the United Provinces of the Río de la Plata and the subsequent establishment in 1817 of an independent government in Santiago by O'Higgins. The Carrera family, which was dispersed across several countries from 1814 to 1824, left a rich archive of correspondence that documented both intimate relations and partisan plots. Although their family drama takes us beyond the territory of Chile (see map in the introduction), their actions and words allow us to trace their mobilization of kin ties for political ends. Their many letters, moreover, allow for an in-depth analysis of the prevailing assumptions of how men and women were expected to act depending upon their roles within the family. In addition to exploring the Carreras' own, sometimes conflicted, feelings about the degree to which political goals and familial responsibilities were or were not compatible, this chapter considers how the measures taken by the authorities in power reveal the degree to which men and women would be held responsible for their own actions as well as those of their kin.

Family Networks as Political Networks

The Carreras traced their lineage in Chile back four generations to 1640.[9] Ignacio de la Carrera Cuevas was born in Santiago in 1747 and in 1773 married Francisca de Paula Verdugo Fernández de Valdivieso y Herrera, daughter of one of the judges on the audiencia whose ancestors had arrived in Chile in 1576. Ignacio de la Carrera inherited wealth that his father had made from mining while serving as governor in the north, but made his living principally from the family estate San Miguel del Monte, to the southeast of Santiago. As a prominent member of colonial society, he joined the militia and served as a colonel in the royal cavalry, but otherwise held few official posts prior to 1810. Four children survived into adulthood: Javiera (born in 1781),

Juan José (1782), José Miguel (1785), and Luis (1791). The three sons all attended the military academy, and Javiera briefly entered a convent but opted to marry rather than take religious vows. By most accounts, Javiera was precocious and intelligent, José Miguel charismatic, and Luis good-natured and well liked; Juan José, by contrast, was reputed to convey an attitude of entitlement despite sharing few of his siblings' more endearing character traits. Although there remains no correspondence from their youth, later expressions of affection suggest that the family was loving and close. Francisca de Paula Verdugo had been a noted hostess of social gatherings who particularly enjoyed the visits of foreign travelers; after her death in 1805, Javiera took charge of the household. Although only twenty-four at the time, Javiera had already been widowed and remarried, with two children from the first marriage with Manuel José de la Lastra (Manuel and Dolores) and on her way to bearing five more (Pío, Ignacio, Domitila, Santos, and Pedro) with her second husband, Spaniard Pedro Díaz de Valdés. As a widower, her father Ignacio also relied on his sister Damiana, who had been widowed around the same time, and her children Manuel and Dolores Aráoz Carrera.[10]

Ignacio de la Carrera and Francisca de Paula Verdugo were respected but not particularly remarkable members of the local elite, and it is unlikely that anyone before 1810 would have predicted the public family drama to come. Middle son José Miguel found himself in trouble with the law on two occasions: trying to seduce a married woman and killing an Indian in the course of a conflict over cattle between the family estate and neighboring community. His father attempted to avoid scandal by shipping him off, first to Lima and then to Spain, where he was present for the invasion of Napoleon in 1808. José Miguel joined the volunteer regiment of Madrid, and distinguished himself on the battlefield. Over the course of a year he was promoted several times, from lieutenant to sergeant major, and put in charge of recruiting soldiers for a new corps of Hussars of Galicia until he was wounded in battle and requested leave to return to Chile. Although José Miguel was committed to fighting the French invasion, he felt that officers from the colonies were not treated fairly in Spain, and upon receiving news of events in Chile he wished to play a role in his homeland. Javiera was the first family member in Chile to be affected by the unfolding imperial crisis when, in April 1810, the unpopular interim captain general Francisco Antonio García Carrasco removed her husband from his post as chief counsel and judge advocate (*Asesor Letrado and Auditor de Guerra*). Soon after taking office in 1808, García Carrasco had warned the king "of the deplorable state of this kingdom, owing to the partisan spirit, alliances and connections

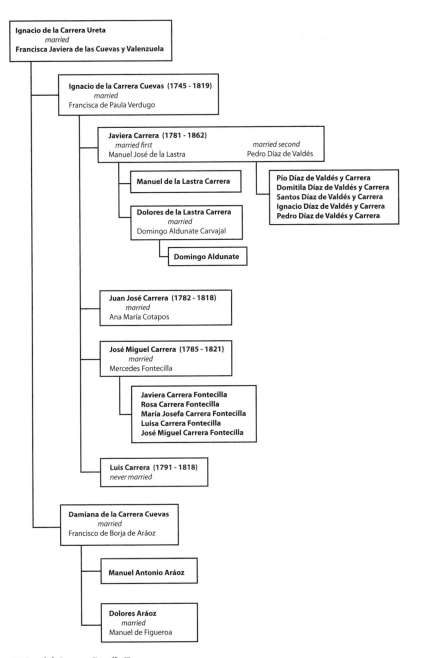

1.1. Partial Carrera Family Tree.

among the ministers on the audiencia as well as between them and Chief Counsel don Pedro Díaz de Valdés."[11] Further on in his report, he elaborated that several of the audiencia judges as well as Díaz de Valdés were married to women from Chilean families, a circumstance that required special dispensation for colonial administrators and raised suspicions that they would favor local over imperial interests. While Díaz de Valdés set out for Spain to protest his dismissal, his wife and in-laws became caught up in the rising discontent that resulted first in the audiencia's appointment of a new captain general and ultimately in an open assembly that led to the establishment of a nine-member governing junta that included Ignacio de la Carrera. Among the body's early measures was to prepare for the defense of the kingdom, including the establishment of the Battalion of Veteran Grenadiers under the command of Sergeant Major Juan José Carrera.[12]

The junta also called for elections to a Congress and prominent Chileans began to coalesce into conservative, moderate, and radical groups. As the *vecinos* of Santiago prepared to elect their delegates in April and the junta increased its communications with its counterpart in Buenos Aires, royal troops mutinied against orders to relocate toward the Río de la Plata and called for the reinstatement of García Carrasco as captain general. The key role played by Luis Carrera in mobilizing his artillery regiment to put down the revolt and protect the junta was an early indication that the power base of the Carreras would be in the military. Ignacio de la Carrera reportedly advocated for the banishment of Colonel Tomás de Figueroa, the leader of the uprising and the father-in-law of his niece Dolores Aráoz Carrera, but in the end signed the death sentence along with other members of the junta. By the time Congress convened on the symbolically important date of July 4, 1811, it was clear that moderate delegates held a majority and were unlikely to implement major reforms to government, much less declare independence from Spain. The radicals, therefore, began to conspire under the leadership of members of the Larraín family, and Juan José and Luis Carrera attended their meetings. Three weeks after the opening of Congress, José Miguel Carrera and Pedro Díaz de Valdés returned from Spain. José Miguel quickly apprised himself of the political situation and began advising his father and siblings on the best course of action. It was he, rather than his older brother Juan José, who played the most visible role in a coup on September 4 to purge Congress of its conservative-leaning deputies. And he again, on November 16 and 17, who turned the bayonets against the Larraín clan, dissolved Congress, and established a new three-member junta under his control.

1.2. Javiera Carrera. *Source:* Benjamín Vicuña Mackenna, El ostracismo de los Carrera (Santiago: Imprenta del Ferrocarril, 1857), 120.

1.3. José Miguel Carrera. *Source:* Narcisse Desmadryl, Hermojenes de Irisarri, and Miguel Luis Amunátegui, *Galería nacional, o, Colección de biografías i retratos de hombre célebres de Chile,* 2 vols. (Santiago: Imprenta Chilena, 1854), 2:2.

José Miguel Carrera complained that members of the extended Larraín family had been appointed to most of the government positions, including as officers of the militia, and justified his coup as saving Chile from becoming the "patrimony of that family."[13] Enemies of José Miguel Carrera would, of course, later make the same charge against him. Moreover, reprisals by the central government in Santiago against first patriots and then royalists in Concepción created further rifts among Chileans that threatened the image of an emerging nation as family. Although José Miguel was determined to bring the south under central control, he acknowledged in 1812:

> Never as much as now had we as brothers and sons of Chile dissented among ourselves, and never had the kingdom's troops set out on a horrific campaign in which victory would defeat us and in which our security and defense drowns us in our own blood. If we arm ourselves and the sword cuts our differences, the damage remains in our own house, to our own people and our families, whatever the result of our conflict.[14]

It would be simplistic to reduce the politics of this period only to family rivalries. Ties of blood or marriage were no absolute guarantee of political cooperation. In September 1812, for example, relations between José Miguel and Juan José soured; the former attributed the discord to the latter's belief that as the eldest brother he should play a more prominent role and to pressure from his in-laws following his marriage in June to Ana María Cotapos de la Lastra, whose family had ties to the Larraín clan.[15] It is true, nonetheless, that frequent intrigues and turnovers in power raised the importance of trust. The Carrera brothers were soon reconciled, and if Juan José was not always enthusiastic in following the leadership of his younger brother, he certainly closed ranks when he perceived that his family was under attack. Luis, as the youngest, never challenged José Miguel's leadership, always mobilizing the troops under his command in defense of his authority. Javiera meanwhile served as the official hostess for public events organized by the government of the still single José Miguel, most notably the second anniversary of the junta in 1812 when, despite the absence of any declaration of independence, she provocatively wore jewelry that featured a crown turned upside down.

From 1811 to 1814, the Carrera and Larraín factions alternated in power and exacted retribution against each other. The Carreras twice accused their enemies of plotting assassination attempts; in one a conspirator allegedly revealed that at dawn on November 27, 1811, "on the gallows will appear a father and four Carrera offspring."[16] Those found guilty, including members of the Larraín clan, were imprisoned or banished. These conflicts allowed royal reinforcements under the command of General Gabino Gainza, who had landed in January 1814, to advance quickly as far as Talca, about halfway to Santiago near Concepción. There O'Higgins and Gainza signed a treaty in which the former agreed to recognize the constitution promulgated in Spain in 1812 and to reaffirm Chile's allegiance to King Fernando in exchange for the continuation of limited home rule and free trade. O'Higgins did not, however, negotiate the release of José Miguel and Luis Carrera, who had been captured by Spanish troops. The brothers escaped and managed to seize control of Santiago. As the Carreras and O'Higgins renewed their conflict, Viceroy Abascal rejected the treaty and sent a third expedition to Chile under General Osorio, which landed in the south in August 1814. Although the patriots briefly set aside their differences, each side blamed the other for the patriot loss at Rancagua on October 2, 1814. Osorio meanwhile treated all who had participated in the various Chilean governments and military forces since 1810, regardless of their family affiliations or position as moderates or radicals, as traitors to the crown. While his offspring fled over the Andes, Ignacio de la Carrera found himself exiled to the penal colony in the Juan Fernández Islands along with others who held his sons responsible for the patriot defeat.

This rivalry continued among the Chileans who sought refuge in the United Provinces of the Río de la Plata during the royalist reconquest of Chile.[17] As the émigrés made their way into Mendoza, the governor of Cuyo province, José de San Martín, favored O'Higgins and his allies. When the latter accused the Carreras of stealing funds from the Chilean treasury before fleeing, San Martín ordered their detention. Luis blamed Juan Mackenna, married to Josefa Vicuña Larraín and friend of O'Higgins, for turning San Martín against them and killed him in a duel to defend the Carrera family's honor. While San Martín and O'Higgins formulated a strategy to retake Chile with a main expedition from Mendoza accompanied by diversionary crossings of the Andes both to the north and south, José Miguel pitched his own plans to the central government in Buenos Aires. In November 1815, José Miguel left for the United States to solicit financial support and naval forces for a plan to retake Chile by sea. When he returned with a fleet to Buenos Aires in February 1817, he learned that San Martín and O'Higgins had already launched their campaign. Rather than accept José Miguel's offer to reinforce the Army of the Andes by landing his fleet on the coast of Chile, authorities in Buenos Aires seized the ships and placed him along with Juan José under arrest. In a request to Supreme Director Juan Martín de Pueyrredón for release to a third country, José Miguel highlighted the persecutions his family had suffered:

> With my father imprisoned on Juan Fernández and all my siblings as émigrés in these provinces, there is not a single person left in Chile who can claim what belongs to us. . . . My wife, who is pregnant and is caring for two young daughters, has been forbidden from joining her mother, the only means to avoid indigence. . . . My sister is in the same situation or even worse considering that five of her young children are in Santiago with their father, who as a Spaniard should not be relied upon.[18]

In April, as yet unaware of the release of his father along with the other prisoners from Juan Fernández, José Miguel managed to escape to Montevideo, leaving behind his wife and siblings in Buenos Aires.

As he had during his journey to the United States, José Miguel relied upon his relatives—siblings, in-laws, cousins, and nephew—for support in his ongoing schemes to return to power in Chile. They attempted to maintain good relations with allies in the United Provinces—foreigners as well as other Chilean exiles and locals disaffected with the regime in power—and they provided José Miguel with updates on the political situation. In all these efforts, correspondence was critical.[19] Their political rivals knew the power of such communication and worked to intercept their letters. The Carrera missives frequently conveyed to the receiver instructions on how to send future communications: whom could be relied upon to carry the letters and what alias should appear on the envelope. Furthermore, in the event that such letters nonetheless fell into the wrong hands, they developed a code, substituting letters of the alphabet with others or with numbers, in which the most sensitive material could be written. On July 8, 1817, for example, José Miguel sent his sister Javiera lengthy instructions. He advised her to number all her letters to him, so he would know when some might have been intercepted, and to make use of their secret code. Indeed a paragraph of this letter was in cypher. He counseled her on whom and whom not to trust, but also that she should not let on to "false friends" that she no longer had confidence in them.[20] He also relied on Javiera as a conduit to get coded letters to his allies and to receive news from Buenos Aires and Chile.[21] He provided her information on troops sent from Spain to quell the South American rebellions and urged her to write him all the news she had in return.[22]

Although in July and August 1817, José Miguel seemed to be counseling caution—"Let us watch and learn, but not increase the number of our enemies"—his siblings were discussing plans to return to Chile.[23] As critical as correspondence was, face-to-face meetings were equally important to forging alliances and making plans. Javiera hosted a salon (tertulia) at her residence in Buenos Aires that became, according to Benjamín Vicuña Mackenna, "like a piece of Chile which the émigrés savored with eager ravenousness."[24] This historian and statesman, friend of José Miguel's son as well as grandson of Juan Mackenna, attributes to Javiera an ill-fated plan for small groups, the last two under the leadership of Juan José and Luis respectively, to slip into Chile and attempt to overthrow the government of San Martín and O'Higgins. She certainly was influential; in a trial one year later against several foreigners for plotting with the Carreras, intercepted letters refer to Javiera's role as a conduit for correspondence and praise her "heroism."[25] Nonetheless, Vicuña Mackenna's account has a romantic tinge that may exaggerate her role: "The impetuous refugees in Buenos Aires, who had not been called to test their mettle in the Chilean military camps, thus took refuge in that circle of emotions that seduce and enchain when a woman evokes them, with her magic wand of inspiration and enchantment, from the hearts of those who love and suffer."[26] Javiera's eldest son, Manuel de la Lastra, José Miguel's servant, José Conde, and a few others had gone ahead to meet at the family hacienda of San Miguel. Luis left Buenos Aires in July and Juan José followed in August, both accompanied by one companion and under assumed names. Luis was recognized in Mendoza and detained on August 5. Thus alerted to the plot, the authorities captured Juan José on August 20. The brothers admitted to attempting to cross into Chile but denied a conspiracy to overthrow the government; the case against them, therefore, was based almost entirely upon the confession of Luis's travelling companion, Juan Felipe Cárdenas.[27]

The two Carrera brothers were held in solitary confinement for months, while authorities in Buenos Aires and Santiago investigated the alleged collaboration of residents in those cities, and their relatives on both sides of the Andes attempted to advocate for more humane conditions and a fair trial. José Miguel also tried to recruit the wife of Juan José, Ana María Cotapos, to aid an escape, writing her in code to ask permission to visit her husband and to borrow money from his father to bribe the guards: "Imitate the heroic Madame Lafayette," he urged, "who saved her husband from the terrible clutches and vigilance of Louis XVIII."[28] There is no evidence whether Ana María seriously considered this request, but younger brother Luis did start ingratiating himself with prison guards, at least some of whom were Chilean. By February 1818, he had recruited some to assist in an escape plan that would also result in another attempt to enter Chile where, depending upon who was testifying, the Carreras would either join the continuing struggle against royal forces in the south or attempt to overthrow the O'Higgins government. One of the recruits, however, alerted the authorities. The trial for the earlier plot had been delayed by questions about whether it should be judged in the United Provinces (where it had been conceived) or in Chile (where it was to have been carried out). With the revelation of this new conspiracy, which allegedly involved killing or at least overthrowing the local governor, officials initiated a new trial confident of their jurisdiction. On March 6, 1818, Luis offered a full confession in exchange for leniency for the guards and for his brother Juan José who, he claimed, knew of the plan but had not participated. Governor Toribio de Luzuriaga assented to the terms, but as the prosecution proceeded news arrived on March 24 of the royalist victory over patriot troops five days earlier at Cancha Rayada near Santiago.[29]

During the ensuing weeks, the slow movement of communication throughout the region enhanced the drama of unfolding events. The mail between Santiago and Mendoza usually took about a week, and another

1.4. Luis Carrera. *Source:* Benjamín Vicuña Mackenna, *El ostracismo de los Carrera* (Santiago: Imprenta del Ferrocarril, 1857), 164.

ten days or so to reach Buenos Aires. On March 8, Ana María, writing from Santiago to her sister-in-law Javiera in Buenos Aires, was discouraged by the recent news of the new trial against the brothers and frightened by the approach of royal troops toward the capital.[30] After the patriots forced the royalists to retreat at the Battle of Maipú on April 5, however, she had reason to hope that her husband might be pardoned. She appealed to San Martín through an intermediary and met in person with O'Higgins who promised her that, by early the following year, the Carreras could freely return to Chile without threat of prosecution. Fearing it might be a trap set to capture José Miguel as well, Ana María emphasized the importance of tact, telling Javiera to advise her brothers not to speak out against the governments of either Chile or the United Provinces. Heartened by the celebrations in the capital, she wanted to believe the assurances of O'Higgins: "God willing, so that I can bury myself with my Juan in the countryside, which is all I long for."[31] Two days later in Buenos Aires, although not even the news of the Maipú victory much less Ana María's letter would yet have arrived, Javiera too had reason to hope. Writing to her husband, she expressed her confidence that the next day the Congress of the United Provinces would resolve the case of her brothers and asked him to share this information with her father and Ana María. Each woman posted her letter unaware of the news she would hear shortly.

In Mendoza, where these letters would cross, Governor Luzuriaga was increasingly worried by the reports from Chile about the royalist advance. Although by the end of March, official memoranda detailed plans to defend the capital, refugees, exhausted by their flight across the Andes, kept straggling into Mendoza and spreading rumors that royalist guerrillas were also crossing farther south, perhaps with assistance from the region's indigenous warriors, and that they planned to free and arm the many Spanish prisoners-of-war detained throughout the province of Cuyo. Some of the trial witnesses had alleged that the Carreras similarly intended to recruit royalists, so Governor Luzuriaga intensified security at the jail and wrote to his superiors in Buenos Aires for authorization to proceed with sentencing. On April 4, the prosecutor requested the death penalty for both brothers, on the grounds that exile to a third country would neither adequately punish their crimes nor assure the security of either Chile or the United Provinces. On April 7, with no response yet from Buenos Aires, Luzuriaga consulted several attorneys who confirmed his authority, given the threat of a royalist invasion, to carry out a sentence without allowing for appeal. On April 8, at three in the afternoon, Luis and Juan José were informed that they would be executed, and by six, after they had confessed and made their final dispositions, they walked out of the jail for the first time in over six months to face the firing squad.[32] A few hours later, the courier dispatched by San Martín from the field of battle at Maipú arrived with word of the patriot victory and, according to the account he later gave to historian Diego Barros Arana, verbal orders to suspend any action in the trial against the Carreras.[33]

Their hopes of early April dashed, surviving family members redoubled their efforts to return José Miguel to power and to exact revenge in the name of those to whom they henceforth referred as "our martyrs." José Miguel in Montevideo issued a manifesto calling for Chileans to join him in opposing the "despotic" regimes in Buenos Aires and Santiago, including among his rallying cries: "The innocent blood of the Carrera and Rodriguez families!!!"[34] (Manuel Rodríguez had been a friend of José Miguel; although he worked as an advance spy for San Martín, O'Higgins did not fully trust him and was accused of ordering his assassination in May 1818.) Pedro Díaz de Valdés worried about the depression into which his wife Javiera had fallen and counseled her to trust in God, seek a state of Christian resignation, and return to Chile.[35] Whether or not she followed the first piece of advice we cannot know, but she certainly continued her political activity in Buenos Aires. Ana María's parents, similarly concerned that grief was taking a toll on her health, sent her to convalesce in the countryside or, as she put it in an October letter to Javiera, to put a distance between her and the "cruel assassins who sacrificed the purest innocence to their horrific ambition."[36] That letter was the last of the Carrera correspondence to reach its addressee until almost a year later.[37]

In November 1818, Chilean authorities intercepted a handful of letters, mostly written by José Miguel, with notes added by his wife Mercedes Fontecilla as she sent them on to the next couriers, including her mother Rosa Valdivieso and her sister-in-law Ana María Cotapos. Former Carrera associates as well as Ignacio de la Carrera and two cousins were detained, one of the latter apparently for no reason other than his relation to the Carrera family, but Javiera's son Manuel de la Lastra escaped into hiding. Valdivieso and Cotapos were confined to convents, but Ana María's mother and the wife of a Carrera cousin avoided prosecution by refusing to receive letters sent after the trial had begun and turning over the male courier to the police. José Miguel chided one anonymous recipient for not writing to him, claiming that "Neither the world, nor the revolution have ended."[38] The sections translated from code allegedly urged the assassination of O'Higgins and San Martín to avenge the deaths of the Carrera brothers. Authorities subsequently seized a trunk addressed to Valdivieso and filled with inflammatory manifestos printed by José Miguel. Congress granted O'Higgins's request to dispense with the usual formalities of the justice system in order to prosecute the defendants for treason.

Given the summary nature of the case and the ongoing state of war against internal enemies, prosecutor José Gregorio Argomedo (who had himself been tried for conspiracy against the Carreras in 1811 and 1812) recommended in January 1819 that the state could justify banishing and/or confining the defendants based upon presumptions (such as their kinship with the Carreras) rather than full proof. Appealing several times to familial metaphors, he lamented, "Humanity trembles to contemplate that many times a good son must witness the death of a bad father, owing to the difference in [political] sentiments."[39] Once the revolutionary government had stabilized itself, he pointed out, "these deceived brothers would then realize their error, they would detest it, and the sweet Mother Fatherland (*Madre Patria*) will again receive those sons separated from her affection . . ."[40] The next day, the defendants were exiled to various places. Valdivieso (José Miguel's mother-in-law) was confined to a convent in Mendoza, where the abbess was ordered to monitor all her visits and correspondence, and Ana María Cotapos was to be placed under house arrest in a village in northern Chile.[41] Meanwhile in Buenos Aires, Javiera also came under suspicion of participating in the conspiracy. The president of the United Provinces asked San Martín and O'Higgins whether "I should eject from the country or send to you this troublesome woman."[42] The decision was to imprison her in the interior town of Luján, but she was later transferred to a convent closer to Buenos Aires.

These measures likely deterred most former supporters of the Carreras from further participation in plots within Chile, but José Miguel persisted with his plans on the other side of the Andes. In June 1819, he wrote his will in Montevideo, with instructions for the education of his children, and by July he had crossed back into the United Provinces where he allied himself with the governor of Santa Fé, Estanislao López, who was fighting against the central government of Buenos Aires.[43] Although he was frequently on the march, he could spend some time with his wife Mercedes and she assisted his efforts. For the first year, he and his allies experienced good fortune, even briefly taking the capital in February 1820. The following August, however, Carrera's troops suffered a major defeat and Mercedes was briefly a prisoner of war. López's forces remained strong, but in November he signed a peace treaty with the province of Buenos Aires that required him to end his support for Carrera. In October, Carrera had begun to recruit expatriate Chileans and to form alliances with indigenous groups for yet another expedition to Chile, writing to Javiera in Buenos Aires: "you will see me restore our beautiful Chile or die with glory."[44] As always, he enlisted her to solicit allies for assistance and financial aid, urging her to leave no stone unturned. He confessed that lack of funds was hindering him from properly outfitting and arming his troops; Mercedes had been able to complete jackets and caps, but they had no cloth for the shirts and pants. He promised to write again and urged Javiera to speak to their friends and send him all the news she heard.

In early December, Carrera's forces, allied with indigenous warriors, attacked the town of El Salto. Accounts of atrocities against the civilians further damaged José Miguel's reputation and forced Javiera and other friends of the family to flee Buenos Aires for Montevideo.[45] For months, Carrera and his remaining soldiers retreated to the territory controlled by their indigenous allies. During this period, Javiera wrote to him desperate with worry from not having received any news. Despite her lament that most of their allies in Buenos Aires had turned against him, she tried to cheer him with the scene of her hosting their close friends in Montevideo: "all together we celebrate your triumphs and everyone makes a toast, but no one can love you as much as your lonely and unhappy sister."[46] In August 1821, Carrera again attempted to fight his way over the Andes to Chile but was captured within ten days and taken to Mendoza. In contrast to the lengthy detention and two trials against Luis and Juan José, José Miguel's fate was decided quickly. On September 4, he asked his companion in arms José María Benavente to look out for his children and wrote Mercedes a farewell note. Refusing a blindfold, he then went to face the firing squad.[47] An anonymous letter writer reported that he died a hero, proclaiming to those who had gathered to watch, "that he would die for the rights of his Homeland (Patria)."[48]

Mercedes made her way to Montevideo, where she requested a copy of José Miguel's will and began petitioning for permission to return to Chile.[49] Despite the pleas of Pedro Díaz de Valdés and her children, however, Javiera Carrera stayed on in Montevideo. Although she variously blamed poor health, blockades, and financial difficulties for the delay, she was also hesitant to return to a Chile governed by O'Higgins.[50] In October 1822, she expressed her ambivalent feelings to her son Pío:

> My son I do not have to give you firm explanations for all your arguments about my natural resistance to live in a country that is terrible and disastrous for me. . . . God willing my presence will not be the ultimate ruin for all of you and, far from bringing you relief and advantage, increase your tears and miseries; of course since my Valdés and my good children want me present in that country and not in another I will go with resignation and even calmly because even the sacrifice of my life is [illegible] in order to prove to you my tender, my intimate love, and I hope that you, darling (mi vida), in reflecting fairly will not mistake the sharp pain in my heart with desire for vengeance much less detachment from my beloved family.[51]

In 1823, O'Higgins was forced to resign, and a year later Javiera finally boarded a ship bound for Chile where she hoped "the loving arms of my children" would support her as she faced painful memories.[52]

The Carreras threw themselves into the politics of independence and saw the fate of their family as closely associated with that of Chile. As the reprisals against them by those in power mounted, patriotic and familial interests could even become conflated, leading José Miguel to write of his plans in 1818: "The Chileans will be free, my loved ones will be avenged."[53] They formed alliances with those who shared their ideas, from Chile to the United Provinces and even the United States. Kin were critical to the formation and maintenance of these networks, especially as the need for trust increased. Nephews, cousins, and in-laws fought alongside José Miguel or attempted to carry out his plans in Chile. Sisters, wives, and mothers-in-law were the conduits for conspiratorial correspondence as it traversed multiple borders in South America. Aware of the strength of bonds of blood and marriage, the authorities on both sides of the Andes were quick to detain Carrera relations whenever they suspected a plot was afoot. Hence the same kin they mobilized to pursue their political plans from 1811 to 1821 suffered retribution when those plans failed to come to fruition. The roles particular relatives played in these efforts, and the punishments they faced, varied depending not only upon their gender but also their position in the family.

The Politicization of Family Roles

Unsurprisingly, men and women played distinct roles in the independence wars and ensuing partisan conflicts. While the Carrera brothers held political and military commands in the emerging republican public sphere, Javiera and her sisters-in-law served in support roles. Ana María Cotapos frequently and effusively thanked her sister-in-law Javiera "as the most loving mother" for caring for her husband Juan José while in exile.[54] She returned the favor by looking after Javiera's father when she returned to Chile in 1817. With the arrest of loved ones, however, their roles as family caretakers could justify women's actions in public. When first Luis and then Juan José were imprisoned in Mendoza in 1817, Javiera maintained a frequent correspondence with a friend in that city, Tomasa Alonso Gamero, who did all she could to intervene on the brothers' behalf. The government had made Alonso Gamero's husband Manuel Muñoz y Urzúa, a member of the last patriot junta in 1814, responsible for keeping accounts of the expenses of the brothers' detention and prosecution and deducting it from the money seized from them upon their arrest.[55] Nonetheless, Alonso Gamero was the one overseeing arrangements. Indeed she reported that the government had given her the money captured with Juan José, although certainly her husband Muñoz officially would have had to acknowledge receipt of the funds. Later she also received funds from Ignacio de la Carrera for Luis and from Ana María Cotapos for Juan José.[56] She informed Javiera that she had hired servants to attend to the brothers' needs, although they had to go through the guards to bring in food and take out laundry as the prisoners were held incommunicado. She tried to send them cigarettes and the occasional treat but complained that the guards stole a share of everything.[57]

Caring for prisoners added a political dimension to women's customary role that could evolve into broader intercession. On September 9, Alonso Gamero confirmed that she had immediately delivered to Governor Toribio de Luzuriaga the letter Javiera had addressed to him. In response to subsequent expressions of anxiety for her brothers' wellbeing, she further promised Javiera that she would "pay a visit to the wife of Luzuriaga and I will convey your feelings to her and ask for her assistance."[58] In this case, however, a female touch does not seem to have been effective. A month later, Alonso Gamero reported that she would deliver a letter Javiera had written to the governor's wife, but did not hold out much hope that it would make any difference because she had seen many letters written on behalf of the prisoners and yet the authorities had not taken any measures to improve the conditions under which they were being held.[59] By mid-December, Alonso Gamero's tone had changed from consoling to discouraging, explaining that she had not written in the last two posts because she had no good news. Muñoz had met with Luzuriaga, she reported to Javiera, to inquire why the prisoners were still shackled, to which the governor responded that he had orders "to treat them with consideration, but also attend to their security." Lamenting that they were being tried by their sworn enemies, she advised Javiera to work in Buenos Aires to ensure that any sentence in the case would have to be confirmed by authorities in the capital.[60]

Javiera Carrera had indeed been petitioning the authorities in Buenos Aires since learning of her brothers' detention. She repeatedly protested to Supreme Director Juan Martín de Pueyrredón that her brothers deserved a fair trial and decent treatment, and she subsequently tried to hold him to his assurances.[61] She also appealed to Governor Luzuriaga in flattering terms, expressing her confidence that someone with his "virtues" would not be indifferent to a letter from a woman who hoped he could relieve the suffering of her brothers.[62] Possibly as a last effort as their detention stretched into a seventh month, she also appealed to the Congress of the United Provinces. Although in this petition, like the earlier ones, she emphasized the rights due to citizens, she opened with a more plaintive and feminine tone:

Reduced to a true state of orphanhood, without a father, without a husband, without children, and fighting continuously between grief and dejection caused by the misfortunes that for some time afflict disproportionately one wretched family, nothing affects me more, Your Sovereignty, than the thought of two brothers accused before the law when that law is ignored in the procedures that should guide the examination and clarification of their crimes.[63]

In mid-April, she wrote to her husband with misplaced confidence that Congress would act on behalf of her brothers.[64]

Meanwhile, Ana María Cotapos and her mother María del Carmen de la Lastra were making appeals to authorities in Chile, both on behalf of the brothers imprisoned in Mendoza as well as of the friends and relatives, including their father, who had been detained in Santiago on suspicion of collaboration. On October 10, 1817, Ana María wrote to Javiera about the arrest of her father two weeks earlier, having delayed conveying the bad news, she explained, until there were some signs for hope; at least the state of incommunication had been lifted, she reported, and she promised to visit him every day.[65] Meanwhile, Ana María begged for news of her husband Juan José, about whom she had heard only rumors that he may have been detained. By November, she knew the worst, writing to Javiera that she had cried so much that her eyes had turned into canals. But she had also written a petition to Pueyrredón, of which her mother had sent a copy to Manuel Belgrano, one of the leading patriots from Buenos Aires. Ana María also appealed to Governor Luzuriaga, who had allowed her to exchange letters with her imprisoned husband.[66] Ten days later, she admitted to having taken to bed for three days under the stress of anxiety ("un histérico furioso"), but then forced herself to get out and work on behalf of their imprisoned loved ones, "since my life matters little as long as I can relieve the suffering of my unfortunate companion."[67] She reported that she had personally visited all three members of the governing junta, the minister of war, General San Martín, and the ambassador from Buenos Aires to Chile, and that she was also preparing a written plea. All these officials assured this worried wife that they would advocate for fair treatment of the Carrera brothers, but none claimed the power to intervene in the trial. By the following March, Ana María was discouraged, even wishing for death. All the petitions had been in vain, she lamented, and she had no money to travel to Mendoza in an effort to work more directly on the behalf of the prisoners. She advised Javiera to mobilize all her contacts in Buenos Aires to request from the government permission for them to go into exile in a third country.[68]

Relatives advocating on behalf of imprisoned loved ones spoke in gendered voices that reflected their roles within the family. José Miguel Carrera, from exile in Montevideo, had also written in protest about the cruel treatment of his brothers and father to the Congress of the United Provinces, but his style was much more of a declaration than a plea. Whereas Javiera had begun her petition by calling attention to her pitiful state as a woman alone, José Miguel opened with his right "Authorized by nature and by the law to demand the considerations of humanity" and called upon the delegates to hear "in my voice the expression of the truth so that you enact your decrees according to the principles of justice."[69] Distinct expectations of familial roles similarly shaped the attitudes and responses of officials toward such appeals. Authorities in both Buenos Aires and Santiago sent the female relations of the Carreras away with reassurances, however vague or unfulfilled; to have treated them coldly would have clashed with the very criticisms patriots leveled against royalists for their cruel treatment of women and children.

Even within these gendered differences, moreover, there were subtle distinctions in the expectations of the various roles played by women and men as mothers and fathers, wives and husbands, sisters and brothers, and daughters and sons. In general, as reflected in women's legal status and the attitude by political authorities toward them, women were expected to be loyal to their husbands. Spanish law had for centuries required that a wife share her husband's domicile and obey his authority. In times of war, therefore, it was assumed that wives would similarly support and follow their husbands' political choices, rather than act independently. Such a belief meant that wives could pose a danger in times of crisis but made it easier to pardon their actions once order was established. The inverse, that out of love and self-interest wives might influence their husbands to abandon the dangers of political action, was a concern that was less often explicitly expressed. Throughout the colonial period, men's allegiance to Spain had been predicated upon a paternal model of loyalty to the father king. Republicanism posited that men, in contrast to both women and royal subjects, were able to make independent political decisions and were willing to sacrifice their own personal and familial interests for the general good. In the practice of Chileans during the independence struggles, however, there did seem to be an assumption that men's political allegiances would most likely lie with their natal family (father, brothers, and sons) rather than with their kin by marriage. Moreover, although republican philosophers posited that male citizens should be free to act in the public sphere without regard for personal interests, men expressed their aspirations to fulfill their paternal responsibilities.

Ana María Cotapos and Mercedes Fontecilla were able to align their political interests with their obligations as wives. They married Juan José and José Miguel Carrera respectively after the start of the independence period, so their personal choice of a marriage partner presumably matched their political sympathies. Subsequently, their fidelity to their husbands was simultaneously loyalty to a particular partisan faction. Benjamín Vicuña Mackenna quotes a letter from Rosa Valdivieso to her daughter Mercedes reflecting such expectations: "It gives me great satisfaction to know that you have borne these upheavals full of resignation and fulfilling your duty to recognize the merit of your husband."[70] Ana María, more of whose letters have survived in the archives, was particularly effusive about her love for Juan José and anguish at his arrest and execution. In her first letter to reach her husband after his detention in Mendoza, she noted that it had been a year since their separation and declared: "If I knew, my beloved Juan, that my death could bring about an improvement in your fortune, I would gladly offer it up."[71] Ten days later she wrote to Javiera—whose father, brothers, and oldest son were all in prison—that she was fortunate at least that her husband was free since "that love is the greatest in the world and I see mine in the hands of his enemies."[72] In another, she assured Javiera that she frequently visited her father, now under house arrest, but that "Whenever I go, I am like a fool peering through the windows of the rooms that had belonged to my Juan and I water the shutters with my tears."[73] When she learned of the execution of her husband, she became so ill and distraught that her family moved her from Santiago to the countryside.[74] Over four months later, Ana María expressed her hope to Javiera that they would one day be able to embrace and grieve together, but that "Since I have already lost forever my beloved, for whom I desired to live, only death can calm my desperation; but in the midst of that [desperation] and without spirit, I am always your faithful one."[75]

In her correspondence, Ana María never wavered in her devotion to her husband and denounced what she considered the injustices committed against him. Her loyalty was above all personal, and her letters, in comparison to those of other members of the family, were less overtly political. In June 1817, she recounted to Juan José, whom she addressed as "My desired one, my darling, my delirium, my only love," her difficult trek over the Andes through a snow storm to return to her parents' home in Santiago.[76] Over

1.5. Ana María Cotapos. *Source:* Benjamín Vicuña Mackenna, *El ostracismo de los Carrera* (Santiago: Imprenta del Ferrocarril, 1857), 166.

1.6. Juan José Carrera. *Source:* Benjamín Vicuña Mackenna, *El ostracismo de los Carrera* (Santiago: Imprenta del Ferrocarril, 1857), 162.

and over, she told him how miserable she was to be apart from him. For one paragraph, she switched to code, for which a recent translation has been published. Although that section included the statement that those in power were tyrants and her hatred for them grew daily, she emphasized to Juan José that he should not worry that her return to Chile would lessen her faithfulness to him personally: "*And take pride, my precious, that every day my honor and good name rise more and more. Only my tico chino [term of endearment] has any sway over his unfortunate Ana. In all things, I am subject to nobody other than to my little pigeon.*" She warned him, moreover, to think of her before acting rashly: "*And so, my soul mate, relieve me soon, soon, with your appearance; but, my little boy, out of your love for me no longer avenge yourself as you had planned. . . . request permission for us to retreat to the countryside . . .*"[77] She repeated this wish in the section no longer in code: "I desire nothing else but to live peacefully with you and only in a foreign country can we achieve that because here the revolutions will never end."[78] Indeed, during this time, both Juan José and Luis seemed to be contemplating exile in the United States. Although it may have been a cover for their ill-fated attempt to enter Chile, even José Miguel in Montevideo seems to have believed they were headed north rather than west until July 1817, when he wrote Luis: "You left without writing to me and without notifying me of your plan."[79]

For his part, throughout their time in the United Provinces, Juan José was very solicitous of his wife's comfort and safety. Vicuña Mackenna depicts Juan José in a lesser light than his brothers in all but one respect: "As a husband no one could equal his tenderness, his dedication, or his faithfulness."[80] Like his brothers, he had been ordered by San Martín to leave Mendoza soon after their arrival in the wake of the defeat at Rancagua; Juan José appealed, unsuccessfully, that he had already paid in advance to rent a house for his wife and they could not be separated. A draft protest he penned in 1817 returned to the theme of what his wife had suffered and how he had been prevented from assisting her at various times: "forced to leave in a complete state of orphanhood and poverty my unfortunate wife, that woman who, in order not to live among tyrants, took on all kinds of dangers and discomforts, abandoning her home and crossing the Andes at a critical moment."[81] After slipping out of Buenos Aires in August 1817, he explained his secret departure to Javiera as a need for some time to think about what he should do and expressed his concern that "Ana and all my family will one day criticize my conduct, and will look back on me as only a criminal deserving of their scorn and contempt."[82] Among the options he was pondering, therefore, was to await his share of their maternal inheritance and use the funds to take Ana María with him to the United States. Instead he was apprehended on the way to Chile. On September 9, he wrote from jail to his wife, claiming "I undertook my desperate journey in order to search for you." He insisted that he had no intent of promoting revolution in Chile, reminding her that he had not wanted anything to do with José Miguel's planned naval expedition. "Farewell Ana of my heart," he signed off, "be steadfast and patient, assured that even amidst the greatest agonies I will be yours deliriously and every day more loving."[83] His protestations that his attempt to enter Chile had nothing to do with politics were certainly shaped both by the possibility of the letter being intercepted and a desire to console his beloved wife, but taken together with the earlier missive to Javiera, they do suggest at least ambivalence about his brother's aspirations to return to power. If so, this vacillation was influenced at least in part by his desire to live out a normal, married life. Ana María certainly believed so; upon learning that Juan José as well as Luis had been detained, she wrote to Javiera not of the justice of their cause, but of their innocence.[84] She may, thus, be an example of a wife who, motivated by love, put the safety of her husband and the goal of a shared life above political ambitions.

None of the letters that Mercedes Fontecilla wrote to José Miguel Carrera have been archived or published, but her actions and other correspondence

1.7. Mercedes Fontecilla. *Source:* Benjamín Vicuña Mackenna, El ostracismo de los Carrera (Santiago: Imprenta del Ferrocarril, 1857), 105.

demonstrate that she was both loyal wife and dedicated political collaborator. They married on August 20, 1814, and within six months, at the age of fifteen, she accompanied him over the Andes fleeing from the victorious royal troops. Although they were frequently apart during the following seven years, she decided not to return to Chile with her sister-in-law Ana María.[85] In this period, she bore five children: four girls, of whom the first was named for her Aunt Javiera, and finally in 1821 a boy named for his father, fulfilling the latter's wish that "our surname continue."[86] This son was born in Rosario, up the River Plate from Buenos Aires, while José Miguel was carrying out his campaign across the pampas. Within a month of the birth, Mercedes informed Javiera, in a letter filled with news of the battles, that she would have to be moving soon. Other than back pain from the labor, Mercedes made no complaints; she had not heard from José Miguel in over a month and was starting to be concerned, but figured that his enemies would quickly announce any defeats in the newspaper.[87]

José Miguel's letters express his love for his wife and children and his aspirations to fulfill his responsibilities as a husband and father, but unlike Juan José only rarely did he confess to disillusionment with politics. When he believed she would return to Chile in 1817, he was sad but ready to endure their separation: "You, my beloved Mercedes, and my children, are the only ones whose memory sweetens my sorrows. Only you have my heart and my trust."[88] The most difficult separation for him seems to have been during his exile to Portuguese occupied Montevideo in 1817, where he was more re moved from the sphere of politics. Vicuña Mackenna claims that he sent over two hundred letters to his wife from Montevideo, compared to relatively few during his journey to the United States the year before.[89] In mid-May, he certainly sounded desperate for news from her, writing: "Without your company I cannot accommodate myself, I now feel that I should separate myself from revolutions and search out peace and happiness in retirement, in the company of my *negra* [term of endearment]. Let's go to Chile and in the countryside we can leave aside the days of anarchy and craziness."[90] Such outbursts were unusual, however, and there is no evidence that he ever seriously considered abandoning his quest for power or that Mercedes ever asked him to do so. Nonetheless, José Miguel did express to his sister his frustrations at not being able to fulfill his paternal responsibilities while on military campaigns: "I am useless and shameful. I have abandoned my Mercedes and two little girls."[91] Several years later, on the eve of his execution, he wrote to Mercedes: "I will die with the only regret of leaving you abandoned with our young children in a foreign country, without friends, without relatives, without resources."[92]

The officials of the O'Higgins regime would not accept a wife's loyalty to her husband as an excuse for explicitly political activities, such as Cotapos's serving as a conduit for conspiratorial correspondence. Although Cotapos attempted to depict her correspondence with her brother-in-law in 1818 as merely personal, the prosecutor confronted her with the fact that his letters were in code. She denied knowing that particular code and only admitted having corresponded with her "martyred" husband using a different cypher: "Because it would have been shameful for others to read the expressions of love and affection between a husband and wife, but that after the defeat of Cancha Rayada, having been promised that he would be freed and they united, she destroyed the code along with his letters, which she laments to this day for not having them as consolation."[93] Juan José had similarly testified in his trial a year earlier that the code he used with his wife was to prevent their personal communications from becoming public.[94] The prosecutor in

Cotapos's case, however, regarded such excuses as "the most unbelievable, futile, and frivolous."[95] Found guilty of conspiracy, Cotapos and Fontecilla's mother were sentenced to confinement. In recognition of their dependent status as women, unlike the case of Juan José and Luis, the state would pay their room and board for the duration of their detention.[96] In March 1819, Ana María's mother appealed her daughter's confinement and exile to the north on the grounds that she was ill and that mercy could help commemorate the upcoming anniversary of the Battle of Maipú. In addition to insisting upon her daughter's innocence, Carmen de la Lastra offered as a guarantee that she would not abuse a pardon: "a large family, imbued with gratitude for the good will of Your Excellency, that will not cease in showering you with blessings."[97] Unmoved, O'Higgins granted permission only for Cotapos to remain in the Augustinian convent of Santiago until she was well enough to go into exile."[98]

Although women were held responsible for collaborating with their husbands, once the latter were dead, contemporaries could understand why wives had aided them and they could be forgiven. In October 1821, a month after the execution of José Miguel Carrera, Miguel Zañartu, the Chilean ambassador in Buenos Aires, informed O'Higgins that his widow was living in extreme poverty in the town of Rosario. Any danger Mercedes Fontecilla posed had passed, he pointed out, since "with the dog dead, the rabies is gone." Allowing her to return to Chile, therefore, would be good public relations for the government and for O'Higgins personally, who could put on his epitaph: "He was as generous as he was courageous."[99] By December, he relayed an official request from the Foreign Relations Minister of the United Provinces to allow relatives of the Carreras to return to Chile and to regain their sequestered property.[100] The following March, he reiterated the request for a safe conduct for Fontecilla:

> For me the highest recommendation on her behalf is having been the wife of an enemy. A well-governed sense of pride would be offended at extending hate beyond the grave and you, who have given so much proof of magnanimity in your public life, should distance yourself from any suspicion that you needlessly persecuted the innocent remnants of those miscreants.[101]

The English traveler Maria Graham, moreover, was surprised to receive a visit in 1822 from the mother and sister of bachelor O'Higgins, when she was staying in the Cotapos home. "But now that there is not one of the Carreras left, and that faction is believed to be at an end," she reflected, "it is surely the business of those at the head of the affairs of Chile to buy golden opinions of all sorts of men; and I have no doubt but they are glad I am here as an excuse to call without the formalities of reconciliation."[102] Like the Carreras, the women of the O'Higgins family played an important role as social mediators.

The relationship of family to politics was much more complicated for Javiera Carrera. She advocated for the independence of Chile simultaneously with her brothers and followed them over the Andes. She then remained in exile even after their deaths, refusing to return to Chile until O'Higgins was not only out of power but out of the country. These choices meant a decade-long separation from her husband and most of her children.[103] Thus, she clearly placed her political ideals above her duties as wife and mother. Indeed she likely acted against the wishes of her husband, Pedro Díaz de Valdés, who was a Spaniard and not a clear partisan of independence. Their letters expressed affection, but also resentments: he thought she had acted rashly by going into exile and stayed away for too long, while she chastised him for not writing to her often enough, for not adequately protecting her family's interests in Chile, and for not sending her sufficient financial support while she was abroad.

On the eve of Chilean independence, however, Javiera had been dedicated to her marriage and her husband's career. Díaz de Valdés arrived in Santiago in 1800 to take up the post of Chief Counsel, and before the year was out he had wed the young widow, almost twenty years his junior. All went well until Captain General García Carrasco removed him from the post in April 1810. Javiera supported his going to Spain in order to appeal the decision. Her letters to him as he made his way, accompanied by her son Manuel from her first marriage, over the Andes and on to the port of Buenos Aires from May to July relay a mixture of domestic news and the intrigues of the viceregal court. She lamented their "cruel separation" that did not allow them to talk in person and entreated him for letters and news before signing off "until the Lord grants me the pleasure of seeing you as your most beloved desires from the bottom of her heart" or as "your love until death."[104] As she repeatedly expressed her concern for his comfort and safety, the drowning of her first husband Manuel José de la Lastra on the same route exactly twelve years earlier was undoubtedly on her mind. She sent Díaz de Valdés a light-weight mattress so that he would not have to sleep on hides, scarves to keep him warm, and the best muleteer to serve as his guide, while dispensing advice on reducing the effects of altitude through rest and the right kind of wine.[105] She approved his efforts to discipline Manuel, while also entreating him in each missive to give her "Mañungo" a big hug from his mother.[106] And she proudly conveyed news of their young children, as well as preparations for the birth of "the one whom we do not yet know but is already jumping."[107] Nonetheless, she used as much ink on political news and advice. She reported on the visits she received from prominent members of the municipal council and royal administration, urging Valdés to follow up with letters to them, and denounced those who failed to pay her a call or inquire about her husband. There was certainly no dearth of news in 1810. She informed him of García Carrasco's arrest of three leading notables and the ensuing protests that removed him from office. Although the responses of Díaz de Valdés were not preserved, one can see from her letters that the two of them were also discussing the rumors from Spain of Napoleon's invasion and their repercussions in Río de la Plata.[108]

The rapidly unfolding events of the next four years refocused much of Javiera's efforts on the careers of her brothers, although she did intervene with the new authorities to have Díaz de Valdés reinstated in office despite his failure as a Spaniard to request a letter of naturalization.[109] Then with the patriot defeat at Rancagua, she was the one to make the difficult journey over the Andes, taking with her the youngest son Pedro, named for his father and born a mere week after the establishment of the junta in Santiago on September 18, 1810. One of her first letters to her husband, dated November 15, 1814, in Mendoza, exclaimed: "Valdés: I never believed that your indolence would be so great in the face of the serious hardships we have suffered."[110] "Your sudden decision to cross the mountains despite what we had agreed, Javierita, has caused much harm," he countered.[111] She tried to justify her decision by claiming that just for being a Carrera, she would face persecution in Chile: "Despite your insistence that women have no political opinions, I have the sin of being a Carrera, and for that they [the royalists] will have destroyed my home. Now you should do me the justice of believing that I have left you and my beloved children, not because I prefer others to you, as you have unjustly said to me many times, but by the necessity imposed by destiny."[112] In another letter she again alluded to his opposition to women's involvement in politics, averring, "If I had influence, it was all exercised on behalf of you [and the children]."[113] He assured her that the rumors of royalist atrocities were false and that "our very kind General" (royalist commander Osorio) had signed an agreement with the government in Buenos Aires to allow Chilean women to return from exile. He urged her to make arrangements to come home soon, since he could not take care of everything and ended the letter with greetings from the children, who "clamor for their mother."[114] Two years later, his tone had softened somewhat, but he still urged her to take advantage of a pardon offered by the royalist authorities in order to return to Chile.[115]

Javiera's correspondence suggests that the distance from her father and later her brothers was at least as hard to bear as the marital separation. Her letters to her husband still used endearing terms but did not display the ardor of those from 1810. In July 1817, Javiera wrote sadly to her husband that her brother Luis had left her alone in Buenos Aires, practically sighing: "without a homeland, without a father, without you, without my children, without my brothers."[116] Her letters repeatedly expressed her worries about her father, both his failing health and the political reprisals taken against him by first royalists and then O'Higgins because of the actions of his sons. Back in 1810, she had written to Díaz de Valdés of how she had responded when her father suffered an attack of indisposition, decamping to his house and keeping four doctors on hand for the first ten hours.[117] Her inability to rush to his aid when he really needed it, therefore, was maddening. When Osorio imprisoned her father on the island presidio of Juan Fernández, she criticized her husband for failing to prevent his arrest: "I believe you could have prevented it, just as my own father and I have acted on your behalf thousands of times."[118] Later, Ignacio de la Carrera tried to reassure his daughter of his robust health, thanking her for her concern about bundling up against the cold, but pointing out that the winter in his country home was nothing compared to what he suffered on Juan Fernández and citing a couplet learned in his youth: "So accustomed am I to hardship / That when I encounter relief / I beat a hasty retreat / Judging it to be my enemy."[119] On August 23, 1819, Javiera tried to hearten her father with examples from the Bible of staying strong in the face of misfortune and entreated him to take care of himself as his life meant so much to her.[120] She had not yet received the notice of his death four weeks earlier. Two years later, after Javiera's last brother had been executed, Díaz de Valdés, acknowledging that her spirits must have fallen ever lower, advised her to take care of her health and to ask God for strength in resignation.[121]

Politics also competed with Javiera's duties as a mother. Every letter to her husband emphasized how much she missed the children and conveyed to them her greetings and love. She expressed particular concern about her daughter Domitila, who presumably needed a mother's guidance more than her sons. Shortly after crossing the Andes, she wrote special instructions about to whose care to entrust Domitila "for whom I sigh so much."[122] Three years later, her sister-in-law Ana María Cotapos, returning to Chile, offered to look after her daughter: "I will regard her as a daughter and it would be a pleasure to care for her."[123] In addition to sadness caused by separation, she was frustrated at her inability to exercise her maternal authority. A letter from her husband in 1816 informed Javiera that her older daughter Dolores from her first marriage had married, without being able to wait for her mother's permission. To make matters worse, Dolores was demanding more money from her paternal inheritance, claiming that her allowance from Javiera had been insufficient.[124] By late in her exile, even her younger children were able to correspond with her directly, and the communications were clearly tense. In August 1821, she reassured her son Pío that she was working hard to return to her family: "Then I will squeeze you in my arms, my love, and in the meantime you are intimately in the heart of your very loving mother."[125] Six months later, still in Montevideo, she chastised him for the tone of his letters: "I cannot help but have observed for some time your brevity and tone that before was more expressive and less laconic."[126] In response to the concerns he had expressed over the fate of his patrimony without her in Chile to recuperate it from state seizure, she urged him to follow advice she was sending with a relative in order to set himself up in business. At the same time, she expressed concerns to her husband about rumors that Pío was going to marry someone of whom she did not approve.[127] She must also have chastised her eldest son, Manuel de la Lastra, because he responded with a long defense of the sacrifices he had made for the family, first in exile and then in hiding in Chile. "I have been a victim of my own [relatives]," he exclaimed, "I have been a victim of the love and support I have always professed for them, and I will be a victim again when justice and circumstances demand it."[128]

For as hard as she tried to mother her children from across the continent, Javiera Carrera, unlike her sisters-in-law, did not fulfill feminine ideals. It is difficult to know how harshly her contemporaries judged her. Her husband and children clearly grew impatient over time, but other relatives and friends did not criticize her decision to remain in exile. The head of state in Buenos Aires once referred to her as a "troublesome woman," but many of the period's leading figures treated her with respect and spoke highly of her.[129] History, however, has been less kind. In his eulogy delivered ten days after her death in August 1862, Vicuña Mackenna struggled to justify her actions to a generation whose women, "angels of the home," were dropping their patronyms to take on the surnames of their husbands. He referred to her as an "illustrious Chilean" and "the last spark that still remained from the dimming beacon of 1810," but acknowledged to his audience, "of course it is more difficult for us today to absolve her of her unnecessary participation in the public affairs of her homeland, as meritorious as she may have been."[130] He depicted her, therefore, as a mother in Buenos Aires to all the exiled sons of Chile and insisted, "One could accuse her of having loved too much, but never of the offence of egoism, which is the negation of all love."[131] By 1878, Vicente Grez also acknowledged Javiera Carrera's important role in his book on the heroines of independence but criticized her for pride and lavished greater praise on those women who acted simultaneously on behalf of their husbands and the homeland. "But exile and misfortune," he allowed, "purified this woman of whatever errors she may have committed."[132] One hundred years later, Jerome Adams summed up his unflattering English-language portrayal of Carrera by the title "Ambition's Sister."[133] By sharing the politics of her brothers rather than her husband, Javiera Carrera failed to fulfill contemporary expectations and suffered the judgment of later generations. She had acted more like a man, whose loyalties were presumed to lie with his natal family rather than relatives by marriage.

The case of Javiera's father reveals that men could be suspected of partisanship with their blood kin, regardless of their own actions. As one of the leading patricians of Chile, Ignacio de la Carrera was elected to the junta established on September 18, 1810, and like many of his colleagues, he likely favored an increased role for local notables within an imperial framework rather than separation from Spain. Nonetheless, with the restoration of royal rule, he was exiled to Juan Fernández and his property seized. He returned to Santiago with the other prisoners in April 1817, only to find himself under constant suspicion by the O'Higgins administration. While other patriots immediately recovered the assets seized by the royalists, Ignacio complained to his daughter in July that his petitions went unanswered and powerful members of the new government had been installed in his houses. They were emptied of furniture, moreover, and one had been reduced to a pigsty.[134] Each time government officials suspected a conspiracy involving his children, they imprisoned him. Yet there is no evidence that he encouraged or even supported his sons' ongoing efforts to return to power. José Miguel, for his part, expressed his surprise and concern that his father was sending him neither letters nor financial support.[135] Shortly after his return from Juan Fernández, Ignacio cautioned Javiera to trust no one and to correspond only with him and her husband.[136] In September 1817, he informed her that it had been a mistake for her son Manuel de la Lastra and José Miguel's faithful assistant José Conde to have returned to Chile.[137] When he was released from jail to house arrest in November only to find out his sons were in prison in

Mendoza, he exclaimed in a letter to Javiera, "I cannot understand the great madness carried out by your brothers," attempting to return to Chile instead of seeking asylum in the United States.[138] He asked her not only to appeal to officials in Buenos Aires to improve the conditions of their detention but also to pray and carry out spiritual devotions, since their fate was in God's hands.

Whatever his opinion about his children's political intrigues, Ignacio de la Carrera felt great sorrow over their misfortune. Upon his own release from prison on February 12, 1818, as part of a general amnesty to celebrate Chile's declaration of independence, he pleaded with the government to extend its pardon to his sons and offered to serve as their guarantor.[139] His letters to Javiera were affectionate. In August 1817, he sent her a brief note expressing his hope that the lack of correspondence from her recently was not an indication of illness and signing off "wishing to see you before long in the arms of your most loving father."[140] Despite his offspring's age and distance, Ignacio de la Carrera also continued to fulfill his role as family provider to the best of his ability. Shortly after his return from confinement on Juan Fernández in 1817, he promised Javiera that he would try to expedite the partitioning of property from their mother's will to her and her brothers and that he would use proceeds from the wine harvest or sell some cattle to send them some financial assistance.[141] He repeated such assurances eight weeks later, expressing his sadness at the difficult circumstances in which she and Luis were subsisting in Buenos Aires.[142] In the meantime, in response to an order to contribute four thousand pesos toward the war effort, Carrera offered the government the use of one of his properties because he needed cash to support his household, five grandchildren, and his daughter and daughter-in-law in Buenos Aires.[143] In November, he temporarily had to reduce aid to Javiera because he was sending two hundred pesos each month on behalf of her brothers imprisoned in Mendoza.[144] In December, he again asked her to be patient as he was supporting as many members of the family as he could while also paying off his debts in order to preserve his honor as a gentleman.[145] José Miguel also expected financial support from his father but asked on behalf of his wife "six-months pregnant, without any funds, separated from her family in a foreign and enemy country. I appeal to you, my beloved father. . . . I beg you to help Mercedes so that she can make the trip to Santiago and that when she arrives you receive her with the hospitality owing to a daughter whose virtue has been proven many times over."[146] With his sister, however, he did not worry as much about masculine pride, complaining to Javiera that in Montevideo he was penniless and asking her to share funds she might receive from their father.[147]

The O'Higgins administration had similar expectations of don Ignacio as a provider. In addition to detaining him several times, officials in Chile held him responsible for his sons' debts. In June 1818, only a few months after the execution of Juan José and Luis, John Skinner of Baltimore asked the Chilean government to cover a loan of four thousand pesos he had made to José Miguel Carrera in 1816 to transport troops and arms to liberate Chile. O'Higgins ordered Ignacio de la Carrera to pay, and when he pointed out that he was not a party to his son's debt, the government initiated proceedings to seize the cattle on his San Miguel hacienda. Protesting these measures as a violation of his property rights, Ignacio unsuccessfully proposed instead that the state return to him a house and rural property still held in sequester, so that he could take the funds out of José Miguel's maternal inheritance.[148] In March 1819, Ignacio tried to save his valued estate by renting it out to Diego Antonio Barros (father of future historian Diego Barros Arana), who agreed to pay in advance to cover Skinner's credit.[149] Within days of having paid off José Miguel's debt, Ignacio received a bill from the O'Higgins administration for those costs of the trial and execution of Juan José and Luis that had not been covered by the funds seized with them or sent by their relatives.[150] By the end of July Ignacio had died, of grief according to Vicuña Mackenna. State attorney José Gregorio Argomedo immediately advised O'Higgins that José Miguel's share of the inheritance should go to pay urgent military expenses, and so the government sold the cattle that Ignacio had taken such pains to keep to renter Barros, who was only too eager to purchase them at a bargain price.[151]

The contrast between the fates of Javiera Carrera's father and husband are striking and reveal the differing expectations of men toward their natal or affinal families. Pedro Díaz de Valdés miraculously weathered the rapidly changing political regimes of 1810 to 1824, owing in part to his studious attempt to appear neutral but also because his relation by marriage to the Carreras helped him when they were in power without harming him once they were out of favor. The formation of the first junta in 1810 found Díaz de Valdés on his way to Spain to appeal his destitution from royal service by Governor García Carrasco. Upon his return in 1811, he was able to secure an appointment with the first autonomist government of Chile. In 1813, he found himself again temporarily out of a job when the government passed a law prohibiting employment of Spaniards who had never sought naturalization in Chile, but he was quickly reinstated thanks to his wife's influence.[152] With the return of Spanish rule from 1814 to 1817, Díaz de Valdés worked with the royalists while his father-in-law Ignacio de la Carrera was imprisoned on Juan Fernández. In response to Javiera's recriminations of not helping her family as much as they had favored him, he assured her of his efforts to protect their family property by renting from the state one of their confiscated houses. "My conduct during this time is a long story," Díaz de Valdés wrote obliquely, "I'll save it for when we see each other."[153]

Having been retired at half salary by the Spanish government and unable to secure a position after 1817 under the O'Higgins administration, Pedro Díaz de Valdés was able to support his household only partially from his own income. When his father-in-law died and the Carreras' property was sequestered, therefore, he requested a maintenance stipend from the government payable from the proceeds of the rental of the San Miguel hacienda: "Honor, character, and circumstances urgently oblige me to disturb your lordship in order to explain the pressing need to provide even the bare necessities for [my wife] and five children, the cost of which, even tightening our belts, will amount to an allowance of at least one hundred pesos monthly."[154] The O'Higgins administration agreed to ninety pesos monthly and ordered Díaz de Valdés to share some of the amount with Dolores de la Lastra, Javiera's daughter from her first marriage, whose husband Domingo Aldunate claimed never received sufficient support from her mother.[155]

Although Díaz de Valdés had to request assistance in order to fulfill his role as family provider, he likely spent more time supervising the rearing of his children than would have been common for fathers at the time. All his letters conveyed news of their growth and education as well as illnesses and setbacks. He had mostly praise for Pío, the eldest, but informed Javiera of various discipline problems with Ignacio.[156] He felt particularly challenged by raising their daughter, Domitila: "She is lively and very mischievous and so requires the utmost care and vigilance."[157] When Javiera left in 1814, Díaz de Valdés followed his wife's advice in recruiting a woman, Manuela Sánchez, to help care for their daughter, but when Ignacio de la Carrera suggested sending Domitila to be with her mother in Buenos Aires, Díaz de Valdés reported responding, "For Heaven's Sake: until when does Javierita plan to stay in Buenos Aires because she should come here rather than have the girl sent there."[158] Instead, as she grew, Domitila spent much time with her maternal great aunt, Damiana de la Carrera. Díaz de Valdés was, he concluded of his paternal labors, "a slave to the education and rearing of the children."[159] How difficult it must have been, therefore, when a few months after this exclamation, he learned that Javiera had sent their youngest son Pedro, affectionately called Perico, to a boarding school in Baltimore. He reminded her that they had always discussed sending the children to Spain for their education, where his relatives would lovingly look after them. He worried particularly that Perico might relax his Catholic devotions among Protestants. Nevertheless, he also acknowledged the pain that Javiera must have experienced upon the separation from this "little angel," and as he acquired more information from visiting North Americans about the school and the presence of other students from Catholic countries, he came to terms with her decision.[160] Even Javiera acknowledged that Valdés, as she always called him, was a dedicated father doing his best to supervise the rearing of their children on his own. In response to a letter from him about Domitila taking ill, she confessed, "you have acted in my place and the satisfaction I derive from this reassures me that with your care she will quickly recover."[161] And several times she advised Pío to set a good example for his younger siblings by "taking care not to upset your virtuous father in even the smallest way."[162] The advice on fatherhood from his uncle, the Bishop of Barcelona, apparently paid off.

Clearly, it was assumed that men were more likely to be swayed by the political preferences of their male blood relatives than those of their wives or in-laws. The 1818 trial over the conspiratorial letters yields an apparent exception that reaffirms the general principle. Cleric José de la Peña resided in the home of Fontecilla's widowed mother, Rosa Valdivieso, and was so much part of the family that her children referred to him affectionately as taita or "little father." She testified that she shared all her daughter's letters with him, while he protested that he had expressed his disapproval of those with political content. The interrogator confronted his denials of complicity by pointing out that "the fact of living so many years in the house of José Miguel's mother-in-law, would compel him out of gratitude not only to belong to the faction of that troublemaker, but also to do anything that his mother-in-law demanded of him."[163] In the eyes of the authorities, Peña was no independent citizen capable of acting upon his own ideals, but a dependent hanger-on of a woman from a powerful family.

In most cases, however, men's family connections were presumed to come second to politics. Needless to say, in contrast to the censure faced by Javiera Carrera, fathers pursuing their political careers were expected to leave behind their children in the care of others. But even while fulfilling the republican expectation of sacrificing their own personal interests for public service, men had been raised to regard filial and paternal responsibilities

Acuérdate que somos soldados chilenos i que debemos morir como tales....

1.8. The execution in 1818 of Juan José and Luis Carrera with the words Luis reportedly said to calm his brother: "Remember that we are Chilean soldiers and should die as such." *Source:* Benjamín Vicuña Mackenna, El *ostracismo de los Carrera* (Santiago: Imprenta del Ferrocarril, 1857), 120.

as part of their masculine identity. In a letter to his own father, José Miguel included copies of newspapers from the United States to show the esteem in which he was held in that country and looked forward to the day when "I can have the incomparable satisfaction of squeezing you in my arms and dedicating myself exclusively to your service."[164] He later expressed to his sister his frustrations at not being able to care for his wife and children while on military campaigns or after his death. Juan José had no children, but he too was distraught at the thought that his death would leave his wife alone and unprotected. Ana María had written to Javiera a year earlier, "Luis is today the most fortunate because, after all, he is single and therefore can choose his own path."[165] A witness to the brothers' execution reported that Juan José lost his composure and refused even to receive his last rites until Luis, the only bachelor, called to him: "Let us calm ourselves! Remember that we are Chilean soldiers and should die as such."[166]

....

Such a dramatic concluding speech demonstrates that the novelistic case of the Carrera family fulfills many of our expectations of republican characters and plots but also offers some surprises. As was true in many parts of Europe and the Americas in this period, men took the leading roles on the public stage, while women primarily helped from the sidelines or played in the Greek chorus condemning injustice and calling for mercy. Nonetheless, women's presumably private correspondence and social networking could serve explicitly political ends, and they would be held responsible for their actions. Indeed it was expected that wives would further the causes of their husbands; hence they had to be watched closely in wartime but could be treated with sympathy in periods of national reconciliation. Male blood kin of one's enemies were also regarded with suspicion, but husbands were presumed to act independently of their wives and in-laws. A woman who abandoned husband and children to conspire with her brothers, by contrast, was a target of criticism not only from her contemporaries but also from many historians. Once they no longer posed a threat, the Carrera brothers were forgiven their ambitious partisanship and recognized as early heroes of independence by subsequent Chilean governments. Mercedes Fontecilla and Ana María Cotapos are generally remembered as beautiful, self-sacrificing wives rather than political activists. Javiera Carrera, by contrast, is identified along with her brothers for her key role in their movement, but for the same reason often painted as ambitious and domineering beyond what was considered proper for a woman.[167]

The extensive surviving correspondence of this prominent family allows us to analyze in depth how familial relationships influenced both the political actions and contemporary expectations of men and women according to their varied roles in families. Although famous, the Carreras were not exceptional in their experiences. Chapter 2 will trace how the wars affected numerous families within Chile, both patriot and royalist, as well as their deployment of paternalist rhetoric to criticize their opponents.

CHAPTER 2

Reconquest and War to the Death: Patriot and Royalist
Families Face Sanctions and Separation

On November 6, 1814, royal soldiers turned up at the grand residence of Ignacio de la Carrera with orders for his arrest.[1] Carrera had served as a member of the first junta established in 1810 to govern Chile during the captivity of King Fernando VII. Although this assembly swore its allegiance to the Spanish monarchy, Carrera's son José Miguel had subsequently overseen the drafting of a constitution for Chile rather than recognizing the charter issued by the Spanish Parliament in Cadiz. All three sons had then resisted the expeditions sent by the viceroy of Peru to pacify Chile, and a month earlier had fled over the Andes days before General Mariano Osorio restored royal authority in Santiago. The Carrera patriarch, therefore, was boarded onto a ship, crowded with some forty other notable members of Chilean society suspected of treason, and sent to the penal colony in the Juan Fernández Islands.

The physical conditions on the desolate island were a shock to those, like don Ignacio, who had lived in luxury. Primitive housing offered little protection from the cold, wind, and storms, and meat rarely appeared in their rations. The only comfort available to the prisoners was the company and solidarity of their peers. Together they drafted petitions to the viceroy and the king proclaiming their loyalty and appealing for better treatment, but Carrera's signature does not often appear with the others. The supplicants highlighted their own innocence by casting the blame for the disorders in the Kingdom of Chile upon the Carreras. Life on Juan Fernández for don Ignacio, therefore, was not only hard but also lonely. Almost a year into his confinement, however, Carrera was able to summon three of his fellow detainees—Agustín de Eyzaguirre, Enrique Lasale, and Agustín de Vial—to witness the writing of his final will and testament. There he declared that he did not know the reason for his imprisonment, noted money he had spent on behalf of his sons, increased the inheritance shares for Javiera and Luis, and appointed as his executors his sister Damiana de la Carrera, her son Manuel Aráoz Carrera, and Manuel Barros. He also ordered a bequest of two hundred pesos for Santiago Parada, the servant who had accompanied him to Juan Fernández.[2] Shortly after dictating his will, Ignacio de la Carrera also signed, along with these witnesses and thirty other prisoners, a plea to the captain general to put into effect a royal amnesty for those Chileans who had not emigrated in the wake of the restoration.[3]

The richly documented drama of the Carrera family demonstrates how kin ties could facilitate the planning and execution of political activities as well as the expectations of contemporaries about the degree to which various family members would be held responsible for those actions. Although most Spanish Americans assumed women were generally apolitical, they did expect that the loyalty of wives to their husbands would extend beyond the domestic realm and into the public sphere. Women like Ana María Cotapos and Mercedes Fontecilla, who collaborated politically with their husbands, were held culpable as long as those movements were active but could be forgiven once the danger had passed. A father like Ignacio de la Carrera, on the other hand, was held responsible for his son's actions and debts regardless of his own guilt or innocence. The experiences of the Carreras, though seemingly drawn from the annals of truth stranger than fiction, were not unlike the travails of other Chilean families between 1814 and 1823.

Indeed, the Urrejolas of southern Chile offer an interesting parallel to the Carreras. Although the Urrejolas had been in the Americas for only two generations, patriarch Alejandro had established himself as a wealthy and prominent resident of Concepción, where he and several sons served in various capacities on the cabildo. In 1776, from his earnings as a merchant, he purchased the hacienda Cucha-Cucha from the Crown after it was confiscated from the expelled Jesuit order. He had twelve children, of whom ten survived into adulthood to have their lives disrupted by the wars of independence. In contrast to the Carreras, all the Urrejolas were fervent royalists. Agustín and Luis were both elected deputies from Concepción to the Congress of 1811, only to be purged for their conservative beliefs by the Larraíns and Carreras. Agustín, a canon of the Cathedral of Concepción, successfully appealed to Ignacio de la Carrera, who was known for his more moderate positions, to persuade the junta to grant him a passport to travel to Lima. Urrejola later continued on to Spain where the king appointed him bishop for the Philippines, but he died before being able to take office. In contrast to his father, when José Miguel occupied Concepción in 1813, he was less lenient in his treatment of members of the Urrejola family, unknowingly foreshadowing reprisals his own relatives would later face. Francisco de Borja Urrejola worked to provision royal troops, and Carrera detained his wife, María del Carmen Díaz de Lavandero, for corresponding with her husband and for "promoting conversations opposed to the [political] system, her salons and visits are with the Saracens [an insulting term for royalists]."[4]

Several of the Urrejola brothers joined the royal army as soon as a Spanish expedition landed on the southern coast, and Luis in particular rose through the ranks and distinguished himself in various battles. In May 1814, when José Miguel and Luis Carrera were prisoners of the royalists, Luis Urrejola granted them permission to visit the wife of the intendant of Chillán, which they used as an opportunity to flee. Urrejola may have facilitated their escape in the hopes of reigniting internal conflict within the patriot ranks. A year later, Captain General Osorio dispatched Luis Urrejola and Juan Antonio de Elizalde to Spain to convey congratulations from the subjects of Chile to the restored Fernando VII, and while there they advocated for an amnesty for those like Ignacio de la Carrera who had played lesser roles in the events of 1810 to 1814. Luis would never return to his homeland, holding positions in both Spain and the Philippines until his death in 1845. The eldest daughter María Josefa Urrejola, fearing retribution from the patriots when they returned to Chile in 1817, escaped to Lima where she died in 1821. Her sister María Manuela, a nun in the Trinitarian convent of Concepción, was forced to flee south of the Biobío River into Mapuche territory the following year when Spanish commander Juan Francisco Sánchez evacuated the city and retreated.[5]

This chapter will analyze the impact of the wars of independence upon many Chilean families, some prominent like the Carreras and Urrejolas, and others more humble. Although political disputes between members of the same family occurred, most Chileans turned to and trusted their relatives as they built political alliances. Many were then separated from loved ones as some were detained and others fled, either across the Andes, south of the Biobío, or to royalist Peru depending upon their political affiliations. The first part of the chapter examines how patriots detained during the reconquest period and their families used the very rhetoric of royal paternalism to protest their treatment by the captains general. The second part traces how the patriots subsequently targeted royalists in part based upon their kin ties. In war torn southern Chile, in particular, patriot officers attempted to keep royalist families from communicating with one another, ostensibly to combat espionage but also, I argue, to demoralize the enemy. Some correspondents were prosecuted when the letters through which they attempted to maintain contact were intercepted. As with the Carrera correspondence, moreover, these missives reveal Chileans trying to live up to their familial responsibilities despite the hardships and hazards of war.

Tyrannical Patriarchs and Weeping Wives

In the wake of their defeat at the Battle of Rancagua in 1814, some patriots, including the four Carrera siblings and Bernardo O'Higgins, were able to flee over the Andes and take refuge in Mendoza and other parts of the United Provinces of the Río de la Plata. Others, like Ignacio de la Carrera, either were unable or chose not to emigrate and so remained to face sanctions by first Governor Mariano Osorio and then his successor Francisco Casimiro Marcó del Pont. Juan Egaña, who had served in both Congress and one of the governing juntas during the Patria Vieja, later recounted that he had believed "the proclamations and solemn assurances of peace, amnesty, and fraternity that were repeatedly promulgated." Because the juntas had never disavowed the authority of King Fernando VII, Egaña said he remained without fear in Santiago. Within a month of the restoration of royal rule, however, all those suspected of participating in the revolution were suddenly arrested within two nights: "At the same time, the dungeons, jails, churches, and barracks filled up with illustrious citizens."[6] Agustín de Eyzaguirre, a merchant who had served on the municipal council in 1810 and the junta in 1813, protested that he had been taken into detention despite being ill in bed at the time.[7] A joint petition from prisoners in 1816 recalled that they had welcomed General Osorio, had sworn loyalty to royal authority, and had declared to him "that we were his brothers."[8] Yet Governor Osorio soon ordered Egaña, Eyzaguirre, and many other prominent Chileans suspected of having collaborated with separatists to be held at the presidio in the Juan Fernández Islands and their properties seized pending prosecution for treason.

The conditions on the island were a shock to the prisoners, who were used to living in comfort. They complained to royal authorities of shortages of food and medicine and of huts that provided little protection from the elements, which included cold winds and frequent, fierce storms. Manuel de Salas ticked down the list: "A horrible climate in which nothing grows and to where we are forbidden from bringing anything; scant and rotten food; houses that are entirely ruined and without the means to repair them; the absence of any assistance, or even any comfort, for our ailments; weakness from advanced age."[9] Many of the prisoners were elderly, and all began

2.1. Juan Egaña, writer and congressman; he was exiled in 1817 to Juan Fernández and later served as head of the central Sequestration Commission and author of the 1823 Constitution. *Source:* Narcisse Desmadryl, Hermojenes de Irisarri, and Miguel Luis Amunátegui, *Galería nacional, o, Colección de biografías i retratos de hombre célebres de Chile,* 2 vols. (Santiago: Imprenta Chilena, 1854), 2:36.

2.2. Agustín de Eyzaguirre, Chilean merchant and statesman exiled in 1817 to Juan Fernández. *Source:* Narcisse Desmadryl, Hermojenes de Irisarri, and Miguel Luis Amunátegui, *Galería nacional, o, Colección de biografías i retratos de hombre célebres de Chile,* 2 vols. (Santiago: Imprenta Chilena, 1854), 1:227.

to show the toll of living on the island. "Everything here deteriorates," lamented Egaña, "and we are mutually surprised to see how much more each of us shows our age, since we are suffering this climate."[10] Physical deprivation also contributed to feelings of shame and humiliation. Some patricians, Egaña noted, had even become incontinent and had to sleep in soiled bedding.[11] Undoubtedly concerned for their reputations, the exiles further protested that Juan Fernández had always been the destination for atrocious criminals who had been spared only the death penalty.[12]

For all their physical suffering, the prisoners equally denounced the mental anguish that resulted from their separation from family as well as the privations and affronts to which their loved ones on the mainland were subjected (and from which these once powerful patricians were unable to protect them). In a petition to Captain General Marcó del Pont in June 1816, they recounted the terror they had experienced when "we were snatched, when we least expected it, from the arms of our wives and young children" and added to the list of physical discomforts was the "cruel memory of the anguish that closes in on the people who are as dear to us as life itself."[13] The very first paragraph of Egaña's lengthy memoir about Juan Fernández ends with concern for his family as he remembered "the tears, orphanhood, abandonment, and destitution of my wife, beloved children, and the thirty individuals who make up my unfortunate family."[14] Rhetorically, the detention of the patriarch, even though he was still living, reduced all members of the household to the status of orphans. This theme continues to punctuate the rest of the account. He despaired at the offensive treatment of his loved ones at the hands of the royal officials. When soldiers occupied the interior rooms of the family home in Santiago, his "innocent and tender" daughters not only had to serve them but also to "listen to their coarse conversations."[15] His sons went into hiding, but Mariano Egaña was discovered and sent to join his father on the island presidio. Juan Egaña's wife, Victoria Fabres González de la Rivera, was left to hold the household together as best she could. Egaña paints a picture of her receiving the news of the seizure of his country estate: "There was my wife, alone, afraid, surrounded by the tears of the whole family . . . and without anyone to whom she could turn or seek advice, just the manager of my farm at the door who came to inform her that they had taken it from her."[16] Eyzaguirre's wife, Teresa Larraín, similarly protested that soldiers had threatened her when she was unable to pay levies, given "the few means available to a woman with family but without her husband, without her dowry at her disposition, and to whom they have not restored her sequestered assets."[17]

In addition to recounting the fate of his own family, for whom he could no longer provide, Egaña vividly related stories that demonstrated how royal officials consistently refused to respect the relatives of patriots, particularly violating codes of conduct toward women and children. He recounted, for example, that a Pablo Romero had tried to defend his home from attack by royalist guerrillas until a bullet pierced the heart of his wife, who was on her knees praying; seeing that the guerrillas had also set fire to the house, he turned himself in not knowing the fate of his four children left behind, "increasing with their tears the torrents of blood that flowed from the body of their mother."[18] He spent pages on the long tale of Candelaria Soto, a lovely seventeen-year-old who caught the eye of the royal governor of Concepción.

When he failed to woo her, he accused her of treason. Egaña re-created (or created) part of the dialogue from her trial. Candelaria defended herself in the gendered terms of an innocent maiden: "I do not know how you can accuse me of deserting the flag, which would be a military crime, nor treason, which can be committed only by those who handle public and political affairs." But the judge declared: "you shall serve as a warning so that the insurgents know that neither sex, age, nor status can excuse them from their crimes." When she was sentenced to a dungeon used for common criminals, Egaña claimed that she tried to commit suicide rather than face such dishonor, but that finally the man from whom he heard the story convinced the guards to allow her mother to accompany her there in order to guard her virtue.[19]

The prisoners expressed the mental anguish that they experienced in terms of separation from family, and they used stories of the retribution taken against those loved ones to depict the royal authorities in Santiago as immoral, tyrannical, and hence illegitimate. Meanwhile, their wives launched a campaign on behalf of their husbands, pleading with royal authorities to act in a paternal and benevolent manner. As soon as Eyzaguirre was detained, Teresa Larraín began to petition royal officials in Chile, Peru, and Spain. She enlisted the services of Manuel Antonio Echevarría, who also represented at the court in Madrid her brother-in-law Miguel de Eyzaguirre, a judge on the Audiencia of Lima. In her first missive to Echevarría, she hoped that a letter would be sufficient for him to act with her power of attorney because the notaries were too afraid to write up an official document for her.[20] She followed up with a lengthy exculpation for the part her husband had played in Chilean politics since 1810 and included a plea for mercy addressed to the king.[21] Many of those detained blamed the rebellion on the Carreras and celebrated their defeat by the royal expedition. Teresa Larraín went further to characterize the conflict in familial terms: "After a governing junta was established in this kingdom," she wrote to Fernando VII, "two rebellious Families seized the Arms, took control, and disturbed the order of everything." She did not attempt to make a legal argument for her husband's innocence, but rather pleaded that "the unfortunate situation of an abandoned woman, surrounded by family full of anguish and without the least refuge, will be the target upon which could shower the pious effects of the Royal Mercy with which Your Majesty has regarded your vassals."[22] In a petition to the viceroy, Larraín highlighted the sorrow of the prisoners' families in a manner that would become ubiquitous: "Just relating these events," she penned, "renews the sorrow that they cause me so much that my eyes feel flooded with tears."[23] Appealing to the captain general to carry out a royal pardon for all but the most criminal rebels, she offered to raise funds among the families to pay the costs of a ship to bring back their loved ones, promising that he would see the power of "the love that we profess for our husbands."[24]

These expressions of love and shedding of tears as the wives pleaded with first Osorio and then Marcó del Pont for the pardon of their imprisoned husbands became a powerful image in discrediting royal authority in Chile between 1814 and 1817. Egaña later wrote that upon receiving letters from Juan Fernández detailing the horrendous conditions, "the government palace, where almost all our families gathered in one day, was flooded with their tears."[25] Indeed, within days a pregnant Catalina de Echanes appealed to Osorio on behalf of her husband Mateo Arnaldo Hoevel: "do not let it be said that a heartbroken woman who once came and watered your plants with tears," she entreated, "left unconsoled and oppressed."[26] Although pleas by women to the king or other royal officials asking mercy for loved ones had a long tradition in Spanish society, at some point the Juan Fernández prisoners devised a strategy of coordinated action in person as well as in writing. Draft "Instructions" marked "top secret" (*especial reservado*) among the papers of Agustín de Eyzaguirre detailed seven steps that should be taken by relatives to advocate for the prisoners. Among the recommendations were to lobby various parties with influence to advocate on the prisoners' behalf: members of cabildos, prelates, any commissioners who might arrive from Spain, and nuns. Relatives were to prepare the ground by circulating a letter from Egaña detailing the terrible conditions on the island, "in order to win over justice with compassion," before presenting the prisoners' formal petition. Particularly striking was point four: "It is expedient and necessary that every day our families take turns gathering night and day at the General's house to wear him down until he grants favorable measures. Do not deceive yourselves, this is of the utmost importance if you do not want to lose us." The coordinated nature of this campaign was underscored by designating Eyzaguirre's house in Santiago as the headquarters for raising funds and directing actions.[27]

Although the tears proved unable to move the captains general to bring home the prisoners from the Juan Fernández Islands, inflexibility in the face of weeping women went against the official image of the royal government and took hold in the public imagination. When Osorio had taken his oath of office, he had announced "that he did not wish to be regarded as a warrior chief who dominates by force and terror, but rather as a tender, loving, and beneficent Father."[28] Osorio even expressed concern to his treasury ministers about the "repeated outcries from the innocent" over the manner in which property sequestration was carried out. "Let us wipe away so many tears," he suggested, "let us avoid so much anxiety and grief and in this way we can give happier days to those that fate believed she had brought misfortune." They recommended allowing family members to administer sequestered property after posting bond in order to "dry [their] tears" and to prevent royal authorities from "becoming an object of public hatred."[29] Similarly, the women's petitions to the king may have contributed by January 1816 to his issuing a general pardon for all those except the revolutionary leaders who had fled across the Andes. The text of the pardon was delivered first to Osorio, who had been recalled to Lima, and he began to publicize it much to the chagrin of his successor. The news must have reached Juan Fernández around the same time as Santiago, because in June 1816 the prisoners wrote to Captain General Marcó del Pont calling attention to the "paternal" sentiments of the king, whose heart suffered upon seeing his vassals in such misery, and expressing their hope that he would follow that example because the fate of their "disconsolate families" was in his hands.[30] In late August, José Antonio Rodríguez, an attorney on the Santiago Audiencia, advised Marcó del Pont to publicize the pardon widely along with the promise of the minister of the Indies that the king "would treat those who have gone astray mercifully and would receive them like a father, completely forgetting their crime."[31]

Under pressure, Marcó del Pont finally published the pardon on September 4, 1816, over three months after its arrival in Santiago, but added dire warnings that the government would monitor even the "most hidden thoughts" of Chileans and take measures against any who did not demonstrate complete loyalty.[32] Moreover, he expressed his concerns about the pardon to the minister of the Indies as justification for the continued detention on Juan Fernández of those who had not fled to Mendoza, he claimed, because they could not take with them their families and haciendas.[33] In addition, he recommended that various judges on the audiencia be transferred to other posts because of their marriages to Chilean families.[34] Marcó del Pont expressed concerns that the women's actions would embarrass the government, but his response was to take tougher measures rather than to yield. In October 1817, a year after publishing the royal pardon, the captain general ordered María Palazuelos, wife of prisoner José Portales (and mother of future statesman Diego Portales), confined to a convent. Her crime had been to go "from door to door asking for alms from well-known royalists, saying that she was requesting funds in order to redeem a captive Christian; and this greatest insult to authority and this strategy to show the tyranny of the Spanish Government, so often proclaimed by the revolutionaries, could not be tolerated."[35] Marcó del Pont's refusal to show clemency hence became a failure of paternalism that discredited his authority.

The image of the weeping wives was so well known that it was repeatedly invoked in the legal transcripts of a marital dispute of the era. An analysis of this lawsuit, like the petitions on behalf of imprisoned relatives, reveals the multilayered relationship between public matters and domestic affairs. On October 31, 1814, shortly before forty-two Chileans were exiled to Juan Fernández, Mercedes Fontecilla (not the wife of José Miguel Carrera of the same name) presented herself to the recently restored royal officials and requested the return of her dowry from Felipe Calderón on the grounds of adultery. She asked the authorities to take quick action to prevent his fleeing with her assets "because he has been one of the most decided and public supporters of the revolutionary and insurgent party on account of which he feared the arrival of royal troops."[36] The lawsuit followed the slow course of mutual recriminations and presentation of evidence typical in such cases. She accused him of having an affair with a slave, of not providing for her when he went to Peru on business, and of destroying her dowry papers upon the death of her father. He countered that he was an able administrator of her dowry and inheritance. Calderón denied Fontecilla's contention that he was a security risk by explaining that he had in fact protected their joint interests by hiding, like other merchants, when troops approached in order to avoid looting of his shop.[37] They had sufficient property to merit the costs and time of litigation—at one point Calderón estimated the value of his wife's dowry and inheritance at 22,000 pesos in urban and rural property, livestock, and jewels—but they were not among Santiago's elite. She had filed in ecclesiastical court for an official separation, and their lawyers argued over the financial technicalities of whether or not he should pay alimony (he asserted that she had a higher income stream) and lose administration of her dowry before a final sentence in that case.

Although Calderón mentioned politics a few times in three hundred, double-sided manuscript pages of this initial suit, for the most part his lawyer attributed his wife's supposedly false accusations to material desires beyond her station and "the weakness characteristic of the ignorance of her sex."[38] Over the course of two years (1814 to 1816), the decisions made by judges at various levels showed no particular favoritism to one party or the other.[39] Two years after Fontecilla initiated proceedings, a judge denied

Calderón's effort to make his wife responsible for two thousand pesos exacted on him by the royal officials, pointing out that a wife was not legally liable from her own assets for a husband's debts and that he had not proven that her accusation (that he had sided with the insurgents) resulted in that levy.[40] On the other hand, the court also ordered Fontecilla to turn over to her husband any income she collected on their rental houses. She appealed the order but then desisted on January 17, 1817 (as San Martín and O'Higgins secretly began their ascent over the Andes), so that the parties could settle accounts.[41]

The story of the turbulent marriage, and the association between the independence struggle and depictions of ideal Chilean wives, was taken up six months later in a lawsuit filed this time by "the citizen" Calderón in the courts of the restored republic. Claiming that ecclesiastical authorities had never approved a permanent separation, he requested custody of their daughter and the right to administer the joint marital property. Moreover, he attributed their marital conflict explicitly to political disputes: "At the very time of the installation of our national Government, the domestic disagreements with my wife began, caused principally by our differences of opinion." Specifically, he identified her as a supporter of the Carreras, to whom she was distantly related, while he opposed their seizure of power. More seriously, he accused Fontecilla of having reported his support for the insurgents (presumably the anti-Carrera faction) to the royal authorities who imposed upon him fines and ultimately arrest.[42] Indeed her decision to withdraw an appeal over rents in the initial case coincided with his being shipped off to the Juan Fernández presidio, where he remained for about two months before all the prisoners were liberated by patriot forces.[43] Appealing to the notion that women were inherently apolitical, her lawyer countered that the couple's dissension was rooted in his infidelity, "not political opinions in which the [female] sex always cedes to the gentle influence of the husband."[44] But these were not apolitical times, and Calderón's lawyer contrasted the behavior of Fontecilla with that of other wives of incarcerated patriots:

> In Chile, whose women have been models of conjugal virtues, should we allow such a horrible example of immorality and cold cruelty to go unpunished? [This woman was] . . . unmoved by the tears and the most heroic tribulations of the other wives who, throwing themselves at the feet of the tyrants, pleaded for mercy and proclaimed the innocence of their persecuted husbands.[45]

Her lawyer acknowledged the pleas of these prisoners' wives, but also dryly noted that their husbands had been on the penal island for two and a half years, rather than just a few months, and that their assets had also been seized.[46]

As the new case entered its ninth month of various judicial decisions over who would control a particular asset or another, and with Fontecilla receiving slightly but not dramatically less favorable rulings than in the initial lawsuit, Calderón decided to escalate. In July 1818, a few months after the patriot victory at Chacabuco, he accused his wife of treasonous acts that had put his life in peril.[47] He proceeded to present witnesses who testified that Fontecilla recruited soldiers from the infamous royalist company of Chiloé, who were lodged at her home, to stake out her patriot husband to see which women were visiting him. Other witnesses reported that even her brother had tried to dissuade her from accusing her husband of association with the insurgency, and the lawyer who filed her lawsuit in 1814 similarly stated that he had advised her against making such references in the written complaint.[48] On August 18, 1818, the state-appointed prosecutor (fiscal) José Gregorio Argomedo backed Calderón's charges. By accusing her husband of being a rebel and using royal soldiers to spy on him, she had indeed put his life in danger, if not immediately then as a result of what he would suffer on "the Island of Hell." Argomedo recommended she be confined to a convent, "until the example of those virtuous souls achieve her reform and repentance," and that Calderón be awarded administration of her property and custody of their children.[49]

With this formal criminal charge, the trial entered the lengthy stage of presentation of evidence by each side. Fontecilla's lawyer argued that Calderón was well known for his patriot sympathies and since he was not imprisoned until over two years after his wife filed for divorce, her accusations were not the cause. Rather, he was caught up in the "grasping of a drowning person, that Marcó committed in the death throes of his regime, banishing all those who were said to be Patriots despite the tears and efforts of their wives and families."[50] He also contrasted Calderón's mere fifty-six days of detention to the terms suffered by others, asserting that it was ridiculous to request all of Fontecilla's property in compensation. Calderón's lawyer continued to juxtapose Fontecilla's "monstrous" behavior with the example of the "best [women] in the entire world who chose poverty and nourished themselves with their tears so as not to expose even the smallest fault of their husbands."[51] Her attorney, therefore, countered that a cruel and adulterous Calderón hardly lived up to the model patriot husband in "virtuous Chile":

"They expect heroic actions, to which no one is obligated, from the weaker sex. And instead of motivating them with a model on the part of the stronger sex, they exhibit only crimes."[52] Simultaneously, the divorce case proceeded in ecclesiastical court until May 1819, when Fontecilla was awarded a permanent separation on the grounds of her husband's adultery.[53]

By the time Fiscal Argomedo was called upon to issue his final recommendation, more than a year and a half after the initial charge of treason, he still affirmed Fontecilla's guilt on the grounds that her intent in accusing her husband of being an insurgent was to harm him and keep the attention of royal authorities on him even if he was not immediately arrested. But, "considering the moderation with which our Government has been treating this kind of crime," he no longer called for her confinement but only that Calderón be awarded administration of his wife's property, which would not normally result from a separation in which the husband was found guilty.[54] When the three justices on the superior court finally passed their sentence on January 24, 1821, Chile's independence was almost secured; rather than highlighting political dangers, therefore, they lamented the damage to the social order inflicted by the public and shocking accusations made by both spouses. They awarded one-third of the income generated by Fontecilla's assets to Calderón, reserving the other two-thirds for her maintenance and that of their daughter. Acting to protect the honor of the latter, moreover, they prohibited the presentation of any further material by either side, ordering the case to be filed away in the "secret archive."[55] Although Calderón did receive his third until at least 1836, the justices' goal of burying the ugly matter was not achieved: Calderón and Fontecilla continued to fight in court over payments until 1845, and as late as 1829 he was still calling her a *goda* ("Goth"), an insulting term for a royalist.[56]

This couple, like many families, had been caught up in the politics of independence. Political prisoners and their loved ones suffered the mental anguish of separation but also publicized their plight as a way to discredit the royal government as failing to live up to its paternalist principles. Fontecilla, by contrast, initially sought the protection of royal officials in disputes with her husband only to find, with the return of the patriots to power, that her behavior would be contrasted with the model of the weeping women who publicly advocated for their absent husbands. The rancor that had developed between Fontecilla and Calderón differed little from that of other unhappy couples who went to court before and after independence, but the intensity of the period from 1814 to 1818 politicized their domestic disagreements. Other women might place their love for men above politics, as with an anonymous young woman in southern Chile who urged her betrothed in 1814 to desert the patriot army and flee with her to Lima where her father could set him up in business: ". . . you do not need a uniform to live brilliantly and with as many comforts as you could wish for; and so come; let's go to Lima; leave aside bullets; don't risk your life."[57] In contrast to the criticism leveled against Fontecilla, who fell short of the "heroic actions" expected of women during wartime, this woman's fears were understandable; the official who sent her letter to O'Higgins noted simply that she hoped to save her husband.[58] Such a distinction was similar to that between Javiera Carrera, who put politics above her marriage, and Ana María Cotapos, who wished to escape politics in order to make a life with her beloved Juan José.

Family Correspondence as Alleged Espionage

As in the case of the Carreras, royalists and patriots alike were suspicious of their enemies' family members. As part of his case to attribute his arrest to his wife's accusations, Calderón pointed out that others with the same patriotic sympathies had not been punished unless "it was feared that they exercised influence owing to their talents or Family relations, which did not apply to me."[59] Likewise, upon their return from exile to Chile in 1817, patriot leaders viewed relatives of suspected royalists with apprehension. In April, O'Higgins named the wives of various royalist officers who should be confined to monasteries and watched closely to prevent them from sending or receiving correspondence, and then extended the order: "As a last resort, shut up in that convent all the harmful godas, especially those who are related to the enemy by marriage or other ties, and hold them responsible for paying their monthly maintenance."[60] Even in the absence of other evidence, family relations alone could be enough to recommend extra vigilance. The governor of San Fernando expressed such concerns to O'Higgins about Salvador Olaguer Feliú: "There is nothing said against him, indeed generally people assure me that he was in favor of Chile's freedom and against the sentiments of his father. Nevertheless, given the importance of the latter in the royal army and their close kinship, it seemed appropriate to me to send the son to the central authorities."[61]

In contrast to Santiago, where by 1819 Argomedo noted the government acting with greater leniency toward its opponents, tensions between patriots and royalists intensified as the conflict in the south settled into an extended civil war. These were years of a "war to the death" in the southern region of Chile, and to contemporaries the outcome was still unknown. Moreover, this phase of the war had a great impact upon the civilian population, as first one and then the other army occupied towns, forced large-scale emigrations, and set fire to houses and farms. The patriots both denounced the abuse and murder of women and children by royalist guerrillas and their indigenous allies, and used such acts as justification for their own executions of prisoners and of civilians suspected of being spies, including women.

From 1817 to 1820, the city of Concepción and its port Talcahuano changed hands five times, and smaller towns such as Chillán and Los Angeles experienced even more frequent turnovers. (See map 1.1 in the introduction.) In January 1818, after a long and unsuccessful siege of Talcahuano, where the royalist army was entrenched, the patriot forces retreated from Concepción to central Chile, taking with them 50,000 civilians and setting fire to the countryside so that "the enemy would not find in its path more than a desert, houses without people, fields without crops or cattle" according to orders issued by O'Higgins.[62] Ten months later, the royalist forces, fearing a patriot attack by sea, withdrew from Talcahuano first to Los Angeles and ultimately to Arauco, accompanied by civilians, including María Manuela Urrejola and her sister Trinitarian nuns of Concepción, who feared retribution for their decision to stay under royalist authority.[63] "I have come amidst an Army," wrote one of the nuns of her ordeal, "surrounded by enemies, crossing mountains and rivers, sometimes on foot and other times on horseback . . . not a day passed when I did not fall two or three times, usually flat on my back."[64] The nuns would not return to their convent until Christmas of 1822 as skirmishes in the south persisted.

Military historians attribute the ability of the royalists to hold out in southern Chile for so long partly to the failure of patriot forces to follow up adequately on their victories, allowing their enemy to regroup time and again south of the Biobío, where they had the support of many Mapuche leaders.[65] Chile's most prominent historian of the nineteenth century, Diego Barros Arana, acknowledged that much of the region's creole and mestizo population also had royalist sympathies, joining guerrilla bands, provisioning the army, and providing intelligence. He asserted that the royalist spy network in the south was so effective that patriot officers regarded the region's civilian population with mistrust.[66] At the beginning of their siege of Talcahuano in April 1817, the commanding officer issued an edict that all those caught providing food to or maintaining correspondence with the enemy would be executed, and in September O'Higgins assured San Martín that he was patrolling the lines and setting traps to cut off all communication.[67] Women were chief among civilians suspected of aiding the royalists.

Of seventeen people from the towns of Talca, Parral, San Carlos, and Linares who were identified in an 1817 military communiqué as likely royalist conspirators, fourteen were women.[68] Two years later, Commander Ramón Freire again ordered the removal of families of suspected royalist guerrillas to prevent their sheltering the enemy.[69] When the mayor of Concepción heard in July 1817 that Manuel Bello, his cousin Benito Lazo, and José León were taking provisions into Talcahuano, he immediately ordered the arrest of their sisters and brother; nonetheless, the siblings insisted that they were not on good terms with the alleged smugglers and so had no knowledge of their activities.[70] Although there was only one witness in another smuggling case, the governor of Quillota was convinced of María Luisa Flechar's guilt because her son was in a prisoner-of-war camp for royalists. O'Higgins ordered Flechar to report to the central authorities in Santiago.[71]

A court martial in Concepción against silversmith Juan José Caro for allegedly harboring his son Antonio, a presumed enemy spy reporting back to royalist officers in Talcahuano, reveals the atmosphere of mistrust and fear that dominated the south. Neighbor Valentina de Acosta testified that on the evening of October 2, 1817, a man arrived at Caro's house and looked all around before entering; she was suspicious since no one should have been visiting Caro after dark "especially because as a royalist he has been prohibited from socializing with others."[72] Officers detained Caro, his wife Narcisa Villaseñor, and daughter María Dolores Caro and began to interrogate other members of the household as possible witnesses. Journeyman Ignacio Mendoza said he did not live in the house and so had no knowledge of visitors.[73] Juan Bustos, a ten-year-old indigenous servant, concurred that Antonio had visited the house once, but that he could not hear what he and his parents discussed. When pressed to declare whether Antonio was a spy, Bustos offered that "given the efforts of Antonio Caro to remain silent and hidden when he arrived, it seems that his primary objective was to spy on the Patriots."[74] He thought his older sister, also a servant, might know more. María Bustos denied any knowledge of the alleged visit but did report that the family frequently expressed royalist sympathies and that Villaseñor had set her to work baking bread to send to Talcahuano. Asked if the family respected her, Bustos replied "Juan José Caro, his wife, and family profess a bitter hatred toward her, because when the family speaks against the Patria and in favor of the King, she strongly disagrees with them."[75]

In their statements, all three family members not only denied that Antonio had visited but also claimed they were patriotic Americans, the term for those born in Chile and other parts of Spanish America.[76] Caro's widowed daughter-in-law, Milagro Hurtado, whom María Bustos had identified as a patriot, similarly characterized the accusation as the false denunciation of someone who had completely forgotten "humanity, charity, and Religion." Moreover, she identified the evening visitor as Juan Tobar, who worked herding cattle for the patriot army.[77] Given this new information, the interrogators arranged a judicial confrontation between the Caro family and their indigenous servants. They all stuck to their original stories, except for young Juan Bustos who, "pale and quiet," responded to the judge's question of who had visited, "it must have been Juan Tobar."[78] Called to testify, Tobar admitted that he had dined and slept at the Caro house several times, but added that one time he had heard the sound of horses and then saw some people enter the house. When asked whether he worked for the army out of conviction or for the money, he acknowledged his wages but insisted that he did it because he was a patriot "as this was a powerful motivation that dominated all his passions, to such an extent that he would like to see . . . exterminated all those against the American system." He did not know before that the Caros were royalists, he concluded, but now that he had learned that their son was a spy he hated them as enemies.[79] Whether out of fear or conviction, a witness who might have cleared the family's name instead chose to denounce them.

The prosecutor's summation, which ends the case, demonstrates the heightened tensions of the war, especially in the south, and the tendency to pass judgment on thin evidence. The initial depositions (presumably the neighbor and the two servants), he asserted, left no doubt: "all three point directly to the crime of high treason that today characterizes the infamous, perfidious, and de-naturalized Juan José Caro, his wife, and children: the trial leaves no doubt that the criminal Caro and his family are professed Enemies of the American Cause and for this reason concealed the espionage."[80] While it was true that these three witnesses had all characterized the Caro family as expressing royalist sympathies, only Juan Bustos had identified the mysterious visitor as son Antonio, and he had later retracted that statement. Nonetheless, the prosecutor recommended that Caro, his wife, and daughter be sent into detention in far northern Chile and their property confiscated. He added that journeyman Mendoza, who had lied under oath about not living in the household, should do six years hard labor without pay and tethered by a chain. Although the final sentence is missing from the trial, the process of taking testimony and the prosecutor's assessment demonstrate that merely receiving a visit from a son who was suspected of working for the enemy was considered a crime during wartime.

In addition to such trials, patriot concerns over espionage resulted in the archiving of numerous intercepted letters, rich sources with which to analyze the impact of the war on families as well as their response.[81] The correspondence seized by patriot officers in southern Chile was often prosaic and the content ranged from family news to occasional political or military references. But even those letters whose main objective was to communicate love and concern for absent relatives entered into the public sphere upon being captured by the military forces. During the state of war, to send such letters was considered to be a high crime of treason and the authors and carriers were prosecuted. In such a context, whether conspiratorial communications or the most intimate note, to write became a political act.

The letters, many in shaky script and riddled with misspellings, nonetheless adhered to a similar model. The following brief missive demonstrates in a few words the most common elements of this type of correspondence:

> My esteemed Cruz I celebrate your good health and that of all those of your household and in particular that of my father and carmelita and rosita and Jose Maria and Siriaco here there is no news only that we are very afflicted with this damned patria that is not a patria but a hell and I do not see a time when I will be with my loved ones [los míos] send me some pounds of sugar and tobacco and send me news of how you are and Josefa gave me a pound of tea for my sister carmen. [signed] You know who.[82]

As in this example, almost all the letters open with warm greetings—father, sister, or lady of my heart or of my affection—and sign off from your daughter, brother, or wife "who desires to see you." In between, their authors related the current state of the family: here we are well, or ill, or afflicted, or "with our souls still in our bodies," and we hope that you find yourself in good health.[83]

Despite the largely cheerful greetings at the beginning and end, the letters leave a vivid testament to the toll that war and forced migrations had taken on families. Upon retaking Concepción in late 1820, royalist officer Mariano Ferrabú wrote to his sister about their miraculous victories, but also observed, "they no longer take prisoners, the Fields are sown with Cadavers."[84] Another soldier at the same time told his brother they were holding off on attacking Talcahuano, where the patriot forces had taken refuge, to save the lives of innocent families and "so that less blood is spilled than has been the case."[85] And priest Juan Antonio Ferrabú asked Tadea Concha to assure Carmelita that although her Aguayo, presumably her husband or son, was working for the insurgents in Talcahuano, the royalists were trying to get him to desert and that even if they took that port "nothing would happen to him, unless it were to occur in the conflagration that war brings in its path."[86] Manuel de Mier's story of what had happened to him in the two years since having to abandon Nacimiento conveys some of the confusion and chaos of the era. "I assure you there was much disorder," he related to Manuel Pantoja in late 1820, "the Soldiers took the boats and left us civilians and families abandoned on the shore." A boy took him to where he could cross the river in a small craft and after three days a don Lorenzo sent for him to go to Monterrey. There Mier joined up with women named María Antonia and Conchi with whom he continued on to Arauco. But in a patriot attack, he got separated from his family for a time. Meanwhile Lorenzo went to Valdivia where he first got into trouble for criticizing royal Commander Vicente Benavides and then was captured by patriot troops and taken to Concepción. Somehow Lorenzo ended up again among the royalists in Rere where Benavides was ready to execute him until other officers interceded.[87]

A major objective of the correspondence was to locate relatives and reconstruct family networks torn apart by forced and voluntary migrations as well as acts of war. Carmen Nova wrote from the town of Santa Bárbara, along the Biobío frontier, to her sister Rosario, most likely in Peru based upon references within the letter. Carmen commiserated with Rosario over the fate of Rivas, either a relative or common friend, who had been captured by patriot forces, but passed on the news that he had been spared execution and was instead sent to Santiago. In turn, Carmen thanked Rosario for sending her information: "I have received much joy from the news that you sent about Manuelita of whom I knew nothing since we were separated in Concepción."[88] Other times the news was not good. One woman wrote that God must be punishing her for being too attached to her loved ones: "I have no news from home not even whether they are alive or dead, last year I learned that they had taken Silveria and Ilaria prisoners and had banished them to I don't know where, I have heard nothing about Acuña, whether alive or dead, because I have not received any letter."[89] The writer also informed the recipient that she had moved from Tucapel to El Rosal in search of a confessor, and then could not move again because she was caring for a very ill Juliana. Letter writers recognized that news traveled slowly and was not always reliable. "In this war," María Jesús Riveros wrote to her *comadre* (a bond created by serving as godparent) Rosario Nova, "as soon as one receives word of one thing, another is contradicted."[90]

Correspondents faced great difficulties getting their letters out, and clearly many never arrived at their intended destination. Several nuns began letters by saying that they were going to write quickly, having just heard about the arrival of a boat, not waiting to see if it brought them any letters to which they could reply, because in the past they had missed the opportunity to send their own before it set sail again. Similarly Mier informed Pantoja that he had already written two letters but that each time when he sent them, they failed to reach the boat before it departed.[91] Angel Gatica wrote from Concepción in 1820 to Clemente Lantaño conveying his sympathy for what he had suffered during a royalist retreat from Valdivia and particularly the separation from his wife Juanita and the rest of his family; Gatica added that mail to Valdivia was being intercepted or he would have tried to get word through to Juana.[92] Less frequently, correspondents expressed relief at having received a letter, or could share news such as: "we have heard that Doña Mercedes is alive in Los Angeles."[93]

Although one person actually wrote the letter, almost always he or she represented a larger community of extended family and friends, referring to others who sent their greetings: "Remember me to Panchita who will not forget to entrust me to God and to Chepita Martinita Juana Rosa and to Jose Ramon and . . . also to my comadre Nicolasita"[94] or "a thousand remembrances to Doña Agustinita and Josesito from my mother, tell Martines not a day goes by that we do not think of him and we do not lose hope of seeing him, tell pepa oyague and her Mother that their family is well."[95] Sometimes, in addition to sharing words, the writer also tried to make a physical connection: "I'm sending for you an ounce of snuff and a half bunch of tobacco, please give my mother 2 pesos as a token to show that I am thinking of her" or "I know that sugar is very scarce so I'm sending you a pound."[96] The nuns profusely thanked those who sent herbal tea and cloth from Lima but asked also for devotional items, lamenting their state of spiritual as well as physical hunger.[97] Of course, everything was scarce during wartime and so such packages were often a necessity, but they were also an attempt to reestablish physical contact with friends and family. Material accompaniments to written sentiments, moreover, reflected the importance of familial networks of support and care.

As well as trying to locate and stay in touch with loved ones, some letter writers referenced the fulfillment of, or failure to fulfill, expected family roles particularly as providers. Manuela Somonte wrote from Concepción in October and November 1820 to a Rafael who was her godson, and possibly also her stepson, chiding him for the lack of communication:

With great Pleasure I Write This so that you will Know of Our Existence since thanks to the Mercy of God we are All Surviving Although You must Believe we are Dead since you Have not Written any letter even though we are so defenseless, after all your father has Not missed any opportunity to Write us even though he is So far away and Among His Enemies 50 leagues beyond Buenos Aires And he always Asks us for News of your whereabouts And he says that Eduardo is Supporting him With His work.[98]

She then went on to recount what they had suffered, especially without a man to help: fleeing through Mapuche territory with Commander Sánchez, "Walking all Day Without Eating from dawn To dusk through mud and Potholes Sinking Up to our Knees,"[99] and "Going up and Down the mountains without even a Flask of water to Drink."[100] For five months, she reported, they had received a stipend (presumably from the royalist army), but for another six it was reduced to half. Then it ceased altogether, she reported, although she found out some refugees were still secretly receiving pensions. "Think how sad it would Be to See Your poor Siblings Dying of Hunger," she remarked pointedly.[101] During the time they were apart, she continued, "Juanito has grown by leaps and bounds, it took much effort to Hide him from the fury of those Bloodthirsty pirates [i.e., the patriots], At last General Benavides has Rescued them and has given Juanito the Post of Cadet In the Battalion of Concepción." She finished, like so many other correspondents, with greetings from all the family, noting how much Juanito (presumably his little brother) wanted to see him and that his little sister asked that he send her a blouse since she had almost no clothing. Then in the margins, she added a postscript letting him know that they had just heard that his father had been transferred with the other prisoners of war from Las Bruscas to the city where she assumed the recipient of the letter to be (probably Lima): "this news has given us Great Satisfaction, I don't Know If It Is True And so Let Us know as soon as Possible."[102] The news reports and requests were aimed at getting Rafael to provide for his siblings, given that his imprisoned father was unable to fulfill these paternal duties.

In addition to sending greetings to and from a multitude of relatives and friends within the text of the letters, their authors constructed networks to write and send the letters. Those persons anxious to communicate with family members would try to find out who would be traveling across enemy lines, such as between Concepción and the port of Talcahuano. Many couriers were poor women who hid notes in their petticoats or bodices, according to the reports of the soldiers who searched them. Having captured one, the military investigators could often follow the thread to expose a larger network of relatives, friends, and servants. María Josefa Ponse, captured in 1817, confessed that when don José Ordóñez, chief of the royalist forces in Talcahuano, found out that she wanted to go to Concepción he gave her a letter to deliver to a Señora Antonia Andariena, whose son was serving in the Spanish army. Ponse (the letter carrier) said that she already knew Señora Andariena as a friend of her patron or employer. Upon arriving at the house, she spoke with Andariena's daughter who sent Ponse to hide out in the home of a doña Rita. Andariena's servant testified that Ponse had come to the house on various occasions with messages from royalist officers, and that her employer told her to keep quiet about these visits. The servant also said that neither Andariena nor her daughter knew how to write, but that a friend, doña Nieves, frequently visited them. The daughter and Nieves insisted that they knew nothing about the letters, but the authorities found another note signed by Nieves in the same handwriting. Andariena confessed to her own communications with the enemy but at first denied the participation of the other young women. Nevertheless, when her interrogators confronted her directly with the notes with matching handwriting, the scribe recorded her response as:

That out of respect for the friendship and good harmony that she has with Doña Nieves she had tried not to reveal her name, hoping to avoid any cause for harming her but now that the fact has already been discovered and her denial in addition to being useless would make her a criminal, and out of consideration for the truth and the oath she has sworn she confesses to have seen Doña Nieves write it, having composed and dictated it together.[103]

The main objective of the intercepted letters was to communicate personal news, but many also discussed the war and politics. For the most part, such references were very general: such and such general has arrived in port, the patriots have set siege to Talcahuano, they are making us emigrate to such and such a place (often "among the infidels"), the royalist forces are advancing. Letters reported, for example, that "the patriots have taken talcaguano with all the families there and the general has them besieged so that they find themselves very afflicted without having any consolation neither by sea nor by land . . ."[104] or "now Our Chief has the Enemy well cornered and all the frontiers are in our control."[105] Correspondents often also expressed their sympathies for the royalists and complained bitterly about the abuses of the enemy:

Merceditas I assure you that this unfortunate town [is] in the utmost desolation now it is not even a shadow of what it once was I don't know when Our Lord will raise his arm of Justice that so Rightly he has brought down upon us. The houses burned, the insurgents destroyed them in order to build up their own; where you lived has been reduced to nothing but the foundation.[106]

Such passages were sometimes underlined, presumably by the patriot officers who regarded such views as treasonous whether or not they provided any real intelligence. Much less frequently, they might reveal specific news about numbers of troops and their movements, the delivery of weapons, or the arrival of a flotilla with the objective of aiding the royalist forces.

Even soldiers tended to write as much personal news as descriptions of battles. One wrote from Concepción to his cousin in Lima in November 1820. Although the royalists had just taken that city after a series of victories along the frontier, he said he was not writing to recount these glories, about which his cousin could read in the newspaper, but rather "to let you know that I am healthy and nothing has happened to me other than that every day I have more work to do."[107] Although he asked his cousin to send him some books with military tactics and regulations, he also sent his greetings to eight people by name and "lastly to all my friends." Finally, he regretted that the imminent departure of the boat left him no time to write additional letters, and so asked his cousin to write on his behalf to his father in the town of Castro on Chiloé Island in the far south.[108]

Concern that letters might contain intelligence was one reason that patriot authorities seized all correspondence and prosecuted those who carried it. Women were frequently both the authors and couriers. "It is the experience in all the Revolution that the Enemy has sustained its Espionage inflicting incalculable evils upon the Republic by means of the women," one high officer declared. "Your Lordship is well aware of it and the pity and leniency with which they have been regarded have not had the proper result since they still persist in their obstinate opinion."[109] As the war intensified, therefore, the patriots zealously prosecuted such women without regard for the supposed "weakness of their sex" or for the personal nature of much of the correspondence. In 1817, for example, Carmen Belmar was captured during the siege of Talcahuano when she returned to Concepción from that port carrying letters. When she was asked if she understood the seriousness of the crime, she responded: "she knew that it was wrong to go to the enemy but she had no other means of seeing her only brother and that in order to return, after having learned of the death of her brother, it was necessary to accept letters to obtain her way out."[110]

One of the letters Belmar carried was written by royalist officer José Sirilo [Cirilo] Retamal to his wife and dealt only with family news, following the same model (and lack of punctuation) as so many others:

> My most beloved and esteemed Wife of all my heart in company of my beloved children and my esteemed Doña Maria Balencuela and my dear Mother Doña Mauricia de Opaso: Manuelita I write to tell you that I find myself in this fort of talcaguano in complete health and also I tell you that I have written you so many letters and I have not had any answer Manuela I send you an ounce of snuff and a half bunch of tobacco: on my part you will give two pesos to my mother as a sign that I remember her and I do not notify you of the departure because it is not appropriate to do so without anything else to add your most esteemed husband who desires only to serve you.—Jose Sirilo Retamal[111]

Retamal's intent was to let his loved ones know he was still alive and to fulfill his role as a husband and son who could provide, in however small a measure, for his family. He purposely withheld political messages and military intelligence from his letter, but in the midst of war, even the personal was political and the supposedly private was public.

The defense lawyer assigned to the women accused of carrying this and other letters cited the same justification Ana María Cotapos offered for corresponding with her husband in code. "Could these women be accused of a crime?" he asked rhetorically. "No: we would say that the laws of nature, of friendship, of conjugal love, cannot be restrained by anyone, when they proceed in good faith and without malice."[112] The prosecutor, however, asked for the maximum penalty according to the edicts issued by the patriot officers:

> and the crime having been proven, and in virtue of their sex: I conclude for the Patria that Carmen Belmar and Carmen Valdes be condemned to suffer the capital punishment of death so that by this example the scandalous communication with the enemy will be cut off and it will serve as a deterrent to others who might attempt it: Maria Fajardo and Manuela Nuñes must witness the punishment of their companions and then be exiled to some presidio.[113]

The president of the military tribunal agreed with the prosecutor, but the other members apparently could not bring themselves to carry it out, reducing the penalty to one hundred lashes for Belmar (who had carried the letters) and exile and detention during the duration of the war for the other women, who had sent and received correspondence.[114]

In some cases, the political intent of the correspondence was clear. In the southern fort of Valdivia in 1820 there was a conspiracy among men and women to motivate and aid royalist guerrillas in an attack on the city. They sent letters to their sons and brothers who were hidden in the mountains. The principal correspondent was the sister of one of the guerrillas; even some men dictated their letters for her to write. In one she declared:

> My esteemed and beloved I will celebrate infinitely that upon receiving this that your condition continues unchanged. This is simply to tell you that a very good opportunity has presented itself to shake off this heavy yoke that torments us so much. This plan can be accomplished on Sunday, which is the day of My Lady of Mercedes, and these [soldiers] have a very great ball they will all be drunk and so we can achieve victory easily taking them by surprise. Commit yourself, valiant champion, to defend the just cause as all the Valdivianos are ready to aid you to take up arms and to ferry you on boats.[115]

The chief of this guerrilla band was Andrés Palacios, and his own family displayed more concern for his safety than commitment to the royalist cause. His brother Valentín Palacios testified he had tried to get his brother to turn himself in to the authorities to which Andrés responded by pointing a pistol at him and speaking out against the patriots. Since then, Valentín continued, he had not written to his brother and spoke rarely with their parents.[116] The maternal aunt of Andrés had similarly advised him to surrender to which he had reportedly replied "that first they would have to catch him."[117]

The guerrilla leader's father, Ramón Palacios, denied being part of the plot but did confess to having sent letters and supplies to his son, some written apparently by his daughter Severa.[118] One of those letters, dated July 15, 1820, and addressed to "My very beloved son," reads like many of the other captured missives, expressing best wishes for his health and conveying, "I and all those in our Household send the best, although wishing very much, on the other hand, to see you." The letter then took a surprising twist, revealing that his father had been imprisoned twice and that the governor of Valdivia advised the recipient to turn himself in: "why do you want to be mixed up in such a scheme, you should come back, you have been pardoned on his word of honor."[119] The trial transcript began on November 7, 1820, and includes a letter from Andrés Palacios to the governor of Valdivia dated November 24 thanking him for not executing his father and asking that his family members be released. He implied that he might be ready to switch sides, but feared being deceived and wanted assurances.[120] Apparently, patriot officials were using Ramón Palacios as a hostage in an attempt to negotiate his son's surrender. A memorandum on December 3 confirms that another message had been sent to Palacios but that he had not yet replied and that there were rumors that Benavides had communicated with him about recent royalist victories in the Concepción area. On December 4, 1820, the military tribunal condemned four men, including Ramón Palacios, to be executed by a firing squad, but the sentence was not carried out until December 12 when they decided negotiations with the guerrillas would not be successful. Furthermore, when the trial transcript reached Santiago, the judge advocate (*auditor de guerra*) recommended the death penalty as well for Micaela Ocaña and Dolores Moreno, mother and daughter, who had coordinated the correspondence with the guerrillas:

> Their punishment must serve as a warning for those who would similarly cooperate with the enemies of order. Thus these two perfidious women should die, unless out of great mercy Your Excellency wished to commute the punishment to a decade of incarceration, where day after day they would feel the enormity of their treason.[121]

The ultimate fate of the women in the Palacios trial was not recorded, but in another case Josefa Garrido was condemned as a spy and shot within twenty-four hours. She insisted that she had crossed enemy lines (in this case the Biobío River) only in search of food for her family, an appropriately gendered excuse. The letter that she carried, from José Antonio Roas to his cousin, was one that mixed concern over the situation of his family with some general news about the war and politics. Embracing the role of devoted son, he asked his cousin to tell his mother:

> Do not forget your son born of your womb and do not think that he has forgotten you, that some day, which God will choose, he will serve and attend you with honor in closing mother I do not have more to say except to tell my brothers that they not go around wasting time and that they not lose their honor of being upstanding men [*hombres de bien*] since I am doing the same.[122]

In spite of her protests of innocence, Garrido was able to reveal specific details about the whereabouts of royal officer Benavides, the number of troops and arms he commanded, and his plans of attack. Therefore, based upon no evidence other than her confession, the sergeant major denounced:

she has not foregone any personal sacrifice with the singular aim of satisfying the implacable hate she harbors against the system of her own country; and so it is that without any consideration she should suffer the indicated punishment in order to serve as an example to others of her sex.[123]

The next day she was shot.

Undoubtedly, some letter writers and couriers were spies, and thus their correspondence provided intelligence that might aid one side or the other on the battlefield. Nevertheless, that the vast majority of letters lacked any tactical information, and some did not even express political opinions, suggests that the effort to intercept such communications went beyond the prevention of espionage. The war in the south was fought not only over territory, but also over hearts and minds. The forced emigrations and sieges were aimed at isolating the enemy from the region's population and demoralizing soldiers and civilians alike by preventing them from knowing the fate of their loved ones. Letter writers challenged such a strategy, insistently publicizing their existence along with that of their mothers, spouses, sisters, brothers, and children. Moreover, as collective works, carrying news and greetings among multiple relatives and friends, they attempted to knit together both kin networks and political communities. This state of total war explains why the military prosecuted not just obvious spies but also those who carried even the shortest and most intimate notes.

....

The conflicts of the independence period affected almost all families. As in any war, households lost breadwinners as they were recruited or forced into military service. There was little distinction between home front and battlefield, especially in the south, where the war arrived on Chilean thresholds. In some cases, family members were taken away as prisoners, in others entire households were forcibly relocated. Assumptions that kin would share political opinions led to the surveillance and often detention of the relatives of known partisans. Wives of the prisoners on Juan Fernández mobilized a coordinated campaign to plead for mercy and advocate for their release, and patriots publicized the cruel treatment they allegedly received to undermine the efforts of royal governors to present themselves as benevolent patriarchs. Royalists in the south ignored orders against communication, smuggling out letter after letter in an effort to contact loved ones and discover their whereabouts. Some of the correspondence, like that of the Carreras, had explicitly tactical goals. Other missives were politicized by the context of psychological warfare.

The war also made more difficult the fulfillment of family roles. Patriot and royalist men alike struggled with the tension between serving a cause and continuing to protect and provide for their wives, children, and other family members. Along with their letters, in which they often acknowledged their roles as devoted husbands or sons, royalists tried to send material support, however small, to their families. Patriot officers also worried about their families. Juan Manuel Cabot, a resident of Buenos Aires who came to Chile as part of San Martín's army, requested a leave to assist his wife in Mendoza, where her mother had died. His declaration that he could no longer "observe my wife's suffering with indifference because I love her more than my own existence," however, made his superiors suspect an insufficient commitment to the cause.[124] More commonly, officials stationed in different parts of the country requested and offered assistance to their colleagues' relatives. Treasury official Domingo Pérez wrote to O'Higgins from Santiago in 1817 that he would take care of his mother and sister, insisting "they should not ask anyone else because I will provide all that is necessary."[125] In return, he asked that O'Higgins help out his widowed mother should she request his aid in southern Chile. Others requested lenience for relatives whose sympathies may have been on the other side. José Antonio Rodríguez, who had served as a royal judge and prosecutor during the reconquest period but switched his loyalties after Chacabuco, asked O'Higgins to show mercy toward his mother, sister, and nieces whom he feared had been convinced to take refuge among the royalists in Talcahuano.[126] In both 1814 and 1817, moreover, the warring armies arranged for exchanges of officers' wives and family members—including the mother and sister of O'Higgins—who were held in the opposite camp.[127] Reconstructing these familial networks of care would remain a priority during the period of nation-state formation after the war.

Men's political roles might make more difficult their fulfillment of paternal and filial responsibilities, but these duties were rarely in direct conflict. As in the case of the Carrera family, societal expectations were that single women would be loyal to fathers and married women would follow their husbands. Hence the pleas of the wives and daughters of the Juan Fernández prisoners were effective in shaping public opinion both at the time and in historical accounts. Vicente Grez, whose 1878 book was one of the first to memorialize the heroines of independence, recounted the story of young Rosario Rosales, who insisted on accompanying her elderly father to Juan

Fernández, and that of an anonymous wife who almost drowned trying to follow the boat that was carrying away her husband.[128] In early 1818, the patriot *Gazeta de Santiago de Chile* published a letter from Mercedes Rosales de Solar offering to donate cloth to the hospital on the grounds that "As mother, sister, and wife of Chileans prepared to spill their blood to defend the Freedom of their HOMELAND, I have considered it my duty to come forward and assist in any way that I could, because my sex does not excuse me from the obligations of being a Chilean." The editor offered her as "a perfect model of the civic virtues that all those of the fair sex should embody," that is, a woman who supported both her male relatives and the cause to which they were willing to sacrifice their lives.[129] By contrast, the patriot press satirized royalist women as old, ugly, and under the sway of their confessors, "petrified along with the sad monuments of the old servitude." Although they joked, therefore, that few men would be converted to royalism out of love, suitors were advised to educate young women on the benefits of independence.[130]

Other sources suggest that officials feared that such women would instead use their influence on male kin in a reversal of proper familial and gender roles. When arms were found in the house of Gabriela Velasques in San Felipe, about 100 kilometers north of Santiago, witnesses were quick to identify her as a royalist who had swayed her daughter, son-in-law, and grandson to her cause.[131] A year later, to the south in Pichidegua, witnesses similarly reported that María Jesús Romo influenced her husband to persecute patriots during the reconquest period; one reported even hearing Manuel Donoso tell his wife on the verge of tears: "Madam, if I had not married you I would have been a patriot with the patriots and a royalist with the royalists, but because I am married to you I have been a Royalist to the patriots and a patriot to the Royalists."[132] Depicting royalist women as exercising an unfeminine power over weak men in their families was in the same vein of political propaganda that portrayed royal authorities as tyrants rather than benevolent fathers. Letters and trial transcripts reveal more complicated cases in which family loyalties might be divided, or in which women might be forced to choose between being faithful to a husband or to a cause. Indeed, as we shall see in chapter 3, patriot authorities pressured the Chilean-born wives of Spanish émigrés to switch their loyalties from their husbands to the symbolic fathers of the new nation. Those who complied expected those officials to take on the responsibility of providing for them and their children, particularly if the state had seized their family patrimony.

CHAPTER 3

Émigrés, Refugees, and Property Seizures:

Chilean Officials in the Role of Family Providers

On January 16, 1816, the following notice appeared in the official royal gazette of Santiago: "The house of Don Ignacio de la Carrera, located on the Street of the Augustinian Convent, four blocks from the central plaza, has been put up for auction, for either purchase or rental."[1] The house had been valued by the royal treasurers at 13,693 pesos, along with the residence of his daughter Javiera at 18,117 pesos and that of his son Luis at 39,901.[2] Various notes about the furnishings as well as his other properties, including the hacienda of San Miguel in Melipilla and the smaller estate of the Conventillo he had purchased from confiscated Jesuit properties, are scattered throughout accounts related to the seizure of properties of suspected insurgents after the royalist restoration of 1814. One of the entries notes that an auction to rent out San Miguel had been canceled, and that the property instead would be turned over for administration by Pedro Díaz de Valdés, husband of Javiera Carrera.[3] The Carreras were not alone in facing the seizure of their property. Governor Osorio, citing various Spanish laws and ordinances, had ordered the sequestration of all property belonging to either prisoners or émigrés who had taken refuge in the United Provinces, to be held until their cases were sentenced, at which point confiscation could be one of the penalties. But unlike other patriots who returned to Santiago in 1817, Ignacio de la Carrera could not immediately recuperate his assets. At the end of July, almost four months since his return from the presidio in the Juan Fernández Islands, he lamented to daughter Javiera that he had nothing but a few changes of clothing. He was staying with her husband because someone had filed a petition to prevent the return of his own house; her house was also in litigation.[4] Exactly two years later, following the death of Ignacio de la Carrera, state attorney José Gregorio Argomedo requested that his properties again be sequestered to cover debts and penalties of his sons.[5]

In addition to seizing the property of their domestic enemies, officials of the O'Higgins government sequestered all assets of royalist émigrés. In June 1817, Ignacio's niece María de los Dolores Aráoz (she did not use her full surname of Aráoz Carrera) appealed a sequester order against 10,177 pesos that her husband had left in safekeeping with Mariano Serra, who had fled Chile after the Battle of Chacabuco. Her own husband, Manuel de Figueroa (son of Tomás de Figueroa, who had led a failed royalist uprising against the Chilean junta in 1811), had left for Spain on business before that battle, she claimed, and so should not be considered an émigré subject to sequester. She protested that the money included her dowry, her share of joint property, and the patrimony of their children for whom she now could not provide even their daily bread. Although she expected her full share returned, in the meantime she requested a pension that would provide necessary living expenses for herself and her children "as has been done for others whose husbands emigrated to Lima."[6] State attorney José Gregorio Argomedo scoffed at the claim of Dolores Aráoz and her characterization of her husband:

> I can never forget the political conduct of this individual. Can anyone prove that he was not a fervent enemy of the State, of our Cause? Can Doña Dolores really say so? How could one ignore the determination with which, from the time of the tyrant's invasion [1814], he persecuted those patriots who had put down his father's uprising? . . . Oh, Your Excellency, how our clemency is abused![7]

Argomedo recommended that no dispensations be made for her until the government had established regulations on the matter and she recognized the errors of her husband, who was "Ungrateful to her and to their children, since with his political opinion he has undone the favor granted to him of entrusting him with the hand of an American woman."[8]

During the independence war, the kin by blood or marriage of known partisans also came under suspicion of political involvement even in the absence of corroborating evidence. Although some relatives faced arrest and prosecution, the most common penalty that affected families was the loss of property. In 1814, royal officials seized assets belonging to Ignacio de la Carrera owing to his membership in the 1810 junta. The reluctance of patriot officials to return his property after 1817, however, rested primarily upon the resistance of his offspring to O'Higgins and San Martín. Aráoz Carrera, as both the daughter-in-law of a royal officer and relative to the Carreras, similarly elicited little sympathy from the O'Higgins administration. The reaction to her petition also hints at an emerging national identity figured in familial terms: although in practice husbands were not expected to align themselves politically with their in-laws, in patriot rhetoric Spanish royalists were denounced for "betraying" their American-born wives and children. This language could nonetheless put patriot officials in a bind; although it justified their seizure of royalist assets, it also invited a comparison of their treatment of enemy families with the failed paternalism of royal authorities between 1814 and 1817 that they had so vehemently condemned.

This chapter examines policies and practices of property seizure (secuestration) during the wars of independence to 1822, with particular attention to the petitions of affected family members.[9] Initially both royal and patriot officials treated wives' share of marital assets in a manner similar to procedures for handling property claims during suits for ecclesiastical separations. Women who sued husbands for divorce under canon law (separation without the right to remarry), like the case of Mercedes Fontecilla against Felipe Calderón, could request alimony while testimony was presented; if their spouses were found guilty, they could then request possession of their dowries and shares of joint assets.[10] Until 1821, many wives (if not the unfortunate Dolores Aráoz) who pleaded that they could not feed themselves or their children without access to the property seized from émigré husbands, were granted temporary pensions under the same terminology as alimony and child support (*alimentos*) upon condition that they shift their loyalty from their "ungrateful" husbands to the new paternalist state. As military conflict began to decline in 1821, the Senate proposed conditions under which full rights of possession might be restored to those who had been wrongfully accused of supporting the enemy and even to repentant royalists who wished to rejoin "the greater Chilean family." The initial beneficiaries were American-born women and children, but in southern Chile, where the commander of royal troops had forced civilians to emigrate, Governor Ramón Freire and other authorities were increasingly sympathetic to pleas of innocence even from the region's male inhabitants.

Property Seizures in Law and Practice, 1813 to 1820

The seizure of property belonging to suspected enemies on both the royalist and patriot sides is critical to understanding the relationship between families and the state, because the policy forced officials to decide the extent to which wives and children would suffer the consequences for the actions of their heads of household. Unfortunately, there is perhaps no subject more difficult to track through the archives and shifting legislation. Procedures and record keeping were often arbitrary, inconsistent, and prone to corruption during wartime, and all branches of the government struggled with how to reckon accounts in the aftermath. Officials had no qualms about seizing enemy property on the grounds that confiscation was a penalty for the crime of treason, but many complications ensued.[11] Quickly, wives petitioned for the return of their dowries and their share in joint marital property; these women or other guardians also protested on behalf of children who immediately lost the financial support of their fathers and faced the future loss of their inheritance. Technically, confiscation was a penalty to be applied after a criminal trial, though property could be held by the state in sequester (*secuestro*) prior to sentencing. But as implemented in Chile, especially between 1817 and 1820, anyone who had emigrated was considered guilty and their property treated as if it already belonged to the state. Initially perishable goods were auctioned before they spoiled, but eventually much real estate was also sold or given away. When suspects were later found innocent or pardoned (in most cases there was never a formal trial), they or their heirs demanded the return of property often no longer in the possession of the state.

Both royalist and patriot officials ordered the seizure of enemy property between 1813 and 1819 as a punishment and a means of raising funds. On April 15, 1813, the Chilean junta issued an order for the sequestration of assets in Chile belonging to residents of Peru in retaliation for a similar order issued by the viceroy in Lima against property there owned by Chileans.[12] But the confiscation of all kinds of property, from merchandise and cash to houses and rural estates, began in earnest during the Spanish reconquest period. Within a few days of occupying Santiago, Governor Osorio's legal adviser indicated the Royal Instruction for Intendants called for the sequestration of enemy property.[13] By January 1815, Osorio circulated lists of alleged insurgents, some imprisoned in Chile and others who had escaped, with orders to begin prosecution and to hold their property in case a guilty sentence led to permanent confiscation of their assets.[14] In April, he issued another order requiring anyone with knowledge of any funds left in safekeeping by insurgents before they fled over the Andes to report it within three days.[15] Spanish officials usually followed the principle that the property should be held until the end of a suspect's trial. With the exception of perishable items, which were auctioned off, seized properties were generally rented rather than sold.[16] The income generated by the seizures from 1813 to 1816 amounted to about 24,000 pesos, less than 2.5 percent of total state revenue during that period.[17] Of course, abuses likely occurred; people later protested that the royalists had seized and sold horses and cattle without any prior judicial sentence.[18]

Despite this attempt to follow the procedures as laid out under Spanish law, complaints did arise, particularly from the wives of the suspected rebels. As early as February 1815, Osorio wrote to the treasury ministers, who were charged with overseeing the property seizures, that "Among the matters that most concern me and especially weigh upon my heart are those of seizures and sequesters and the way in which they are carried out; the repeated clamors of the innocent affect me personally." Urging them to seize only property belonging to the accused and to sell only perishable items, he portrayed himself as a concerned father figure: "We will wipe away so many tears and avoid so much anxiety and unease, and in this way we will bring happier days to those whom fate had attempted to bring misfortune."[19] The ministers responded with a long defense of their conduct, pointing out that they had proceeded against only those on the lists prepared by Osorio himself. Although aware of the laws against selling nonperishables, they had also followed the governor's own orders to turn some silver into coins, to donate clothing to the royal troops, and to sell property belonging to several of the suspects. Moreover, they had complaints of their own about the stratagems of the insurgent families to hide items or claim exemptions based upon dowries: "We can assure you that this duty is dreadful and odious and not even an angel descended from heaven would be capable of proceeding in a manner that would satisfy those who do not want their property sequestered."[20] They concluded by asking to be relieved of this duty. Shortly thereafter, the king issued a pardon for suspected sympathizers of independence who had remained in Chile rather than fleeing to Río de la Plata. Although those who swore their loyalty to the royal government were promised the return of their properties, Marcó del Pont did not fully implement the terms of the pardon.[21]

Needless to say, numerous families were either harmed by or hoped to benefit from these property seizures. Nonetheless, royal authorities do not seem to have contemplated using these assets to aid the victims of war. In early February 1817, the commanding officer of the royal battalion from Valdivia requested permission to pay the wives of soldiers taken prisoner half their salary. On February 11, legal counsel advised the captain general against making such an exception to the regulations on the books governing public expenditures:

3.1. Bernardo O'Higgins, supreme director of Chile (1817–1823). *Source:* Narcisse Desmadryl, Hermojenes de Irisarri, and Miguel Luis Amunátegui, *Galería nacional, o, Colección de biografías i retratos de hombre célebres de Chile,* 2 vols. (Santiago: Imprenta Chilena, 1854), 1:70.

> The damages of war are immense and the costs too great for any state to be able to compensate those who suffer them: in addition to the Soldier, the Civilian suffers when his hacienda or house is sacked or his assets are consumed to maintain the army; many also perish in the fires, murders, and other atrocities when towns are stormed; but despite all this, their families and children are not supported by pensions for life.[22]

Marcó del Pont's decision is not recorded; given the ensuing events, the matter was likely dropped.

On February 12, 1817, patriot troops defeated the royal army at Chacabuco, and within a week O'Higgins issued a decree claiming for the state property of all prisoners of war and émigrés; those found to be hiding such assets would be shot.[23] On March 12, the decree was extended to include the property of anyone living in Spanish dominions, unless they had been exiled for their support of independence, on the grounds of reciprocity for royalist seizure of patriot property.[24] In the first month, ninety-seven denunciations of property belonging to émigrés were recorded in the account book for the Santiago area; informers were rewarded with one quarter of the assets seized.[25] The implementation of the decree during the first months appears to have been disorderly, especially out in the provinces. An official from Vallenar in the north reported that the estates of Spaniards had been looted. Although he claimed to have recuperated many of the goods, he recommended against prosecuting those responsible since so many people had been involved.[26] In Santiago, secretary of state Miguel Zañartu complained to O'Higgins that everyone was trying to profit from the sale of merchandise seized from the shops of fleeing Spaniards:

> Those claiming a share in sequestered property have risen up in force. I have had to resist the Prosecutor, Legal Adviser, Attorneys, and claimants. Few, very few, indeed I would say no one looks out for the public interest. They believe that State property is the prize for those in favor or those who lobby most.[27]

Between 1817 and 1824, 762,017 pesos officially entered the national treasury from the sale and rental of sequestered property. Income from sequestration constituted the single largest revenue source in 1817, surpassing even customs duties, and provided 14 percent of all revenue in the first two years of the new government.[28] Further, some houses and haciendas seized from royalist émigrés were given to patriots seen as deserving of compensation, from fairly humble folk up to leaders such as José de San Martín and Ramón Freire; it is unclear whether such properties were included in treasury revenue calculations. Finally, the families of suspected royalists complained that officials took additional goods, which they left off the official inventories.

Gradually, the new state tried to regularize the process. On April 23, 1817, Zañartu issued a brief set of instructions for the Sequestration Commission; although they required strict record keeping, they also authorized its members to seize, rent, and sell properties.[29] A decree on September 20, 1817, aimed at getting more accurate information by clarifying that to qualify for a reward, denunciations had to be specific and documented.[30] In May 1818, O'Higgins issued rules that required frequent reports from local authorities to the central Sequestration Commission, and established procedures for conducting inventories and appraisals of property.[31] But a year later, O'Higgins was still dissatisfied with the performance of the local commissions, noting that the seized properties were not producing the anticipated level of income for the government, and ordered local officials to refer all protests to the regional governor-intendents for decisions and then on to the executive for final approval.[32]

Juan Egaña, back from his imprisonment on the Juan Fernández Islands, served as head of the central Sequestration Commission. Upon his resignation in April 1819, he took credit for having made more professional the administration of matters related to sequestration. He claimed to have organized and indexed two trunks and a bag full of disorderly papers that he had inherited, as well as keeping track of the voluminous correspondence between his commission and the local ones as well as other branches of government. In cooperating with a total of 473 lawsuits, he and his employees did not charge fees for issuing reports and opinions and dealt with the public in a humanitarian and courteous fashion "so that this odious commission has not resulted in any complaints nor any tears shed."[33] He took particular pride in the efficient use of the scant resources and income acquired from the sequestered properties in order to care for all the war refugees from the forced evacuation of Concepción. Spending, according to his own accounting, a mere eighth of a peso per day per person, he nonetheless ensured that none went hungry or homeless, and that those able to travel could make the return journey.[34] Regardless of the veracity of Egaña's claims, he highlighted the crucial areas in which the politics of wartime sequesters intersected with the well-being of families on both sides of the conflict. The relatives of those whose property was seized as well as those who claimed to have been their victims, appealed first to the Spanish authorities and then to the national government to ensure the basic survival of families through the provision of support termed *alimentos*.

Support Pensions for Families Affected by Property Seizures

Captain General Osorio in 1814 was flooded with petitions from wives protesting that their dowries were included in assets that had been seized and that they were unable to support their children without the income provided by such properties. Catalina Echanes, whose husband Mateo Arnaldo Hoevel had been exiled to the Juan Fernández Islands, appealed to the governor in particularly emotive terms when the administrator assigned to her estate told her he could no longer pay her a monthly stipend of twenty-five pesos:

> The consternation of this so unexpected blow has almost made me lose my mind; I looked at my little children, some still nursing, and with eyes

filled with tears I told them: "can it be possible that the crime of your father could extend to inflict upon you the punishment of being victims, even before you know what malice is" . . . then a small hope in the secret part of my heart said to me: "appeal to your protector, appeal to his lordship Osorio, who could not allow you and your children to perish."[35]

Teresa Larraín, whose husband Agustín de Eyzaguirre was also a prisoner on Juan Fernández, complained that she was being taxed two hundred pesos a month for war expenses, even though she was no longer in possession of the family's property.[36] State attorney José Antonio Rodríguez was sympathetic to such requests. Repeatedly, he asserted that a man's responsibility to pay back his wife's dowry took priority over his debts to the state and that dowries, if not a wife's share of joint marital property, were also exempt from a sentence of confiscation.[37] The treasury officials tended to take a harder line, citing in one case a law that called for the loss of all property in cases of lese majesty, and required full documentation for any claimed dowries.[38] Spanish officials during the reconquest period responded to the pleas of wives in two ways: either allowing them to manage the property under question, after providing guarantors to ensure the assets would be available at the time of their husbands' sentencing, or awarding them a portion of the rent paid upon seized property by a third party to cover their families' maintenance.[39] Many preferred the first option, as they feared the deterioration of their estates under the management of a renter.

After the reestablishment of the patriot government in 1817, women from royalist families also asserted their entitlement not only to their own dowry but also to a support pension payable out of the husband's property. In March, Isabel Villota, the wife of a Spanish merchant who had fled to royalist Lima, protested that much of his confiscated property actually belonged to her in the form of her dowry as well as her half of all jointly acquired marital assets; she claimed that by law a wife should not lose her belongings because her husband had committed a crime. When the commission charged with the property seizures reported that it would take some time to inventory and calculate the value of those goods, Villota requested an interim pension in order to feed her seven children and the servants who cared for them. She boldly argued, moreover, that it "should not be charged to my dowry or marital share, but rather should be paid out of my husband's belongings because the right of children to support rests in his property."[40] Although no decision was recorded in this case, her claims likely spurred officials to begin contemplating these questions.

3.2. José Gregorio Argomedo, legal advisor to supreme director Bernardo O'Higgins; he also served as a judge, congressman, and president of the Supreme Court. *Source:* Narcisse Desmadryl, Hermojenes de Irisarri, and Miguel Luis Amunátegui, *Galería nacional, o, Colección de biografías i retratos de hombre célebres de Chile*, 2 vols. (Santiago: Imprenta Chilena, 1854), 1:33.

State attorney José Gregorio de Argomedo, who had deferred offering an opinion in Villota's case until he had more information, called in April 1817 for some rules regarding dowries and other debts. By the end of the month, Argomedo (whose own property had been seized during the royalist reconquest) had written up a long legal opinion justifying sequestration but also offering some guidelines for implementation. He began by contrasting the leniency of the patriot government to that of the former Spanish regime. The royalists, he asserted, had seized and sold off properties without following legal procedures; moreover, they had imposed levies on the families of patriots well beyond their means and then authorized officials "to violate all morality, all social bonds and all manner of justice, with the daughters, wives, and family of the unfortunate party until payment was made."[41] Claiming that the government was allowing many Spaniards opposed to independence to live freely in Chile, he concluded that any who fled must truly have been enemies of the Americans and charged they had taken public monies with them. He assumed, moreover, that the friends and families of the émigrés shared their opposition to independence and had no secure rights to the abandoned property, whereas patriots who had suffered under the Spanish tyrants deserved compensation. Argomedo argued that in law, dowries deserved no special treatment but then conceded, "what are we to do with Chilean women and children? We must protect them."[42] He proposed a solution similar to that arrived at by the royal officials, that wives either receive a pension for alimentos or be allowed to manage urban and rural properties in return for paying interest to the state. In this way, the state would not immediately have to return full possession of properties equivalent to the wives' dowries:

> No solution could be fairer. During peacetime, these women would not have any right to recuperate their dowries as long as their husbands were living and they had not received an ecclesiastical separation; with much less right should they be able to reclaim them from the goods presumably belonging to the State, especially since their fugitive husbands ran off with great sums with their [wives'] knowledge.[43]

Argomedo thus linked public policy to family law.

By July 1817, O'Higgins echoed Osorio's earlier paternalist concerns that in the haste and confusion of war, the shares of wives and creditors in confiscated property may have been overlooked and that it was now time to "silence the clamors of the many unfortunate ones."[44] Argomedo's proposals served as a general principle, although there is no evidence that they ever became official regulations. Instead, at least through 1818, O'Higgins and his cabinet ministers responded to such petitions on a case by case basis, influenced by the reputation and wealth of the family making the request and the potential public relations impact of the decision, particularly when the welfare of children was at stake. For example, while some wives were evicted from their houses, others were allowed to stay if they paid rent, and some were simply put back in possession of their dwellings. In cases where the claim to ownership was more tenuous, the claimant less influential, or there was not the specter of hungry American children, the state was less obliging. Siblings of the deceased Dominga Vásquez, for example, were unable to convince authorities that they, rather than her son in Spain, should be considered the rightful owners of her house. Property belonging to the son, a resident of Spanish dominions who presumably was not responsible for supporting his aunts, would be subject to sequestration.[45]

Even as they seized valuable estates, the authorities usually treated with respect the wives of Spanish merchants who came from prominent local families and likely had relatives on the patriot side. Isabel Villota, the wife of Spanish merchant Nicolás Chopitea, was allowed to rent her sequestered residence at an annual rate of two hundred pesos in addition to paying the interest on any debts mortgaged to the house.[46] In September 1817, she purchased the house from the state at auction but then transferred the deed to José Casimiro Alvano the following July when he helped her acquire a passport that would release her husband and allow the Chopitea family to leave for Spain.[47] María Loreto Iñiguez y Landa, the wife of the wealthy émigré Rafael Beltrán, claimed a dowry of 12,000 pesos as well as half of the substantial property acquired during their marriage. She said she accepted the divine punishment of being separated from her husband but appealed to the government's benevolence. Argomedo argued against her claim to marital property, but suggested a support pension that was set provisionally at fifty pesos a month.[48] In other cases, lack of influence seems to be the only possible explanation for less favorable treatment. Rafaela Cantos and her Spanish husband, Juan Rosellón, managed a modest shop in Valparaíso, building up a capital of about 5,000 pesos from humble beginnings. She claimed that he tried to hide from other Spaniards after the Battle of Chacabuco but was found and forced to emigrate with them to Lima. Witnesses did not corroborate her story of Rosellón's reluctance to flee, but they did affirm that her brother and sons were active patriots. Nonetheless, Argomedo argued, "if we open the door to the division of marital property, it will be necessary to close the door on sequestration." Although he conceded that she might qualify for some small assistance, no decision was recorded in the case.[49]

Although many of the families of émigrés subject to the seizure of their property were wealthy merchants and landowners, others were even humbler than Cantos. On Christmas Eve, 1818, almost two years after the initial sequestration decree, the official in charge of the port of Valparaíso reported to the central Sequestration Commission that the wives of Spanish fishermen had appealed to him regarding the recent seizure of their husbands' boats: "these unfortunates have no wealth or industry other than these small and insignificant vessels in order to support their families; if they are taken away, they will perish from poverty." He protested that the crimes of the fathers should not extend to the children who would grow up to defend the new, liberal state. Juan Egaña recommended following the strict procedures that he had helped to establish:

The families of the fugitive owners of the canoes find themselves in the same situation as others who have been coldly abandoned by their cruel Fathers in order to follow principles that are destructive to the land that has shown them consideration and good fortune. Therefore, they have no particular rights; but if it was to the pleasure of Your Excellency you could grant them the favor of allowing them to purchase the crafts at two thirds, or if you are feeling generous even half, of their assessed value.

O'Higgins decided that the families should be allowed to buy back the boats at half their price or receive half the proceeds from their sale to the public.[50] While the authorities may have considered these generous terms, since wives of merchants like Villota paid the full price to recover sequestered property, these fishing families had far fewer resources at their disposal.

In addition to those lacking influence, wives who adopted the wrong attitude harmed their chances of a favorable settlement with patriot officials. Rafaela Donoso apparently made the same mistake as Dolores Aráoz Carrera of initially trying to defend her husband's innocence, rather than denouncing his crimes. Insisting he would never have joined the royalists, she lamented that he was dead rather than missing. Argomedo responded that they would consider her case when she presented more documentation of her dowry, but that in the meantime she could console herself that Melchor Rojas must indeed be alive and with the enemy, and that the government "would overlook the arrogance with which she compares the patriotism of her denaturalized husband with that of Your Lordship."[51] Within a few months, however, officials in Santiago, if not the province of Colchagua, again sounded sympathetic. When Donoso protested that even her own clothing and jewels had been seized, forcing her to beg to feed her seven small children, Egaña noted that it was a general principle to show compassion to those unfortunate enough to have tied their fate to the enemy. Argomedo, in a reversal from his earlier opinion, recommended that she be allowed to administer the hacienda and that an investigation be launched into possible abuses in the seizure of her personal belongings.[52]

Manuela Acuña, like other wives, insisted that her husband was innocent, having traveled to Lima for reasons of health rather than politics. Perhaps she hit the right note by not asking for the return of her dowry but just appealing to the government's mercy and compassion for a support pension. She indicated that the belongings seized from her husband's shop were precisely those that "he believed would cover my subsistence during our separation and, bathed in tears, he had told me this upon his departure."[53] Argomedo responded favorably because the request would make no legal precedent and offered an opportunity to strengthen the bonds between family and nation:

> According to a strict interpretation of the law, Your Excellency has no obligation to assist the wife of a husband who is ungrateful to the land that gave her to him. But a beneficent government, which acts with liberal conduct, could not see her perish without feeling grief. Were it to your liking you could exercise some of this liberality toward a young woman who, wounded by necessity, could deviate from her honorable conduct, by assigning her a small pension.[54]

The acting executive concurred, granting her 1,000 pesos from the seized property and calling attention to the benevolence of the new government in honor of the celebration of the Virgin of Carmen. A woman, whose virtue in normal times rested on obedience to her husband, would be provided for upon transferring her loyalty to the new paternalist state.

A few women who actually criticized their husbands, even indirectly, were able to recover property rather than simply receive pensions. Francisca Maceyra claimed that her émigré husband, far from building upon her dowry of 2,500 pesos, had lost money in his commercial enterprises. Argomedo, noting that the sequestered house in question rented for only seven pesos a month, recommended that:

> Considering this circumstance and that of having eleven American children, this attorney believes it to be a duty of Chilean charity to show compassion, letting her keep the house under the condition that, since she is now separated from her ungrateful husband, she be warned that she has no excuse for not proving her true devotion to our [political] system and educating her children according to such sacred principles, inculcating in them ideas of love for their native country; and that if, on the contrary, she should fail to do so in any way, she will not receive any special legal consideration despite her sex.[55]

This order to shift her loyalties was striking given the legal obligation and custom that wives obey their husbands.

Eustaquia Tapia was even more pointed in disavowing her émigré husband. "If [José] Moreno was an enemy of the American Cause," she declared, "by the same action he became an antagonist of his own American children." Local authorities in the town of Quillota, moreover, provided Tapia with a good character reference, noting that she was not "one of those arrogant and loudmouthed Americans, but rather she has been observed to remain silent and retiring in the bosom of her family." Ironically they were praising the domestic virtue of a woman who had rejected her husband. Argomedo was clearly pleased at this opportunity for good public relations:

> It would offend the Supreme Beneficence of Your Excellency if we were to oppose the favor requested by a sad American family for possession of a place, worth only eighty pesos, in which to live. Since an ungrateful Father abandoned them, you can take them in and thereby educate this poor family about the better principles of love for our system.[56]

The executive branch immediately ordered that the house be returned to her.

María Antonia Wassermayer y Zedrón did not condemn her husband, the director of the Royal Tobacco Monopoly, who had accompanied the retreating Spanish army, but did highlight the vulnerable position in which she and her children found themselves. She sorrowfully recounted how, during the day in which Concepción had been left unprotected by either army, her house had been looted, leaving her without so much as a bed and "without any hope for educating and feeding [my seven children] other than the Christian charity for which I would be forced to beg." In order to provide for them, she appealed to the new authorities to return the 1,510 pesos seized from her husband's belongings. In this case, Argomedo was not consulted and the treasury officials were uncharacteristically generous, suggesting paying the amount back at 80 pesos per month: "It is very just, Your Excellency, to assist the helpless and there is not one reason to make these unfortunate creatures die of hunger since surely they played no part in the crimes of their Father."[57] Patriot officials were particularly moved by cases where children, as well as their mothers, would suffer hardship from the loss of property.

Grown children of émigrés who still resided in Chile were also generally successful in claiming assets that would constitute their inheritance. In July 1817, the junta turned over the property seized from émigré Antonio Cabrera to his son and three daughters despite inadequate documentation, because "although they are children of an ungrateful and foreign Father, their own sentiments are most noble, just, and loyal to the current American system."[58] Sons of two émigrés were also allowed to remove cattle they claimed as their own property from the sequestered estates of their fathers. The "citizen" Blas Reyes, as he referred to himself, contrasted his own patriotism with his father's criminal actions and even offered to change his patronym from Reyes (Kings) to Patria (Fatherland): "it is an honor to be known as the Citizen Blas Patria, just as the republican Tarquino erased this name out of abhorrence to the Kings with the same surname who were expelled from

Rome." His request was successful. As Argomedo pointed out, not only had he proven his separate ownership, but also "was deserving of recognition as a son, convinced by Justice, who knew how to show respect toward a patriarch but also remain firm in his own correct opinion, so contrary to the unjust position of his Father."[59] During wartime, authorities assumed that married women would support their husbands and men would ally with their natal kin. In the effort to gain their loyalty for the new nation, however, they advised wives to reject émigré husbands and rewarded sons for not following the dictates of filial obedience when it would take them down the wrong political path.

Providing for the Victors and Victims of War

Few wives and children of royalist émigrés were immediately successful in recovering their dowries and inheritances from sequestered assets, but a significant number were identified as deserving of pensions owing to their American birth and/or willingness to shift their loyalty to the nation's founding fathers. A new government that made public displays of largesse toward the relatives of its enemies certainly could not ignore the suffering of the civilian populace that had supported the cause of independence or at least remained neutral.[60] Surviving documentation does not reveal the uses to which royal officials had put sequestered property beyond rental contracts, but there is ample evidence that Chilean authorities immediately started redistributing the assets seized from émigrés. Although they auctioned off the rental or sale of some houses in an effort to generate income, military officers and displaced patriot families were allowed to live in others rent-free.[61] At the end of April 1817, for example, Dominga Romero appealed to O'Higgins for assistance and compensation. Royalists had seized a ship carrying merchandise belonging to her husband, Mateo de Astorga, and had then forced him to quarter Spanish officers; his widow claimed he subsequently died of shock and shame. Moreover, she noted that her son-in-law Francisco Perales also died in service to the patriots, having served as a guide for San Martín. Throughout her petition, although still unsure what to call the independent country, she emphasized family ties, both real and symbolic:

> Your Excellency, I raise for your consideration the situation of my family; we find ourselves without the comforts that we used to possess, without a loving and honorable Father who provided for all our human needs. . . . Today we appeal to you as our only refuge as the general Father of the

inhabitants of this Kingdom [reino] and devoted champion of those who have distinguished themselves in the service of America . . . [62]

O'Higgins gave the family a house in Valparaíso abandoned by a royalist named Gutiérrez.

A decree in March 1818 proclaimed that soldiers, officers, and civilians serving in administrative posts for the armed forces would be rewarded from property and other assets seized from the enemy.[63] It likely emboldened supporters of independence to petition for grants of rural property. Ramón Pardo claimed that he had served as a volunteer soldier since 1813 and was imprisoned for almost a year during the royalist reconquest; his request for land and a house in Chillán was approved by O'Higgins in 1819 as long as the total value did not exceed 200 pesos.[64] O'Higgins granted María Cornelia Olivares property in Chillán worth 1,000 pesos, owing most likely to her noteworthy actions as a woman since her petition reminded him that:

> Your Excellency deigned to recognize me as one of the most meritorious female citizens in the State of Chile for my unwavering adhesion to the patriotic system, for having announced in the midst of the enemy the imminent arrival of the liberating Army, and for having suffered as a result of raising that cry; I withstood the greatest insults without allowing them to defeat my spirit, even when they cropped my hair and eyebrows and put me out for public ridicule tied by my arms to the pillory of the Plaza from ten in the morning until two in the afternoon under a burning sun.[65]

On a much larger scale, seized haciendas were given to prominent leaders such as José de San Martín and Ramón Freire as recompense for their services to independence.[66]

Just as understandings and practices of kinship in Chile were hierarchically ranked, the paternal government cared for refugees to varying degrees based upon their class and status. In December 1817, patriot officers arrested Spaniard Vicente García on suspicion of supporting the royalists and dispatched him to a prisoner-of-war camp on the other side of the Andes. Although he convinced them of his innocence within a few days, illness prevented him from returning to Santiago for several months. During his absence, authorities in Santiago ordered the sequestration of his house and belongings. "My family evicted and unable to locate a place to take refuge at last found asylum in one of the rooms facing the street, pertaining to an unfortunate maid who took them in," García later recounted, "and from there, shedding tears and without anyone to assist them, they began taking steps to request restitution."[67] In the meantime, Carmen Prieto, a refugee from Concepción and the mother of Lieutenant (and future General and President) Manuel Bulnes, moved into García's house. When García returned and filed a protest in May 1818, governor of Santiago Francisco de Borja Fontecilla proposed that his family be allowed to use a few rooms off the patio but refused to dislodge Prieto,

> since nothing is more in accordance with human rights than to protect and support the emigration of all those individuals who, fleeing the furor of the enemy, abandoned their homes out of love and support for the liberty of the country, utilizing when possible the assets of those who are in fact dissidents and enemies of the holy cause of America among whom Vicente García is reputed to belong."[68]

When García appealed again, state attorney Argomedo was uncharacteristically sympathetic, recommending that García's family occupy the main house but provide some rooms for the refugees. Nonetheless, he warned García that his punishment would double should he prove in fact to be an enemy despite the equity dispensed by the government.[69] In August, however, Prieto still had refused to move, and rather than enforce the order, O'Higgins decided she should be allowed to stay in the main house given that she had lost everything in Concepción and that it would be only a temporary arrangement.[70]

Francisca Ursúa, by contrast, narrowly escaped bondage. In a petition, she explained that her parents, too poor to support her, had given her to don Mariano Olave, and since then, she had passed through many households; that she worked as a servant was too obvious to state. She emigrated from the south to Santiago with one lady who, when she returned to Concepción, abandoned Ursúa. Finally she was evicted from her last place of employment upon getting married. An official working for the Sequestration Commission, finding her homeless and alone, assumed she was a slave subject to seizure. Given the lack of evidence as to her bondage, however, Ursúa was granted her freedom.[71] In August 1818, Egaña had proposed rounding up the slaves of émigrés, whom he identified as vagrants, and putting them to work—five years in the navy for men and seven years in hospitals for women—until they earned their freedom. Children could be sold, but their new owners would be required to educate them and set them free at the age of twenty-three.[72]

The new government distributed both urban and rural properties seized from royalists to reward and compensate supporters of independence.

Although some of the modest properties went to relatively humble folk, the majority who petitioned the new authorities for assistance received smaller allotments in cash, cattle, or other foodstuffs to provide for their basic subsistence (alimentos).[73] O'Higgins responded personally to individual requests but also pledged to provide for the thousands who had evacuated the southern province of Concepción.

In December 1817, after his attempts first to besiege and then to assault the royal army in Talcahuano were unsuccessful, O'Higgins decided to retreat to Santiago. In order to deprive the royalists of support and provisions, he ordered the region's civilian population to accompany the patriot troops, evacuating with their cattle and burning all crops left behind. O'Higgins appealed to the need for national unity in the language of family:

> The fatherland [patria] calls upon you to make this great sacrifice. The enemy should not find in its path other than a desert, houses without inhabitants, fields without crops or cattle. The army will protect you during the retreat and our Northern brothers will receive you with hospitality until the soil of Chile is free from those who are trying to submit you again to odious servitude.[74]

Jorge Beauchef, a French officer who had joined the Chilean army, later recalled that exodus: "What a sad spectacle! Nothing was so heartbreaking, not even the fate of the wounded!"[75] Upon the arrival of tens of thousands of refugees in central Chile, O'Higgins called upon their "brothers" to take families into their homes, "because our interests are reciprocal and nature has united us in such a way that the prosperity or misfortune of some is in fact common to all."[76] Some patriotic citizens with means did receive displaced families from the south, but voluntary efforts alone could never meet the needs of so many people. Therefore, just as a father was obligated to support his children, the government decided to use property seized from royalist émigrés to provide support pensions (pensiones alimenticias) to the most needy.[77]

Proposed regulations from Rancagua's Sequestration Commission indicated that refugees from Concepción should stay either in houses seized from royalists or in those of private individuals. In the latter case, in order to reduce the hardship to the host, a homeowner could bar refugees from the interior rooms dedicated to his or her own family, could prevent people from coming or going at night or bringing in additional guests, and could prohibit refugees from bringing their animals into the house. Having offered a place to stay, moreover, homeowners were exempted from providing food.

Instead, state authorities would start to slaughter confiscated cattle and distribute meat rations to displaced families.[78] In March and April 1818, the government ordered Spaniard Josefa Dumont, widow of royalist José Gregorio de Toro, to provide the equivalent of 7,000 pesos in cattle; when they discovered that the cattle were not worth much, they demanded a forced donation in cash and ended up seizing jewelry and silver items as collateral.[79] By June, Egaña lamented that, owing to a hard winter, the available cattle were extremely gaunt.[80] A few days later, O'Higgins approved Egaña's proposal that when the government's agent was unable to acquire animals he should pay the refugees in cash as a substitute for their daily meat rations.[81] Throughout September, Egaña urgently requested wheat seized from émigré José Prado and sheep from the estate of Rafael Beltrán to make up for the shortage of beef cattle.[82] By early October, rations to families in Rancagua ceased until Juan Guerrero came forward with a donation, for which the state transferred to him 2,000 pesos worth of credits owed to a deceased royalist.[83]

The coordination of housing and rations was an administrative challenge. In July, Juan Egaña, head of the Sequestration Commission, informed O'Higgins that it was difficult to ensure distribution of food rations in Santiago without a secure place to store provisions; he suggested using one of the carriage houses of the Mint where several women related to soldiers had camped out.[84] In August, he received permission to auction off some items belonging to royalists that he had discovered were still in the possession of informers and used the proceeds to help defray the costs of relocating the families from Concepción. A memo from November 1818 included a list of 161 refugees housed in the Foundling Home; among them were families with up to eight children.[85] Despite all the difficulties, Egaña insisted that his commission was fulfilling the state's promises to the refugees. In December, in response to a complaint from two sisters that they were not receiving rations, Egaña denied the charge and assured O'Higgins that "The people to whom I give food assistance (alimentos) number 4,122, and not a day goes by that even one family lacks such aid."[86] That the state was acting as the primary provider for more than four thousand civilians in the area of Santiago alone indicates that patriot leaders took seriously their proclaimed role as fathers of the new nation.

Providing for refugees in rural areas challenged the government's efforts to demonstrate benevolence toward wives of prominent émigrés. One year after the forced donation imposed upon Dumont, the government seized one of the largest and wealthiest estates in Rancagua, the Hacienda de la Compañía, which had been part of her son's entailment. No response was recorded to Egaña's query whether he could distribute 200 cattle from the hacienda or whether that property was only being held awaiting a judicial sentence against its owner.[87] He did send two families who, "after having proven their adherence to the American cause under the most atrocious persecution by the Tyrants, find themselves homeless and reduced to begging during their emigration from the far south," to be housed on that estate, with rights to graze their horses and to food rations. Two weeks later, he also sent Santiago Pantoja with eleven family members and Felix Sepúlveda with twelve along with their animals, indicating that every day they should receive sixteen pounds of meat or its equivalent in other foodstuffs as well as enough flour to make twelve loaves of bread.[88] But in August 1818 the administrator of the Hacienda de la Compañía informed Egaña that 200 refugees were living on the estate and causing significant damages.[89] They turned out to be a group recently arrived from the southern town of Nacimiento, and Egaña agreed that they should be assigned enough land on the estate to house them and their mounts but with orders that they should not "invade" other areas of the hacienda. Although he also indicated a group of two hundred was entitled to rations from either one steer, ten sheep, or two bushels of beans, he suggested that those who could work as *peones* either on La Compañia or other estates in the area should support themselves from their own wages.[90] Clearly, class affected the amount of aid to which one was entitled.

Josefa Dumont in the meantime was pursuing a lawsuit that claimed that once her son had joined the Spanish forces, his sister Nicolasa de Toro became the heir to the estate because the terms of the entailment prohibited its possession by a criminal. In July 1818, she complained to the judge that the estate's products were being sold off against the law, particularly in a case that called for protecting the interests of a minor. The local governor of Rancagua confessed that he had been ordered to send all the wheat from the region to Valparaíso, but that he had taken only a few cattle to feed the refugees. The judge informed Dumont that she would have to file charges in a higher court.[91] By January 1819 Dumont complained to O'Higgins that what had once been a herd of five to six thousand cattle had been reduced to three hundred, fulfilling her fears that under state management the estate would lose its value. She reiterated an earlier offer to rent the estate and rebuild its herd because of her interest in recovering possession at some point. Whereas she had originally offered 6,000 pesos per year, without cattle the rental value of the estate was calculated at only 3,700. Nevertheless, O'Higgins accepted the offer.[92]

By this time, impoverished refugees were wearing out their welcome. Early in the year, Egaña suggested that it was time to stop feeding them and order their return south: "For ten months already without fail, we have been feeding, dressing, healing, and assisting this throng of people."[93] In February 1819, O'Higgins ordered the itinerant families to return to their homes in Concepción, which had been retaken by the patriot army from royalist forces, and thereby relieve the government and inhabitants of the central valley from paying their support pensions.[94] Although the proclamation called upon residents of towns to assist refugees as they passed through and promised additional aid to poor families, relocating those families for a second time could not occur overnight. On March 6, Egaña sounded a more sympathetic note toward the refugees who had been evicted from their housing before being provided with the means to travel. Rather than provide them shelter, O'Higgins empowered a commission to quickly round up the necessary carts, horses, and mules.[95] Egaña assured him that "an exact account of all that has been given them is recorded in the passports they have been provided as proof of the Government's generosity."[96] In April, the official in charge of administering sequestered property in Rancagua informed Egaña that he was providing for two families, including that of the bishop of Concepción, who had been traveling south but had been forced to return when the party encountered bandits and possibly royalist guerrillas in Talca.[97] Almost two months after his decree, O'Higgins again paternalistically exhorted the refugees to return: "Citizens: march to your homes crowned with the blessings of your brothers in Santiago. Care for the security of those provinces that have cost us so much blood and sacrifice." The generous assistance they had received over the course of a year ought to have convinced them, he proclaimed, that they were "the favored sons of the Fatherland."[98]

Initial Policies on Property Restitution, 1819–1822

Increasingly confident that they ultimately would prevail over royal forces, Chilean officials began turning their attention to reconstruction and reconciliation. As relatives of émigrés continued to press for the return of properties, therefore, they found judges and political authorities more sympathetic. The shift occurred first in the south, where many of the émigrés were not Spaniards fleeing to Lima but rather Chileans following the orders of the Spanish commander to evacuate south of the Biobío River in October 1818, in a mirror image of the earlier patriot migration north. Moreover, while the vast majority of Spaniards fleeing central Chile had been wealthy male merchants and landowners, the royalist emigration in the south included women and children and depleted the region of the farmers necessary to its economic recovery.

As the patriots gained control of Chilean territory, multiple decrees and laws attempted to address the disputes arising from sequestration. The government wished to promote reconciliation by pardoning all but the most fervent enemies of independence, but without taking responsibility for abuses that had been committed or suffering any financial consequences. In 1819, O'Higgins had to pass judgment in a dowry dispute that raised doubts about the legality of the sales of sequestered real estate, which had been carried out without judicial sentences of confiscation, without the approval of the head of state, and in most cases without the opportunity for all affected parties to testify.[99] Most of the sales had been made while O'Higgins was on military campaign in the south during 1817 and 1818. Backed up by the testimony of his secretary of war, José Ignacio Zenteno, O'Higgins insisted that among the detailed (but secret) instructions he had transmitted to General Hilarión de la Quintana, whom he left in charge of the government during his absence, was a prohibition against disposing of any real estate held by the state.[100] State attorney Juan de Dios Vial acknowledged Quintana's lack of authority to make the sales but warned of the crisis that would ensue should they be nullified, most notably a public loss of confidence in the government. He proposed that the failure of O'Higgins to protest or overturn the sales in almost two years constituted "a tacit approval that has diluted the prohibition and leaves the sales secure."[101] A majority of justices on the appeals court concurred in September 1820.[102] A week later, the Senate expressed its approval, noting that secret instructions did not carry the force of public law and that to reopen the matter would result in endless litigation.[103] With the assent of these two branches of government, O'Higgins proceeded to approve retroactively the sales regardless of the irregularities in procedure.[104]

On May 7 of the following year, however, the Senate laid down principles for the return of property under two circumstances. First, individuals who could prove that their assets had been seized under the false assumption that they had been opponents of independence should receive any property still in possession of the state, though not be reimbursed for any income or profits the state had earned during the intervening years; such persons were also free to sue for damages those who had falsely identified them as royalists. Second, the confiscation of the property of those who had in fact fled the country because of their opposition to independence was justified, but the executive could return such belongings, in whole or in part, to those who repented and returned in order to "unite with our greater family."[105] An additional door opened in September 1822 when the government issued an amnesty for any men born in Chile or married to Chilean women, who had fled because of their political opinions, to return to the country so long as they had not participated in murder or mutiny.[106] Strikingly, both laws were aimed in part at family reunification, both at the level of actual households and the metaphorical level of the nation-state, the "greater" Chilean family.

Once opened, these doors would lead to multiple complications and lawsuits. The state faced a loss of rental income from sequestered properties returned to their original owners, as well as the possibility of having to make financial reparations. In 1822, therefore, O'Higgins decreed that in the case of returned property, individuals should pay a one-time assessment of 4 percent of the value in order to cover "the costs and expenditures the state had assumed in order to seize and maintain it."[107] The potential social costs were equally high. The government immediately faced the dilemma of trying to reincorporate émigrés who claimed either their innocence or their repentance while not harming the interests of Chileans who had supported and often made sacrifices on behalf of independence.

The first lawsuits after the Senate allowed for the return of sequestered property to innocent parties and the consideration of restitution for repentant royalists were filed in Concepción where the circumstances were distinct from those in the rest of Chile. The opinions of the inhabitants of this province, regardless of socioeconomic status, were essentially split on the issue of independence. Therefore, the region suffered the effects of prolonged warfare, including economic devastation and multiple displacements of people. Some émigrés were, like the majority elsewhere, either Spanish bureaucrats or merchants, but many were Chilean-born family farmers; moreover, while some fled as far as Peru or Spain, the majority went shorter distances into Mapuche territory. On the one hand, many patriots resented Chilean-born royalists, whom they regarded as having forfeited their birthright nationality, almost more than Spaniards. On the other hand, it was questionable how many had fled the patriot army voluntarily, and the region could not recover if it remained depopulated. As early as May 1819 Governor Freire had invited émigrés to return, promising amnesty and the restoration of their property, but many stayed with the royalist forces for another year or two. The mercy initially shown mostly toward women gradually prepared the way for the vindication of men as well.

3.3. Ramón Freire, military officer who served as governor intendent of Concepción (1818–1822) and later as supreme director and president of Chile (1823–1827). *Source:* Narcisse Desmadryl, Hermojenes de Irisarri, and Miguel Luis Amunátegui, *Galería nacional, o, Colección de biografías i retratos de hombre célebres de Chile*, 2 vols. (Santiago: Imprenta Chilena, 1854), 2:53.

Petrona Mantega used the legal subjection of her sex to the authority of patriarchs—both familial and governmental—to excuse her own migration. Her case illustrates well the multiple disruptions of the war, especially for inhabitants of the south. Witnesses testified that she had first followed the patriot orders to evacuate Concepción in late 1817, getting as far as the Itata River where bandits prevented her party from proceeding. She returned to Concepción, therefore, and remained in that city even when Spanish troops withdrew to the port of Talcahuano in 1817. She claimed that she wished to remain even when the commander of royal forces, Juan Francisco Sánchez, took control of the city and ordered the civilian population to move south of the Biobío the following year; she was required, however, to accompany her husband (a Spanish surgeon with the royal army) and to obey the orders of Commander Sánchez as well as the natural law of survival, as those who did not evacuate were threatened with execution. When royalist officer Vicente

Benavides briefly held Concepción again in 1820, the then widowed Mantega was able to return for good.[108]

Although her house had burned down in 1817, in March of 1822 Mantega received permission to rent the hacienda she had inherited from her parents, which had been seized by the patriot government when she retreated with the royalist forces. Without this farm, she lamented, she would "not have any place to take refuge with my family, all minors, nor any way to feed them."[109] Then she began a lawsuit to have the sequestration lifted using every possible argument. Her husband, according to witness Bernardino Pradel, "was a man endowed with beautiful qualities and so peaceful that he would not be capable of raising arms against the Nation."[110] Moreover, Mantega claimed, he had contributed only his surgeon's salary to household income whereas she had brought all the property in question to their marriage. As for whether her property should be subject to seizure, she claimed that no one had ever heard her express political opinions contrary to independence, and that she had emigrated only out of fear of losing her life. Mantega, like others in these petitions, further claimed that properties had been returned to others who had collaborated with the enemy, "men who soaked the Republic in blood."[111] Finally, once an obedient wife and then an unfortunate widow, Mantega appealed to the new government that as "a beneficent Father, it could make a characteristic gesture of generosity to aid the innocents who cry out to me for their daily bread."[112] Three months into her case, the local treasury officials in Concepción recommended the hacienda be returned to her on the grounds,

> that owing to the rigorous order of the detestable Sánchez she followed her husband to the other side of the Biobío: That as a surgeon he was obligated to follow the military corps to which he was attached: That he did not raise arms against the Fatherland, nor do harm to any of his neighbors: That he was of a kind and charitable character, and that he has left behind underage children.[113]

Although it would take many more months of going through bureaucratic channels and multiple consultations in Santiago as well as Concepción, Mantega finally got an affirmative sentence from the Supreme Court in June 1824.

Appealing to the 1821 Senate resolution, Antonia Padilla, the widow of a former royal bureaucrat, made a similar argument to Mantega in reclaiming a house. Although the house was in Santiago, Padilla's husband José Gundián had relocated his family in 1815 to Concepción where he had been appointed to the royal tobacco monopoly. Witnesses on behalf of Padilla characterized

Gundián as someone who tried to stay out of politics. Francisco Echague wrote that the Chilean government, presumably between 1810 and 1814, had granted Gundián naturalization, and Manuel de Matta noted "that if he did not demonstrate himself to be a committed patriot, neither does anyone say he was an enemy of the patriots."[114] With the arrival of O'Higgins in 1817, the family followed the orders of Spanish commander Sánchez to retreat to Talcahuano, and Gundián died in an epidemic that broke out during the siege. Widowed and with nine "American" children, Padilla boarded a ship for Lima rather than evacuate south of the Biobío, "venturing the fate of such a large family, in order not to be victims of the confusion and disorder."[115]

After Padilla's petition languished for five months, she again appealed to O'Higgins: "How could a hapless American woman surrounded by nine unfortunate children, unable to provide them even the most basic education so that they could be useful to their Fatherland, be left lacking when some assistance, to which by right she is entitled, could improve their fate?"[116] In September 1822, commissioners agreed that the house could be returned to Padilla, whose pitiable situation in Talcahuano "almost" justified her decision to flee wherever she could. Whatever responsibility she might retain for her actions, moreover, her decision should not "harm her minor children who were not free to oppose her."[117] Ten days later, Padilla and her children were able to move into their former home. Unfortunately, it is not recorded whether or not the buyer, Santiago Muñoz Bezanilla, protested or was reimbursed. Later, as a liberal representative in Congress from 1824 to 1829, Muñoz Bezanilla did propose a bill to expel enemies of independence from Chile and seize their assets, and he advocated for the rights of those who had purchased sequestered properties from the state.[118]

Treasury officials in Concepción, nonetheless, sounded a note of caution about returning sequestered assets, owing in part no doubt to the imminent loss of revenue in the already impoverished province. In 1822, Casimiro Tapia appealed to Governor Freire that, terrified by rumors that the patriot army was advancing south "to slit the throats of the inhabitants of all ages," he had fled with the Spanish army and then failed to return fearing capture either by royal troops or Indians.[119] Treasurer Juan Castellón, without commenting on Tapia in particular, offered an alternate explanation. He noted that many émigrés returned only after the major victories against royal troops commanded by Benavides in November 1820 made them lose hope that the forces of the king would ultimately triumph: "From their obstinacy has resulted the sacrifice of so many illustrious defenders of our Liberty: the general ruin of the fortunes of all; and the deplorable state of annihilation to which the reserves of the public treasury have been reduced."[120] Arguing the justice of having sequestered assets meet these shortfalls, Castellón suggested that those who recovered properties should pay a percentage of their value in taxes for a period of ten years. Perhaps unsure how to balance the negative opinion of Castellón with the favorable recommendation on behalf of Tapia by the local governor of the town of Linares, Freire simply sent the case on to higher officials. For the time being, only women and children were seen as deserving of protection.

The Plaza de los Reyes family included patriot sons as well as their Spanish father. They had been able to recover their sequestered property in 1821 but protested the assessment of a fee for administration in the interim when the state in fact had been earning income on the property. Lorenzo Plaza de los Reyes described the region in 1818 as under the utter tyranny of Sánchez and his indigenous allies:

> The slightest suspicion was punished by execution, and continuous emigrations resulted from his plans. He ordered entire villages to leave their homes and march to the interior of the province. From these decrees no one was exempt: neither the old woman, the young orphan girl, nor the disabled and impoverished who had no funds with which to undertake a move. Should one decide to tempt fate by remaining there, he was immediately the victim of the ferocious Indian who, authorized by the Spaniard, entered the villages to murder all whom he found there.[121]

Hence, claimed Plaza de los Reyes, his father (perhaps owing to old age) was forced to follow the Spaniards in their retreat all the way to Valdivia: "It was either go or die."[122] The son remained to manage the family estates only to find them seized first by Sánchez and then by the returning patriot army. He and one brother were imprisoned by the royalists while another fought with the patriots at the Battle of Maipú, and yet they found themselves punished rather than rewarded: "because our progenitor was forced to flee, we find ourselves dispossessed of the only property that made up our patrimony."[123] The case contains no response to their appeal to have the fee waived.

The case of Juan Bernardo Ruiz, by contrast, demonstrates the growing opinion that most people who evacuated south of Concepción under royalist orders did so involuntarily and that punishment should not be extended to family members. The case was filed by the estate executors, José Liborio and Manuel Ruiz, because Juan Bernardo Ruiz had died shortly after returning to patriot-controlled territories. However, both the local head of the Sequestration Commission and the treasury accountant advised Freire that since Ruiz had failed to seek amnesty during the stipulated term, his property rightfully belonged to the state. His nephew, José Liborio, then appealed personally through his friend Juan Antonio Bello to intercede with O'Higgins on behalf of his numerous relatives. When the state attorney in Santiago insisted that the proper jurisdiction for the case was Concepción, the local treasury accountant reiterated his opposition in 1822 on the grounds that everyone used the excuse that they were forced to emigrate and that Ruiz had given no public indication before his death of a change in political opinion. Nevertheless, in August a local judge declared that the witnesses had sufficiently proven the involuntary nature of Ruiz's evacuation, that he had died back in Concepción under the protection of the new Chilean state, and that therefore the property should be awarded to his heirs, all Chilean citizens.[124]

Although there was not complete consensus, by the end of 1822 most officials in the south believed that men as well as women had been subjected to sufficient terror to relieve them of responsibility for having followed the orders of Sánchez to evacuate Concepción and other towns. The goal of the government to retain wealthy inhabitants in the province allowed other men to recover their property even during the first half of that year. Manuel Pantoja, a merchant based in Concepción since 1795, claimed that his trip to Lima in the fateful year of 1817 had been for reasons of business and not politics, and owing to the state of war he could not return until San Martín took Lima. The local head of the Sequestration Commission was skeptical, pointing out that his departure came after the patriot victory of Chacabuco and during the royalist retreat to Talcahuano. Nonetheless, the mere testimony of two witnesses that Pantoja had been a civilian passenger on board the Spanish brigantine *Santa Mariana* convinced the Concepción accountant and then Governor Freire of his innocence. Undoubtedly, that a wealthy Spaniard was willing to resettle in the region and proclaim his allegiance, however belatedly, to "our sacred cause of America" was also persuasive.[125] Juan Antonio Fresno, born in Spain but naturalized as a citizen, had apparently established himself as a Chilean through lengthy residence and prodigious paternity. In 1822, Fresno asserted that he had arrived fifty years earlier, at the age of twenty-two, and married into a poor family. Since then he had not only built up the family's fortunes but also multiplied their numbers with nine children and eighteen grandchildren. In addition to supporting his descendants, he claimed that through his good deeds "thousands have enough to eat."[126] Despite these good deeds, some had avenged the patriot defeat at Rancagua by looting his properties; therefore, he had taken to burying his wealth. When one of his renters dug up a cache of gold in 1817, the government seized it. In 1822, however, no official opposed his request to have the gold returned, instead citing him as a good father and a supporter of Americans.[127] For Fresno and Chilean authorities alike, his responsibilities as a patriarch were inextricably intertwined with his duties as a citizen.

....

Property sequestration was critical to the patriot strategy for defeating the royal army because it deprived the enemy of resources while sales and rentals provided much-needed revenue to fund troops and reward supporters. Officials of the O'Higgins administration asserted that the policy was both necessary and justifiable in wartime, because royal authorities had taken similar measures against the patriots. The seizure of cattle and crops also allowed paternalist authorities to provide for the thousands of refugees who had dutifully fled the southern theater of war. In order to win over the population who had either remained neutral or even harbored royalist sympathies, agents of the new regime also had to distinguish their policies from the tyrannical abuses against innocent families of which they had accused captains general Osorio and Marcó del Pont. Granting pensions to those wives of émigrés who showed sufficient contrition and to children born in Chile demonstrated the benevolence of "the American system" and laid the groundwork for constructing national identity on the basis of familial ties. Gaining support for the patriot movement in the south, whose inhabitants had borne the brunt of the war, would be particularly challenging. As their confidence in ultimate victory increased, Freire and other officials in the region of Concepción tried to woo back émigrés, many of them native to Chile, by promising amnesty. Depicting the royal officers and their Mapuche allies as particularly cruel and bloodthirsty both served as good propaganda for the new government and justified returning some of the sequestered properties to those who repented and requested to join "the greater Chilean family."

The 1821 Senate resolution signaled the transition from a period of war to a period of reconstruction. That process was especially critical in the ravaged south, where agricultural production and commerce had collapsed. Government officials were eager to pass the responsibility for providing for the region's impoverished inhabitants back to male heads of household, like Pantoja and Fresno, willing to turn their efforts toward economic recovery. Nevertheless, the 1821 resolution was only a first step toward regularizing procedures regarding sequestered assets. Although it was rhetorically easy to invoke the new nation in familial terms, actually reconciling the competing interests of patriots and returning émigrés would prove challenging. As they debated laws and policies regarding sequestration, authorities would also turn their attention to other areas in which the new state had an interest in guaranteeing financial support to dependent families: either directly through pensions to military widows and orphans or indirectly by adjudicating claims brought by wives and offspring against patriarchs for failure to provide. The role of these policies in nation-state formation will be the subject of Part II, "Reconciling the National Family."

PART II
RECONCILING THE NATIONAL FAMILY

CHAPTER 4

Constituting the Greater Chilean Family: Nation-State Formation and the Restitution of Property

The executors of the estate of Ignacio de la Carrera lost little time after Ramón Freire replaced Bernardo O'Higgins as head of state in 1823. For four years, they had bided their time, accepting out of necessity the rental of the San Miguel hacienda to Diego Antonio Barros. In September, nephew Manuel Aráoz finally expressed his frustration to Freire: "The lawsuit of which I attach a copy for Your Excellency is a portrait of scandal and an example that confirms the repeated lessons of the revolution in which the victor and the vanquished are alternately judged to be the traitor or savior of the Fatherland." He pointedly inquired whether there was any difference between the movement led by José Miguel Carrera against O'Higgins from the one led by Freire that had secured the abdication of the latter earlier that year: "then we shall see if we do not all deserve the confiscation that has been carried out against the fortunes of the former and his siblings." Protesting that there had never been any trial and that the renter had been allowed to purchase the estate's cattle without approval of the executors, he concluded that "Under cover of the term *sequester* (because there is no sentence, nor could there have been one, of confiscation) a true despoilment has been committed."[1]

With the issue revived, the treasury ministers tried to determine whether the accounts in their archive would show the funds O'Higgins had accused José Miguel Carrera of stealing before fleeing Santiago in the wake of the defeat at Rancagua in 1814. On June 19, 1824, the judge ordered the sequester order lifted but left open the possibility for the government to sue the heirs of Carrera should it be determined that he absconded with government funds. But renter Barros appealed, claiming that because he had not been cited and given the opportunity to testify, the sentence should be voided.[2] A year later, finally back from her ten years in exile, Javiera Carrera entered a plea: "I shudder at the memory of these events, whose mere mention renews the bitter grief for my dearest loved ones: but I still have other loved ones in my tender children that obligate me to overcome this profound sorrow so that hunger does not end up sealing our fate." She protested that there was still no decision on the validity of Barros's purchase from the state of San Miguel's cattle, even though the court had lifted the sequester and ordered all property returned to the Carreras. "The spirit of partisanship, always superior to the interests of patriotism, threw itself upon our patrimony with as much right," she noted ironically, "as Osorio upon the wealth of those who went into exile and of the lion upon the prey he is devouring."[3] Although the final sentence about the cattle is missing from the documents consulted, Javiera did manage to evict the renter and take up residence at her family estate.

The wars of independence had torn apart many Chilean families. Fleeing Spaniards often left behind American-born wives and children, who found their properties subject to seizure by the new government. Some of the proceeds of those confiscations were used to support patriot families affected by the war, particularly the thousands of residents of the southern provinces who were ordered to evacuate so that they could not provide provisions, willingly or not, to the royalist troops who controlled that territory in 1818. During the years of the most intense conflict, 1817 to 1820, patriot officials targeted properties of suspected enemies, whether they were wealthy landowners or modest fishermen. The administrators appointed to manage the process complained bitterly about the tactics employed by relatives and friends to hide assets and evade sequestration. On the other hand, even in the midst of conflict, officials often honored the Spanish legal principle that dependents were entitled to support (alimentos); therefore, even if they did not immediately return properties, they might allow wives and grown children to manage estates, live in houses at reduced rents, or even collect pensions payable out of the seized assets of their principal breadwinners. As "Americans," these women and children had a symbolic kinship with other Chileans, and patriot leaders, acting as benevolent "fathers," urged them to disavow their kin ties to the Spaniards, who had ungratefully abandoned them, and transfer their allegiance to the new nation.

During the 1820s the new government initiated policies statesmen hoped would facilitate reconstruction and reconciliation. As skirmishes continued along the southern frontier, the authorities were eager to resolve civil conflict in that region, where royalists were not only wealthy merchants from Spain but also local farmers. Gradually, relatives of royalists in the center and north also saw their fortunes change, as class increasingly trumped political affiliation as a desirable criterion for citizenship. The new leaders believed that economic recovery depended upon successful, large-scale producers and merchants, and they were willing to overlook past offenses in the name of progress. Finally, even some Spaniards returned and tried to recover their assets in Chile. If property had been administered by the state or rented out, its return was relatively unproblematic, but disputes naturally arose over real estate that had been sold. Seizures that had occurred rapidly and somewhat haphazardly between 1817 and 1820 remained a matter of both litigation and legislation well into the nineteenth century.

This chapter analyzes the attempts to resolve these property disputes during two periods of nation-state formation. From 1823 to 1829, the legislature played a powerful role under the protection of the new supreme director and commander-in-chief Ramón Freire. Using the rhetoric of family, representatives hotly debated the respective rights of Chileans who had endured the devastation of war and émigrés who returned to reclaim their property. Moreover, the credibility of the new state could be undermined if authorities did not uphold seizures and sales carried out during the war. In 1829, the House of Representatives (*Cámara de Diputados*) finally passed a bill that allowed former royalists to request monetary compensation from the state under certain conditions, but not to recuperate real estate that had been awarded or sold to third parties. Before the Senate could consider the legislation, however, civil war broke out that resulted in the defeat of Freire. The more conservative regime established in 1830 left these property disputes principally to the courts, and judges were increasingly sympathetic toward the original proprietors and welcoming of returning émigrés. Presidents and their finance ministers after 1830 put a priority on consolidating the national debt, which they believed would encourage economic investment and development, and on regularizing diplomatic relations with Spain. Distancing themselves from the early, postindependence state, these later administrations saw their credibility tied to paying back debts contracted during the war. Both the 1835 debt law and the 1844 treaty with Spain contained articles that recognized the need to resolve claims arising from wartime property seizures, but put off the matter for future legislation. Finally in 1853, when few royalists were still living, Congress passed a law that recognized as part of the national debt almost all claims arising from sequestered property, whether filed by the original owners or more likely by their Chilean-born heirs. Although in retrospect the link between public policy on property and the politics of family may have been overlooked at each point in this long process, elected officials justified their respective positions by highlighting how different policies would affect Chilean families.

By creating an opportunity for former royalists to recuperate property seized by patriot officials, the 1821 Senate resolution had opened the door to conflicting claims that would be difficult to resolve. In May 1823, shortly after coming to power, Freire noted that he was daily receiving numerous requests for restitution and that, while some of those affected had already received favorable decisions, others in similar cases had not. He asked the Senate, therefore, to formulate a law that would establish clear procedures for the return of sequestered properties. Initially, perhaps arising from his experiences with the émigrés in the south, Freire was sympathetic to those who had lost their property, lamenting that many "sons of the nation [*hijos del país*]" were affected and that it had brought about the "ruin of many families."[4] But the situation in central Chile was still polarized. Within ten days of Freire's request, governor of Valparaíso José Ignacio Zenteno, former minister of war under O'Higgins, sent a cautionary memo to the executive branch about "the general resentment that I observe in Valparaíso among those persons most committed to the mother Fatherland [*madre Patria*]." Property values in the port city had risen by three times since 1817, an increase Zenteno attributed to the free trade policies of the independent state, and he emphasized that returning royalists who recovered their real estate should have to pay the difference either to the state or to those who had purchased it from the state. Like Freire, he raised the specter of family suffering, but in this case of those who had shed blood in support of the patriot cause while the émigrés looked on "from afar (and perhaps) with a smiling countenance upon the desolation of the country, the death of a husband, the absence of a father, of a brother, etc."[5]

By July 1823, the Senate drafted a set of principles to guide lawsuits over sequestered property, taking into account the concerns expressed by both Freire and Zenteno. The senators tried to balance making those who had harmed the cause of Chilean independence pay for their crimes while leaving some inheritance for their innocent children. They acknowledged, moreover, that the way in which sequestration had been carried out could have affected persons who were not guilty or might be deserving of lenience.[6] Several points dealt specifically with the families of émigrés: wives could recuperate their dowries and minor children their own assets technically still under the management of fathers. Moreover, the wives and children of those enemies whose property had been legitimately seized would be assigned a pension [*cuota alimenticia*] calibrated to their social status and the value of the confiscated assets.[7] Freire, possibly more attuned by this point to public opinion in central Chile, suggested some changes to the guidelines. First, he recommended that they make abundantly clear that simply the act of emigrating constituted aid to the royalist cause, and hence an act punishable by confiscation, and that exceptions should be made only for "women or children who were required to follow their husbands or fathers" and for those who subsequently repented and rendered services to the cause of independence. Second, he asserted that in cases in which seizures were overturned, the original owners were entitled to some kind of indemnification but those who had purchased sequestered real estate should not be forced to sell it back to the state.[8]

These guidelines apparently did not have the force of law, and there is no evidence that judges heeded them in their deliberations. As early as March 1824, Freire requested the suspension of all such lawsuits currently in the courts, and in April of the following year, Congress issued such an order until the legislature could pass a law that would establish clear procedures pertaining to sequestration.[9] For almost three decades, bills were drafted but not passed, and although the court of appeals had promised to notify all judges of the congressional order to suspend cases related to sequestration, at least some lawsuits proceeded and resulted in inconsistent sentences.

In 1825, Representative Fernando de Vera proposed a bill that would have endorsed the status quo, by both upholding the validity of sales of sequestered property by the state and confirming those sentences that had already returned property to the original owners; henceforth he favored first the rights of buyers and secondarily of heirs in Chile of émigrés.[10] A year later, Representative Ignacio Molina, from southern Chile, made a proposal to return sequestered properties while Representative Pedro Mena, who had served on the Sequestration Commission in Quillota and had purchased several properties in 1817, put forward his own bill to legitimate the titles to all such properties sold by the state at public auction. Both bills were sent to committee, but Congress adjourned without acting upon either.[11] Molina was frustrated but persistent; when he raised the matter again in 1828, he lamented that the courts had ignored the order to suspend lawsuits over sequestered property. "In the meantime, anxiety and vexation continued," he asserted. "Everyone knows it: there is no other branch of public administration more enveloped in darkness and confusion."[12]

A few weeks later one such property owner submitted a complaint to Congress. María Dunn, the widow of Englishman Ricardo Dunn, recounted how a house in Valparaíso had changed hands numerous times. Seized in 1817, when Modesto Novajas fled to Lima, it had been purchased at auction by Juan Tortel, who sold it to Carlos Delegal, who sold it to Dunn. Each purchaser had invested in improvements, raising the value of the house but risking loss should the royal army prove victorious. When the royalists were defeated in Peru, however, Novajas returned and successfully filed suit to recover his properties; the judge ordered Dunn to turn over the house and left him recourse only to sue the person from whom he had bought it. María Dunn protested the sentence to Congress, pointing out that many lawyers had assured her it violated the law, but also appealing for protection as a widow charged with caring for her orphaned children.[13] Dunn's petition was sent to a committee charged with evaluating whether it fell within congressional jurisdiction, and no further action was recorded. On almost the same date, the town council of Quillota also sent a letter to Congress (though it did not enter the minutes until a few months later) on behalf of the wives and children of émigrés who had been dispossessed of their patrimony. Returning their property, the councilmen argued, was both a matter of justice and would also stimulate their eternal gratitude to the new state for protecting them.[14]

Meanwhile, Representative Molina raised the issue again as urgent in January 1829, putting forward a bill that favored the return of properties to all except those who were still in exile or had committed acts against independence for which they had not repented.[15] Whereas several months earlier, he had called attention to the rights of purchasers, he now emphasized justice for Chileans who had lost their property to sequestration:

> At least three quarters of these rural properties belong to Chileans, and although Spaniards are officially prisoners of war in our country, they have been given rights that put them on equal standing with the true children of Independence; meanwhile our own compatriots, repentant sinners, are considered as if they were prisoners of war, stripping them of their interests and imposing upon their children the punishment for a crime that their fathers committed.[16]

His bill had three articles. The first simply called for the return of sequestered real estate. The second excluded those who remained among the enemy or had committed grave harm to patriots unless they truly repented. The only mention he made of the rights of third parties was to say that property, which had been sold or given away by the government at a time when there were no obligatory heirs living in Chile, would not be restored to returning émigrés. Finally, the third article called for any land remaining after a year to be sold, with two thirds of the proceeds going to the federal government and one third to the local municipality.[17]

The bill was sent to the Committee for Treasury and Justice, which returned it two weeks later, in late January 1829, with amendments to protect the rights of those who had purchased sequestered properties in good faith. The committee members walked a fine line between competing interests and declined to overturn lawsuits that had already been sentenced. The first article was modified to call for the return of any sequestered assets to the original owner or heirs so long as those belongings had not been sold or given to third parties. For properties no longer in the possession of the state, the bill envisioned two scenarios: if a judge had already lifted the sequestration, the owner could choose to recover the property or receive reimbursement for its value, but if a claim had not yet been sentenced in court the original owner could request only indemnification. In the first case, the buyer would be reimbursed by the government for the purchase price and by the returning owner for any improvements made to real estate. Furthermore, the government could reclaim any property sold if the purchaser had not paid according to the terms and deadlines of the contract; such property could then be restored to the original owners.[18]

When the bill came up for debate in October, Rafael Bilbao gave a speech in favor of passage on the grounds that it reconciled the government's credit, the rights of the current owners, and the interests of those who had been unjustly deprived of their property. In contrast to Molina, however, Bilbao's main concern was for the authority of the national state and for Chileans who had supported independence rather than for émigrés:

> The former legislature considered the need to pass a law that would curb the innumerable abuses that have arisen owing to the obscurity and insufficiency of the existing laws in matters of sequestration. . . . The properties in question have from the beginning passed from the care of the Government to the hands of various patriots who received them either in compensation for their sacrifices on behalf of the public good or from judicially ordered sales in which they invested the last remnants of their fortunes left from the storms of war. So it is that the most worthy citizens are frequently the victims of the courts, which confuse true confiscations with transitory sequesters, and in the shadow of this conduct they lay low the credit of the Government, rescinding the contracts which it had guaranteed with the seal of its authority.[19]

After "prolonged" debate (the details of which were not published in the minutes), the House of Representatives approved the first article but sent the rest back to the committee for further revisions. The final law, approved by majority though not unanimous vote, further weakened the rights of the original owners. Article Two declared as property of the state any real estate vacant because the owner or heirs had either died or voluntarily remained outside Chile. Article Three validated sales or donations made by the government of sequestered property, leaving the original owners the right only to request monetary compensation. Finally, those residing in the Americas were given two years to file their claims, while those in Europe would have four.[20] In November, the Senate received the bill and sent it to the finance committee, but the civil war of 1830, which resulted in the establishment of a conservative regime opposed to the liberal Congress that passed the law, interrupted further action on this bill.

The legislative debates in the 1820s demonstrated how difficult it would be to reconcile "the greater Chilean family." In the meantime, plaintiffs continued to bring their claims to court. Given the vague legal context, which rested primarily upon the 1821 Senate resolution, arguments on both sides appealed to principles of family. Several lawsuits arising from sequestration either ended abruptly or were interrupted in late 1822 during the civil conflict that brought down the O'Higgins administration. The change of government may have led to confusion, and some officials may have wished to limit the gains made by émigrés toward the end of the O'Higgins administration.[21] In February 1824, María Juana Maturana was surprised to hear that her house was up for auction by the state. She appealed to the local governor of the town of Chillán: "as you know neither I nor my family have ever left the province nor emigrated anywhere: and although it is true that my husband, back in 1817 when the victorious Patriot Troops arrived in this province, hid for fear of being imputed to belong to the Enemy, this concealment was brief and within two weeks he had returned to the bosom of his family."[22] Fortunately for Maturana, even though her husband was at the time in Lima, the mistake was easy to rectify. Three prominent residents testified on her behalf, and the governor, Coronel Clemente Lantaño, who had switched from the royalist to the patriot army only in 1821, declared the seizure to have been in error.

Others resumed in 1824 efforts to recover property that had been seized years earlier. Lujardo Elgueta of Chillán had followed the royalist evacuation order, but claimed that he had done so to avoid becoming embroiled in politics and had returned at the first opportunity to his homeland "where I have been admitted as a son of Chile."[23] In this case, Governor Lantaño himself served as the character witness, testifying that he had known Elgueta since his youth and "that he did not provide any service to the army of the Goths [royalists] since the entire time they were in charge, he only worked in his shop."[24] Although Elgueta had to wait almost a year before the Supreme Court in Santiago officially lifted the sequestration, the delay was simply bureaucratic not political. When Esteban Fonseca had crossed the Biobío, his small house and plot in Chillán were seized, but he claimed to have cooperated with the patriot government since his early, but unspecified, return. Although Fonseca shakily signed his initial petition to the local authorities, he granted his power of attorney to José María Sierra to pursue the case in court. Sierra referred to the numerous similar cases that pardoned people who fled out of fear rather than political opinion and even others who had actively supported the enemy. Asserting that the property in question was all that Fonseca had to support himself in his old age, Sierra pointed out that "the acquisition of my client's miserable fortune could in no way alleviate the needs of the State, while it would share in the great misfortune of paralyzing a family that could be useful with its subsequent services."[25]

Fonseca's case, like Elgueta's, provoked no controversy, but a second lawsuit, in which he was trying to collect a debt on property he had sold in 1816, was interrupted in April 1825 when Congress ordered the courts to suspend all cases having to do with sequestration.[26] Surprisingly, despite that suspension, the Treasury Ministry allowed the court of Concepción to sentence another case. Spaniard Antonio Fernández applied for naturalization in 1822 and for the return of his property in 1823. Based on his good conduct along with his need to support his Chilean wife and children, a judge lifted the sequestration of his property as long as it did not affect a third party. "Citizen" José de la Cruz Villalobos protested that he had purchased a farm, which the government had seized from Fernández, at a price of more than 40,000 pesos to be paid over nine years and had proceeded to plant grape vines. Nevertheless, the final sentence in late 1825 declared that sale null and void, leaving Villalobos only the option of suing the officials who had illegally auctioned off the hacienda.[27]

The year 1826 would prove busy for sequestration litigation in Concepción. It may have been that the conflicting sentences had resulted in political unrest and confusion, just at a time when the Chilean army was mounting renewed campaigns against royalist guerrillas in the south, termed "bandits," as well as an effort to wrest the southern island of Chiloé from Spanish control. The local treasury officials ordered a new list of properties to be prepared to replace documents that had been lost, and may have been trying to make up for the revenue lost from other properties that had been returned. Carmen Rojas was surprised to find her two houses in Talcahuano on the new list, protesting that she had not left the city in sixty years and that her property had not previously come under a sequester order. Rojas was ultimately vindicated, but the treasury officials insisted that their new records must be the correct ones and acted outraged that a woman would dare to question them. They even tried to turn around the principle of family dependence that usually exempted women of responsibility for their actions. Rojas had let two nieces live in one of her houses until they left for Lima, presumably as enemies of Chile, and the officials argued that these women "obliged to the Aunt who maintained them, would have been dependent upon and in agreement with the political opinion of their protector."[28]

María Jesús Arregui similarly protested that she was suddenly charged rent on her house even though three years earlier the governor (presumably Freire) had recognized the injustice of its sequestration. Arregui protested in highly gendered terms that since becoming a widow in 1816, her conduct had been irreproachable:

> without any aspiration other than providing for my own sustenance and that of my family through personal labor incompatible with my advanced age. I would have been prevented from taking any part in the events of the revolution owing to my age, my sex, and my widowhood.[29]

Her only possible crime, she continued, was to have obeyed the royal order to evacuate in 1818, but she complied out of fear. Her characterization matched the expectations of feminine behavior perfectly. As one of the witnesses on her behalf, tithe administrator Francisco Benismelis, put it, "Her sex, her old age, and moreover her very delusions made her unable to conquer her fears."[30] But in an ironic twist, in order to clear the name of her deceased husband as well, she described his conduct in similar terms:

> Everyone in this town knows that my deceased husband Juan Gualva, although a native of Spain, never acted as one during the era of the revolution, since he never did anything beyond his business as a merchant, nor held any goal other than providing for his family. His passive nature and the hatred he professed for anything having to do with warfare, kept him applied only to his domestic matters without taking the least part in any kind of political affairs.[31]

Both Arregui and her witnesses contrasted Gualva's neutrality with the active opposition of others to independence. "If so many de-naturalized criminals, having seen the first light of day in this land have dared to insult the mother Fatherland and yet have obtained the full restitution of their property," Benismelis pointed out, "why not a poor widow whose only crime is to have been the wife of a peaceful Spaniard whose conduct was spotless."[32] Although Gualva's passivity would be considered unmanly during wartime, during postwar reconstruction the state emphasized men's roles as family providers.

The contrasting attitudes by local officials toward Rojas and Arregui, which placed more emphasis on the women's adherence to norms of femininity than on their political affiliations, demonstrate the depth of sympathy for returning émigrés in the region. Members of the provincial assembly of Concepción, tired of waiting for the national Congress to draft a definitive law on sequestration and taking advantage of the de facto federalism of the period, decided to take action on their own in December 1826. The preamble to their decree reasoned:

> Considering the various calls that have been made by the Governors of this Province, the City Council and the prior Honorable Assembly to return to their original owners the property seized owing to errors of opinion during the war of Independence: the harm that results to the Province and to the entire Republic from having these farms fall into ruin for the lack of cultivation, funds to repair them, and administrators willing to take charge of them. . . . that the Federal Government has already ordered that the most valuable be turned over to those who most mortally wounded the Republic: that the only property to remain under sequestration is that of the most unfortunate who have no influence, favor, nor protection.[33]

Based on such deliberations, the assembly proceeded to state the principles that should govern such matters. First, all assets seized owing to "errors of opinion," that is, opposition to independence, should be returned to their original owners. Second, Congress should set a period within which those living in other countries could return to claim their property. Third, apparently in an effort to balance the rights of various residents in the region, the assembly declared any property that had been sold off by the patriot government should not be returned. The assembly also indicated that it would request the confirmation of the decree from the national Congress "with the persistence demanded by the public interest, for the relief of the unfortunate, and to avoid the complete ruin of the Province."[34]

Entries that followed the decree indicate that local judges and officials began to carry out the orders until the treasury officials in Concepción informed the governor in March 1827 that a provincial assembly had no authority to dispose of national property. In September 1828, Judge Juan José Manzanos tried another tactic, requesting clarification from the Congress about the implications of article 105 of the newly passed constitution that prohibited the use of confiscation as a judicial penalty. Manzanos argued that once confiscation became illegal, it was unjust for the state to continue holding sequestered assets. Like the assembly almost two years earlier, he claimed that most of the properties were modest and belonged to those who lacked the resources to pursue their claims "while their unfortunate, innocent children pine away in the most lamentable state of abandonment [orfandad]."[35] Moreover, he contended that the state was earning little revenue from the properties, which no one wanted to rent, and they were falling into disrepair. "Justice and the prosperity of the Country call out for returning the property," he asserted, "since the benefits of agricultural work rest in the true owners who could make the necessary improvements in both rural and urban properties, which will not occur when they are in the hands of others."[36] Although the Congress told Manzanos to resubmit his query through proper channels, there is no further reference to it in congressional minutes. Nonetheless, the bill approved by the House of Representatives in 1829, but never passed by the Senate, was very similar to the 1826 decree of the provincial assembly.

Further, two lawsuits refer to a presidential decree dated July 8, 1829, authorizing officials in the southern provinces of Concepción and Maule to put former owners in *possession* of sequestered property while awaiting a congressional law that would determine whether or not they could again be declared the legal *owners*. In one, the court in Santiago determined in 1848 that the 1829 decree had not gone into effect, but the treasury ministers in Concepción testified that since August 1830 their office had ceased to administer sequestered assets.[37] In the other, which pitted a war heroine against the mother of a royalist guerrilla commander, the judge implied that he did not approve of the generalized return of properties that followed that decree.[38] The transcript of this case demonstrates how much the situation had changed in Concepción within a decade. In 1820, María Cornelia Olivares, who claimed royal officials in Chillán had persecuted her, was awarded property seized from royalist Juan Antonio Olate valued at one thousand pesos.[39] Ten years later, Olivares filed suit to reclaim that property, which had been re-occupied by relatives of the original owner when she fled the region out of fear of royalist bandits. Olate's mother had no qualms about claiming that she and her defenseless grandchildren were more deserving of compassion than Olivares, whom she characterized as a former maid who claimed to be a patriot simply because she had a sexual relationship with a soldier.[40] Upon appeal to Santiago, neither Olivares nor Olate had anyone to represent them in the capital. The case languished, which meant that Olate likely remained in possession of the property.

With the exception of treasury officials, most authorities in the south were ready to forgive those who had followed the royalist evacuation and reincorporate them as productive citizens. In central Chile, reconciliation similarly began with women and children, but it would take longer before men had much success in recovering property. In the case that María Dunn appealed to Congress, it was allegedly a woman's property that had been seized, but her widower and children, returned émigrés, successfully recovered it by 1829. The case hinged on which members of the family were the rightful owners and whether they could be held responsible for their actions during wartime. In 1817, after the Battle of Chacabuco, Modesto Novajas y Solano, his offspring, and his sister-in-law Josefa Velázquez all boarded a ship bound for Lima, leaving their house in Valparaíso subject to seizure. The government auctioned off the property, which subsequently had been resold several times, ultimately to Dunn. In 1822, Novajas filed suit on behalf of his children, protesting that the sequester order had been against his sister-in-law, but that the house in fact belonged to his wife, who had died twenty years earlier and hence before the war. Because minor children had no choice but to follow their father, he argued, they should still be recognized as the rightful heirs to their mother's house.[41] Although he was careful to acknowledge in retrospect that patriots had treated the enemy with mercy, he recalled his fear during the war about the fate that would await his children if he left them in Chile:

> They were not imprinted with the words "out of love for my patria I have not followed my Father" so that the victor would admit them to his ranks and they would not be affected by the ensuing havoc. They were the children of a Spaniard, and as long as they could not express their own will, held back by their minor age, they would be presumed to hold the same opinion as me.[42]

There was, however, some question as to whether all his offspring had been minors at the time they boarded ships for Lima. If his wife had died in 1803, the youngest must have been at least fourteen in 1817, and later evidence suggested that at least one of the sons was already living and working in Lima. Dunn's lawyer argued that one did not need to be twenty-five to exercise his own will and alleged that the children "were not some innocents but rather men who had already declared themselves against the cause of America."[43] Moreover, he called attention to the injustice and disorder that would result from returning properties already auctioned off by the government: "innumerable contracts that had already been executed would be broken, a thousand buyers would be deceived, a thousand fortunes would collapse, and the fugitives by their mere presence would triumph over those who in good faith accepted the Government's invitation to purchase [property]."[44]

As the case continued, two sons submitted briefs on behalf of the siblings. Manuel Novajas in Chile emphasized their need and dependence:

> The error of [our father] should not encompass us in a blow that takes away the basis of subsistence from a large family. His minor children, who are today devoted to the sacred cause of the Country and did nothing except follow without premeditation the orders of their progenitor, should not be harmed.[45]

Writing from Peru, Agustín Novajas asserted that he and several of his brothers in fact had acted on their own, but on the side of fighting for independence in Chile, La Plata, and Peru. "In this enlightened century," he asserted, "there are no laws, however strict they may be, that punish children for the mistakes of their Fathers."[46] Nonetheless, he did highlight the innocence and dependence of the daughters: "my unfortunate sisters, young ladies living in a miserable hut exposed to the inclement weather without any shelter other than some branches and a straw mat . . . in the Country that witnessed their birth."[47] On their behalf, he called upon the "paternal mercy" of the government.

The logic of family resonated with all the officials who commented on the case as it continued through several appeals to 1830. In 1823, Rafael Correa de Saa and Joaquín de Echeverría, representing the central Sequestration Commission, agreed with the argument that minors were subject to paternal authority and, therefore, Novajas's children could not be considered voluntary émigrés:

> In sum, these unfortunates are Americans and they find themselves today subject to having to beg, and perhaps to prostitution to which so many times poverty has led. Even the least sensitive heart would shudder upon

contemplating the wretched state with which they are threatened if the small assets for which they are asking are not returned to them.[48]

Only state attorney Manuel Antonio Gonzales asserted, in 1829, that the court should abide by the congressional order to suspend lawsuits over sequestration and await a treaty with Spain that would also compensate patriots. He called attention to families on the other side: "One would rejoice that innocents should not pay for the crime of their parents, and truly sequestered assets should be applied toward the relief of so many orphans and widows whom the enemy have left suffering with no fault other than having been children or wives of patriots."[49] Nevertheless, the superior court upheld lower rulings to return the property to the heirs of Rosa Velázquez upon the reimbursement to the purchaser of any investments he had made in renovations and maintenance.

The case of the Novajas family demonstrates that the point at which men became independent and responsible for their own actions was debatable. In 1823, the priest of Pelarco near Talca returned from Peru and filed for the return of his sequestered assets, a debt of 4,000 pesos Ramón Ramírez owed him on account of a chaplaincy established on his farm. The priest, Pedro Juan del Pozo, protested that he had never been prosecuted and found guilty of opposing independence, and he claimed that he had been forced to emigrate to Lima with a brother upon whom he relied for his maintenance. Extending the claims of dependence, Pozo requested the lifting of the sequestration in terms similar to wives asking for support payments to cover their alimentos, a term he used in the case: "I have no other income to provide a decent living. I have not been condemned to die of hunger."[50] The judge agreed, voiding the sequestration so that Pozo could sue the debtor.

By the middle of the 1820s, the national government also began to show more clemency toward former royalist men who had clearly opposed independence and emigrated to avoid patriot retributions; after all, many were wealthy and had ties to prominent Chilean families. Merchant Andrés Carlos de Vildósola was among those who clambered aboard the ships bound for Lima after the royalist defeat at Chacabuco in 1817. Within weeks, officials had collected the keys to his shop from his wife Catalina Castro, and in May and September witnesses informed the government of various debts owed to Vildósola that, if collected, could be included with his sequestered assets.[51] Unbeknownst to authorities in Santiago, Vildósola was signatory to a petition in Lima that called upon the king to order the sequestration of all patriot property in order to compensate royalist émigrés.[52] In August,

Castro, like other wives, approached the Chilean government for support payments to feed her children; she was initially granted 500 pesos payable from the sequestered property, an amount reduced within a few weeks to 250 pesos. In 1821, she complained to the Senate that she was never paid, so that body authorized the return to her of a sugar mill.[53] It is unclear when Vildósola returned to Chile, but in 1826 he filed a suit for the return of his property.[54] Four gentlemen, including Diego Portales, testified on his behalf, claiming that he had intervened with the Spanish government during the reconquest period on behalf of various Chileans including Portales's uncle Santiago Larraín.

Vildósola apparently died soon after filing his claim, because his widow pursued the case in 1827. State attorney Fernando Elizalde was sympathetic, noting that her numerous American children should not be held responsible for the supposed crimes of their father and that other (unnamed) royalists, more fervent than he, had successfully recovered their property. Like Argomedo before him, he pointed out that by showing mercy, the government would demonstrate to the world its benevolence and that the children "would extol such a beneficent government and would become additional columns to support our sacred cause."[55] The judges, however, were not yet prepared to forgive in full. The first sentence in August 1827 determined that Vildósola fell into the second category of the 1821 principles laid out by the Senate—someone who had been an enemy of the state but had repented—and that therefore his widow should appeal to the executive branch, which would determine how much property might be returned. Vice-president Blanco Encalada, however, kicked it up to the court of appeals, which decided on its own to restore a house to Castro but to postpone determination about other cash and goods until a treaty had been signed with Spain.

Cases of returning royalists like Vildósola were, not surprisingly, even more complicated than those who could claim to have evacuated from Concepción fearing retribution from Spanish officers. Merchant Bautista Uría, a native of Spain, first set up shop in Valparaíso in 1806 but joined the exodus to Lima after the Battle of Chacabuco. He returned the following year with the 1818 royal expedition led by Osorio, and some witnesses testified that he fought with the royalists at the Battle of Maipú. It is unclear exactly when his house was seized, but Pedro Chacón Morales purchased it from the government in February 1819. Almost a decade later, in 1828, Uría resurfaced and sued for the return of his house on the grounds that he had never been found guilty in a trial. "It is time to repair the damages produced by a restrictive spirit that violated property rights," he asserted, "and led to a forced redistribution."[56] Moreover, he cited examples of others like him, including the Novajas family, who had recovered their property. Basing his opinion on the 1821 Senate resolution, state attorney José Santiago Montt declared the case under executive jurisdiction to decide whether or not Uría was innocent or sufficiently repentant, and he ordered both sides to present their evidence. Each mounted a comprehensive case and called numerous witnesses over the course of three years.

Juan José Vargas, representing Uría, depicted his actions in the best possible light. He presented a certificate from 1813 in which Uría had not only complied with a levy of 500 pesos to the patriots but also swore "that if having been born in Spain were an indication of little love for Chile, his last drop of blood would redeem that mistaken belief."[57] He called five prominent witnesses, including Diego Portales, to testify that Uría had not participated in the persecution of patriots during the subsequent period of the reconquest, and attributed Uría's emigration to a generalized fear that the patriot victory would lead to retributions against all Spaniards and an urgent need to attend to his business interests in Lima before communication with that city was cut off by the war. When Uría applied for naturalization in 1826, he was vague on the circumstances of his return, noting only that "I finally managed to return to a country that had sheltered me so much and whose recognition is still engraved upon my heart with the firm resolution never again to abandon it; and thus, united with a virtuous Chilean wife, I live peacefully in a country that I am proud to call my homeland [patria natal]."[58]

Chacón called sixteen witnesses to depict Uría as a royalist émigré who returned with the Spanish army in 1818 to fight against patriot forces. General Francisco Calderón testified that Uría had been identified to him as an enemy fugitive, and customs administrator Agustín Beyner characterized Uría as the same as the other Spaniards living in Valparaíso during the war: "namely that of hating any American who had committed himself to independence from Spain."[59] Still Beyner could say only that he had heard but not witnessed that Uría served Osorio voluntarily and had fought at the Battle of Maipú. Chacón discounted the excuse of going to Lima on business given its timing and Uría's risking greater losses by abandoning his more valuable Chilean property. Finally, Chacón called attention to the question of family, which had weighed so heavily in earlier property restitutions; he pointed out that Uría had not married until after the war, and so there were no children whose interests would have been harmed by the confiscation.[60]

The dispute between Chacón and Uría reveals the critical issues under debate over how to evaluate people's actions during the war and the criteria for their reincorporation into the new nation conceived as "the greater Chilean family" in the wording of the 1821 Senate resolution. The hesitancy of government officials to weigh in consistently on one side or the other likely reflects the difficulty of this process as well as the growing political conflict between liberals and conservatives. In 1829 Chacón requested suspension of the lawsuit as ordered by Congress in 1825, but his petition was denied. Instead the court let the parties argue their cases until the controversies threatened to escalate. In his final arguments in 1831, Uría's lawyer hinted that Chacón may have been on the wrong side in the recent civil war.[61] Chacón countered with a request to have Uría answer some questions in a closed hearing, at which point the written record ends. Although the final outcome is unknown, Uría seemed to be in a more difficult position than others who were successful in recovering their property, owing to his close association with Osorio and his lack of family, other than his new wife, who would have shared the consequences of the sequestration with him.

These lawsuits bear out the complaints of representatives in Congress about the arbitrary and inconsistent judicial sentences in cases of sequestration. The question of whether the government could legally dispose of properties held in sequestration, whether by sale or donation, was one of the thorniest problems in the generally confusing matter of property seizures. Although both O'Higgins and the Senate in 1820 retroactively validated the state's prerogative to dispose of sequestered property, courts in Concepción declared some sales in that province null. Furthermore, O'Higgins himself continued to distribute property to reward those who had contributed to the country's independence, and to pit the claims of such patriots against returning or repentant royalists was politically charged.[62] In 1822, for example, the government granted the widow of Lieutenant Colonel Cayetano Letelier, who had died in battle in Valdivia, a hacienda named "Las Palmas" valued at 7,500 pesos; but when Leonarda Sans Merino arrived from France, she discovered that the hacienda had been returned to its owner.[63]

Sans Merino's case ended up on the docket of state attorney Montt, who gave his shifting legal opinion on the question of the government's dominion in sequestered property in a series of lawsuits in 1828, one year before the heated debate in Congress. In late December 1827, Montt weighed in on notorious royalist Rafael Beltrán's efforts to reclaim his sequestered houses. He first noted that only treaties between the governments that had been at war should settle the final decision on claims. In the event that judges lifted sequester orders, he continued, the government was responsible for refunding an equal value to the original owners but should not nullify contracts selling or awarding property to third parties.[64] Just over two months later, Montt reiterated his opinion in the case of Sans Merino, that "governments should uphold the grants and sales of such sequestered properties, because otherwise they would undermine their credit and no one would want to contract with them, and they remain responsible only for the value [set upon such properties] in treaties ratified after the war."[65] By June 1828, however, Montt declined to weigh in on the legality of Chacón's purchase of Uría's house; instead he simply ordered both sides to present evidence.[66] Finally, in September, in a case involving the grant of a hacienda to Ramón Freire, Montt changed his position. He asserted that any disposal of sequestered property after 1818, when the constitution abolished confiscation as a criminal penalty, was illegal.[67] Clearly disputes arising from sequestration, in which families on both sides could be harmed by the consequences, would be difficult for the new state to resolve.

Attempts to Legislate on Sequestration and Restitution after 1830

In the following decade, it would be President José Joaquín Prieto, victor in the civil war of 1830, and his finance minister who would take the initiative on the matter of sequestered property. In September 1832, Prieto asked the Senate to revise its 1821 resolution by passing clear guidelines to be followed by the courts in lawsuits over sequestration. In terms of the first part of that act, he asserted that the courts had generally returned property without sufficiently investigating whether or not the political opinions of the owners had justified confiscation. But he particularly protested the difficult position in which the second part of that act, authorizing the government to pardon repentant royalists, put the executive. Without any clear criteria, the president would face criticism from one side or the other regardless of his decision.[68] In his first memo, Prieto emphasized the need for a law on property restitution, but left it up to Congress to draft appropriate guidelines. The Senate assigned the matter to two committees, where it languished. Just under a year later, in June 1833, therefore, Prieto's finance minister conveyed to the Senate a reminder from the president of the urgency of the issue, this time identifying specific matters that required clarification (such as the validity of sales, criteria for evaluating claims, deadlines, etc.). The president of the Senate assured the minister that the Senate would take care of the legislation just as soon as the finance committee made a recommendation.[69] In

October, Prieto charged a special session of Congress with addressing thirteen matters, including sequestration; legislators managed to get through most of the business but took no action on the latter.[70]

In 1834, Prieto tried a somewhat different tack. Prioritizing the consolidation of the domestic debt to bring public finances into order, he reminded both chambers of Congress in his annual address that in order to proceed on that front, it was necessary to set guidelines on how to deal with the sequestered property.[71] Finance minister Manuel Rengifo reiterated to lawmakers that measures that may have been politically expedient during the independence war had ruinous economic consequences: "Thus when the departure of the enemies of the Republic was promoted in order to consolidate domestic order, we lost not only the industry of many hardworking men but also the fortunes they had acquired and that were taken away at the very time we most needed the productivity they could provide."[72] After waiting a year, the president submitted a draft bill detailing the kinds of debt that the government should and should not commit to repay and invited legislators to amend it as they saw fit.[73] Influential Senator Mariano Egaña (who had been imprisoned in 1814 on the Juan Fernández Islands with his father) argued that dealing with the foreign, rather than the domestic, debt was a more pressing issue. Nonetheless, his colleagues finally began to debate the bill article by article from July through September 1835, and the House of Representatives took up the matter in October.[74] Under the law promulgated on November 17, 1835, the government took responsibility for various debts, including all funds that had entered the treasury from sequestration, whether imposed by Spanish authorities from 1814 to 1817 or by Chilean officials thereafter. Moreover, the government recognized its responsibility to reimburse those who had either purchased or received as compensation for services to the state property that was later returned to its original owners. Article 4, however, left to a future law the procedure by which credits resulting from sequestration would be recognized. The 1835 law was careful to reject any claims that had not been recorded in the offices of the treasury (procedures not always followed during the war according to witnesses), to repay only the value of property at the time of its seizure (not improvements, compensations for damages, or repayment of income), and to set deadlines for filing for compensation (although these deadlines were extended in 1837 and 1839).[75]

In the final years of the Prieto administration, various members of the executive branch reminded Congress that it still needed to pass the law called for by Article 4 of the debt consolidation law that would set criteria for determining which sequestered assets would be recognized as part of the debt, but legislators made no progress toward establishing a comprehensive policy.[76] Prieto had also hoped to normalize relations with Spain, but instead had to divert his attention to the war against the Peru-Bolivia Confederation from 1836 to 1839. War hero Manuel Bulnes was elected president in 1841 and resumed negotiations that resulted in an 1844 treaty, in which Spain finally recognized the independence of Chile. Spain had insisted that sequestered property be returned to Spanish subjects, so the treaty cited Article 4 of the 1835 law, which promised that Congress would establish procedures for certifying debts arising from sequestration.[77] From 1848 through 1853, the Spanish chargé d'affaires and the Chilean minister of foreign relations corresponded over the urgency of passing such a law. Spain expressed concern that the bill under consideration required documented evidence of seizures, rather than witness testimony, and that cases would be decided in Chilean courts rather than a commission with representation from both countries.[78] In regard to the latter, minister Antonio Varas reminded the Spanish chargé d'affaires that although much of the property was originally seized from Spanish subjects, the majority had since then passed (presumably through inheritance) to Chilean citizens.[79]

In 1853, Congress finally passed a bill detailing the criteria for consolidating debt arising from sequestration, and it was signed into law by the successor of Bulnes, President Manuel Montt. Most of the affected parties had probably died, but their heirs could file for compensation. Strikingly, the process was depoliticized: claims could be filed for any property that had been seized, regardless of the circumstances. As with earlier principles, the law limited the credit to the value of the property at the time of its seizure. But certain articles were more generous than prior practice. Article 3 allowed for the presentation of documentary (though not testimonial) evidence beyond the accounts kept by the treasury, as long as the party could prove that the property had been seized on the orders of a competent official. And Article 15 stated that after four years, any unclaimed property would be divided among claimants who had proven they were targets of seizures even if they had not been able to accurately establish the value of the sequestered assets.[80]

Throughout the decades during which laws on how to handle claims arising from sequestration were debated and finally passed, several notable and wealthy royalists pursued lawsuits that demonstrate the complex legal issues raised by the return of émigrés. Although the language of family was less prominent in later congressional debates on debt consolidation and sequestration than it had been prior to 1830, such concerns were still aired in court. One of the longest-running and most complicated lawsuits arising from wartime seizures involved Freire and the Urrejola family, whose lives had intersected with those of the Carreras prior to 1814. Spaniard Alejandro Urrejola purchased in 1767 a hacienda named Cucha-Cucha, which had been confiscated from the expelled Jesuits. His ten children stood to inherit the estate, but patriot officials seized it when they all fled during the war. On September 6, 1821, the government granted the hacienda to Freire as compensation for his many services.

Spanish merchant José Manuel Eguiguren had emigrated to Lima with his wife María Josefa Urrejola, since deceased, while most of his sisters-in-law had followed the royalist evacuation of Concepción south of the Biobío River. Within a year of the 1821 Senate resolution, Eguiguren was pardoned under the second category of someone who repented of his support for the Crown, considering his earlier appeals to royal authorities on behalf of imprisoned patriots and his duty to provide for ten Chilean children.[81] Two years later, he invoked familial rhetoric in a petition to recover the Cucha-Cucha hacienda for his children and in-laws. Claiming that this innocent family, like so many others, had emigrated only under duress, he particularly highlighted the plight of the women and children:

> It is impossible to believe that the weak, delicate, and penniless sex would voluntarily abandon what was most dear and precious in order to follow a wretched Army like nomads into the land of the barbarians where, far from anything pleasant, all would be anxieties, miseries, and fears not only of hunger but of one's very existence at the whim of barbarians without law or religion. No one could ignore the contrast between their domestic lives within their own homes and among civilized society with a nomadic existence without fortune or security. And what should I say about so many minor children tied to the destiny of their unfortunate parents . . . ? Could even the most unfair person possibly fault these hapless victims?

He continued by extending the metaphor of family explicitly into the realm of politics. After noting that the return of many other sequestered estates was helping to secure peace and revive agriculture, he contrasted those results with the negative effects of property still being held by the state or third parties: "One should add that the scandalous abuses taken with these properties brings with it another transcendent harm to the public, namely establishing discord among families." He concluded by appealing to the Chilean magistrate as "the best Father who knows how to gather to his breast even those children who have gone astray."[82]

Freire found himself in a delicate situation: he was championing reconciliation and the lifting of sequestration but did not want to lose his own property. As governor, he had even pardoned the husband of Rita Urrejola, who took her to Spanish-held Chiloé. Freire decided to defend his right to indemnification from the state but indicated his sympathy for the plight of the Urrejola family, particularly the daughters:

> I cannot look with indifference upon the lamentable state of those who can claim a right to the Cuchacucha hacienda, which the former government gave to me as compensation for various credits I had against accounts of the state. . . . You may make this clear to the Madames Urrejola so that they proceed knowing that I will take the greatest satisfaction in their achieving from the courts of justice whatever is due them by right and equity.[83]

Given the high-stakes nature of a case affecting Freire at the height of his power, the lawsuit moved slowly. In April 1827, the treasury officials, who usually sought any avenue to avoid the disbursement of scarce funds, issued an opinion that in the event that the Urrejolas received a favorable sentence, the government should compensate them rather than return an estate no longer in its possession.[84] State attorney José Santiago Montt walked a fine line in his 1828 opinion, justifying wartime seizures aimed at weakening the enemy but asserting that real estate, in particular, should have been held only until the conclusion of the war when its disposition would be set in treaties. He asserted that sales of such properties transacted after the Constitution of 1818, which abolished confiscation along with all penalties that affected anyone beyond the guilty party, were null and void. Arguing "neither could the government official make that grant, nor had the owner done anything to merit the loss of his property," Montt concluded that the government instead should reimburse Freire. The sentence of Judge Palma in December 1828 was similarly partial. He lifted the sequestration of the shares of the inheritance pertaining to Francisco Urrejola and the children of María Josefa Urrejola (the deceased wife of Eguiguren) but found that other family members had yet to prove that they fell under the terms of the 1821 Senate resolution.[85]

The following year, therefore, was filled with the presentation of evidence on behalf of the other heirs. María Ignacia Urrejola had apparently hidden in the woods and countryside of the region along with the children of her brother Francisco. Manuela, a Trinitarian nun, had accompanied her religious order in the royalist evacuation, and her earthly sisters Carmen and Mercedes Urrejola followed behind. Juan Antonio had been forced to evacuate but had escaped and was subsequently appointed as a teacher in the new National Institute. Rita accompanied her husband to Chiloé. The lawyer mentioned Agustín's election to the first Congress of 1811, but not his subsequent emigration. Luis had been posted as a royal soldier to the Philippines, but he had published a paper advocating "reconciliation with the unfortunate Chileans and advocating their restitution to their families."[86] In addition to calling witnesses to affirm the good conduct of the Urrejolas, their lawyer presented copies of Freire's own reports and decrees on the lamentable state of Concepción whose residents had all fled or were in hiding when he occupied the city in 1819.[87] On December 21, 1830, a judge lifted the sequestration on the shares of all heirs of Alejandro Urrejola with the exception of Luis, absent from Chile as a member of the Spanish army, and Agustín, the royalist bishop who had emigrated to Spain. Although this sentence came eight months after Freire's defeat at the Battle of Lircay, the judge still called for it to take effect only after Freire had been indemnified. Four months later, however, the superior court ordered the estate restored to those Urrejolas found innocent or pardoned and simply reserved for Freire (at that point in exile) the right to pursue a separate lawsuit for compensation.[88]

Unfortunately for the Urrejolas, the return of their hacienda, far from resolving their problems, resulted in the very family discord their brother-in-law Eguiguren had decried a decade earlier. The heirs could not agree on who should administer the property. Both Juan Antonio Urrejola and Miguel González (Rita's husband) were named at various points, but neither seemed eager to accept the responsibility. Juan Antonio reported in 1832 that Rita was thwarting consensus among the siblings. The Chilean government, which still held the shares of brothers Luis and Agustín, suggested selling the hacienda and dividing the proceeds, but the Urrejolas refused. Complaining that the Urrejolas never submitted accounts, that each heir simply took what he or she wanted from the estate, and that some grandchild had planted wheat without permission, the treasury officials got a court order in 1834 that the hacienda be put under a rental contract.[89] Presumably the rental simplified the distribution of proceeds as records on the estate did not resurface for another decade when the family finally presented a copy of Agustín's will dictated in Spain in 1824. Agustín made his siblings his heirs but with an extra portion (the one-fifth that Spanish law allowed testators to distribute freely) to his brother Luis. This will led to a reshuffling of shares as the state now remained in possession of only the inheritance of Luis. Finally, yet another decade later in 1854, the Urrejolas appealed for the share of Luis based upon the Debt Consolidation Act of September 15, 1853, which lifted sequestrations still in force against any Spanish citizens. The superior court finally adjudicated shares in 1857, allowing the state to retain the income on the share of Luis up until the lifting of the sequestration in July 1854 but to return the rest of the estate to the Urrejolas.[90] As for Freire, he too had finally benefited from a period of national reconciliation in the wake of the War against the Peru-Bolivia Confederation. He returned from exile in 1842, and in 1845 Congress authorized President Bulnes to work out a payment schedule to compensate Freire with the sum of 20,750 pesos.[91] Stretching over three decades, the lawsuit over the Cucha-Cucha hacienda represents well the difficulty of reconciling Chilean families and adjudicating the sequestration and restitution of property.

The Urrejolas, as residents of southern Chile, garnered more sympathy than Spanish merchants who had been active in supporting the royalist cause. At the time of his capture on a boat headed from Talcahuano to Lima, Rafael Beltrán was one of the wealthiest men in the country.[92] His wife, María Loreto Iñiguez y Landa, estimated the value of lands, livestock, minerals, and merchandise in 1817 at almost 200,000 pesos. State attorney Argomedo noted that the government had seized more property from Beltrán than from any other émigré but did not believe his wife was entitled to half the marital property because it should not be divided up "during the lifetime of the spouses"; instead, like others, she was provisionally granted fifty pesos per month as a support payment (alimentos).[93] The Chilean government granted one of Beltrán's haciendas, patriotically renamed "La Chilena," to José de San Martín, who sold it and was still trying to collect payment in 1833.[94] Beltrán returned to Chile with the Osorio expedition, and after the royalist defeat at the Battle of Maipú, he and others were captured on a ship trying to flee once again to Peru. His wife paid a large ransom to allow him to return to Spain instead of facing trial.[95] Almost a decade later, Beltrán returned to Chile and with his wife began a legal effort, which would last thirty years, to recuperate his properties on the grounds that the seizure and subsequent sales had been illegal.

Although the Supreme Court lifted the sequestration on some vineyards, two other lawsuits in which Beltrán and Iñiguez requested the same for haciendas that had been sold by the government to third parties were inconclusive.[96] Then, in 1840, Beltrán sued the estate of the purchaser of the hacienda "El Parral" in Rancagua. Presumably, the 1835 law on debt consolidation did not provide enough grounds for the lawsuit because it left hanging the specifics of how sequestered assets were to be recognized and affirmed that those who left Chile after the Battle of Chacabuco should be considered political opponents of the state. His attorney instead cited the Senate resolution of 1821, arguing that the time had certainly come to right the wrongs committed during the turbulent years of the independence wars. Beltrán's lawyer also appealed to the argument of family and nationality to counter the assumption that all Spaniards resident in America would have opposed independence: "Related by marriage with local families, rooted in this soil by their landed properties, far from being enemies, they were members of the same Chilean society whose rights were being vindicated."[97] Nevertheless, on December 21, 1847, the Supreme Court reaffirmed the legality of the original seizure as well as the decree of October 27, 1820, which sanctioned sales of such property "although some of the necessary formalities may have been lacking."[98] Beltrán, unlike others, was able to recover only property not in the possession of third parties, most likely because he had made too many enemies during his extensive financial operations at the end of the colonial period.[99]

The family of another wealthy royalist similarly had mixed success in trying to recover the value of sequestered assets. Pedro Nicolás de Chopitea arrived in Chile from Spain at the end of the eighteenth century and built a lucrative business as a merchant. He married Isabel Villota, daughter of Spanish merchant Celedonio Villota, who brought a sizable dowry as well as valuable commercial contacts to their union. With the political crisis beginning in 1810, Chopitea's loyalty to Spain was clear. In 1812, as the Carreras were leading the junta toward independence, an antipeninsular crowd called for Chopitea's head.[100] Under the restoration of royal rule from 1814 to 1817, Chopitea served on the Santiago Cabildo and took on the administration of at least some property sequestered on the orders of Governor Marcó del Pont.[101] When the patriots regained Santiago, Chopitea was in Lima and so the government seized his house, the merchandise in his warehouse, and his account books with notations of money owed to him.[102] Villota first paid a monthly rent of 200 pesos to be allowed to stay in the house and then purchased it back from the government for 13,000 pesos in September 1817.[103] She also petitioned the government to protect her dowry and marital share in the property and to provide a support pension for her children, but the outcome was not recorded.[104] In the meantime, Chopitea joined Osorio's 1818 expedition from Peru. His family later claimed that he stayed in the south and did not participate in any battles, but when the expedition retreated, the ship on which Chopitea was again trying to reach Lima was captured.[105] Like Beltrán, who was on the same vessel, Chopitea paid 40,000 pesos for his release. In order to raise the money, Villota signed the house over to José Casimiro Alvano.[106] Once the transaction was complete, Chopitea, his wife, and children were allowed to leave Chile and settled in Barcelona.

At some point, news must have reached Chopitea in Spain that some former royalists were successfully recovering their properties in Chile. By 1833, Chopitea had traveled to Montevideo but having taken ill sent his son Alejandro on to Chile to represent their joint interests. Alejandro de Chopitea began cautiously in early 1834, defending his father's innocence but less stridently than Beltrán, and initially asking only for the right to attempt to collect any outstanding debts from the sequestered account books. Chopitea emphasized the ties of family that had bound his father to Chile and the consequences suffered by these American relatives: "he was considered a Chilean owing to his long residence in the country and for having married and had children here."[107] "My innocent brothers and I," he added, "have lost a fortune."[108] Crucially, he claimed that his father had left for Lima simply to attend to his business in 1816, *before* the Battle of Chacabuco, and therefore had not fled for political reasons. Moreover, he attributed his return with Osorio to his "desire to return to his adopted fatherland, where his wife and children were, and the hope of recovering his sequestered belongings" and denied that he took up arms or even spoke out unless it was to defend persecuted patriots.[109] After some positive testimony from prominent Chileans, including several of Villota's relatives, the courts authorized him to attempt to collect outstanding debts.

Emboldened by this initial success and perhaps having acquired more knowledge of how these cases worked, Alejandro de Chopitea quickly followed up with a request that the government return any funds it had received from the sequestration on the grounds that his father fell under the first category of the 1821 Senate resolution: a person incorrectly suspected of having emigrated as an enemy of independence.[110] State attorney Elizalde, apparently overlooking Chopitea's presence in the Osorio expedition, concurred that his defense of patriots during the period of royalist rule and his departure for Lima before Chacabuco demonstrated that the sequestration had been unwarranted.[111] Treasury accounts from 1817 and 1818 showed a total value for Chopitea's property of just over 53,660 pesos (though at the time Villota had protested this figure as too low).[112] Alejandro de Chopitea was just on the verge of reimbursement in 1836, when treasury officials called attention to a provision in the recently passed law on the consolidation of the internal national debt that included sequestered assets but excluded "those amounts that the Republican Governments demanded in exchange for commuting sentences imposed to punish political crimes."[113] On appeal to the Supreme Court, the lawsuit languished for several years. In 1841, Alejandro had passed away and his brother renewed the petition to be reimbursed from the treasury; the last entry in the written record was a report from the treasury asserting that the 40,000 pesos Chopitea had paid for his release from prison was not refundable and should be deducted from the total of 53,660 pesos.

By the 1840s, the fortune of the Chopiteas, like that of the Beltráns, took a turn for the worse. In 1846, the heirs tried suing Alvano to return a house on the grounds that the sequestration and subsequent sale had been illegal. In 1852, state attorney Serrano interpreted Chopitea's status under the 1821 resolution distinctly from Elizalde in 1834. Pointing out that he had been captured along with other royalists fleeing Talcahuano, Serrano concluded that he was legally subject not simply to sequester but the confiscation of his property. Moreover, the failure of Chopitea or his family to appeal under the 1821 provisions, overlooking that the family had appealed once they returned to Chile in 1834, indicated that he was in fact guilty.[114] The judge concurred, adding that Alvano had in fact taken a risk in purchasing the house in order to aid the Chopiteas in their efforts to leave Chile.[115]

Attitudes changed dramatically in the 1850s, however, when few royalists remained alive. Under terms of the 1853 Debt Consolidation Act, plaintiffs claiming compensation for sequestered property generally were successful, if not always for the full amount claimed. Credits ranging from 400 to 8,500 pesos, for example, were recognized for heirs of José Morales, Gregorio Martínez, Lucas Muñoz, and Santiago Ascasivar. The latter had emigrated all the way to Spain where he had been awarded the Order of Isabel the Catholic in recognition of his loyalty to the crown.[116] Heirs of Spanish merchant Antonio del Sol successfully filed a claim for just over 30,000 pesos. Most of the amount arose from credits in his account books, and the judge asserted that whether or not the state had ever collected these sums, "the slowness, negligence, or carelessness of the employees of the public treasury, or the concessions made by the government to some of the debtors, should not harm the heirs of Sol, who could do nothing to collect on those contracts."[117] Six years after Rafael Beltrán's death, moreover, even his nephew and heir, Valentín Fernández Beltrán, was awarded at least 38,282 pesos for the value of one hacienda as well as some share of over 16,000 pesos to which a hospital also had partial claim arising from a charitable donation.[118] In 1860, minister of the treasury Jovino Novoa reported to Congress that over 1,000,000 pesos arising from sequestration had been consolidated into the national debt since passage of the 1853 act.[119]

....

Laws on the sequestration and subsequent return of property were complicated, and they were applied inconsistently both during and after the wars of independence. Even though not every case followed the same course, some general principles can be discerned. Chiefly, family ties at various levels were critical. Even during the height of conflict, the government recognized the right of dependents to support payable out of sequestered assets. In the longer term, almost all wives and children, especially if they had been born in Chile, were able to recuperate their shares owing to dowries, joint marital assets, or inheritance. Spanish and/or royalist men related to these presumed innocents were usually pardoned should they decide to return and make Chile their home. Especially in the south, too many men, women, and children of all classes had at least passively supported and followed the Spanish authorities to refuse to reincorporate them as they returned from Mapuche territory. Certainly, some neighbors must have resented the return of those who had informed on them and were loath to give up the houses they occupied because their own had been destroyed. But political leaders recognized that reconciliation was imperative if the region were to recover from the devastation of prolonged warfare. Indeed the language of laws and decrees referred to this process of reincorporation as joining the national family. Class standing also influenced individuals' chances of recuperating properties because the government wanted men with capital to help rebuild the economy. Still, status was intertwined with kinship as elite families usually had members on both sides of the conflict and could provide witnesses, such as Diego Portales, to the good deeds performed by some royalists during the reconquest period in order to offset their later crime of emigration.

Constituting the nation as "the greater Chilean family" was an ideal upon which most agreed, but which was difficult to achieve in practice. The many conflicting claims and interests posed a challenge to the postindependence Chilean state. Although their sympathies varied, all members of the executive and legislative branches recognized that the credibility of the new government depended in part on how it handled these property disputes. In 1829, the Congress was on the verge of passing a law that would recognize claims of émigrés while protecting those who had purchased real estate, as

well as patriot families who had been compensated for losses with sequestered property. The conservative regime that came to power in 1830 initially
left disputes up to the courts, where judges, who often regarded the sale of
sequestered real estate as illegal, were sympathetic to the claims of those who
had lost property. As the Chilean state tried to attract investors and sought
diplomatic recognition from Spain, the executive branch pushed Congress
to include claims arising from sequestration in legislation to consolidate the
national debt. Given the sensitive nature of the disputes, final resolution
was delayed until 1853 when most of those who had been adults during the
wars of independence had died. During these same decades, other matters
of litigation and legislation also tied state formation to the fate of Chilean
families: pensions for war widows and orphans and enforcement of laws
that made parents responsible for supporting dependent family members.

CHAPTER 5

Protecting Soldiers' Patrimony: Expanding Pension
Eligibility for Widows and Orphans

In April 1828, for the third time in as many decades, Javiera Carrera anxiously
waited in Santiago for news that a loved one had safely made the journey over
the Andes to Mendoza. Thirty years earlier, the messenger bore the sad tid-
ings of her first husband having drowned while trying to forge a river along
the mountain pass. In 1810, her second husband crossed successfully and
continued on to Buenos Aires and from there to Madrid; when he returned
the following year, Chile was in the midst of momentous political change. In
1814, Javiera had decided to make the dangerous journey herself to flee the
Spanish forces sent to overthrow the separatist government established in
part through the efforts of her brothers; when she returned ten years later
she chose the route by sea from Montevideo and around the Cape rather
than pass through Mendoza where her brothers had been executed. Now her
eldest son Pío followed the trans-Andean route as a member of the official
commission sent to recover the remains of the Carrera brothers and repatriate them to Chile. "Since your departure I have not had a moment of peace,"
she wrote in the first of four surviving letters during his absence, "always
fearing that the weather will change."[1] Two weeks later she noted her relief
at having received a response from him. "I will see my martyrs passed down
to posterity in proper form and remember with pride that I have overcome
with the power of perseverance all the obstacles put up by the villains," she
rejoiced in her final letter, "This time period is and will be glorious for me,
especially as I reflect upon how my Pío has done his duty in such a satisfac-
tory manner."[2]

The trip was the result of a motion put forward the previous month in
Congress by Representative Manuel Magallanes, who had been an aide-de-
camp to José Miguel Carrera but had returned to Chile in 1817 and fought
under O'Higgins. He depicted the Carreras' struggle as a disinterested

defense of the nation rather than the pursuit of personal ambition. "What act could be more natural and more fitting for a civilized nation after having achieved the high status of an independent Republic," he asked his colleagues, "than to honor their valor and if possible to thereby attest in a suitable manner to the recognition that the Fatherland owes to all its illustrious defenders."[3] The motion was approved and the government moved quickly to make the necessary arrangements to recover the remains from Mendoza and give them a proper ceremonial burial back in Chile.

On June 16, 1828, following the official exoneration of Brigadier José Miguel Carrera, Francisco Ruiz Tagle filed a petition with the government. As the legal guardian of Javiera, Rosa, María Josefa, Luisa, and José Miguel Carrera Fontecilla, he applied to the government for the pension "that the sword of their father earned for them." Ruiz Tagle further asked that the requirement to present official documents (marriage certificate, baptismal certificates, service record, etc.) be waived. The children had been born in distant places, he pointed out, some even in military camps, during the time of the Carreras' "misfortunes." Given the notoriety of the family, surely such papers "far from proving facts, would serve only as pure formulas." President Francisco Antonio Pinto readily assented. "As the government is well aware of all the circumstances pertaining to the death of Brigadier Don José Miguel Carrera, as well as those of his marriage at the same rank and the birth of his five children," he approved payment of the pension, retroactively to his death on September 5, 1821, to be paid to the widow until the date of her remarriage and thereafter to the children until the son became an adult and the daughters married.[4]

In contrast to the volumes of trials, correspondence, and manifestos about the Carreras, as well as to other applications for pensions, this file at two manuscript pages is surprisingly brief. Nonetheless, the spirit of granting pensions to widows and orphans to achieve reconciliation among members of the "greater Chilean family" was not unique to the case of Fontecilla and her children. But before such largesse would be shown toward former enemies and rivals, the persistent petitioning of less famous widows had pushed the government to loosen some of the "mere formalities" of the previous Spanish regulations on military pensions. Spain established a pension system, the monte de piedad or montepío, in 1761 and reorganized it in 1776 with the intent of promoting suitable marriages among military officers and rewarding their service by providing for their widows and children.[5] In order to qualify, officers had to delay marriage until they attained at least the rank of captain, and their prospective brides had to pass muster by presenting testimony of their honorable status and their families' ability to provide dowries. The pension system was designed to be financially self-supporting; all officers had a percentage deducted from their salaries to contribute toward the general fund. The Chilean national state inherited the system at independence but reformed it over the ensuing decades as the denial of benefits to widows and orphans of war veterans who did not meet the highly restrictive requirements of the Spanish regulations became a political embarrassment for the elected executive branch.

The impact of petitioning by and on behalf of war widows and orphans upon the issuance of decrees and laws reforming the montepío system clearly demonstrates the centrality of family to the process of nation-state formation.[6] First and foremost, by appealing to the proclaimed paternalism of postindependence heads of state, widows and guardians pressed the government to broaden its responsibility to care for the dependents of the nation's defenders. Furthermore, changes to the rules of eligibility addressed two specific issues, both related to the family. First was the question of who had a properly constituted family: the Spanish regulations had strict provisions about the rank at which officers could marry and the need for documented permission to do so from their commanding officer (and ultimately the king) that many of the postindependence petitioners failed to meet. Second was the question of who belonged to the Chilean national family: the government was confronted with whether to include beneficiaries of royal officers and family members of patriots who fought on the losing side in civil wars. This chapter will address each matter in turn, although the timing of the respective policies overlapped.

As with legislation on property sequestration and restitution, policies on pensions developed through several periods of nation-state formation. Under the administration of O'Higgins, widows seen as deserving of support, even though they did not meet the requirements of the Spanish regulations, were granted exceptional pensions on a case-by-case basis. By the latter part of the 1820s, Freire and Congress officially expanded eligibility to lower-ranking officers and temporarily waived the requirement of prior approval for marriage. Passing legislation on pensions was easier to accomplish than resolving disputes over property seizures because it did not pit the interests of certain Chileans against those of others. Both treasury officials and a state attorney (fiscal) had to render opinions on applications, after which the president, as commander-in-chief, decided whether or not to approve pensions. The expansion, however, was not revenue neutral, and for decades treasury officials attempted to interpret the changes narrowly in order to keep down public expenditures. The conservative regime that came to power in 1830, however, had similar incentives as Freire to maintain morale within the army that had fought on the winning side in the civil war. President and commander-in-chief Prieto, therefore, continued a generous interpretation of the new pension regulations but discharged all officers who had remained loyal to Freire and thereby made their dependents ineligible for pensions. In the interest of healing divisions within the "greater Chilean family," in the 1840s President Bulnes, the hero of the war against the Peru-Bolivia Confederation, pardoned and reincorporated many of those officers and their families. Finally in the 1850s, at the same time as credits against the state arising from wartime property sequestration were consolidated into the national debt, the executive and legislature codified rules for the montepío to replace the patchwork of laws dating from both the late colonial and early republican periods. The new comprehensive regulations maintained some of the more expansive criteria for eligibility but also introduced reforms to reduce state expenditures and pass a greater share of the burden for supporting dependents back to their families.

Providing for War Widows and Orphans

Although the degree of enthusiasm for the cause of independence varied among those who took up arms or were pressed into military service, in official rhetoric the willingness to sacrifice one's own life for the homeland was the touchstone of emerging nationalism.[7] As Agustín López put it, recalling a fallen companion, "with the heroism fitting of a true Republican and as a good Chilean officer, who preferred to take up a sword and face death rather than fall into the hands of those tyrannical lions the Spaniards who spilled the blood of innocent Americans out of covetousness for our Country, such a one was the meritorious Captain Don José Ignacio Ibieta, who will always be remembered by his comrades in Arms."[8] Such a sacrifice almost always encompassed the soldier's family members as well. Captain Ibieta, who had died at the Battle of Rancagua in 1814, was also remembered by his mother. María Luisa Benavente noted the double loss created by the death of her son, "the Fatherland losing in this young man a defender and I an offspring whom I loved tenderly and whom I will always remember with affection."[9]

Widowed mothers of unmarried officers who died in battle could qualify for the montepío, because law and custom would have required such sons to support them financially.[10] In their applications, therefore, several women highlighted their economic as well as emotional vulnerability. "I dedicated my two sons, from the time they were children, to the honorable profession of soldiering," María del Tránsito Montenegro asserted, "and when I expected to begin gathering the fruit of their labor they brought me the unfortunate news of their disastrous end."[11] Montenegro applied for a pension fourteen years after their death in battle, however, claiming that in her grief and isolation she was unaware of such benefits. In the case of Lieutenant Colonel Manuel Jordán (the nephew of Mercedes Fontecilla and a partisan of the Carreras), treasury officials recommended denial of a pension to his mother in 1828 on the grounds that his widow had already collected the pension before remarrying and that allowing limitless succession would wipe out the nation's budget reserves. The state attorney, however, convinced the president that his mother was deserving as "the one that gave to the Fatherland a son who was capable of preserving the glories of Chile abroad as well as within the Republic."[12] Josefa Claverías, whose son Lieutenant Nicolás Gorigoitía had died at the end of the long war in the south, was more assertive about the state's responsibilities even as she played the role of republican mother willing to sacrifice her children:

> I had no other support than this good son, who out of love never neglected to share his wages with me. In my widowhood I mourn his loss, although I am consoled by his having given his life as a brave defender of the Fatherland. And if [the Fatherland] always favors its meritorious sons, it cannot fail to bestow such recognition upon me, granting me some relief in return for that life taken in its service, a life for which a good Mother can never be fully compensated. . . . Throughout the world, Nations provide aid to the widows and Mothers of those who die in battle. Chile has respected this principle and will not forget it while governed by a veteran soldier who all too well recognizes military merit.[13]

Nevertheless, it still took Claverías seven years to compile all the necessary papers and certifications before her pension was approved.

Claverías was correct that commander-in-chief Freire would recognize the responsibility of the state toward the dependents of those who had sacrificed their lives in service of the nation. Indeed, Chilean heads of state between 1810 and 1850, all of whom were military officers, recognized that the promise of a pension for one's loved ones could be a powerful incentive for men to make a career of military service and to stand their ground during battle. As the state attorney pointed out in 1823, "Without [the montepío] there would not be that stimulus to virtue that motivates the fulfillment of a man's military duties: it truly makes the indifferent one virtuous and the virtuous one a hero."[14] Almost twenty years later, in the case of a second lieutenant who had died during Chile's campaign against the Peru-Bolivia Confederation in 1838, another state attorney similarly affirmed, "Perhaps the pension that he left to his family was this officer's last thought, which diminished the horrors of a battlefield death."[15]

Although death in battle was a dramatic demonstration of patriotism, one that the Spanish regulations had recognized as making the dependents of even subaltern officers eligible for the montepío, the aged veteran was another powerful symbol of heroism and often both a real as well as metaphorical father figure. The state attorney overrode the objections of the treasury officials in recommending a pension for the widow of Captain José Aguila, arguing that "Twenty-one years of service and his unwavering allegiance to the country's independence, on behalf of which he exposed his life so many times, justly demand compensation from the Montepío."[16] Widow Dolores Maturano added that the pension would help her support their son "who, following in the footsteps of his father, some day will likely provide very important services to the Fatherland."[17] Granting a special pension to another widow of an executed patriot provided a similar opportunity to predict that masculine heroism would be passed down through the generations and help to forge unity in the national family:

> The blood of heroes is fertile: it produces those who will avenge the resentments left to them as an inheritance. The son of the unfortunate Moyano will seek, with ardour, satisfaction for the offence committed against his father! We are all one family: the cruelty of the Spaniards forges in us a common cause to resist them, exterminate them, and execrate them with eternal hatred.[18]

This rhetoric credited paternal blood, rather than maternal wombs, with reproductive powers.

Although commanders-in-chief recognized the importance to military morale of providing for the dependents of servicemen, the Spanish montepío regulations under which the Chilean government began operating restricted eligibility to high-ranking officers or to subaltern officers who died in battle. Not only did military personnel need to go through a formal procedure to request a license to marry, which included testimony about the suitability of the bride and her provision of a dowry, but they would be ineligible for pensions if they had married below the rank of captain. When a prospective beneficiary applied to collect a pension, she (most were widows) was required to present that license as well as the ecclesiastical certificates of marriage and the baptismal records of any children. After independence, applicants had to go to great lengths to provide the proper documentation. Those who were unable to submit the ecclesiastical certificates, most often on the grounds that the parish books had been destroyed during the wars, could substitute witness testimony. But there was no recourse for those who could not prove that officers had obtained an official marriage license from their commanding officers. Applicants often became frustrated by all the required paperwork and technicalities of the law. One case of a military officer who had gone on to serve as an intendant governor was delayed as treasury officials tried to find documentation of whether deductions had been made to his salary upon the promotion. Exasperated, the brother who was representing the widow denounced the red tape. "There is nothing unjust nor strange," retorted the treasury ministers, "in executing the Law."[19] Procedures that the treasury ministers saw as protecting the state from undue expenses (and themselves for liability in cases of improper expenditures) were regarded as a bottleneck by applicants.

One way around such technicalities was for the president or the Senate to grant an exceptional pension (*pensión de gracia*). This practice was fairly common during the wars of independence given the need to maintain morale among the troops, recruit new soldiers, and avoid the appearance of abandoning the families of those who gave their life for the new nation. Most often such exceptions were made on a case-by-case basis, but Bernardo O'Higgins did decree a special pension to either the widows or mothers of soldiers who had died at the Battle of Chacabuco in 1817. Declaring public gratitude "for the blood of the heroes sacrificed for the Liberty of the Nation," he generously awarded ten pesos a month to beneficiaries of privates and corporals and twelve for sergeants. Although he regretted that state funds could not be stretched even further, he proclaimed, "The widows and mothers of the victors of Chacabuco deserve the recognition of the Government, for in them lives on the memory of the brave who extinguished tyranny."[20] But such ad hoc solutions could not address the problem in the longer term.

The first legal challenge to result in a new law regarding the payment of pensions, however, did not arise from the question of whether a family had been properly constituted according to montepío regulations, but rather from the area of deciding who belonged to the Chilean national family. In April 1820, Juana de Dios Baeza petitioned O'Higgins to continue receiving the pension that had been granted to her mother in 1798 upon the death of her father, a royal officer, but had not been paid since the fall of the Spanish government. Her request appealed to two arguments. First, she emphasized her pitiful situation as a war refugee who had been compelled to emigrate from her home in the southern city of Concepción to Santiago: "The state of nakedness, hunger, and other accumulated misfortunes in which we arrived caused my mother to exhale her last breath, leaving me an abandoned orphan, and unable to find resources owing to my sex and lack of relatives in this strange land, my fate cannot get any worse, and only from the paternal goodness of Your Excellency do I hope to find relief from my misfortunes."[21] Such an appeal to the paternalism of the new Chilean leaders, particularly O'Higgins, who had ordered the evacuation, was similar to the petitions of other women who were given temporary aid during the war. Baeza further pointed out, however, that because her father had contributed a percentage of his salary to the montepío fund throughout his career, "this is not a gratuitous pension that expires with a change in the sovereign power that had granted it, but rather a debt upon the state."[22] This second argument, that she was legally entitled to a pension as long as she remained single, prompted O'Higgins to ask legislators to clarify the eligibility of all pensioners in her situation. At this time, the treasury officials reported that in general the montepío account had ample funds because officers paid more into it than was ultimately disbursed, owing in part (although they did not mention it) to their own strict interpretation of the rules. The Senate, therefore, passed a law that the Chilean state would continue to pay pensions granted to the family members of royal officers who died before the wars of independence, on the grounds that the nation had inherited both the assets and debts of the prior royal government.[23]

Although the law was careful to clarify that officers who had fought against independence would not be eligible for this benefit, the favorable treatment granted to the families of royal officers became an embarrassing contrast to the denial of benefits to those of many veterans who had fought for independence.[24] It would not be long before pressure began building for further expansion of the montepío. Indeed, the new supreme director Freire, who signed the law, immediately requested of Congress that any benefits granted to these widows and orphans be extended under the same terms to those who had died in service to the patriot cause.[25] With few exceptions, only successful applications for pensions were archived by the Ministry of War; it is impossible, therefore, to know how many petitions were rejected. But shortly after Baeza's successful lawsuit, a petition submitted by María del Rosario Gómez was denied. Gómez's husband, like Baeza's father, had been a career officer in the Spanish army since at least 1780, posted to the indigenous frontier of Valdivia where his father and father-in-law had also served.

Unlike Baeza, he was still living at the outbreak of the independence wars and joined the patriot cause. According to his widow, "While along with the first Heroes of the Nation he was cooperating in the defense of the Common Cause in the interior of the Republic, I endured in this Fort [Valdivia] for this principle the vexations and sufferings inflicted upon my family by the monstrous intentions of our oppressors."[26] Nonetheless, the treasury ministers rejected her claim on the grounds that he had married at the rank of cadet. In October 1824, her case was sent on to the state attorney for his opinion but ended inconclusively.

About a year later, a Josefa Gómez petitioned for a pension and also was turned down because she had married her husband when he was only a private, even though he had attained the rank of captain by the time he died. Determined, she resubmitted her petition, and it was approved without further consultation by the executive council, which was temporarily governing in place of Freire who was out on military campaign.[27] The treasury officials protested that proper procedures had not been followed and refused to authorize payment of the pension. The executive branch, in turn, issued a general decree on February 20, 1826, making dependents of all officers with at least the rank of second lieutenant (*subteniente*) eligible for the montepío as long as they had served the nation for at least ten continuous years and the applicants could present a notarized copy of the marriage certificate (saying nothing about requiring evidence of prior license). A clarification of the decree four days later stated that beneficiaries could qualify under either the Spanish regulations, which set a minimum rank rather than a minimum term of service, or the new rules.[28]

The preamble to the decree clearly articulated its political intentions and pro-family stance: (1) officers who had won the country's independence were still being held to colonial laws and specifically the "impolitic, unjust, and contradictory montepío regulations," (2) that all officers paid into the pension fund even though families of only a few ever benefited, (3) that the code discouraged soldiers from forming families and therefore limited the ability of the nation to progress and prosper, and finally (4) that the strict limits of the pension code penalized precisely "the most meritorious servants of the nation who, moved and animated by the echo of liberty and patriotic enthusiasm, had flown to take up arms" without considering the impact on the fortunes of their families.[29] Six months later, when Congress was back in session, provisional President Manuel Blanco Encalada asked legislators to formally ratify the decree in order to guarantee that dependents of "the most hardworking and meritorious" soldiers would not be excluded from the pension system simply for marrying before reaching the rank of captain. He reiterated that the executive branch had been moved by "the misfortune and orphanhood" to which widows and families had been reduced when "soldiers who had dedicated their lives to serving the Republic had no other patrimony to leave their children than poverty and bitterness."[30] It would be more than two years, however, before Congress took action.

In March, the state attorney recommended approval of Josefa Gómez's pension under the new decree, and commander-in-chief Freire authorized it. The treasury ministers then tried a new tactic, asserting that the decree should not be enforced until ratified by the legislature, or that at least they should be freed from any financial responsibility should the decree later be overturned. An exasperated Freire expressed surprise that these officials were dragging their feet despite admitting "the powerful motives" behind the February decree, and declared it effective immediately.[31] Taking advantage of this new opportunity, the first Gómez, María del Rosario, made her fourth request for a pension. Despite Freire's orders, the treasury officials still opposed implementing the decree until it was ratified by the legislature but found some royal order from 1790 that they believed applied sufficiently to her situation to approve the montepío without creating a precedent for the new criteria.[32] Doña Dolores Maturano similarly reapplied despite a finding by the treasury officials to await ratification of the law. On this second request, the officials also asserted that she had married her husband before he entered military service and was ineligible on those grounds. The state attorney disagreed, citing the officer's merit and lengthy service.[33] Nonetheless, on January 27, 1829, the treasury ordered Maturano to provide evidence that her marriage had taken place after her husband began his military service. Four days later, the Congress finally ratified the 1826 decree, and Maturano got her pension under its terms in March.[34]

Under the 1829 law, a special military court was charged with evaluating the legitimacy of marriages and the filiation of children, based either upon documentation or witness testimony, in the frequent cases in which parish records had been destroyed during the war. Compared to earlier bottlenecks, this process became routine and relatively quick. Treasury officials could no longer delay implementation of the new terms, which explicitly waived through 1828 the requirement to have received official permission to marry as well as making even second lieutenants eligible after ten years of service.[35] Nevertheless, for years these bureaucrats would try to limit the effects of the law through two main tactics: by trying to narrow the window of the waiver for marriage licenses and by looking for ways to exclude years of service from the required minimum of ten.

Although no comprehensive records remain of rejected petitions, evidence of the treasury officials' strategies survives in pension files that were ultimately approved. In May 1829, for example, they denied the claim of María Sambuesa on the grounds that her husband had served for only eight years in Chile, his prior duties having been fulfilled over the Andes in the United Provinces of the Río de la Plata. Fortunately for Sambuesa, the state attorney accepted her alternative argument that her husband, a captain, had acquired prior permission to marry because the marriage certificate indicated that the ceremony had occurred only after the proper formalities had been carried out.[36] Thus she qualified under the Spanish regulations if not the 1829 law. Similarly, the treasury officials turned down the request of Josefa Obando because when her husband's years of service as a cadet were subtracted, he was two and a half months short of the ten required years at the time of his death in 1833. Again fortuitously, Obando was able to make an alternative claim. At the time of their marriage her husband had taken a leave from service and so was not required to request prior permission. According to the Spanish regulations, dependents of a married officer who joined (or rejoined) service at the rank of captain or above were eligible for the montepío.[37]

Almost a decade after the passage of the law, the treasury ministers were still interpreting it in the narrowest possible terms. In 1837, Dolores López, widow of Second Lieutenant Manuel Romero, "without any refuge or protection than the numerous military services of my Spouse," appealed to the president as a "merciful Father accustomed to drying the tears of an unfortunate family."[38] López and Romero had married in 1833 with prior permission of the government and he served twelve years before his death, but the treasury officials asserted that the 1829 law had done "nothing more than pardon those servicemen who, taking advantage of the disorders that occur in all revolutions . . . violated the requirements of the military montepío regulations by contracting marriages when and how they wanted without requesting the proper license." The law did not cover marriages after 1828, they continued, "because it was necessary to begin calling and guiding things back to order."[39] López insisted that pensions were authorized under *either* of the law's two provisions: the waiver for unlicensed marriages before 1828 and/or making eligible all those who had served ten years from at least the rank of second lieutenant. The state attorney agreed with her interpretation, asserting that "No one can doubt that the objective of that Law was to benefit widows and orphans from the military class by broadening enjoyment of the *monte* as far down as the subaltern rank of second lieutenant."[40] In this case, the treasury officials stood their ground against the counsel of the state attorney, but López's right to a pension was approved on appeal to the superior court of the treasury.

The treasury officials' strategy of attempting to interpret narrowly the waivers for unapproved marriages and reassert control over the nuptials of servicemen would continue for decades with little apparent success. In 1834, the officials turned down the petition of María Rita Polloni on the grounds that her marriage to a then *second lieutenant* in 1800 *preceded* the grace period of 1810 to 1828. Once again, the state attorney came to the widow's rescue pointing out that the intent of the law was to waive the marriage regulations up to 1828 and the 1810 date simply referred to the beginning of the independent Chilean government.[41] The treasury officials then turned their attention to the end of the period, being vigilant to prevent the waiver from extending past 1828, especially when the new national military ordinances (*ordenanza*) of 1839 reiterated the requirement that soldiers and officers get prior approval from the government before marrying. In 1840, the officials denied the application of María Antonia García on the grounds that the new ordenanza overturned the 1829 waiver on unapproved marriages. García's fiancé at the time, Santiago Lincongur, had actually requested and obtained permission to marry in 1826 at the rank of captain, but the officials argued that then supreme director Freire's permission was invalid because at the time he had delegated his powers to an executive council while he led the final campaign against the royal army in Chiloé. The state attorney successfully countered that Freire would not have delegated powers related to his role as commander-in-chief and that because Lincongur died just prior to the implementation of the new ordenanza, he would still fall under the law of 1829.[42]

In the next case to arise, the officer in question, Captain Rudecindo Granadino, had died *after* passage of the new ordinances, so his widow Juana Inostrosa was requested to provide proof of their permission to marry. Granadino had joined the patriot army in 1817 at the age of thirteen and was promoted to second corporal only in 1824 and then second lieutenant (the lowest rank at which officers became eligible for the montepío) in 1830. By the time of his death in 1840, he had served in the military for twenty-three years but mostly as a noncommissioned officer. His commanding officers testified that they did not start to keep records of marriage licenses until 1827, but that Granadino surely would have been punished had he not requested the required permission.[43] Their word was good enough for the state attorney, and President Prieto approved Inostrosa's pension. A few months later, the treasury ministers were ready to deny a pension to Isabel Herbert, who could not find a copy of the permission granted for her marriage to Miguel María Occarol (a native of Ireland), who had died after the 1839 ordenanza. But on October 14, 1840, the government quickly issued a decree grandfathering into the ordinances of 1839 officers who had married without permission prior to 1828.[44] Although presidents and legislators alike hoped to regulate marriages among servicemen, they repeatedly relented rather than appear callous toward the wives and children of the nation's defenders.

In the 1840s, the treasury officials tried a new tactic to restrict how years of service were calculated. In 1839, with Chile's victory over the Peru-Bolivia Confederation, the government rewarded those who had fought in the war: officers at the rank of lieutenant and above were promoted one rank and all servicemen were allowed to double the time served in Peru on their records.[45] Treasury officials turned down petitions for pensions that counted this double time toward the total of ten years to qualify under the 1829 law. But when Mercedes Pérez requested a pension on the same grounds in 1846, minister of war General José Santiago Aldunate decided to investigate further. In this case, state attorney Antonio Varas agreed with the interpretation of the treasury officials that such service bonuses could be considered in retirements but should not count toward the years required for pensions. The question was then elevated to a military court whose justices studied the decrees in question and determined that they did not explicitly exclude application to the pension system. The victory over Peru and Bolivia, coming shortly after the assassination of Portales, had been crucial to establishing the popularity and legitimacy of the conservative regime in Chile. Therefore, it is not surprising that General Manuel Bulnes, who had been elected president as a war hero in 1841, decreed on September 23, 1847, that service bonuses could be counted in the years required for eligibility in the montepío.[46]

In 1849 treasurer José María Berganza made yet another effort to severely limit the impact of the 1829 law. After computing the length of service of José Manuel Molina, who was promoted to second lieutenant in 1837, Berganza made the startling claim that the government had been misinterpreting the law for twenty years, because it should have extended eligibility only to officers who had served at least ten years starting in 1810. Therefore, he reasoned, "it had as its objective only to grant a special favor to those who had fought since the very beginning of the War of Independence."[47] He urgently called upon the president to end the prior expansive interpretation of the law because "not much more time will pass before the value of the montepío pensions absorbs a very considerable part of the nation's expenditures."[48] It was the duty of treasury officials to keep government expenses to a minimum. The responsibility of the state attorney was to interpret the law as it affected state interests, including, at least in practice, protecting the executive branch from political embarrassment. In this case, it was not difficult for the state attorney to fend off this latest attack on veterans' families. The 1826 decree, he pointed out, had set no starting date for the calculation of services, and if 1810 had been added to the 1829 law it clearly was intended to exclude years of service in the royal army not years of national service regardless of when they began. He then painted his own grim picture of a future based upon the treasurer's interpretation: "In a few years all those who started their military service in 1810 will have disappeared and the pension law would expire with them."[49] This argument convinced President Bulnes, who approved the pension for Molina's widow. A few years later Congress passed an even more expansive interpretation of the service period, allowing years at all ranks (even privates) to be counted toward the minimum of ten.[50]

The expansion of the montepío system did not encompass all soldiers, but it certainly incorporated a class of people who never would have qualified under Spanish law. According to data compiled by Sergio Vergara Quiroz, 383 (45 percent) of the 844 pensions granted between 1819 and 1884 went to the families of officers who had died at a rank below captain and hence would have been ineligible prior to the 1829 law except in some cases of battlefield deaths.[51] The wars of independence had provided opportunities for relatively humble soldiers to rise slowly through the ranks. Some of their families may not have even realized they could qualify for the montepío. In 1831, fourteen years after her husband's death, Antonia Mateluna petitioned for a *pensión de gracia* on the assumption that she would not qualify according to the regulations. Mateluna, identified on the certificate of her marriage to Juan Ferreira in 1806 as a *parda* (partial African ancestry) and the daughter of unwed parents, was clearly from the lower strata of Chilean society. She alluded to the legacy of slavery by asserting that her husband, "guided by an innate desire to be free, gladly embraced the cause of Independence and in accordance with this principle abandoned the only work that could have provided a subsistence for his family."[52] Ferreira had joined up before 1814, and after the Spanish reconquest had to go into exile in Mendoza from where he returned with San Martín's expedition in 1817, finally dying at the Battle of Maipú. In a rare instance, the treasury officials actually pointed out that if she could prove he had died in battle, she would qualify for a pension under the terms of the 1817 decree issued by O'Higgins.

The 1829 law went further to reward the career service of upwardly mobile officers regardless of whether they died in battle or not. José Plaza, whose widow qualified for a pension thanks to the new law, had risen through the ranks, beginning as a first corporal in 1810 and dying thirty years later as a retired sergeant major. On the certificate of his marriage to Tomasa Henríquez in 1811 neither she nor any of their parents had an honorific don or dona, and the "D" before his name had clearly been added later.[53] Justo Urra started at an even lower rank, joining the army as a private in 1817, participating in the final battles against the royal army, and then continuing his military career after independence. In 1825 he was finally promoted to second corporal and a year later, when he married Norberta Chaparro, he had risen to first corporal. As with the previous couple, their names on the marriage certificate were not preceded by honorifics. In 1837, at the beginning of Chile's war against the Peru-Bolivian Confederation, Urra had risen to the rank of captain, and he was fatally wounded in that war's decisive battle of Yungay in 1839. At the time of his death, he had served more than twenty-two years, including over ten at and above the rank of second lieutenant, but left his widow, by her own characterization, "reduced to the most fearful misery."[54] She had by then, nonetheless, earned the respect of being addressed as a "doña," and the state recognized its obligation to support her with an annual pension of 188 pesos in compensation for her husband's service and sacrifices.

For families of humble origins, even a modest military pension could make the difference between poverty and a decent standard of living. As Luisa Arriagada, a lieutenant's widow, pointed out in 1834, "it is the only recourse on which the family of a soldier can count."[55] At least some officers consciously planned for their families' fate. In 1833, Juan de Dios Ugarte, having lost his copy of the official military license to marry Carmen Molina in 1825, asked his commanding officers to testify that he had followed proper procedures. He then requested and received certification from President Prieto that his widow would qualify for the montepío because "he has no other patrimony than his modest income for the support of his spouse and children . . . since otherwise at my death that unfortunate [lady] would be left begging for sustenance."[56] His foresight paid off. After his death in 1842, the treasury officials still required witnesses to testify under oath that he left no will, but they did not question his marital status. Although families of servicemen who never rose to the rank of second lieutenant would neither pay into nor benefit from the montepío, the postindependence state did paternalistically provide for the dependents of many more officers than had the colonial regime.

Reincorporating Widows and Orphans into the National Family

War widows, particularly those from a humble background, persisted throughout the early republic to have their families recognized as properly constituted and entitled to benefits from the montepío fund to which their husbands had contributed. Others, more often from prominent families and married to high-ranking officers, patiently had to await auspicious moments to petition for their reintegration into the national citizenry, figured as "the greater Chilean family." Scholars have identified the importance of periodic pardons and amnesties of male political figures to Chilean political culture.[57] An analysis of pensions demonstrates that women and children, more easily seen as innocent and deserving of compassion than one's former enemies, were often the first beneficiaries of such measures. Specifically, caring for the families of former political rivals could be the first step toward reconciliation.

The civil war that resulted in the establishment of Chile's enduring conservative regime in 1830 had adverse consequences for numerous officers. Ironically, one of the final acts of the liberal regime established by Freire had been the expansion in 1829 of the montepío system. When his forces were defeated by the conservatives under the leadership of Prieto at the Battle of Lircay, all officers who had remained loyal to Freire were cashiered. As early as 1835, moderate conservatives were proposing the reinstatement of at least some of those officers, but an attempted invasion of Chile by Freire in 1836 and the assassination of Portales in 1837 further polarized partisan divisions.[58] By the end of the decade, however, the war against the Peru-Bolivia Confederation created a climate ripe for reconciliation. On the one hand, fighting against an external enemy unified national sentiment within Chile. On a more pragmatic level, the war also created a need for experienced military officers, some of whom were reincorporated.[59]

In 1838, widows of officers who had fought under Freire began petitioning the government for extraordinary pensions, knowing that their husbands' official separation from the army disqualified them from the montepío.[60] Carmen Mújica was one of the first, indicating in her petition to President Prieto that as a widow with five children under the age of twelve, she had appealed in 1836 to the legislature for a special pension, "and although this request was well received by the patriotism and wisdom of the Nation's representatives, ultimately it was not approved because higher priority issues took precedence and absorbed the full period of the sessions."[61] Her deceased husband Ramón Picarte had joined the patriot army in 1810 as a sergeant and had risen to the rank of general commander when he was cashiered in 1830. This second petition fared better; Prieto approved a monthly pension of twenty-five pesos in recognition of "the gratitude that the Nation owes to the first and oldest defenders of its independence."[62]

Once the precedent had been set, it did not take long for other widows to follow suit. Within a month, Francisca Fuenzalida, widow of Manuel Urquizo, cited the Picarte case in her petition to President Prieto. Noting that her initial request in 1836 had not been approved, "since then, submerged in sorrow and bitterness on account of my lack of resources, . . . I resigned myself to waiting for another time that would be more fortunate for me."[63] The following year, Josefa de la Puente claimed that her husband, Captain José Domingo Meneses, had simply followed the orders of his superiors during the political conflicts of 1829 and 1830. "Today, Sir, that the Fatherland is celebrating the magnificent triumph of arms in Yungay" (over the Peru-Bolivia Confederation), she hoped that the president "would deign to look with compassion upon the wife and small children of a soldier who employed his best years in the service of his homeland."[64] Prieto granted her a special pension in March 1839. Two months later, he issued a general decree to restore the decommissioned officers to their employments and honors so long as they presented themselves before a deadline, had joined the army prior to 1826, and had not committed any crimes or treason since 1830.[65] Article 3 made the widows and orphans of any affected officers who had died in the interim eligible for an official montepío pension.

Because the special pensions were at lower rates, widows who had received them reapplied for official montepío pensions, but some subsequently got tangled in the red tape that characterized the normal procedures. Josefa Demetria Ureta had successfully appealed to Prieto in 1838 as "a father of the Homeland, a chief who knows how to appreciate and distinguish the merit of his soldiers, and that with such qualities he could not look with indifference upon the tears of children whose father had so many times exposed his life in defense of his Fatherland."[66] Yet when she reapplied after the 1839 decree, the treasury officials raised the objection that the couple's marriage had preceded by two weeks the official license issued by the government. Fortunately for Ureta, she was saved by yet another decree: that of

October 14, 1840, grandfathering in the waiver for those who had married without the proper permission.

Even the October decree could not help Fuenzalida when the treasury officials pointed out that she had married Urquiza in 1830, past the grace period, and about six months after he had been decommissioned and therefore of civilian status. But the state attorney intervened, arguing that since Urquiza had been separated from the service, he could not possibly have requested permission to marry and should be treated like other officers who enter military service already married.[67] The same argument rescued Teresa Lazo, widow of Lieutenant Colonel José Castillo. Castillo had been exiled to Peru for his loyalty to Freire in 1830, and when the invading troops from Chile arrived, he rushed to join their cause. He was rejected and had to serve instead among Peruvian troops that were also fighting against the Confederation. But now, proclaimed his widow in 1841, "civil war has disappeared in Chile, and enlightenment seems to have disarmed the parties, removing that hate and partiality with which they had persecuted others without consideration of their principles, conscience, and honor."[68] Dolores Ross, or someone representing her, took this precedent one step too far; the treasury officials called for a careful inspection of the parish books that revealed that someone had erased the date of her marriage to Colonel Bartolomé Asagra in January 1830 and replaced it with the month of May to make it look as if he had married as a civilian after the Battle of Lircay. Her pension was rejected, and it was recommended that charges of fraud be filed against the offending priest.[69]

Treasury officials continued to be vigilant, but the spirit of amnesty and reconciliation continued in the early years of the Bulnes administration. In September 1842, treasury officials rejected on a technicality the pension application of Rosa Muñoz, the widowed mother of deceased Second Lieutenant José Soto Aguilar, because the 1839 decree rehabilitating the decommissioned officers had mentioned only their widows and orphans in the article on montepíos. Within the month, Congress passed a law ratifying the 1839 decree and specifically including widowed mothers of unmarried officers among those eligible for pensions.[70] The case of Muñoz was reconsidered the following year and was on the verge of approval when the military court questioned whether the Battle of Lircay, where Soto Aguilar died, should be considered an act of war or a mutiny. An in-law representing Muñoz argued that Soto like all honorable soldiers was simply following orders and that not to include him in the rehabilitation would be to recall "the fanatical thirst for politics that no longer exists."[71] The court and president were finally persuaded to grant the pension in 1846.

The question of whether to rehabilitate officers who had died in the Battle of Lircay also arose in the case of the orphans of Guillermo de Vic Tupper. Their guardian, Jorge Huneeus, argued that rather than beginning to pay their pension from the date of the rehabilitation decree (May 31, 1839), they should be eligible from the date of their father's death on the battlefield (April 17, 1830). An interim state attorney issued an opinion in July 1840 sympathetic to the needs of orphans and attentive to the important services Vic Tupper had provided to the country, but finding no justification in the law to make the pension retroactive. Huneeus appealed after the passage of the October 1842 rehabilitation law, and the military court was divided on whether an officer could be decommissioned without official notification. Vic Tupper died before news could reach him of the April 15 law, cashiering officers who remained loyal to Freire, and thus he had no opportunity to put down his arms to save his position. The case then passed to a civilian judge, who upheld the denial of retroactive benefits on the advice of the state attorney, who could find no legal basis for a pension however unpleasant it was to oppose the children of an independence hero. But the children's guardian appealed yet again to the Supreme Court, which decided that indeed Vic Tupper could not be cashiered without notice and that his children should enjoy a pension from the date of his death.[72]

Throughout the 1840s, Bulnes took on the role of benevolent father of the nation, repeatedly issuing pardons and even appointing some liberals to his cabinet in an attempt to reunite the "greater Chilean family." As the son of a royalist officer, the nephew of President Prieto, and the son-in-law of opposition candidate Pinto, Bulnes symbolically represented the potential of elite families to coalesce as they had before independence set off rivalries for political power. Those divisions erupted again, however, during the 1851 elections that pitted conservative Manuel Montt against General José María de la Cruz, a hero of both the war of independence and the expedition against the Peru-Bolivia Confederation. Cruz was no liberal, but those who had been excluded from power since 1829 saw him as their best hope. Mercedes Fontecilla, whose son José Miguel Carrera Jr. was wanted by the authorities on charges of subversion, led a delegation of ladies dressed in mourning to appeal for the protection of Cruz. Cruz and his supporters refused to recognize the legitimacy of the vote count that designated Montt the winner. Shortly after stepping down from office, therefore, Bulnes returned to the battlefield in order to defend the government of his successor from the armed opposition during the civil war of 1851. After the Battle of Loncomilla in December, during which some two thousand soldiers perished, Bulnes reached out to negotiate with Cruz, who happened to be his cousin as well as former comrade-in-arms. Although Bulnes fulfilled his promise to Cruz to advocate a general amnesty, Montt refused. Early in his term, this first civilian president would favor pensions for the families of soldiers who fought on the winning side in 1851, as well as those from earlier conflicts. By the mid-1850s, however, Montt would push for reforms to the montepío system, which would ultimately reduce the number of beneficiaries and hence state expenditures on military families.

Codifying Pensions: Apogee and Decline of the Paternal State

Throughout the 1830s and 1840s, treasury officials had tried to interpret narrowly the criteria for montepío eligibility set out in the 1796 Spanish regulations and the 1829 law in order to limit state expenditures. Meanwhile, widows and the guardians of orphans also continued to appeal to both the executive and legislative branches when their applications for pensions were denied. The early 1850s mark the high point for generous interpretations of the law in granting montepío pensions. In 1852, María García petitioned Congress for a special pension. Her husband Manuel Enrique, who had risen slowly through the ranks from sergeant in 1826 to lieutenant in 1838, had died the following year of illness while on the campaign against the Peru-Bolivia Confederation. As a poor woman living in Chiloé far from the capital, it had taken her ten years to compile the documents to apply for the montepío, which then had been denied because Enrique had not served ten years since his promotion to second lieutenant in 1837. Upon consultation, Congress passed a law clarifying that all service at any rank should be included when computing years toward the minimum of ten required by the 1829 regulation. Within six months of the enactment of the law, García was granted her pension.[73] In a surprising reversal in roles, even treasurer Ignacio de Reyes argued in favor of a claimant whose eligibility was unclear. Lieutenant José Luis Poblete had died at age twenty-two, one of numerous casualties in the critical Battle of Loncomilla in 1851. When his mother applied in 1852 for a montepío, it was actually the state attorney who, although he praised the young man's willingness to sacrifice his life to defend the government, asserted that not having served ten years excluded his dependents from eligibility. Reyes, by contrast, argued that the intent of the 1829 law had been to overturn only the restrictive criteria of the Spanish regulations, not the article granting pensions to the families of those who died in battle. Any other interpretation made no sense, he argued, "both the sentiments of the heart and the well-known interests of the Nation would be abandoned if this unfortunate mother were denied the scanty bread which the law grants her owing to the death in battle of her son, who spilled his blood in defense of the constitution and the constituted authorities."[74] President Montt, citing similar precedents, agreed with Reyes and approved the montepío. In another case, Reyes regretted that Captain Manuel Rodríguez, who had been wounded at Loncomilla but did not die until over a year later, did not fall under the regulation that granted montepío eligibility to those who died in battle or "shortly thereafter." Nonetheless, his widow's application was sent to the court of appeals for consultation, which recommended approval.[75]

Despite the effort to institutionalize the process, the government continued to award special pensions for those considered deserving. Some exceptions incorporated other kinds of dependents, such as sisters, or addressed cases where the officer had barely fallen short of ten years of service, but the most common impediment continued to be having married without prior license from a commanding officer. In 1853, when a congressional committee passed along its recommendations on requests for special exemptions from military regulations on marriage, Representative Ramón Rengifo pointed out that he and his colleagues were frequently voting on such petitions and that most widows were successful in finding a congressman to support their cases. He proposed, therefore, simply extending the exemption to all who found themselves in similar circumstances.[76]

The officer in the case prompting legislators to enact a general policy, Major Gaspar Calderón, had died almost a quarter century earlier. When his widow Micaela Solís applied for a pension in 1844, she found herself in a literal "Catch-22," falling in the cracks between the criteria defining a properly constituted family and determining membership in the Chilean national "family." Calderón entered the service in 1820 at the rank of second lieutenant, married with prior license in 1823, had a child in 1828, was promoted to major in 1829, and finally died at the Battle of Lircay fighting under the orders of Commander Freire. After the amnesty for such veterans, his widow initially applied under the terms of the 1829 law, but the treasury officials calculated that he fell just short of completing ten years of service. The state attorney considered that because he had died in battle, she would qualify under the prior Spanish regulations, which had never been abolished by the laws expanding eligibility. Given the impasse, the case was sent to court in 1844. The treasury officials reiterated their argument that she did not qualify under the 1829 law because Calderón had not served a full ten years and that law made no provisions for those who died in battle; they added that the

Spanish regulations did grant pensions to widows of those who died in battle but only if they had married at the rank of captain or above. The judge agreed. The public defender representing Solís appealed to the Supreme Court, arguing that the waiver for irregular marriages before 1828 ought to apply in this case. He also pointed to the Vic Tupper precedent, without acknowledging the difference in rank. Finally he tried appealing to the justices' political sensibilities. He pointed out that war widows enjoyed a respected social status in Chile and that the elderly and poor Solís was especially deserving of protection. Furthermore, Calderón had been willing to make the ultimate sacrifice for his country because he knew the fatherland in turn would take care of his family. "With his life he paid for the pension that his son and wife claim today," concluded Solís's attorney.[77] Nonetheless, in June 1845, the Supreme Court denied her right to the montepío.

In 1853, Solís petitioned Congress for a special pension, and her case led legislators on October 25 to issue a blanket amnesty for widows and orphans of officers who had married prior to that year without following all the proper procedures, with the caveat that payment of the pension would commence from the date of approval rather than retroactively to the date the officer died. Within days of the publication of the law in the official newspaper, María del Rosario Campos, widow of Sergeant Major Domingo Binimelis, reapplied for a pension. Her original petition in 1844 claimed that they had married after Binimelis had received an honorable discharge from service, but both the state attorney and the treasury officials insisted that he had been on a temporary leave and still should have requested permission to marry. Under the new law, President Montt approved her pension in less than a week.[78] Other women similarly reapplied or applied for the first time and also received pensions under the new exemption.[79]

As a result of favoring applicants in interpretations of both the 1829 law and earlier Spanish regulations, along with the passage of time, pensions were awarded in the 1850s to a relatively diverse array of Chileans. Several prominent heroes from the independence period died in this decade, and their widows qualified for the montepío regardless of the sides taken by their husbands during civil conflict. Ramón Freire, who had returned to Chile in 1842 under amnesty, died coincidentally the day after the Battle of Loncomilla. The following year, conservative President Montt approved a pension of 1,125 pesos annually to his widow, Manuela Caldera, and their youngest son Francisco de Paula, who had been born in 1837, the year of Freire's failed attempt to return to power.[80] A few years later, General Joaquín Prieto, who had defeated Freire at the Battle of Lircay in 1830 and was president at the time of Freire's attempted invasion in 1837, passed away at age seventy. Despite his forty-eight years of military service, he had not achieved as high a rank as Freire, so his widow, Manuela Warnes, was awarded an annual pension of 625 pesos.[81] These same years also saw the passing of two officers who had switched from the royalist to patriot side only late in the wars of independence. Clemente Lantaño had been born and raised in southern Chile, and his service to the royal army earned him induction into the Order of Isabel, established to honor subjects from the American colonies who remained loyal to the Spanish king. In 1821, after transferring to Peru, he finally reached out to San Martín to offer his services to the patriot forces. Upon returning to Chile, he helped fight against guerrillas who held out in the southern provinces into the 1820s. In 1854, Lantaño's widow Juana Pedro Bueno, who had married him fifty years earlier in Chillán, was awarded an annual pension of 500 pesos.[82] Sergeant Major José Antonio de Zúñiga was still fighting for the royalist cause as late as 1824 when he married María Vivanco in Mapuche territory. But he died alongside three of his sons defending the government against the liberal opposition in the civil war of 1851, and so Vivanco qualified for the montepío.[83]

Alongside such prominent figures, the widows and orphans of career military men from more humble backgrounds also qualified for the montepío in the early 1850s. Francisco Gómez and Juan de Dios Ancieta had both signed up for frontier service under Spanish rule at the beginning of the century and continued their careers in the Chilean national forces, rising to the rank of captain and lieutenant colonel respectively before their deaths in 1853 and 1854.[84] Juan Torres joined up as a private in 1817, after the patriot victory at Chacabuco, but fought in all the subsequent significant battles for which he received several decorations: Cancha Rayada, Maipú, the independence of Peru, the seizure of Chiloé from Spain, the campaign against the Peru-Bolivia Confederation, and finally Loncomilla where he was wounded. His long service and attainment of the rank of lieutenant colonel earned his widow Mercedes Labarca and children from a first marriage an annual pension of 375 pesos.[85] Inocencio Ponce served for almost twenty years, with a few leaves, but his widow María Dolores Pérez qualified for the montepío only because he was finally promoted to second lieutenant in 1855, one year before his death at age forty. That promotion likely also entitled her to put a "doña" before her name on the application, a sign of status lacking on their marriage certificate.[86]

In 1856, minister of war Antonio Varas reported to Congress that the government was paying out montepío pensions to widows of 243 officers, from second lieutenants to generals; another 63 recipients of special pensions brought the total to more than 300. The cost of these pensions, along with salaries for active-duty and retired officers, had become a major expenditure for the Chilean state. Manuel Montt, Chile's first civilian president, proposed reducing the officer corps by offering a sum of money, calibrated to rank, to officers who would in turn renounce their families' eligibility for the montepío. Theoretically, those who accepted the incentive could invest in enterprises that would yield a higher income and ultimately a patrimony they could leave to their heirs. Regardless of whether or not they achieved such financial success, officers who took the deal acquired with it full responsibility, in life and after death, for providing for their dependent family members. Even before this proposal, Montt had also urged Congress to adopt new comprehensive regulations for the montepío to replace the patchwork of rules resulting from the Spanish laws, which had never been abrogated, along with the various modifications passed since independence. Although he did not emphasize cost savings, the issue was in the background.

Whether or not to preserve the requirement that servicemen receive prior permission from their commanding officers before marrying dominated the 1854 debate over the new regulations in the Senate. Andrés Bello proposed abolishing the requirement for a separate military license to marry as unnecessary and inappropriate in a republic. Senator Bello was particularly influential. Although a native of Venezuela, he moved in 1829 to Chile, where he was the founder and rector of the national university; in 1855 Congress would discuss and approve a civil code authored principally by Bello.[87] Nonetheless, minister of war Pedro Vial Gómez stood firm against Bello's opinion on this matter. Even though officers were no longer required to marry high-status brides as under the Spanish regulations, he argued that the rule preserved the dignity of the institution by preventing soldiers from marrying women of loose morals. Moreover, the licensing procedure provided information to the state that could help prevent fraudulent claims. Bello offered a different reasoning on both counts. First, he noted that by law soldiers under the age of twenty-five needed the permission of parents or guardians to marry and that these family members would have a strong interest in preventing inappropriate matches, whereas the law trusted the judgment of all men over the age of majority. Second, he agreed that soldiers should be required to inform the government of their marriages and the births of children who would be eligible for the montepío, and that such notice would be as likely to prevent fraud. "The law should not interfere in domestic matters," he declared on the floor of the Senate.[88]

Despite Bello's influence and eloquence, three of his colleagues spoke in favor of preserving the rule that servicemen request permission to marry. Senator and former liberal vice-president Francisco Antonio Pinto asserted that when young men enlisted in the armed forces they left the authority of their fathers (*patria potestad*), and so the state must take on the paternal role of guiding them in making sensible decisions about matters like marriage. Senate president Fernando Lazcano agreed that if requiring servicemen to seek approval to wed from both parents and their commanding officers could prevent even a few bad marriages, the rule was worth keeping.[89] Senator Diego José Benavente, who himself had married the widow of José Miguel Carrera, raised the larger issues of whether marriage among servicemen was desirable at all and the growing cost to the state of paying pensions. The ideal army, he pointed out, would be made up of single men who would not be distracted from service and military discipline by concerns about their families. This sentiment was a far cry from the decree of 1826 that had denounced the Spanish montepío regulations for discouraging marriage. If soldiers were to get married, he continued, the government had an interest in whom they wed. In the end, by a vote of 10 to 4, the Senate not only reaffirmed the requirement for a military license to marry but also added an explicit reference to the law requiring paternal consent as well in the case of minors.[90]

The House of Representatives similarly debated the marriage rule when the legislation reached its chamber in 1855, but some deputies also raised issues related to the standard of living for officers and their families. Representative Francisco Angel Ramírez, a career military officer and graduate of the National Military Academy, articulated the paternalistic position toward servicemen. As a member of the House Defense Committee, he supported the rule requiring prior permission for marriage for reasons of military discipline. Although he thus agreed with Senator Benavente that married officers were easily distracted from dedicating their full attention to the servicemen under their command by "the love for their families, taking care of their children's education and many other affairs," he nonetheless advocated for military families who conformed to the regulations.[91] "When entire populations went to war, those communities rightly provided for the families of those who fell in combat . . . ," he declared, "and the obligation to compensate families became even more just when permanent armies were established and formed."[92] Therefore, Representative Ramírez proposed various measures to alleviate economic hardship on military families, including paying pensions from the state's general funds, rather than deducting contributions from officers' salaries, and increasing pension amounts. "Because if a state has the obligation to indemnify third parties for any assets it seizes during a war," he argued, likely alluding to the recent recognition of compensation for past sequestration in the 1853 Debt Consolidation Act, "it makes no sense not to adopt this same protocol when dealing with those who risked or lost their life in its defense."[93] Although Article 1 of the new montepío regulations did commit the government to make up any shortfalls in the montepío funds, as these made up "a charitable institution with the objective of aiding the families of servicemen," legislators voted against Ramírez's broader reforms.[94]

While Congress debated marriage requirements and funding for pensions, one significant change to the montepío regulations went into effect without discussion. As long as both the Spanish regulations and the 1829 law had been in force, widows of officers could qualify either from having married husbands with the rank of captain or higher or because their husbands had reached the rank of at least second lieutenant after ten or more years of service. The new comprehensive law of 1855 stipulated that dependents became eligible only after officers had served ten years unless they died in battle or as a result of injuries sustained in combat.[95] By applying the minimum length of service to all officers, the law was more equitable than the regulations it superseded, but it reduced the pool of eligible beneficiaries. Two years later, the more hierarchical restrictions of the Spanish law reemerged in a modification to the general army ordinances. Having persuaded Congress to preserve the rule for prior permission for marriage, the government in 1857 ordered commanders not to approve wedding licenses for servicemen below the rank of captain, except under special circumstances, in order to "avoid those hardships that could befall subaltern army officers who married young and without sufficient resources to cover the additional responsibilities they acquired with that new civil status."[96] Although the explicit concern expressed was not to burden lower-paid servicemen with financial responsibilities to provide for families, the unstated outcome would reduce state expenditures on pensions, especially for families from the lower classes. Given the patterns evident in montepío applications during the previous decades, mobility through the ranks was possible but slow, leading most servicemen to prefer marriage at lower ranks.

....

Numerous decrees and laws gradually expanded the number of families eligible for the montepío in early republican Chile. Such reforms did not encompass all servicemen, but this analysis of pension files shows that treasury officials were frequently frustrated in their repeated attempts to interpret eligibility rules strictly and narrowly. Although relatives of those on the losing side of civil wars might temporarily lose eligibility, moreover, periodic pardons and amnesties reincorporated them into the national family and restored their benefits. It was the persistence of widows, mothers, and other guardians that set precedents for changes in those laws, extending the benefits of the montepío to many more families than would have qualified in the colonial period. The wars of independence had created a new political climate in which, for liberal and conservative regimes alike, the embarrassment of appearing to have abandoned veterans' families outweighed possible budget shortfalls. In the wake of devastating wars, Chilean heads of state took on the paternal obligation to provide for the dependents of those who had given their lives in service to the new nation.

As state institutions matured and stabilized by the 1850s, however, the executive and legislative branches reevaluated the extent to which the montepío system had expanded and the burden it placed on state revenues. A majority of congressmen agreed with the minister of war that the state should maintain its paternal authority to approve or prohibit the marriages of servicemen. Nevertheless, by narrowing the circumstances under which permission to wed would be granted, by requiring even high-ranking officers to serve at least ten years before their dependents would become eligible for the montepío, and by failing to raise pension amounts, the new regulations passed between 1855 and 1857 reduced the state's paternal responsibility to provide for military families. Those who still did qualify, moreover, were encouraged to take a one-time payment in exchange for forfeiting future eligibility. This trend, in which the earlier concern over paternalist responsibility shifted by the 1850s to an emphasis on patriarchal authority, would parallel the judicial enforcement of laws on child support and custody among civilians.

CHAPTER 6

Enforcing Paternal Responsibilities: Legal Disputes over Family Maintenance and Custody

More than thirty years had passed since Javiera Carrera returned to Chile from a decade of exile in Buenos Aires and Montevideo, and she had achieved her dream of recovering the family hacienda of San Miguel, which had been sequestered by the state for the alleged crimes of her brothers. She then sold her main residence in Santiago and took out loans in order to purchase the shares in San Miguel from the other heirs of her father Ignacio de la Carrera. Entrusting the cattle and crops to a manager, she supervised the workers who planted and tended the gardens where she received visits from friends and relatives. She was at this country home in July 1855, when officials from the district court of Santiago notified her that grandson Domingo Aldunate y Lastra had filed suit demanding a support pension. Because Spanish law categorized alimentos as urgent cases in which the litigant's survival might be at risk, Aldunate simply had to present witnesses that he was too ill to work, his father too poor to support him, and that his grandmother was "my only ascendant [relative] who has a great fortune." On July 20, Judge Manuel Valenzuela Castillo, citing Title 19 of Law 5 from Partida 4 of the Spanish code, ordered Carrera to provide Aldunate an interim monthly allowance of twenty pesos while the full lawsuit proceeded.[1]

The ensuing litigation, in which Aldunate requested an ongoing allowance of seventy pesos, lasted over a year and built up more than one hundred pages of testimony and summations. Although the legal case rested principally on arguments of need along with class status and the responsibilities thus entailed, it also revived criticisms of Carrera's negligent mothering during the wars of independence. Back in 1819, after the death of Ignacio de la Carrera and seizure of his estate, Domingo Aldunate Sr. requested an immediate inheritance for don Ignacio's grandchildren, including those from his marriage to Dolores de la Lastra, because the Carrera siblings, as criminals, should forfeit their shares.[2] Pedro Díaz de Valdés, meanwhile, petitioned for a support pension on behalf of his wife Javiera and their children. The government granted Díaz de Valdés ninety pesos per month from the rental of the San Miguel hacienda, on condition that he share a portion with Javiera's adult daughter Dolores, who complained she had been neglected.[3] Dolores died in 1847, and eight years later her son, Javiera's grandson, revived stories that upon going into exile in 1814, Javiera had abandoned her daughter in a convent, where she had to sleep on the hard floor because her monthly allowance of six pesos was insufficient to purchase a cot. If Madame Carrera thought she could also abandon her grandchildren "in the arms of mendicancy," as Aldunate Jr. charged, "for such cases exist the Law, justice, and the Magistrate whose protection I take the liberty of seeking."[4]

Aldunate invoked these memories in order to highlight a past injustice as well as garner sympathy for his own situation. According to the *Siete Partidas*, the Spanish laws still in force in Chile, the two principal grounds for a maintenance allowance were the need of the supplicant and the means to provide of an ascendant family member. There was no age limit to qualify for a support pension, but certainly an adult male had to provide convincing evidence of his inability to support himself. Aldunate alleged a combination of health problems and status concerns that prevented him from securing suitable employment. Along with other Chileans, he tried his luck in gold-rush California, "that graveyard of men and investments," as he called it, but came home broke and presumably disabled, although he was initially vague about the medical condition that prevented him from working.[5] When Carrera's lawyer pointed out that Aldunate was a mature and robust man, he bristled that "Such a reason would be fine for a descendant of peons or the grandson of some poor person; but not for one of a wealthy lady like Doña Javiera de Carrera. Occupations should be matched to families. Even if I were robust, which I deny, it would still not do me any good to work as a peon, muleteer, servant etc."[6] Nine months into the lawsuit, Aldunate presented doctors' certificates that he suffered from heart and liver problems.[7] Carrera's lawyer countered that there were many honorable occupations that did not require physical exertion and that, almost four decades after independence, all Chileans should earn their own living "even when they descend from persons of a more superior lineage, a circumstance that does not grant anyone more rights than another in a republic and under the Constitution that governs us."[8] The medieval laws on family support, however, stipulated that pension amounts should be calibrated according to one's social status.

In addition to establishing his own need, Aldunate faced a double challenge in order to sue for maintenance: he first had to prove that his own father was unable to support him and second that his grandmother did have the means to provide. The first point was particularly delicate: Aldunate's father was in poverty because he had lost his wife's ample dowry of 18,000 pesos in unsuccessful commercial ventures. In her deposition, Carrera mentioned rumors that Aldunate's father had poorly managed her daughter's dowry, but her grandson insisted that his father's business had gone bankrupt owing to the opening of free trade, not through any fault of his own.[9] Carrera's attorney, in the meantime, presented prominent witnesses (including three senators and a superior court judge, which suggests that she remained politically connected) who testified to the unseen expenses behind what the grandson claimed was a "great fortune."[10] They emphasized the debts she had incurred (some of them had even made loans to her) in order to buy out the other heirs to the hacienda and to maintain the property, as well as her lack of a decent house in Santiago.[11] Over a year after Aldunate filed his suit, the judge absolved Carrera of paying him an allowance on the grounds that her expenses outweighed an estimated annual income from the hacienda of 9,500 pesos, that Aldunate was not too ill to hold a job that did not require physical labor, and that he was still in line to receive an inheritance of 500 pesos from his mother's estate.[12] Aldunate appealed, and the superior court ordered a new medical exam. Physicians certified that his enlarged heart could fail if he overexerted himself but did not believe he was "completely disabled for more or less passive occupations."[13] Based on this report, the superior court reinstated the monthly allowance but reduced the amount from 20 to 17.25 pesos.

That an adult man could successfully sue his elderly grandmother for financial support in 1855 seems to indicate that family law in Spain and Spanish America remained unchanged over centuries. Although the general principle of familial responsibility to care for one another did endure, as reflected in wartime efforts to maintain networks of care, magistrates subtly adapted its application to shifting political situations during the transition from colonialism to independence. The most important code, the *Siete Partidas*, was adapted from Roman and canon law in the thirteenth century under the supervision of King Alfonso X. Although subsequent compilations were published—the Laws of Toro in 1505 and the *Novísima recopilación* in 1805— they did little to modify sections on family law. Over the first half of the nineteenth century, judges in Santiago cited the Partidas repeatedly to order family heads (usually fathers but occasionally mothers or grandparents) to provide for dependent relatives of all ages, including offspring born within and out of wedlock. Moreover, when fathers who had been ordered to pay child support sued for custody of those offspring, they were rarely successful. Although the Partidas remained in force until the Chilean Civil Code went into effect in 1857, Spanish law often granted relatively wide discretion to judges. This flexibility in interpretation is reflected by trends in which successful child support lawsuits actually increased during the 1830s and 1840s, after which judges started to reduce such stipends in the 1850s even before passage of the new code. During the unstable years following the wars of independence from Spain, Chilean magistrates did not simply apply family law inherited from Spain. Rather, they chose to enforce paternal responsibility as part of a larger effort to build national unity upon a foundation of domestic order. Indeed, plaintiffs trying to recover sequestered assets and applying for pensions, as analyzed in the preceding chapters, often invoked the same legal obligation to provide for dependents but argued in these cases that the responsibility had been transferred from fathers to the state. These connections have been obscured by the categorization of cases in the archive, but they would have been evident to judges and attorneys who issued opinions and sentences across the various types of lawsuits.

This chapter is based upon an analysis of lawsuits over maintenance, defined broadly under Spanish law to include financial support provided to any family member, and child custody in the judicial district of Santiago between 1785 and 1855.[14] Approximately one-quarter of maintenance suits ended without a definitive sentence; in some cases, plaintiffs may have run out of funds to pursue the case, while in others, the parties may have settled out of court. Moreover, these cases do not represent all support pensions; some husbands, parents, and grandparents would have fulfilled their responsibilities willingly (even if grudgingly) without waiting to be sued; indeed some plaintiffs alleged that the defendants had been providing at least some support and that they went to court only when such payments ceased.[15] In many cases, it is difficult to determine the socioeconomic status of the parties involved, particularly for female plaintiffs who rarely were identified by profession or employment. Given that financial settlements ranged from a few pesos to one hundred pesos monthly, the cases do cover a wide cross-section of the population. Although the surviving records are not comprehensive, an indication of general trends in the number and kinds of lawsuits will supplement the qualitative analysis of testimony and sentencing. Judges consistently enforced paternal responsibility, even when men drew credible contrasts between their own honorable standing and the lack of virtue in the women who brought suit against them. Nonetheless, class and status did affect the outcomes of judicial disputes. Wealthy and powerful men could rarely evade the obligation to support their offspring, even when they denied paternity or alleged filial disobedience; they were more likely, however, successfully to exercise the patriarchal authority that accompanied the fulfillment of such responsibilities, particularly by the 1850s. Poor, unmarried mothers, by contrast, often were regarded as unfit parents. In some cases, judges believed young people were better off in the households of nonrelatives with greater resources, even if they would be treated more as servants than foster children. This chapter will analyze first maintenance and then custody disputes, since the latter often arose out of the former. Countersuing for custody of children could be a way to strike back at the initial plaintiffs (usually mothers) and an attempt to exercise the authority providers expected to enjoy over those dependents they supported.

The Paternal Obligation to Provide

Spanish laws on family maintenance were embedded in principles that emphasized unequal but reciprocal relationships within families. The Siete Partidas, influenced by Roman and canon law but codified under royal jurisdiction in thirteenth-century Castile, articulated the duty of parents to provide for their children. Such a responsibility extended to most children born out of wedlock, who were identified as "natural" offspring, but fathers had no obligations to "infamous" illegitimates born of adultery, incest, or relationships with priests. Legitimate offspring, like Javiera Carrera's grandson, were entitled to parental maintenance even as adults if they were unable to support themselves at a level befitting their status. Judges were to expedite support lawsuits, especially if the claimants were minors; in the case of out-of-wedlock offspring, for example, courts could require provisional payments even prior to a definitive finding of paternity. The Partidas used the term *crianza* (rearing), but in lawsuits such support came to be called "pensiones alimenticias" or simply "alimentos," which, in addition to food, usually covered shelter, clothing, and even education, all calibrated to one's station in life. Most commonly, fathers provided for their offspring, but Spanish law required all ascendant and descendant family members with means to support those in need. Adult children were to support elderly parents who had fallen into poverty.[16] Similarly, men were responsible for maintaining their wives, even after an ecclesiastical separation, but a woman with a substantial inheritance might be ordered to provide for a husband who lost his fortune.

The few scholars who have examined the application of these laws in Spain and its colonies tend to focus on out-of-wedlock offspring and the contentious, high-stakes conflicts over inheritance and status, rather than considering the full range of familial responsibility to provide for various dependents.[17] While in earlier periods women who bore children out of wedlock often sued for breach of promise to marry, studies of Lima and Mexico found that alimentos lawsuits increased in the late eighteenth century.[18] The Royal Marriage Pragmatic of 1776, which empowered parents to oppose marriages on the grounds of social inequality, may have made it harder for unwed mothers to construct credible claims of betrothal promises. A royal order in 1787 to shift jurisdiction over *financial* matters resulting from marital separations from ecclesiastical to secular courts may also have created a new venue for support claims.[19] The little research that has been done suggests that postindependence courts in Spanish America continued to hold fathers responsible for supporting out-of-wedlock offspring, until new civil codes promulgated during the second half of the nineteenth century reinforced the authority of male heads of households over wives and minor children and restricted the options for paternity suits.[20]

Although few in number, the diversity of maintenance claims in late-colonial Santiago for which a written record remains suggests the breadth of the obligation to provide. That only seventeen such lawsuits are archived, either under Real Audiencia or Judiciales de Santiago, for the period between 1785 and 1810, implies that most responsible parties fulfilled their duties to support dependents, either voluntarily or after pressure from local authorities in oral hearings. Most claims that did end up in court reflected either particularly acrimonious alimony disputes between spouses (eight cases) or unusual circumstances in which the rationale had to be demonstrated.[21] The four claims for child support were the minority: one legitimate son sued his widowed mother over access to the family's rural estate; two out-of-wedlock offspring successfully pressured for settlements from their fathers' estates; and only one extant lawsuit from 1805 involved an unwed mother winning child support from a living father.[22] Six cases were filed against parties who were neither husbands nor fathers: two involved sibling disputes over inheritance or reimbursement for care provided; one father was allowed to take out a loan against his children's inheritance; a couple successfully sued for compensation from the estate of an aunt for whom they had cared; a minor sued his guardian over his allowance; and a wife requested a maintenance allowance from her husband's estate before the executors settled with creditors.[23] The lawsuits that held persons other than parents responsible for support help explain why subsequent claims for maintenance against the state, arising from property sequestration and military service during and after the independence wars, were credible and often successful.

Just as Chileans called upon new authorities to act like the benevolent father figures they claimed to be, they also expected judges to enforce the duties of actual fathers who survived the wars. During the years of greatest instability, from 1810 to 1830, only one or two maintenance suits per year left a record in the archives and these differed little from those during the late colonial period. Beginning in the 1830s, however, the number of lawsuits steadily rose and the proportion filed on behalf of offspring—both legitimate and out-of-wedlock, minors and adults—increased in proportion to separating spouses.[24] The reasons for these increases are difficult to determine, but that parties resorted more frequently to litigation certainly implies a rising contentiousness over respective responsibilities. It is plausible that political rhetoric and state policies affirming paternal obligations emboldened more offspring to press their own fathers (and in some cases mothers or grandparents) to provide.[25] Male heads of households, citizens of the new republic, protested many of these claims on the grounds either that adult offspring should be self-supporting or that they did not recognize paternity of children. Nevertheless, judges in Santiago, drawn from the same elite families, repeatedly ordered responsible parties to provide for dependent relatives of all ages born both within and out of wedlock. Rather than requiring strict adherence to clear rules, the existing Spanish laws and judicial procedures gave wide discretion to judges in determining paternity and assessing patriarchal duties relative to filial obedience.

The largest single category of plaintiffs in Santiago maintenance suits between 1785 and 1855 was divorcing wives (just over a third of the total); before 1820 claims by wives constituted about half of all lawsuits and such cases continued to form a plurality until 1845. Of course, children were included in the calculations of many of these pensions. Moreover, these cases tended to be the least complicated: proof of marriage was easy to provide and the law clearly required husbands to support wives who were legitimately separated from them. Suits for temporary separations or "permanent" divorces (i.e., spouses lived apart but could not remarry) were decided in ecclesiastical court, but once the vicar either had certified that proceedings were underway or had passed a sentence, civil courts set the amounts for alimony and legal expenses and oversaw the division of marital property. Husbands often complained about these arrangements, alleging that wives wanted to live apart in order to pursue dissolute lifestyles. In 1845, for example, a state-appointed attorney complained on behalf of Carmen Carrasco that since filing for divorce, her husband "has been incapable of even throwing a piece of bread to his daughter." "This cruel indolence of an unnatural father and ungrateful husband cries out to heaven," he proclaimed. Her husband countered that she was not pursuing the divorce case consistently, alternately reconciling and then leaving him again, because "women always aspire to liberty without limits."[26] But such allegations of immorality or misconduct, rooted in Spanish concepts of honor and Christian precepts, had relevance only to the outcome of the ecclesiastical suit. Civil courts adjudicated alimony according to means of the provider and needs of the recipients calibrated to their social status.[27] The wife of a carpenter, for example, was awarded eight pesos per month (after requesting twelve).[28] At the other end of the social ladder, Silvestre Valdivieso was ordered to pay eighty pesos a month to his wife, Rosa de la Cerda, and when he was in arrears, she successfully petitioned for the seizure and auction of a house valued at over 20,000 pesos to cover the debt.[29]

Claims for alimony brought by wives who were pursuing or had been awarded ecclesiastical separations were legally clear, but the implications of such cases were problematic for the larger philosophy that domestic harmony and unity undergirded social peace and order. The Church favored temporary over permanent separations in the hope that couples would reconcile, and secular judges encouraged spouses to come to amicable financial arrangements in the meantime. The worst-case scenario was represented by the separation of Carmen Goycolea and Manuel Rosales in 1833. The initial sentence ordered him to provide her one hundred pesos each month as well as additional annual amounts of two hundred for clothing, one hundred for legal expenses, and supplies of staples from their hacienda (e.g., beans, wheat, lard).[30] But over the next twenty-three years, in addition to continued litigation between the couple over compliance and amount, their children and their children's spouses sued both parents for shares of those support payments.[31] In 1843, for example, Judge José Antonio Argomedo, son of the state attorney who had advised O'Higgins on pensions payable out of sequestered property, asserted that although Goycolea had custody of the children when they were young, the obligation to support a married adult daughter whose husband was not a sufficient provider fell first upon her father and only secondarily on her mother. Although the appeals court overturned his decision and ordered Goycolea to share part of her settlement with the daughter, ultimately all the funds came from Rosales's annual payments.[32]

Lawsuits brought by legitimate offspring against their parents or grand-parents, like those of the Rosales-Goycolea family or Domingo Aldunate, had been rare before 1835 but increased significantly thereafter.[33] Plaintiffs did not have the burden of proving paternity, but parents objected to providing for progeny who ought to be capable of supporting themselves and whom they often characterized as ungrateful and disobedient. Nonetheless, such claims were almost always successful. In 1845, for example, Ricardo Evans Price was incensed when his son, Ricardo Jr., successfully petitioned the court for an interim monthly allowance of twenty pesos. The father narrated the many investments in educational and occupational opportunities that his son allegedly squandered. He had employed his son himself at an annual salary of seven hundred pesos until a position opened at another merchant firm. When the son refused to take that opportunity, supposedly complaining about "so much working, so much writing," the father sent him off to work for his former partners in Peru, but Ricardo Jr. quit after four months. The father's lawyer contended that far from being rewarded for such ungrateful behavior, which "would mortally wound paternal authority and destroy all the bonds within families," the son should be punished. During the course of the full trial lasting three years, the son married against his father's wishes, moved in with his mother-in-law, fathered his own child, and secured a position paying about fifty pesos a month but continued his suit on the grounds that this salary was insufficient to maintain "the social position, comforts, and expenses that are necessary in order to maintain the rank and decorum to which his rich family is accustomed." The judge and later the superior court agreed. Pointing out that the younger Price had attempted to live within his means and that according to the Fourth Partida "support [alimentos] should be awarded according to the wealth of those who give and the need of those who receive," the court actually increased his monthly allowance to forty pesos.[34]

Price, as an immigrant merchant, may have been particularly shocked by Spanish law on child support, but fathers born and raised in Chile also protested what they considered outrageous demands. In perhaps the most striking case of a father unable to get the court to recognize his patriarchal prerogative to deny support to disobedient offspring, José Miguel Bascuñán complained to police that his daughter had been stolen from his home. "What has become of domestic order! Of proper upbringing! Of Fathers!," he exclaimed, livid with paternal rage. To add injury to insult, a year later his son-in-law filed a lawsuit for maintenance on behalf of his wife and infant daughter. In addition to fulminating against his daughter's ingratitude, Bascuñán objected that he had opposed the marriage precisely because he knew the suitor would be unable to support her. "There is no doubt that a father should support his children when they show him proper love and respect," he affirmed in recognition of paternal responsibility. "But when they abuse him, violate him, and break into his house," he continued, "he should disinherit them in order to prevent such scandals in the future and the corruption of public morals."[35] Like other Chilean patriarchs, Bascuñán emphasized his authority and the reciprocal nature of familial duties. The Partidas did indeed allow parents to disinherit disobedient children, but set a high bar and gave judges the discretion to evaluate charges of filial insubordination.[36] In this case, the daughter was over the age of majority and did not, therefore, require parental permission to marry. Nonetheless, her maturity and independence of action did not necessarily exempt her father from his obligation to provide. The judge ordered Bascuñán to pay his daughter a monthly allowance of twenty-five pesos or to provide her with a dowry sufficient to get her husband established in business.

In the greatest change from litigation patterns during the late colonial period, lawsuits brought by or on behalf of children born out of wedlock increased both in actual numbers and proportion compared to other kinds of plaintiffs from the 1830s to the 1850s.[37] That such children would need support payments is not surprising, but their success at winning them is striking given the prejudices against out-of-wedlock children and their presumably immoral (and often poor) mothers. Although the law required men to support the children they fathered out of wedlock, judges had considerable discretion in determining the responsible party. Predictably, defendants maligned the mothers' reputations, claiming that their multiple sexual partners made it impossible to establish paternity. Yet testimony that a woman had only one partner during her pregnancy, regardless of her prior or later relationships and conduct, usually persuaded judges. Indications that the defendant had paid a midwife and/or wet-nurse or had shown signs of affection toward the child were considered further evidence of presumed paternity, even when he later insisted that he had been deceived.[38]

The dispute between Juana Barra and Narciso Pérez Cotapos was typical. When she sued him for child support in 1833, he protested that she had not been a virgin when he met her, that she slept with numerous men during the same time period, "selling her body," and finally that their relationship had ended thirteen years ago. Barra, represented by a public defender, presented three witnesses (one woman and two men all at least forty years old and presumably neighbors), who testified that at the time of her pregnancy,

Cotapos was the only man who visited Barra. The female witness further recalled Cotapos playing with the child, and a fourth witness admitted that Cotapos had recruited him to serve as the godfather though he claimed not to know whether or not Cotapos was the father. When Cotapos, the brother of Ana María Cotapos who had married into the Carrera family, called his witnesses, his strategy had shifted from trying to deny paternity to pleading insolvency. Although his deceased wife, Juana Salinas, had brought him a dowry valued at nine thousand pesos, he claimed that most of the capital had been lost in unsuccessful business ventures and that he needed to reserve what was left for their legitimate children. Both the judge of first instance and the superior appeals court awarded Barra a modest monthly stipend of six pesos, although she agreed at an oral hearing to a reduction of one peso.[39]

During the lawsuit, Cotapos ceased to deny paternity, but in other cases judges ordered men to pay child support despite their presentation of evidence that called into question the identity of fathers. In 1835, Isidro Garcés resolutely refused to recognize paternity of a girl, baptized a year and a half earlier, alleging the immoral conduct of her mother. He denounced Isidora Grandón, stating that her house was always full of male visitors and that every night "there was disorder, dancing, and wild partying until late into the night." Unlike Cotapos, Garcés also presented witnesses willing to attest to her loose lifestyle, including a man who said that after flirting with him at a party, Grandón had invited him to visit her presumably "to satisfy that which he had insinuated to her, and therefore the witness was persuaded that she had no modesty." Moreover, seven months after filing charges against Garcés, Grandón gave birth to another girl whose father was identified on the baptismal certificate as Felipe Jara. Nonetheless, Grandón presented witnesses, including a priest, who testified that she had behaved properly during her relationship with Garcés and to his having paid the child's nursemaid. Her older daughter's baptismal certificate, moreover, recorded Garcés as the "legitimate" father; Grandón explained that she recorded the child as "legitimate" because Garcés had promised to marry her, but when it became clear that he was not going to fulfill his word, "she no longer allowed him to visit her." The judge found Garcés to be the father of the older girl (though not the infant) and ordered him to pay three pesos in monthly child support.[40] He was not the only judge to grant wide latitude in evaluating a woman's morals. The only witnesses who could positively identify Lázaro Tomás Ramos entering the room of Mercedes Canales, a charge he adamantly denied, were her own relatives. The vagueness of this evidence split a four-judge panel, but the fifth brought in to break the tie supported an order for Ramos to pay Canales five pesos monthly in child support.[41]

Unmarried mothers usually obtained a positive (if often modest) judgment. Some even got the courts to enforce collection of unpaid child support. In 1822 Mercedes Rojas went to the commanding officer of Coronel Francisco Ibáñez to complain that after promising marriage and fathering three children, he had suddenly abandoned her. The commander sent her away after a lecture about the perils of prostituting herself, but she appealed to O'Higgins who ordered that her case be heard in the military court. There Rojas presented letters from Ibáñez that made clear his earlier promises. After professing his affection and how much he missed her while out on campaign, he wrote that she should remain faithful and that he would do right by her: "have no doubt that I will fulfill my word in spite of all the obstacles."[42] Confronted with this evidence, Ibáñez agreed to pay monthly child support of nine pesos. When Rojas returned almost a decade later complaining that he was in arrears, the military docked his paycheck to make sure she got her support payments. In 1834 Ibáñez protested these deductions, and his lawyer argued that the original settlement had not followed proper procedures. Nevertheless, in 1836 the court still ordered Ibáñez to continue payments. At some point during these fourteen years, Rojas had married and then divorced another man, but these subsequent events did not affect the obligations of Ibáñez toward his children.[43] At a time when commanders-in-chief were expanding eligibility for military pensions for legitimate widows and orphans, they were not going to allow living officers to shirk their responsibility toward their children, even those born out of wedlock.

Class and race prejudices often shaped efforts by defendants to malign plaintiffs' reputations. In 1845, Lorenza Mazuela claimed that, believing his marriage promises, she had consented to a relationship with Bernardo Cadiz during which they had four children. When he married a different woman and stopped paying the monthly stipend of eight pesos for child support, Mazuela filed suit. Cadiz was a young retail merchant, employed by his father, who claimed that he did not have enough income to support both his out-of-wedlock and legitimate children. He denied that he had ever promised to marry Mazuela, whom he identified as a laundress or servant, capable of working to support herself at a standard of living appropriate to her low social class. His lawyer made explicit such insinuations: "This woman from the dregs of the common people, an Indian of unknown or illegitimate parents, . . . had already experienced the causes and effects of a dishonest and corrupted life." Mazuela denied ever having worked as a servant, but admitted having had a child with a different man before meeting Cadiz.[44] Juan Manuel Palacios used similar terms to denigrate Mercedes Ayala, who filed suit against him in 1855: "This Mercedes So-and-So is the daughter of a laundress, and has never lived at her mother's side nor been subject to her authority, leading instead a licentious life: currently she is pregnant . . . therefore there is no way to know who is the father of the child for whom she requests support." Palacios denied that he had ever even entered her room and presented witnesses who convinced the court of the mother's "licentious conduct."[45] These women of low status were particularly vulnerable to moral attacks, but judges still found the probable fathers liable for child support, ordering interim monthly stipends of six pesos to Mazuela and fourteen to Ayala until the definitive conclusion of their lawsuits.

Although Chilean judges in the early nineteenth century set a relatively low bar for proving paternity, poor women were less likely to have the time and resources to pursue a case to a final judgment or seek enforcement of rulings. Some, therefore, settled along the way. Six months after Mazuela filed suit against Cadiz, he was sentenced in the initial, supposedly expedited, phase of his trial, to pay six pesos per month until the definitive sentence. Two months later, he still had paid nothing and the presentation of evidence by both sides dragged on. Finally, almost a year and a half after her initial petition, Mazuela agreed to accept a one-time payment of 250 pesos, most of which would be held by a third party who would pay her monthly interest of 2 pesos, an amount the court later acknowledged was insufficient to cover her family's expenses, but by then the deal had been struck.[46] Venancia Torreblanca, one of the few plaintiffs who did not even claim the right for a "doña" before her name, had gotten her child's alleged father, José Moraga, to agree before a justice of the peace to pay a mere three pesos per month for the short period of only a year and a half.[47] He subsequently recanted, protesting that the charge was an affront to his honor as a married man. "I believe, Sir, that there can be no Law that condemns me to support a natural child," he added, "when I have three or four legitimate ones at my side for whom to provide." Of course, ignorance of the law was no excuse and the judge upheld the settlement, but nine months after her initial complaint, Torreblanca's breast milk had dried up as a result of illness, and she needed cash to pay a wet nurse. Desperate and lacking resources to keep pursuing enforcement of the sentence, she finally agreed to a one-time payment of twenty-five pesos, turned over by Moraga's father.[48]

Although women of low status and few resources faced an uphill battle in court, many successfully sued for child support, if only a modest one-time lump sum. Those lawsuits for support of out-of-wedlock offspring that were not successful tended to be those filed after they were adults and/or the alleged parent had died. In 1845, for example, José del C. Letelier filed suit on behalf of his wife, María Jesus Bernal, for one sixth of the modest estate (143 pesos) of José Bernal; he claimed that his wife was the natural daughter of Bernal's deceased son Narciso. The only surviving legitimate offspring of José Bernal and his widow both admitted that they had heard these rumors, but their lawyer quickly discounted their testimony as that of old women and pointed out that an earlier lawsuit brought by the child's mother had been unsuccessful. The judge ruled the evidence of paternity insufficient.[49] The evidence in three other cases from 1850 was even weaker. In one a nineteen-year-old girl, raised by her godparents after the death of her mother, filed suit against her alleged father, who died shortly thereafter leaving an estate valued at only two hundred pesos. Before his death, carpenter Mateo Icarte admitted to having had a relationship with the girl's mother, but claimed that a medical condition prevented him from fathering children. Moreover, the girl's best hope for a witness, her mother's employer in whose house she had been born, denied knowing Icarte. The court ruled against the plaintiff.[50] Even more difficult to prove was the claim of a fifty-five-year-old woman against the estate of her alleged father, who had been dead for twenty-six years.[51] These lawsuits, unlike the successful ones analyzed above, shared three factors that made judges less sympathetic: they believed low-status adults should work to support themselves, the passage of time lessened the credibility of witness testimony, and they were more hesitant to grant rights to inheritance as compared to monthly stipends.[52]

As with the lawsuits filed on behalf of out-of-wedlock children, demands by legitimate offspring occasionally failed, but for different reasons. In these cases, minors were at a disadvantage because they were expected to eat at their parents' tables rather than live independently on allowances. In 1819, Pedro Calancha sued his mother for support, complaining that she was trying to deny him his paternal inheritance. Alfonsa de la Rosa countered his charges by presenting receipts totaling 128 pesos she had spent during the past two years on clothing, a horse, and other expenses for her son and by pointing out that much of her deceased husband's estate was tied up in the house in which she and her son both resided. Complaining that she often had to call upon the authorities to help her discipline him, she declared her willingness to turn over guardianship to someone else to free herself of his constant insults. In this case, the mayor of Santiago (serving in his capacity as a judge of first instance), called the two parties to an oral hearing where he refused to let the mother resign her responsibilities but admonished the son to treat her with due "obedience, submission and respect" and to keep his expenses within the family's means.[53] In 1855, Alejo Grez managed to get a court-ordered interim allowance, but his father Bartolomé Grez recounted his numerous efforts to get his son a good position, naming top public officials as contacts. As in the case of merchant Ricardo Price, the defense lawyer argued that it would be difficult to find a father who had done more on behalf of his son, and that if he were forced to accede to every caprice it would threaten the social fabric: "Few sons will want to stay at the side of their fathers and subjected to them from the moment in which the latter are obligated to support children to live in full liberty, without recognizing any authority other than their own passions."[54] Given that Alejo Grez was under twenty-five and therefore still subject to his father's patria potestad (the legal term for paternal authority), the superior court in this case agreed, revoking the interim allowance and requiring the son to return home if he wished to be financially supported by his father.

Judges usually concurred with claims that support for minor, legitimate children hinged upon their living at home under parental authority. When plaintiffs alleged that they would be mistreated, however, judges were hesitant to force the issue. In 1816 widow María de los Dolores Cubé filed suit against her father-in-law Raimundo Molina to financially support his grandson. After living in his house in rural Aconcagua for two months, Cubé moved to Santiago to be with her own mother, alleging that "because of his [Molina's] wife's bad-tempered personality, a moment did not pass in which she did not throw in my face the support that they were providing me." Molina denied that his wife had a difficult personality, countering that by going to court Cubé had acted out of a "restless spirit, disturbing to the order and peace in which families should live." Moreover, he insisted that his only obligation was to support family members living within his household: "The Law cannot oblige me to do more than this unless there are new laws that allow and declare that children inherit during their parents' lifetime." When Cubé responded that there were additional reasons for her departure that she preferred not to state explicitly but related to tight living quarters, Molina changed his tactic. He demanded that the child should come live with him when he turned three, that is, past the age identified by law when nursing children should be with their mothers. Then if Cubé wanted to continue her independent lifestyle in the city, he continued, "let her work to support herself and leave off from so much visiting and other pastimes." Nonetheless, all Molina's arguments failed, and he was ordered to pay one half peso daily to Cubé for the maintenance of his grandson. When he appealed in 1818 to the new independent government, pleading poverty because his farm had been looted during the war, the judge refused any reduction in the allowance. Further, the public defender of minors ruled that since Cubé's husband had died intestate without appointing a guardian, the law granted custody to the mother.[55] His more limited authority as grandfather rather than father, in addition to the insinuation of abuse, weakened Molina's claim that he was responsible only for dependents under his own roof.

From independence to at least 1850, while the Chilean state was administering paternalist policies in other areas, judges enforced the fulfillment of patriarchal responsibilities within households. Although many cases continued to address alimony for wives who had been granted ecclesiastical separations, lawsuits brought by or on behalf of children increased in the 1830s and 1840s. Perhaps most surprising, given the lack of attention they have received in the scholarly literature and the difference from our own times, were the successful claims brought by adult offspring. One might expect judges in a period that emphasized the independence of citizens to discount such plaintiffs, but instead they upheld the principle that parents had a lifelong responsibility for their legitimate offspring. The needs of children born out of wedlock, often to poor mothers, are more obvious to our eyes; Chilean magistrates also enforced paternal responsibility in these cases and often granted the benefit of the doubt to children in cases of disputed paternity. The increasing number and proportion of maintenance suits brought on behalf of children, especially for those born out of wedlock, would become more controversial by the 1850s, particularly as sentences often denied men the authority they expected to exercise in return for serving as providers.

Custody Disputes: Adjudicating the Authority of Providers

In the majority of maintenance suits, fathers (and occasionally other family members) were forced to comply with their responsibility to care for their offspring. A common response to an order to pay alimentos, therefore, was to insist that the recipient receive that support at the provider's table, rather than receiving a cash allowance. Only under exceptional circumstances would judges deny fathers' demands that legitimate children past infancy but still under the age of majority receive support in the paternal home. Nevertheless, Spanish law did grant judges the discretion to evaluate the nuances of each case within the general guidelines. The Partidas did not clearly distinguish between financial support and custody, nor between legitimate and natural children in this regard. The law in question began by asserting that mothers should support and feed those under the age of three (presumably the average age of weaning) and fathers those older than three, but indicated that in the case of a poor woman, "the father is obliged to furnish her with what is necessary." Fathers often appealed to this article when suing for custody, but the custom seems to have been for children, especially daughters, to remain with their mothers longer. The law continued that in the case of ecclesiastical divorce (permanent separation of bed and board), the party at fault should provide financial support for children, but the innocent party "should bring them up and have charge of them." Finally, the article in question concluded that if a mother who had custody of children married, "she should not then have the care of them, nor is the father bound to give her any property for this purpose, but he should take charge of the children and rear them if he has the means."[56] Since only annulments, but not separations, allowed remarriage, presumably this final point applied to children born out of wedlock. Fathers retained official guardianship and authority over legitimate children even when mothers were granted physical custody, but fathers were obliged to support children born out of wedlock without exercising patria potestad.[57]

Thirty-one lawsuits over custody in Santiago courts between 1804 and 1855, a few of which were added on to maintenance suits, included as interested parties not only parents but also siblings, employers, and putative foster parents. That three-quarters of them date from the last fifteen years of this period suggests increasing contention over whether providers should also have custody rights. The law favored fathers in the case of legitimate children and mothers in the case of out-of-wedlock offspring but the relative class standing and reputations of the contending parties influenced judicial sentencing. Although judges rarely considered honor when adjudicating alimentos, moral assessments could influence their decisions on custody. In cases where the courts had doubts about the moral or financial capacity of parents or in which parents had at least temporarily relinquished custody to third parties, it could be difficult, especially for poor, unmarried mothers, to claim rights over biological offspring. Judges ordered some children placed in boarding schools and set visitation terms for each parent. Moreover, despite legal judgments in their favor, mothers could not always obtain enforcement of court orders against resisting fathers or third parties.

Of the custody disputes in Santiago during the first half of the nineteenth century, those between separated spouses were the least frequent, and courts tried to lessen conflict within legitimate families by facilitating mediated settlements. If we include cases between spouses that did not reach sentencing, it seemed to be a slightly more common practice for children to live with their mothers. Manuel Bravo and Rosario Luco, for example, had separated in 1838; he sued for custody of their children, but the court awarded it to her in 1840 "considering their sex and their current stage of infancy." Five years later, he tried again, pointing out that the only surviving child had reached an age, almost ten, at which her virtue was in danger from her mother's immorality. He asked the court to authorize him to enroll her in a school in Valparaiso, where he resided. Luco countered that when their daughter was old enough, she planned to matriculate her in one of Santiago's convent schools. Bravo, perhaps trying to appeal to the republican spirit of the age, contended that the laws, "truly the tutors and guardian angels that watch over and prevent the early perdition of these creatures," should protect the best interests of children. He asserted that a cloistered education would make the girl "unable to properly carry out the social duties to which she is destined," whereas he was "trying to conquer for her a higher rung on the ladder of social considerations by providing her an education more appropriate to her class and the society in which she should circulate." Luco, on the other hand, was adamant that she was the more virtuous parent:

> I am not giving her up . . . because she does not belong to him and both the law and nature reject such an extravagant pretension. I will raise her according to the principles of a Christian education: in due time I will place her in a convent where she will drink from the font of virtue and will be freed from the pestilent habits of the age.

In cases like this, in which there was no compelling difference in the care the child would receive, judges preferred not to take sides; the couple was ordered to mediation and the final agreement not recorded.[58] Given that the mother already had custody and was adamantly opposed to giving it up, the absence of further litigation most likely indicates that the daughter remained with her.

Ignacio Solar and Carmen Cañas, like Bravo and Luco, were in almost perpetual conflict from 1836 to 1844, but because they were from wealthy and powerful families, the courts encouraged them to abide by a series of mediated agreements. She was the wealthier party, and in 1842 he agreed to relinquish his rights to administer her properties in exchange for being freed from making support payments. Moreover, his efforts to gain custody of their children, or at least change the terms of visitation, consistently failed. The initial agreement in 1836 placed Cañas and the children under the authority of her father, the children's maternal grandfather. In 1840, the elder daughters entered schools, and a new agreement had them go to their mother's house on vacation days but allowed their father to visit them there and take them out for excursions. Beginning in 1844, however, Solar began persistently filing complaints that Cañas was not fulfilling the terms of their agreement. Solar felt insulted that when he came to visit his daughters they did not immediately stop whatever they were doing (music lessons, eating a meal) to attend to him, and he requested that a lady living in his wife's house be made to leave. The official mediator found his grievances exaggerated and not technically violations. Frustrated, Solar filed for permanent divorce, presenting letters (not contained in the civil case file) written to his wife as evidence that convinced the vicar that Cañas had committed adultery despite "the proper and decorous exterior conduct observed by visitors to her house during normal hours."[59] Finally, he was successful. Given the ecclesiastical judgment against Cañas in 1847, she was ordered to pay the court costs, but surprisingly seems to have retained custody of the girls despite Spanish law. In 1848, Solar tried to get out of an agreement he had signed, which basically continued the arrangement that he could visit the girls at her home, but in 1849 the judge ruled the agreement binding.[60] Cañas's wealth, status, and connections, combined with Solar's failure to live up to the paternal responsibility to provide for his family, allowed her to maintain custody of their children, an outcome that affirms the discretion judges could exercise when passing sentences.

Fathers who lived up to the expectations of dutiful providers fared better in court, but judges could still decide whether or not to enforce the letter of the law. In August 1848, Josefa Sierralta left her husband's home to move in with her father, sued for an ecclesiastical divorce, and filed in civil court for alimentos. Antonio Gundián, her husband, was one of the treasury officials whose duties included weighing in on all military pension applications. The court ordered his colleague José María Berganza to garnish Gundián's salary in order to make payments to his wife. Because Sierralta had left home on her own, however, their four children remained with their father along with the children from his first marriage. During the course of the divorce proceedings, she was successful in changing the terms of visitation so that the children could come see her twice a week at her father's home. At about the same time, the ecclesiastical court found Gundián guilty of adultery and granted a temporary separation of eighteen months in the hopes that the couple would reconcile for the sake of their children.

Armed with this favorable sentence, Sierralta returned to civil court and won both custody and child support. Obviously upset by this adverse turn of events, Gundián filed his own suit for permanent ecclesiastical divorce based upon his wife's alleged libelous attacks upon his reputation, "the only patrimony on which I can count and can leave to my children."[61] In order to defend his honor, he had his side of the story printed as a pamphlet. "My Beloved Children! Children of my heart!" he exhorted, "Never forget what you have just seen and heard! Always remember that your father has used all available means to avoid the misfortune that your mother provokes."[62] His invocation of honor may have resonated in the court of public opinion, but the vicar saw no new evidence that could justify making the divorce permanent. The most Gundián could achieve was the same visitation rights previously granted to his wife by pleading "that just as it has not been denied to a mother, neither should it be denied to a father."[63] But when she claimed he had failed to return the children after one such visit, the court issued an order for him to do so. In this case, the parties seemed to have been closely matched in terms of status and influence, so the authorities enforced the laws on the books while encouraging the couple to reconcile. Perhaps most surprising, the vicar's faith proved well placed when shortly after the last custody order, the couple reunited.

In the only case in the sample in which the courts definitively granted custody to a husband involved in divorce proceedings, the wife failed to mount a convincing case, instead evading and ignoring orders from both the civil and ecclesiastical courts to appear for mediation sessions. Pascuala Rojas had sued for divorce on the grounds of excessive cruelty and claimed, without presenting evidence, that their infant daughter had died when her husband, José Santos Nuñes, had kidnapped her and given her over to a negligent caretaker. After the judge of first instance ordered her to turn their son over to his father, she appealed. "I am a mother, Sir, who has raised my son at my breast, providing for him and educating him at my own expense and means"; she pleaded, "if he wants custody of our son it is to discharge against him his barbarous fury since he can no longer discharge it against me." Citing the definition of patria potestad from the most widely used legal dictionary, that a father "can subject, correct, and punish his child with moderation, and request the help of public authorities when the child is disobedient," Nuñes requested that the police enforce the custody order. For his part, Nuñes accused Rojas, also without presenting evidence, of holding wild parties every night and being romantically involved with her lawyer. "Will it not break my heart," he lamented, "to see this child dancing those indecent dances (the *samacueca*) and speaking improper words better than he can read and recite Christian doctrine?" After she failed to appear at several court-ordered oral hearings, the superior court decided against her appeal, upholding his right to custody because the boy was over four and the mother "not only does not have good customs and lives in a house of disorder, she maintains illicit and criminal relations."[64] Neither party had presented much evidence or witness testimony in the civil court, but a woman who failed to mount a defense and evaded judicial officials was presumed to be irresponsible and of low moral character.

Fathers did not exercise patria potestad over children born out of wedlock (though many assumed that they did), and the Santiago courts rarely awarded them definitive custody. One of the earliest cases laid out in detail the customary rationale for favoring mothers of such children. In 1819, José Santos Moreno, married and a master artisan, fathered a child with the single Carmen Rodrigues. Only in 1824, when the mother married another man, did he sue for custody, arguing that the stepfather would surely mistreat his daughter, "something that no Magistrate of the Nation with the Christian morality required by the Constitution could allow." Meanwhile he and his wife had a harmonious, but childless, marriage and would welcome the opportunity to raise the girl as their own. The court appointed an inspector to investigate, and all the factors he reported were in the mother's favor. First, the laws did not recognize the authority of men over children outside their marriage. (The inspector did not mention the article that mothers who married someone other than their children's father would lose custody.) Secondly, Moreno had earlier promised Rodrigues's betrothed that he would not sue for custody and the fiancé in turn had promised to financially support the child. Third, it would threaten the harmony of Rodrigues's new marriage if she had to maintain contact with Moreno in order to see her children. And fourth, a young girl needed the care of a mother, not an uncertain father or a vengeful stepmother.[65] Strikingly, at the same time that judges did not require definitive proof of paternity to order child support, this inspector asserted that the adulterous nature of the earlier relationship between Moreno and Rodrigues made his identity as father "uncertain."

Thirty years later, Nicolasa Aguila successfully sued Agustín Ramírez for child support, but when the girl turned three he filed suit for custody appealing to his "unquestionable right" as a father. When her lawyer pointed out that fathers in fact had no legal authority over their natural children, Ramírez changed his tactic, claiming that he did not earn enough as a farm manager to keep paying child support but could provide for the child in his own home. "The sacred duty of a Mother makes me look out for my daughter's future," protested Aguila, and "I would rather sacrifice my own existence" than to see her at her father's side, where she would not receive an "upbringing that protects her from vices." Of the numerous witnesses few supported Aguila's allegations of Ramírez's moral incapacity to parent, but they did testify to her own respectable conduct, which was sufficient for the judge to affirm her custody.[66] In another case, the lower court sentence awarding custody to a natural father was overturned on appeal to the superior court. In 1837, Petronila Muños and Pablo Donnay had agreed in mediation that he would pay seven pesos in monthly child support to a boy whose baptismal certificate identified them as the legitimate parents. Two years later, he sued for custody, arguing that their agreement had been only until the son turned three. Moreover, he presented three witnesses who testified to her drinking problems to justify why he had not followed through on their intended marriage. The judge, citing the Partida law regarding custody going to the innocent party in a divorce, ordered Muños to turn the boy over to Donnay "in order to have him in his care and educate him until he learns some art or industry with which he can support himself." But a few months later, the superior court revoked this sentence on the grounds that the marriage had never taken effect and that natural fathers did not enjoy patria potestad.[67]

In many cases, justices believed that it was in the child's best interests to enter a boarding school rather than live with an unmarried parent; under such circumstances, mothers' ability to oversee the children's education varied. In a lengthy case from 1844, Manuel Portales presented numerous witnesses who claimed to have seen María Marín go off with various men. Nevertheless, she had as many witnesses to her proper conduct and his recognition of their two children, as well as baptismal certificates on which the children were identified as legitimate to support her claim that he had promised to marry her. Although he asked that the children be put in a school in Rancagua where he resided, she presented evidence that they were in a good school in Santiago and ultimately the courts confirmed her right to supervise their education.[68] Although Marín complained of the difficulties of pursuing a lawsuit against a powerful and wealthy man, she must have had at least some resources and connections to marshal respectable witnesses and place her children in a good school.

Other mothers were less fortunate. Despite having been forced to accept a one-time payment of one thousand pesos and to sign a notarized agreement forswearing future legal action, Carmen Astorga quite easily won a paternity suit against the estate of Manuel Cifuentes, deceased, in

1845. Nevertheless, the court just as quickly appointed a guardian for her daughters and ordered them to be enrolled in the French convent school. Astorga protested that the girls were only four and five "and at this age, when they should be at their mother's side, they want to put them in a strict and rigorous school," where they might be subject to the snubs of more elite pupils. Nevertheless, despite her persistent complaints—that the school's director did not allow her the same visiting privileges as other mothers, that her daughters got sick from the harsh conditions and bad food, that she was not allowed to spend the money left over after paying tuition as she saw fit—the court consistently upheld the authority of the appointed guardian over that of the mother.[69]

Although judges usually interpreted the Partidas to award custody of natural children to their mothers rather than their fathers, there were times when concerns about their moral fitness, often closely related to their class standing, trumped that custom. In the late 1840s and early 1850s, around the same time that it became more difficult for unwed mothers and out-of-wedlock children to secure court orders recognizing paternity and requiring fathers to pay support, some judges began exonerating fathers of their responsibility to provide for children outside their custody. Antonia Gacitúa, who filed suit against Francisco Cerda in 1847, was poor enough to qualify for a public defender and none of her witnesses was recorded by the scribe as "don" or "doña" (and one was identified as an artisan). Nine months after she filed charges, Cerda was ordered to pay her ten pesos monthly to support their eight-year-old son, but on appeal the superior court reduced the amount to four pesos. At that point, he requested custody of the child. Gacitúa protested that he had never cared for the boy and clearly did not love him, but both the judge and the superior court ruled "that if the mother resists turning over the child, Don Francisco Cerda will be exonerated from paying the monthly stipend." She apparently decided to forgo child support because when he asked for enforcement of the sentence, two years from the start of the trial, the notary recorded that she had refused to turn over the boy.[70] The absence of further litigation suggests that Cerda would not insist on custody so long as he did not have to pay maintenance.

In one of the maintenance lawsuits discussed earlier in the chapter, defendant Juan Manuel Palacios had convinced the court of his accuser's "licentious conduct"; nonetheless, her witnesses also gave credible testimony that he had installed her in a room in a house he owned and paid her expenses. In 1855, the court, therefore, sentenced Palacios to monthly child support of fourteen pesos, not an inconsequential amount. However, they also gave Palacios the option to take custody of the child, which he did so as not to have to pay the money to the woman who had filed suit. Still denying he was the father, he claimed he had decided to perform an act of charity and save the boy from the bad moral influence of his mother. Unlike Gacitúa, Mercedes Ayala reluctantly conceded, but threatened to return to court should Palacios not educate the boy according to his social status: "Although it is very difficult for me to give up a son over to the authority of a person who has so forcefully resisted complying with the sacred obligations that both nature and the law impose upon a father; nevertheless, thinking of my desire for his future fate, I resign myself to do so." By turning over the boy, the court ruled that she also relinquished her legal rights to represent him in court and, because the father was awarded custody but not patria potestad, granted power of attorney to a third party.[71] In such cases, in return for fulfilling their legal duty to provide, unwed fathers were de facto granted at least limited authority over children by virtue of taking them into their homes.

The clarity of the law with respect to fathers' lacking authority over out-of-wedlock children favored mothers in custody disputes, but a few men found their way around the law, particularly by the 1850s. In a familiar pattern, after being sentenced to pay child support, Napoleon Charpín sued Elvira Jiménez for custody of their son in 1853. Charpín admitted that he did not have patria potestad but asked, "does that prevent one from satisfying the instincts of his heart and the impulses of his conscience to comply with the sacred duty that he has to look out for the helpless creature that he brought into being?"[72] Moreover, he pointed out that neither did the law explicitly grant patria potestad to unwed mothers, and therefore, the court should consider what was in the child's best interests. To that end, he claimed to have more resources and a more stable household. Jiménez tried to strengthen her case by pointing out that a father who had to be sued to provide child support was not very loving, that his wife could mistreat the child, and that Charpín (who was French) was not a Roman Catholic. As in other cases, the judge ruled in her favor simply because fathers did not enjoy authority over such children, but at this point Charpín's strategy took a very different turn. He successfully appealed to President Montt to use his executive powers to change the boy's legal status to legitimate. Such a procedure harkened back to the power of a king to legitimate a person by fiat and was not abolished in Chile until the passage of a civil code.[73] With that decree in hand, he appealed to the superior court, which recognized his patria potestad and awarded him custody. Filled with confidence, he next tried to have complete discretion over the mother's visitation rights, but the courts guaranteed her Sunday visits during school vacation periods.

Charpín appealed to a power above the courts; other fathers simply ignored judicial orders. In 1851, Tadeo Baeza sued for custody of Carolina, age eleven. When her mother, Rosario Ortíz, failed to appear for an oral hearing, he got a court order for police to seize the girl and put her in a convent boarding school for the duration of the lawsuit. At this point, Ortíz did appear, denying that Baeza was even the father and presenting a certificate from another school that her daughter was a pupil in good standing. The superior court upheld the temporary enrollment of Carolina in the convent school, but ordered the judge of first instance to proceed expeditiously and to consider only the question of whether or not Ortíz was a fit parent. When Baeza and the nuns complained that Ortíz was not respectful during her visits to the school, the judge suspended her visitation rights; once again, Ortíz had to appeal to the superior court to have her rights restored. After the presentation of witnesses favorable to both sides, Baeza asked that the case go to mediation. Each party chose a judge, and not surprisingly the two gave different recommendations. José Bernardo Cáceres, in a rather circular argument, asserted that a woman who appeared in a public court and scandalously challenged the alleged father's paternity was not a good influence on a young girl. Juan Carmona argued that Ortíz should be judged by her current, not past, reputation and that a daughter was always better off with a biological mother, even if she were single, than a stepmother (Baeza was married).[74]

By the time a tie-breaking judge decided in favor of Ortíz, Carolina had turned twelve and by law could request her own guardian. In a strategy similar to that of Charpín, Baeza apparently influenced her to name as guardian a friend of his, who immediately authorized her to leave the school with her father. The judicial order for him to turn the girl over to her mother reached authorities in Valparaíso one day after Baeza and their daughter had boarded a ship for Concepción. For the next two years, courts consistently upheld Ortiz's rights to custody, but the distance prevented her from getting authorities to enforce those rulings. Her brother, armed with a power of attorney, actually traveled to Concepción to retrieve the girl, but local officials there, citing the letter of the law, demurred that they could not turn her over to anyone except Ortíz herself. The last document signed by Ortíz was a new power of attorney to Antonio Dias in which, declaring that she was ill, she expressed "her will that her said daughter comes into her power through the intervention of the said Don Antonio, or if she [the mother] should have died that she [the daughter] be turned over to her brother Don Ramon Ortíz whom she has named as her executor and guardian of the minor." The last entry in the court transcripts was an order on June 5, 1855, to the constable of Concepción to turn the girl over to a person named by Dias, but given the absence of a notarized account of the order being fulfilled it is likely that Baeza successfully evaded the law yet again.[75]

Judges often doubted that poor women could be responsible mothers and, therefore, assumed that children were better off in schools or elite households. When Cadiz initially ended the child support he had been paying voluntarily to Mazuela, he sent her a letter in which he recommended that she turn the girls over to a respectable lady who could look after them: "if you do not want them to be as wretched as you, do as I tell you because with a lady to take charge of them they will not have to experience such want and you will free yourself from your sorrows."[76] Such arrangements were commonplace; the girls of course would have been expected to pay their way by working as servants. Half the custody disputes, therefore, were not between mothers and fathers, but rather involved the presence of poor children in wealthier households. In such cases, legitimate fathers were sometimes successful in retrieving their children, but poor, unmarried mothers had even less success against third parties than they had in disputes directly with fathers. Those who raised such children often resisted returning them to parents or other relatives unless they were reimbursed for the costs (explicitly identified as alimentos) that they allegedly had made in rearing and sometimes educating them. Although the Partidas appear to prohibit persons who raised the children of others to obligate service or reimbursement, the 1855 Civil Code charged parents who sued to reclaim children to pay the costs of their upbringing. As with the tightening of paternity proofs, judicial practice began to change prior to the promulgation of the new code.[77]

In 1848, José Rosa Donaire charged that when his wife was dying, she had left their three children in the care of José Ayala, who later refused to return them. Based upon the father's patria potestad, the judge gave Ayala three days to relinquish the children.[78] But even legitimate fathers were not always immediately successful. Esteban Valles filed suit in 1824 to recover his daughter from Ventura Santana, explaining that when he had married fifteen years earlier as a young man without resources, he had felt compelled to turn his daughter over to Santana, because this distant relative of his wife gave him three hundred pesos to help him start in an occupation. He claimed that since the girl turned ten, he had been trying to get her back, but that Santana demanded compensation for the investment he had made raising her. Santana, for his part, claimed to love the girl as if she were his own daughter and had therefore made her his sole heir. In this case, Valles had at least temporarily relinquished his paternal authority, while Santana projected himself as the responsible father figure. The case seemed to be moving toward a mediated agreement, but no final conclusion was recorded.[79]

In one sensational case, arising from the wartime crisis that had disrupted so many Chilean families, momentum seemed to be in favor of the father, but in the end the person in whose household local officials had placed the boy was absolved of any wrongdoing. The incident began in 1829 with a letter (almost certainly ghost-written) to the editor of the newspaper El Centinela, calling for justice on behalf of a father whose son had been kidnapped. José Cruz Salinas claimed that he and his family had settled in the town of Cauquenes in 1826, fleeing the barbarous Indians of southern Chile, only to find that the local officials were even more savage. While he was out of town working, he claimed, a local justice seized his son along with four other children and turned them over to a local military officer who passed them out among his friends "as if they were chickens and turkeys from the first fruits of the tithe." The printed reply of the editors promised to investigate, because "does your son not enjoy the liberty that the Nation promises to each man? . . . In Chile there are no slaves."[80] The court did immediately investigate the case, and Ramón Freire, who had been on campaign in the south at that time, even testified on behalf of Salinas. Several judges, however, reported that they had tried to settle the issue through mediation, and that they assumed that Salinas had been convinced that his son was better off in a wealthier household. The head of that household, Carlos Correa de Saa, testified that Salinas must have been put up to making the denunciation by rabble rousers, because he had taken in the nearly naked and uneducated boy only out of charity. When his father came to check on him, he continued, "We spoke of the harm of returning him to his former misfortune, at the memory of which the innocent child wailed."[81] The lady who had served as an intermediary in placing the child asserted that "in the southern provinces this is a common measure taken by the judges, especially since the war has increased misery and hunger to the point that even the parents themselves beg the local authorities to receive their children and they give them to the governors so that they are placed in service in exchange for their maintenance."[82] Seven months after the newspaper published the story, the superior court ruled no crime had been committed because Correa de Saa had indicated his willingness to turn the child over to his father, were that truly his wish. Therefore, the court did not order the restoration of the child to his father.

In cases such as that of Salinas and Correa de Saa, even in the relatively idealistic decade after independence, class and social status trumped parental authority. In the worldview of the judges, children were clearly better off in wealthy households whose heads would be good providers, even though it was common if unstated knowledge that their status was closer to that of servants than foster children.[83] Five cases in which unwed mothers tried to recover their children from unrelated individuals were inconclusive, implying that the status quo continued. In 1850, a man had left his natural daughter at a school, authorizing the headmistress as her caretaker, and then disappeared. When it became clear that the girl was simply working as a servant, her maternal relatives sued for custody. Her aunt had written affectionate notes in which she assured her niece they were filing legal petitions on her behalf, but these were intercepted by the headmistress and submitted to the court as evidence of foul play. Although the judge of first instance ruled that the girl should be turned over to her mother, the public defender of minors appealed the sentence on the grounds that the girl was better off in a school, apparently overlooking that the reputed headmistress had to have someone sign a legal brief on her behalf "because she did not know how to write." After an oral hearing, another judge ordered that the girl be put under the care of a third party until a final resolution of the case, but the last entries in the written transcript referred to the headmistress demanding to be reimbursed for three years of tuition before she would relinquish the girl.[84] As in other circumstances, the headmistress claimed that if deprived of the child, she should be compensated for having provided for the child's maintenance. In 1845, Juana Núñez sued priest Mariano Muñoz for support of their two illegitimate children; although the offspring of priests were not legally entitled to paternal support, someone went through the entire transcript striking out "sons" and writing in "nephews." In an oral hearing, he agreed to pay her two hundred pesos if she would turn the children over to him and forever relinquish visitation rights. Three years later the priest died, and Núñez sued to recover custody. Both the judge of first instance and the superior court, however, ruled that the priest's executor, his sister, was fulfilling her responsibility in caring for and educating the children and that they were better off with her than with their mother.[85]

In the only case in which a child was taken from a "foster" home and returned to the mother, the class positions were reversed. When Cruz Morán was called in 1832 to assist with a birth, the mother told her to leave the infant at the orphanage or on someone's doorstep. "I could not bear to see that creature abandoned," Morán later recounted, "so I proposed to doña Carmen that she give me the little girl and that my husband and I would raise her and treat her as a daughter." Twelve years later, in 1844, Inocencio María Pizarro, a merchant from Argentina who had been off working in Peru, returned to reclaim his daughter, because, he told the court, she would have entered puberty and he had to ensure that she was well cared for. In his colorful narrative, he told of risking his own life, traveling through war zones, and then searching the streets of Santiago "without any guide to find her other than paternal instinct." In one of the poorest neighborhoods, he encountered a young woman whose "delicate facial features, color, and all her natural appearance contrasted singularly with her ragged dress and the house where I found her." Given that the laws did not give patria potestad to natural fathers, the court ultimately ordered that the girl should be turned over to the mother, who had previously kept her identity secret to preserve her honor, but that the father could choose a school and supervise her education. Morán not only lost the child she considered as her own, but her own ingenuous testimony was used to deny her compensation for having raised her: "such an idea [to request compensation early in the lawsuit] had never even occurred to [Morán] because she considered her as her own daughter." "Her only desire was to have the girl"; Morán had confessed "that she feared they would take her and this loss would be the same as breaking her heart because she loved her so much, and so she hoped to keep her nearby by settling the case."[86]

In litigation over maintenance before 1850, judges rarely doubted charges of paternity brought by single mothers and consistently enforced the obligation of fathers to provide for their offspring. In awarding custody, however, the courts pursued various options depending upon the circumstances. Although they tended to favor mothers over fathers, judges often considered enrollment in boarding schools the best outcome for children. For those who could not afford the tuition, placement in a respectable household offered a good alternative. Once children were no longer in the home of one of their parents, moreover, the courts seriously considered claims of the investments made in feeding and rearing them. Fathers of out-of-wedlock children could not easily turn their provision of maintenance into grounds for custody, but third parties who served as providers might successfully resist relinquishing children unless they were reimbursed. Finally, by the 1850s, the courts began to allow fathers the choice between providing for children within their own homes or not at all. Whatever the outcome of a particular case, the state consistently exercised the prerogative to award custody and, when deemed necessary, to appoint legal guardians for children.

....

Those cases in which rulings departed from Spanish codes and local custom regarding paternal authority and responsibility foreshadowed the dramatic changes on child support, recognition of paternity, and the legitimation of children enacted by the new Civil Code that was passed in 1855 and took effect in 1857.[87] Although the code still required parents to provide for their children, it prohibited litigation against fathers (though not mothers) who denied paternity over offspring outside marriage.[88] Only an explicit declaration by a father to recognize his natural offspring was legally binding, in which case he acquired patria potestad along with the obligation to provide maintenance; in some circumstances such children might also inherit. Although the Civil Code clearly gave men greater leeway over the generational transmission of status and property, its effect on support (alimentos) is less clear. An illegitimate child could summon an alleged parent to an oral hearing to request a lesser form of recognition that carried only an obligation to provide the minimum support necessary for survival.[89] Although the code upheld the principle of mutual assistance among members of a legitimately constituted family, it placed greater emphasis upon filial obedience. Before an article outlining the responsibilities of parents toward their offspring, three articles underlined the duties of children, including the obligation to care for their elderly, infirm, or impoverished parents and grandparents. One of these pointedly reinforced patriarchal authority: "Legitimate children owe respect and obedience to their fathers and mothers; but they must especially submit to [the authority of] their fathers."[90]

The legislature could have tightened laws on support and paternity earlier had members believed that shoring up patriarchal authority, rather than enforcing paternal responsibility, was a priority. Indeed, congressional deliberations did result in the reform of another aspect of Spanish family law in 1820.[91] The Royal Marriage Pragmatic of 1776 had required parental consent for marriage, but minors who believed parental opposition was unjust or irrational could appeal to a judge.[92] Chilean senators identified such disputes as a source of disorder, claiming that "scandalous lawsuits over marital dissension are the most atrocious and fertile seedbed of enmity among families, of indelible defamation for posterity, of insubordination among children, and of the complete ruin of domestic economy." Nonetheless, they also acknowledged the harm that could result from the arbitrary exercise of parental authority against "the freedom of choice among marriage partners."[93] Therefore, they passed a new marriage pragmatic that established a family council, modeled on the French precedent, to arbitrate disagreements between parents and children. They represented the new pragmatic as a "compromise mitigating parental authority in a gentle, secret, and respectful manner by appealing to persons who, having the greatest interest in the happiness of both father and children, shall be governed only rationally by just, beneficent, and sincere motives."[94] Notably, the law also extended the jurisdiction to include offspring born out of wedlock who previously had not had to request parental permission to marry, but were presumably seen by the legislators as part of the larger family.[95] Although lawmakers established these procedures to govern parental authority over their children's marital plans soon after independence, they left to the discretion of judges the determination of paternity and enforcement of the responsibility to provide under Spanish law.

The independence struggles and subsequent civil wars had created deep divisions among the population and disrupted the networks and relations for providing care; the new state, therefore, regarded familial unification and political harmony as mutually reinforcing. In this context, maintenance lawsuits actually increased in the early nineteenth century as compared to the colonial period, and they were almost always successful. By midcentury, however, the priority of state agents shifted from mending families rent by warfare to reinforcing hierarchies of wealth and status. The process of reforming civil law in Chile, as in other Latin American nations, was essential to establishing liberal market economies governed more by contractual than natural obligations. Merchants and landowners, like the indignant patriarchs who had found themselves dragged into court in the early nineteenth century, claimed the right to control their assets. By the 1850s, they were able to persuade judges and lawmakers, most of whom came from a similar class standing, of the need for legal reform. It was certainly no coincidence that in the same decade Congress also codified procedures for returning sequestered assets to the heirs of royalists and reduced eligibility for military pensions. Poor women and children without access to family support networks, rather than being seen as evidence of the unraveling of social order, apparently came to be regarded as a potential labor force who should earn their keep by working, often in the households of their social betters.

CONCLUSION

Despite his own premature death, along with his childless brothers Juan José and Luis, José Miguel Carrera's wish that his name live on was fulfilled. Shortly before his execution in Mendoza, Mercedes Fontecilla had given birth to their fifth child, the only boy, whom they named after his father. Following in his father's footsteps, José Miguel Carrera Fontecilla threw himself into the turbulent politics of opposition to President Manuel Montt, participating in civil wars in 1851 and 1859 for which he was exiled twice to Peru. He would not return to Chile a second time, having died of an illness contracted in Lima in 1860. Though he had not yet reached the age of forty, he had already fathered eight children with his wife, Emilia Pinto Benavente, the niece of former president Francisco Antonio Pinto. In 1864, with the end of Montt's administration and the return of more conciliatory politics, Pinto Benavente received a special pension, equal to that for a widow of a brigadier general, "in honor of the eminent services provided to the fatherland by the Generals don José Miguel, don Ignacio, and don Juan José, and the Coronel don Luis Carrera."[1] Although they named their first son (the second child) José Miguel, it would be his younger brother Ignacio José Carrera Pinto (named after his great-grandfather) who earned greater renown in his generation. His glory and premature death came not from domestic conflict but during his service as an army captain in the War of the Pacific, Chile's second war against Peru and Bolivia from 1879 to 1883.

Javiera Carrera had seven children from her two marriages. None went on to the political prominence of their cousins, but their marriages picked up the tradition of reinforcing kin ties among the elite.[2] Interestingly, conservative politician José Antonio Alemparte Vial, related on his mother's side to both Presidents Prieto and Bulnes, married first Luisa Carrera Fontecilla and, after her death, her cousin Emilia de la Lastra, Javiera's granddaughter through her eldest son Manuel. Shortly after making his mother proud for his role in the commission that repatriated her brothers' remains to Chile, Pío tragically was killed by a relative after an argument; he had not married but had three children out of wedlock. Javiera had also taken pride in the educational attainments of Pedro (Perico) in the United States, and upon his return he married into one of Chile's most aristocratic families. His wife, Josefa Correa Toro, was the daughter of Juan de Dios Correa de Saa and the Countess María Nicolasa Toro y Dumont, whose own royalist mother, for whom Josefa was named, had rescued the family's entailed estate from wartime sequestration. Nevertheless, Pedro and Josefa had no children. Javiera's other children spent quieter lives, but their descendants multiplied and live on in Chile to this day.

By the 1840s, the generation that had reached adulthood before or during the independence struggles of the 1810s and survived to experience the initial decades of nation-state formation in Chile were reaching the end of their lives. With the passage of time, it became easier for the state to affirm the ideal image of the Chilean nation as a harmonious family. Reconciliation among rivals had begun with the amnesty declared by Bulnes in 1841, which paved the way for Freire's return to Chile. When O'Higgins died in Peru in 1842, a month after Congress had voted to pay him a lifetime salary, all government employees were ordered to dress in mourning for a week.[3] Two years later, the government announced its intention to repatriate his remains and commissioned a public statue and a painting to be hung in the "portrait gallery of the eminent men of the republic."[4] It would take another quarter of a century, however, to bring these plans to fruition.[5] Although the Supreme Court returned to the Urrejolas the Cucha-Cucha hacienda, Congress compensated Freire in 1845 for its loss and for his services to the nation's independence.[6] When he died in 1851, the government awarded a sum of 25,000 pesos to be divided between his widow and children in addition to their montepío pension and ordered two weeks of mourning in tribute to his role "in the most honourable deeds of our history and his having gloriously ended the war of independence with the capture of Chiloé."[7] Civilians who had contributed to the establishment of an independent government in Chile also received recognition. When conservative legislator and jurist Mariano Egaña passed away in 1846, Congress designated funds to purchase his books and establish a special collection in the National Library where his portrait and senate chair would also be displayed. In keeping with the state's recognition of the paternal duty to provide, Congress contributed another 1,500 pesos "for the relief of needy families related to the deceased

Senator don Mariano de Egaña whom he had been assisting with monthly pensions."[8]

During the 1850s, official commemoration of independence heroes and events accelerated. French engraver Narcisse Desmadryl and journalist Hermójenes de Irisarri published a two-volume collection of portraits and biographies of "notable men of Chile" in 1854 (from which are drawn several of the illustrations in this book). Irisarri's introduction provided an overview of Spanish colonization and the independence movement that, while not completely ignoring partisan divisions, certainly attempted to downplay such conflicts. Without identifying protagonists by name, he acknowledged that lack of unity had contributed to the patriot defeat in 1814 in Rancagua but insisted that "the bloody dust from the streets of that heroic town honored the brows of its illustrious defenders as much as could have the laurels of victory."[9] The biographical chapters did identify rivals by name, but each depicted its subject in a positive light. Liberal activist and poet Guillermo Matta accused O'Higgins of having ordered the assassination of a rival, for example, but concluded his homage with a call to forgive and unite: "Our emancipation has not been the work of a single man . . . So let us forget the animosities, the shameful factions." "Each man bears his own laurels," he continued, "and where Freire and O'Higgins are found there also appear the figures of Carrera, Rodríguez, Infante, Ibieta, and so many others, thus forming in unity the monument to our independence."[10] Several other contributing authors, such as Diego Barros Arana and Miguel Luis Amunátegui, soon gained renown among Chile's first generation of national historians.[11]

Statues of independence heroes also began to be erected in the 1850s. The first, a bronze cast of Freire, was commissioned privately in 1856 and allowed liberal opponents obliquely to critique the sitting Montt administration. With financial support from Congress, the municipality of Santiago unveiled statues of José Miguel Carrera in 1858 and Diego Portales in 1860. Newspapers noted the passing of other distinguished founding fathers: former presidents from rival parties José Joaquin Prieto in 1854 and Francisco Antonio Pinto in 1858. And 1860 marked the death of Juan Agustín Alcalde, the last survivor of the junta held fifty years earlier on September 18, which had become Chile's official independence day.[12]

The passing of this generation allowed for a shift in historical memory about the crisis of 1810 to 1830 that recast bitter rivals as common compatriots. Such commemorations overlooked how the independence struggles had pitted not only patriots against royalists and Americans against Spaniards but also Chileans against their fellow countrymen. Rather than feeling kinship with a "greater Chilean family," moreover, many had experienced and articulated the political conflict of the wars as one of family disruption. Ties of blood and marriage were critical in forging alliances that relied on trust and loyalty, as exemplified by the Carrera clan, but rivalries between kin groups divided the country's elite. The wars affected more humble as well as eminent households as members emigrated or were forcibly relocated, male providers volunteered or were pressed into military service, and officials seized family patrimony, from large estates to modest fishing boats. Political critique, therefore, was voiced in part against the failure of paternalism. Supporters of independence, in particular, accused royal officials of violating family ties in their campaign against suspected insurgents. After 1817, when patriots dominated the press and increasing swaths of territory, royalists were less able to publicize their grievances, but intercepted correspondence denounced the new authorities for similar abuses against allegedly innocent women and children. Courts martial confirm that Chilean officers carried out retributions against the relatives of their presumed enemies. Once they felt more confident of victory, however, patriot officials began to respond to the petitions from the dependents of émigrés with gestures such as granting support pensions that would allow leaders to publicly enact their self-proclaimed roles as fathers of the new nation.

Measures aimed at reconstruction and reconciliation, within the home as well as the homeland, initiated under the O'Higgins administration, became more institutionalized policies after 1822. Heads of state and legislators from the 1820s through the 1840s attempted to validate the legitimacy of their authority in part through their ability to both reunite and care for all members of the nation figured in familial terms. Achieving these goals was neither easy nor uncontested. Debates over how to handle claims to property seized during the independence war were particularly contentious. Initially the Chilean-born wives and children of émigrés were granted access to, if not full restitution of, sequestered assets. Gradually even former royalists themselves who returned and pledged their allegiance to the independent state were reincorporated into society and were successful to varying degrees in recovering property. The government similarly recognized the claims of widows and orphans of royal officers to the pensions they had been granted before 1810, opening the way for both the expansion of the montepío system to dependents of lower-ranking and long-serving veterans of independence and to the families of former rivals during periods of reconciliation. While the executive and legislative branches paternalistically committed state funds to providing for those who experienced financial losses in wartime, judges enforced the duty under Spanish law of Chilean fathers (or other family members) to support offspring in need, whether born in or out of wedlock and into their adulthood as well as during their minority. The family metaphors invoked during the independence era were more than rhetoric: they both reflected lived experience and shaped public policy.

In the 1850s, as the last of the nation's founding fathers passed away, the codification of laws regulating these matters of sequestration, pensions, and family maintenance marked a subtle but significant shift from an emphasis on paternal responsibility to patriarchal authority and control over patrimony. The 1853 consolidation of the internal debt reaffirmed the property rights of all who had been subject to sequestration, regardless of their opposition to independence, and secured the inheritances of patrician families. Comprehensive regulations of military pensions, which reinstated the requirement of state approval for marriages and their restriction to higher-ranking officers, reversed expansions of eligibility from the previous decades, and the government encouraged officers to accept early retirement packages in return for renouncing future claims to montepío funds. Finally, the Civil Code made the recognition of paternity largely a prerogative of fathers and emphasized filial obedience over paternal provision of care.

The next generation of Carreras and their peers, who came of age in the mid-nineteenth century, carried on a tradition of intra-elite marital alliances that would have been familiar to their grandparents. In addition to strategic decisions about property and the incorporation of new immigrants from England, France, and the United States instead of Spain, matches may have mended partisan conflicts that had divided separatists from royalists or pipiolos from pelucones. The son of unfortunate Dolores Aráoz, cousin of the Carreras and daughter-in-law of executed royalist Tomás de Figueroa, married into the Larraín family, and his son, Emiliano Figueroa Larraín, became president of Chile in 1925. A team of historians tracing the genealogies of the families who settled Chile in the colonial period even asserts that the country's population is literally "a greater family"; the sample family tree they provide of descendants from one settler does indeed include most of the prominent figures who appear in this book.[13] The same surnames recurred repeatedly in congressional records over the nineteenth century, as sons and nephews of earlier legislators were elected to office.

This post-1850 generation, however, lived in a society undergoing economic and cultural change. They courted at salons where they discussed the latest literature from Europe as well as national and global events.[14] Although Peru and Argentina remained common destinations for banished politicians, some used their time in exile to do grand tours of Europe or the United States, an increasingly common practice for elite young men regardless of their political activities. Some pursued professional careers, while others kept abreast of new commercial opportunities for agricultural and mineral exports from Chile, including nitrates for fertilizers. And they used their earnings to build stylish mansions in Santiago furnished with the latest fashions from Europe. These bourgeois trappings reflected a growing gap between the country's rich and poor, one that was increasingly cultural as well as economic. Rural families had been dislocated by ongoing warfare in the early nineteenth century. After 1850, no longer able to subsist as small proprietors or tenant farmers, increasing numbers migrated in search of employment: women to urban areas and men to the mining zones in the north.[15]

In contrast to the relatively broad networks of familial care reconfigured after the crisis of independence, the ability to establish legally recognized families was more closely tied to class after 1855, as insightfully explored by Nara Milanich.[16] The provisions of the Civil Code, which made filiation contingent upon paternal recognition, along with civic registries established in 1884, which recorded only births and marriages within legitimate households, created an underclass of poor Chileans, who lacked official kin ties and their corresponding civil status. In this era of ascendant liberalism, the state claimed expanding jurisdiction over the regulation of families, while also respecting the privacy and liberty of elite men to choose whether or not to recognize offspring and to provide them with an upbringing and education that would set them either on an upwardly or downwardly mobile path. Lawyers and legislators as well as female philanthropists continued to see family as a key to the country's stability and health, but the policies to achieve this goal differed from those of the nation's founding fathers. Increasing numbers of children were admitted to Santiago's public orphanage, but most were then put out to households or artisan workshops to be trained to earn their own livelihood. When custody disputes arose, the principle of reimbursement for the expenses entailed in raising such children, which had already begun to be articulated in the period before 1855, was enshrined in law. The parties simply disputed in court the degree to which children's labor had already compensated some of those costs.

Contestations over the boundaries of family and the respective duties of fathers, wives, children, and agents of the state continued to mark politics in Chile from the late nineteenth century to the present. Just as mobilization for the war against the Peru-Bolivia Confederation in the late 1830s had paved the way for the reincorporation of first widows into the montepío system and then discharged officers into the army, concerns over destitute dependents of the Chileans who sacrificed their lives during the War of the Pacific created pressure on the state to grant new benefits for military families and to establish civil registries of births and marriages.[17] The twentieth century was marked by the rise of labor movements in which a combative masculine ideal expressed in conflicts with bosses was in tension with the image of the responsible workingman who deserved wages sufficient to support a family. Gains in union rights, welfare benefits, and agrarian reform generally reinforced the norm of men as providers and made invisible the labor of women.[18] Finally, as during the wars from 1810 to 1830, Chileans experienced and articulated political conflict from the late twentieth into the twenty-first century partly in terms of family. Opponents of the government of Salvador Allende mobilized housewives to march, banging empty pots to symbolize their assertion that socialist policies deprived households of basic necessities, while mothers carrying placards with pictures of their disappeared children and women dancing the *cueca* without their missing partners called into question dictator Augusto Pinochet's claim he supported the traditional family.[19]

Although scholars have explored the salience of family in modern Chilean politics, its role in the period of independence and early state building throughout Latin America has received less attention. It is difficult, therefore, to assess the degree to which the developments explored in this book may have occurred outside Chile. Since Spanish American nations shared a common legal legacy, it seems likely that the adjudication of family law followed similar if not identical paths at least until the passage of new civil codes. Certainly the few studies on child support for out-of-wedlock offspring in early-nineteenth-century Mexico, Venezuela, and Nicaragua suggest that judges continued to enforce the paternal obligation to provide.[20] This book, however, has demonstrated that Spanish law as written and as interpreted by Chilean judges in the decades following independence posited this responsibility in much broader terms to encompass many dependents: wives, legitimate offspring into their adult lives, grandchildren, and parents. We need much more research into suits over alimentos in Spanish America throughout the nineteenth century in order to trace changes and continuities in the social and legal expectations of household providers.

Not only did judges enforce the legal obligation to provide within families, during the crisis created by the wars of independence Chileans invoked this principle in ways that held the state responsible as surrogate patriarch.

Such linkages become apparent only when we take seriously the family metaphors that infused the political rhetoric of the period and use them as clues for where to search for evidence of policies that affected family subsistence in the era before the welfare state. In the case of wartime Chile, the sequestration and subsequent use of enemy property resulted in an area of state policy and ultimately law in which both those advocating for permanent confiscation and those calling for restitution based their arguments on the consequences for wives and especially children. A study of Córdoba, Argentina, has documented the toll on families of property confiscations, but also the appeals by women and children to protect their shares and successful calls for restitution following the end of the Juan Manuel de Rosas regime.[21] Throughout Spanish America royalists and patriots as well as opposing parties in subsequent civil wars seized property, yet the aftermath of such measures and their implications for state policies related to family largely remains to be studied.[22]

Processes of political reconciliation offer another fruitful area for research that may uncover the less obvious linkages between family and state policy in the early national period. During independence struggles and subsequent civil conflict, Chilean women and children were rarely spared retribution, whether for their own political actions or those of their relations. When victors hoped to pave the way for more conciliatory politics, however, reaching out to the familial dependents of former opponents offered a low-risk opportunity to demonstrate official benevolence and test the waters before declaring broader pardons. Heads of state, such as Freire and Bulnes, highlighted their paternal aspirations through such measures, but we should not assume that Chilean leaders were unique in this regard. Eduardo Posada-Carbó has noted that amnesties for political crimes were common throughout Latin America during the nineteenth century and has called for greater attention to how they arose and were enforced.[23] Most likely, practices as well as rhetoric linking national unity to kinship and family were one important component.

In Chile, one way presidents reached out to the families of former rivals was to grant them military pensions, whether for the beneficiaries of royal officers in 1823, the widow and children of José Miguel Carrera in 1828, or the widows of officers who had been cashiered for their loyalty to Freire beginning in the late 1830s. At a broader level, of course, such pensions marked the most direct manner in which the state took on the paternal obligation to provide. Eligibility had been limited to high-ranking officers under the Spanish montepío system established in the late eighteenth century, but its provisions encompassed military families across the empire. Although postindependence governments throughout Spanish America were low on funds, it would be surprising if Chile were the only nation to continue some system of pensions for military widows and orphans. Chilean presidents until 1851 were all veteran officers of the independence war and recognized that attending to the well-being of military families would contribute to morale and discipline within the armed forces. Other commanders-in-chief throughout Spanish America likely shared such sentiments. Even if Chile were the only nation in the region not only to provide consistently for military dependents but even to expand eligibility, the institutionalization of a pension system cannot be attributed to the relative stability of the Portalian state after 1830, a factor often highlighted as Chilean exceptionality, because the critical legal reforms took place by 1829. Recovering the history of the montepío in Latin America from the late eighteenth century into the nineteenth century is critical, because studies in other parts of the Atlantic world have demonstrated that such benefits to veterans and their dependents were often precursors to broader state welfare programs.[24]

Royal paternalism is commonly regarded as a key element of the durability of Spanish colonialism in the Americas. That family and kinship remained central to postindependence societies and economies throughout the region is also undisputed. It is time to take seriously the familial rhetoric of the independence era, therefore, and to investigate its implications for state building and nationalism. Governance modeled on the family could invoke horizontal ties of national fraternity but also lessen the incongruity of inequalities under a republic: a husband could turn a marital dispute into a charge against his wife for treason, and military commanders were authorized to treat their soldiers as sons rather than as republican brethren. Although scholars should continue to build on important recent studies into citizenship claims advanced by subaltern men in early republican Latin America, we should also consider petitions from both women and men that appealed less to notions of rights than of protections.[25] Such avenues of inquiry further highlight gender as a relational concept that encompasses the exercises of and responses to dominance both between men and women as well as among men. Leaders of postindependence states in formation likely attempted to foster domestic peace in part through refashioning paternal practices from the colonial era that asserted authority over but also responsibility toward dependents. While the link between family and governance should be particularly evident in the adjudication of lawsuits over maintenance and custody and the provision of pensions, less obvious areas of inquiry such as property seizures and pardons are also likely to yield fruit-ful results. Undoubtedly, the policies pursued by other Latin American na-tions will in some cases parallel those analyzed in this book while differing in other aspects. Until larger comparisons can be drawn, both within the continent as well as to other revolutions of the era, the case of the "greater Chilean family" should not be taken as exceptional but rather serve as an in-vitation to explore more broadly the social dimensions of the political tran-sition to independence and nation-state formation.

The general contours of a patriarchal society might give the appearance of continuity between the colonial and republican eras, but closer examina-tion reveals the significant if subtle ways in which the politics of indepen-dence and state building both affected and responded to the experiences and demands of Chileans as members of families. In response to the toll that war and partisan reprisals wreaked upon households, initially presidents, legislators, and judges both took on and enforced paternal obligations to-ward dependents in order to provide for "the greater Chilean family." By the 1850s, confident that public and domestic order had been reestablished, they institutionalized the parameters of state supervision over family life and began to emphasize patriarchal authority over paternal responsibility.

....

As Javiera Carrera entered the final decade of her life, the Chilean Congress passed several pieces of legislation on property, pensions, and paternal au-thority that favored elite heads of household and reversed some of the gains made by unwed mothers and servicemen from the lower classes. Since 1821, when Congress authorized the executive to pardon royalist émigrés who repented and returned to Chile in order to "unite with our greater family," legislators and judges had repeatedly failed to provide clear guidelines to resolve lawsuits over property seized during the independence war. Only in 1853 did Congress finally pass a law that recognized almost all claims arising from confiscations; although most of the original owners had probably died, their heirs—principally members of elite families—could file claims to their patrimony. Two years later, legislators incorporated provisions for military pensions for widows and orphans, which had been passed piecemeal in the 1820s, into comprehensive military ordinances. Although the rules grand-fathered those who had already qualified for pensions based upon length of service rather than rank, strict control over marriages within the military would thereafter restrict the pool of eligible beneficiaries. Finally, Congress approved in 1855 a civil code that mixed liberal reforms with patriarchal principles. When it took effect in 1857, the section pertaining to the family not only reinforced the authority of male heads of household but even freed men from paternity investigations and placed greater emphasis on filial obedience, at least for minors, than the medieval Spanish code it replaced.

Although Javiera Carrera had left letters recording her thoughts and feelings on independence and her family's role in that movement, she remained silent on the larger transformations in law and policy on the family that paralleled the arc of her life during turbulent times. After living most of her life under Spanish law, she dictated her will in 1862, seven years after passage of the Chilean Civil Code, Article 1184 of which increased the proportion of an estate that the testator could freely distribute.[26] After pointedly noting that any claims by other heirs of her parents had been settled and that she had paid for the education of the grandchildren born out of wedlock to her deceased son Pío, she evenly divided half of her assets among her offspring (or their children) as required by the new law. Allowed to draw upon another quarter to increase shares to favored descendants, Javiera so identified her daughter Domitila along with several grandchildren; the grandson who sued her for support was conspicuously absent. Finally from the quarter that the law allowed her to distribute freely, she further increased the inheritance of her favorite granddaughter Adela Valdés de Prieto, "as a demonstration of my gratitude and compensation for the constant and affectionate care that she has shown me," and of her son Ignacio "so that he can provide for his large family." From this portion, she also asked that masses be said for her soul as well as the souls of her parents and other family members, left various legacies to six servants, and directed her executors to give 2,000 pesos to Tomás Reyes to carry out secret instructions. Ill but "in full and free use of reason," Javiera took advantage of a new law to provide for her direct descendants as well as reward those who had served her well or were in particular need, reflecting the family values with which she had been raised and her experiences during independence and nation building.[27]

APPENDIX

Chronology of Events in Chile

March 1, 1781	Javiera Carrera born
September 18, 1810	Governing junta established in Santiago in response to Napoleon's capture of Fernando VII
April 1, 1811	Unsuccessful royalist mutiny led by Tomás de Figueroa
July 4, 1811	Installation of Chilean Congress in Santiago
September 4, 1811	The Larraíns and Carreras purge Congress of conservatives
November 16, 1811	José Miguel Carrera takes charge of junta and dissolves Congress
March 27, 1813	First royal expedition sent by viceroy of Peru lands at Talcahuano
April 1813–July 1814	Patriots fight among themselves as well as against royal troops
August 12, 1814	Royal troops under command of Mariano Osorio land at Talcahuano
October 2, 1814	Battle of Rancagua; royalists take control of Santiago while many patriots flee over Andes
October 9, 1814	Mariano Osorio takes power as governor and captain general
November 1814	Suspected patriots sent to presidio on Juan Fernández Islands
December 1815	Francisco Casimiro Marcó del Pont takes office as governor and captain general
February 12, 1817	Battle of Chacabuco; Bernardo O'Higgins becomes supreme director
April–December 1817	Patriots hold Concepción; royalists hold Talcahuano
April 1817	José Miguel Carrera flees Buenos Aires to Montevideo
August 1817	Luis and Juan José Carrera imprisoned in Mendoza
January 1, 1818	O'Higgins formally declares independence, but evacuates civilians from southern Chile
March 19, 1818	Battle of Cancha Rayada; victory for royal troops
April 5, 1818	Battle of Maipú; victory for patriots

April 8, 1818	Execution of Luis and Juan José Carrera in Mendoza
October 20, 1818	Royal troops evacuate Concepción with civilians south into Mapuche territory
November 1818	Trial of Ana María Cotapos and others in Chile for corresponding with José Miguel Carrera
February 8, 1819	O'Higgins orders civilian refugees to return to region of Concepción
1819–1824	Patriot and royalist troops continue to skirmish in southern Chile
May 19, 1820	San Martín organizes expedition from Chile against Spanish Peru
September 4, 1821	José Miguel Carrera executed in Mendoza
January 28, 1823	Bernardo O'Higgins abdicates; Ramón Freire becomes supreme director
January–June 1824	Freire expedition against royal troops in Chiloe fails
May 1824	Javiera Carrera departs Montevideo for Chile
January 1826	Freire successfully defeats royal troops in Chiloe
August 1828	Congress passes liberal constitution
May 1828	Repatriation of the remains of José Miguel, Juan José, and Luis Carrera
January 31, 1829	Montepío law expands eligibility for military pensions for widows and orphans
May 1829	Presidential elections; Francisco Antonio Pinto wins, but conservatives dispute
October 1829	House of Representatives passes law to regulate lawsuits over property sequestration; never debated in Senate
April 17, 1830	Battle of Lircay; conservatives under José Joaquín Prieto defeat liberals under Ramón Freire
June 1831	José Joaquín Prieto elected president; Diego Portales serves as minister of the interior
May 25, 1833	Promulgation of conservative constitution
November 17, 1835	First Internal Debt Consolidation Act leaves out sequestered property
June 1836	José Joaquín Prieto reelected president
December 28, 1836	Chile declares war on Peru-Bolivia Confederation
October 6, 1837	Mutiny leads to assassination of Diego Portales
January 20, 1839	Battle of Yungay; Chile defeats Peru-Bolivia Confederation
June 1841	Manuel Bulnes elected president
April 25, 1844	Peace treaty in which Spain recognizes independence of Chile
June 1846	Manuel Bulnes reelected president
June 1851	Manuel Montt elected president

September 7, 1851	Civil war
December 8, 1851	Battle of Loncomilla; General Bulnes wins victory for Montt government
September 15, 1853	Second Debt Consolidation Act recognizes sequestered property
August 6, 1855	Passage of new military regulations, including montepío (pensions)
December 1855	Passage of Civil Code (takes effect in 1857)
June 1856	Manuel Montt reelected president
August 20, 1862	Javiera Carrera dies

NOTES

Abbreviations

AFL   Archivo Fernández Larraín
AHNCh   Archivo Histórico Nacional de Chile
CHDI   Colección de historiadores y de documentos relativos a la independencia de Chile
CM   Contaduría Mayor
FAJE   Fondo Archivo Jaime Eyzaguirre
FV   Fondos Varios
JC-Civ   Judiciales de Concepción—Causas Civiles
JS-Civ   Judiciales de Santiago—Causas Civiles
IC   Intendencia de Concepción
MG   Ministerio de Guerra
MI   Ministerio del Interior
MH   Ministerio de Hacienda
RA   Real Audiencia
RCHG   Revista Chilena de Historia y Geografía
SCL   Sesiones de los cuerpos lejislativos de la República de Chile, 1811–1845

Introduction

1. Copy of baptismal certificate in ANHCh, FV, vol. 237, pieza [pza.] 4533. Family patronyms are not consistent in the documents; for example, Carrera sometimes was preceded by de, de la, or y and sometimes not. I have opted for the most common modern usages for names and lowercase for don and doña except when quoting directly from a primary source.

2. Vicuña Mackenna, *Doña Javiera de Carrera*, 24.

3. Vicuña Mackenna, *Doña Javiera de Carrera*, 17.

4. Carrera, *Diario de José Miguel Carrera*, 32. All translations are the author's.

5. Lamar, "The Merchants of Chile, 1795–1823," 139–52, 166, 182–87; Lamar, " 'Choosing' Partible Inheritance"; Lamar, "Doing Business in the Age of Revolution"; Balmori and Oppenheimer, "Family Clusters."

6. Jocelyn-Holt Letelier, *La independencia de Chile*. On commerce and merchant families, see Cavieres Figueroa, *El comercio chileno en la economía-mundo colonial*; Cavieres Figueroa, *Servir al soberano sin detrimento del vasallo*.

7. Barbier, "Elite and Cadres in Bourbon Chile"; Bravo Lira, *El absolutismo ilustrado en Hispanoamérica, Chile (1760–1860)*; Jocelyn-Holt Letelier, *La independencia de Chile*, 74–95.

8. Another branch of the Larraín family was wealthier and most of its members remained loyal to the Crown; Felstiner, "The Larraín Family in the Independence of Chile," 86–102.

9. Cacho, "Reflexiones políticas sobre las provincias del Sur de la América meridonal."

10. For population estimates, see Collier, *Ideas and Politics of Chilean Independence, 1808–1833*, 4–7; Loveman, *Chile: The Legacy of Hispanic Capitalism*, 91 and 96.

11. León Solís, *Maloqueros y conchavadores*; Boccara, "Etnogénesis mapuche;" Pinto Rodríguez, "La Araucanía, 1750–1850;" Méndez Beltrán, "La organización de los parlamentos de indios en el siglo XVIII."

12. According to Arnold Bauer, 74 percent of the population was identified as being of Spanish descent in 1813; Bauer, *Chilean Rural Society from the Spanish Conquest to 1930*, 14–56. On the class structure, see also Loveman, *Chile: The Legacy of Hispanic Capitalism*, especially 90–100. There were indigenous communities in central Chile, and they went to court to defend their access to land, but they did not join together in collective rebellion; see León Solís, "Monarquistas hasta el ocaso."

13. On plebeian forms of resistance during the independence era, see León Solís, *Ni patriotas, ni realistas*.

14. Jocelyn-Holt Letelier, *El peso de la noche*, 33–34, 42, and 163–64.

15. For an overview see Jocelyn-Holt Letelier, *La independencia de Chile*, 157–93; Collier, *Ideas and Politics of Chilean Independence*. On the various and shifting plans for governance in this period, see Guerrero Lira, "Carácter de los primeros gobiernos nacionales, representación y mecanismos de legitimación, 1810–1814."

16. The Juan Fernández archipelago consists of three islands; the presidio was built in 1750 on the island now called Robinson Crusoe. During the colonial period, the prison was referred to as Juan Fernández.

17. For a thorough study of the period, which tries to avoid a nationalist interpretation of the reconquest as especially repressive, see Guerrero Lira, *La contrarrevolución de la independencia en Chile*.

18. Letter from Bernardo O'Higgins to Clemente Lantaño and Manuel Bulnes dated December 7, 1816; reprinted in *Archivo de don Bernardo O'Higgins*, vol. 7, 82.

19. For an assessment of the O'Higgins administration, see Collier, *Ideas and Politics of Chilean Independence*, 225–59.

20. *SCL*, vol. 8, 25.

21. The "anarchy" interpretation dated from Barros Arana, *Historia jeneral de Chile*, vols. 14–16. Collier highlights initial disorder but proposes that the presidency of Francisco Antonio Pinto in 1827 and the 1828 constitution had the potential to establish a moderately liberal government; Collier, *Ideas and Politics of Independence*, 287–322. The most forceful revisionist account, which identifies the period as democratic, is Salazar, *Construcción de Estado en Chile (1800–1837)*.

22. Quoted in Jocelyn-Holt Letelier, *El peso de la noche*, 137.

23. Jocelyn-Holt Letelier, *El peso de la noche*; Collier, *Chile: The Making of a Republic, 1830–1865*, 22–30. For an analysis of political philosophies in the period, see Stuven, *La seducción de un orden*.

24. Fliegelman, *Prodigals and Pilgrims*; Norton, *Founding Mothers and Fathers*.

25. Hunt, *The Family Romance of the French Revolution*.

26. For a call to revitalize family history by exploring the mutual constitution of families and social hierarchies, see Milanich, "Whither Family History?"

27. Desan, *The Family on Trial in Revolutionary France*; Heuer, *The Family and the Nation*.

28. Woloch, "War-Widows Pensions."

29. Heuer, *The Family and the Nation*, 29–40, 46, and 86–98.

30. Desan, *The Family on Trial in Revolutionary France*, especially 222–81; Heuer, *The Family and the Nation*, 13.

31. Fuchs, "Seduction, Paternity, and the Law in Fin de Siècle France," especially 951–53.

32. Heuer, *The Family and the Nation*, 127–40.

33. Woloch, "War-Widows Pensions," 241–50.

34. The post-revolutionary government in the United States also attempted to balance patriarchal authority and responsibility, but policies did not shift as dramatically as in France; Grossberg, *Governing the Hearth*; Kerber, *No Constitutional Right to Be Ladies*; and Cott, "Marriage and Women's Citizenship in the United States, 1830–1934."

35. For example, Salinas Meza, *El ideario femenino chileno*; Salinas Meza and Goicovic Donoso, "Amor, violencia y pasión en el Chile tradicional"; Salinas Meza, "Las otras mujeres"; Cavieres Figueroa, "Transformaciones económicas y sobrevivencia familiar."

36. Felstiner, "Kinship Politics in the Chilean Independence Movement," 58.

37. Felstiner, "Family Metaphors"; Felstiner, "The Larraín Family in the Independence of Chile." For analyses that track how similar elite families built first economic and then political power bases across several generations in various countries of Latin America, see Balmori, Voss, and Wortman, *Notable Family Networks in Latin America*; Balmori and Oppenheimer, "Family Clusters"; Balmori, "Family and Politics"; Lewin, *Politics and Parentela in Paraíba*.

38. For an important interpretation of the role of family in state formation in the period immediately following that analyzed in this book, see Milanich, *Children of Fate*. On politics and family in the twentieth century, see Rosemblatt, *Gendered Compromises*; Rosemblatt, "Forging Families;" Klubock, *Contested Communities*; Hutchison, *Labors Appropriate to Their Sex*; Tinsman, *The Politics of Gender, Sexuality, and Labor in the Chilean Agrarian Reform, 1950–1973*; Thomas, *Contesting Legitimacy in Chile*.

39. Stern, *The Secret History of Gender*; Premo, *Children of the Father King*.

40. On welfare, see, e.g., Salinas Meza, "Orphans and Family Disintegration in Chile"; Arrom, *Containing the Poor*; González, "Consuming Interests." On social policy, see, e.g., Seed, *To Love, Honor, and Obey in Colonial Mexico*; Socolow, "Acceptable Partners"; Chandler, *Social Assistance and Bureaucratic Politics*; Twinam, *Public Lives, Private Secrets*; Twinam, "The Church, the State, and the Abandoned"; Saether, "Bourbon Absolutism and Marriage Reform."

41. Cynthia Milton found that the establishment of the official pension system for widows of royal officials in 1765 reduced the ability of women to appeal directly to the king for charity; Milton, *The Many Meanings of Poverty*, 100–122.

42. Sinha, "Gender and Nation"; McClintock, "Family Feuds"; Sommer, *Foundational Fictions*; Viroli, *For Love of Country*.

43. For an analysis that contrasts the indifference to a national identity among the mass of poor Chileans pressed into military service with the articulation of a notion of rights earned in defending the homeland among the minority of volunteer soldiers, see Pinto Vallejos and Valdivia Ortiz de Zárate, *¿Chilenos todos?*, especially chapters 2, 3, and 6.

44. For a discussion of the flexibility of notions of familial relations in colonial Spanish America, see Premo, "Familiar."

45. My understanding of state formation has been informed by Corrigan and Sayer, *The Great Arch*; Joseph and Nugent, *Everyday Forms of State Formation*; Centeno and Ferraro, *State and Nation Making in Latin America and Spain*.

46. For an overview of the role of women in Chilean independence, see Serrano and Correa Gómez, "De patriota o sarracena a madre republicana." On women and gender during independence and early nation building in other parts of Latin America, see Brewster, "Women and the Spanish-American Wars of Independence"; Arrom, *The Women of Mexico City, 1790–1857*; Earle, "Rape and the Anxious Republic"; Davies, "Colonial Dependence and Sexual Difference"; Davies, Brewster, and Owen, *South American Independence*; Pani, " 'Ciudadana y muy ciudadana'?"; Brown, "Inca, Sailor, Soldier, King"; Brown, "Adventurers, Foreign Women and Masculinity in the Colombian Wars of Independence"; Hünefeldt, *Liberalism in the Bedroom*; Díaz, *Female Citizens, Patriarchs, and the Law in Venezuela, 1786–1904*; Chambers, *From Subjects to Citizens*; Chambers, "Private Crimes, Public Order"; Barragán, "The Spirit of Bolivian Law"; Chambers and Norling, "Choosing to be a Subject"; Zahler, *Ambitious Rebels*.

47. Pinto Vallejos and Valdivia Ortiz de Zárate, *¿Chilenos todos?*; Wood, "Guardias de la Nación."

48. Attention to popular participation and subsequent rights claims has been a critical trend in the historiography on independence since the 1990s; for a few examples, see Guardino, *Peasants, Politics, and the Formation of Mexico's National State*; Guardino, *The Time of Liberty*; Chambers, *From Subjects to Citizens*; Sabato, *The Many and the Few*; Warren, *Vagrants and Citizens*; Méndez, *The Plebeian Republic*; Salvatore, *Wandering Paysanos*; Lasso, *Myths of Harmony*. For the case of Chile, however, there has been less evidence that popular mobilization resulted in political gains; see Pinto Vallejos, "El rostro plebeyo de la independencia chilena, 1810–1830"; Pinto Vallejos and Valdivia Ortiz de Zárate, *¿Chilenos todos?*; León, *Ni patriotas, ni realistas*.

49. Loveman and Lira, *Las suaves cenizas del olvido*.

50. Haney and Pollard, *Families of a New World*, 3–4.

Chapter 1: Kin Mobilized for War

1. ANHCh, FV, vol. 237, pza. 4625.

2. ANHCh, FV, vol. 237, pza. 4629.

3. Letter dated in Concepción, April 20, 1810, ANHCh, FV, vol. 237, pza. 4593.

4. Letter dated April 18, 1812, ANHCh, FV, vol. 237, pza. 4594.

5. Letter dated in Lima, January 18, 1813, ANHCh, FV, vol. 237, pza. 4596.

6. ANHCh, FV, vol. 237, pza. 4596.

7. Letter dated in Lima, February 1, 1815, ANHCh, FV, vol. 237, pza. 4597.

8. ANHCh, FV, vol. 237, pza. 4470, Doña María de los Dolores Aráoz pide alimentos. With the exception of the letters cited in chapter 2, spelling of names has been modernized and made consistent. See chapter 3 on property seizures.

9. By contrast, the ancestors of most patriots had arrived in Chile later; Retamal Favereau, Celis Atria, and Muñoz Correa, *Familias fundadoras de Chile*, 50.

10. For information on the family, see Ondarza O., *Doña Javiera Carrera*; Cox, *Carrera, O'Higgins y San Martin*; Bragoni, *José Miguel Carrera*; and the novelized biography by Vidal, *Javiera Carrera*. For other analyses of the family correspondence, see Davies, Brewster, and Owen, *South American Independence*, 159–82; Soto Gutiérrez, "Entre el discurso historiográfico y la escritura íntima."

11. "Informe de García Carrasco sobre la conveniencia de transladar a otros empleos a diversos funcionarios," *CHDI*, vol. 25, 149.

12. *CHDI*, vol. 25, 348. His cousin Manuel Aráoz was appointed one of the captains.

13. Carrera, *Diario de José Miguel Carrera*, 31. The manuscript was written in 1815.

14. Memorandum to the junta dated May 11, 1812, *CHDI*, vol. 23, 31.

15. Carrera, *Diario de José Miguel Carrera*, 45–47.

16. Testimony of José Santiago Muñoz Bezanilla, *CHDI*, vol. 23, 24.

17. Bragoni, *José Miguel Carrera*, 115–58.

18. Moreno Martín, *Archivo del General José Miguel Carrera*, vol. 18, 160.

19. On the importance of correspondence and sociability to Spanish American politics in the early nineteenth century, see Chambers, "Letters and Salons."

20. *RCHG*, no. 12 (1913): 423–28.

21. Letter dated July 10, 1817, *RCHG*, no. 12 (1913): 432.

22. Letter dated July 24, 1817, *RCHG*, no. 12 (1913): 434; and letter dated August 6, 1817, ANHCh, FV, vol. 237, pza. 4648; also *RCHG*, no. 13 (1914): 457–60.

23. Letter dated July 8, 1817, *RCHG*, no. 12 (1913): 426.

24. Vicuña Mackenna, *El ostracismo de los Carreras*, in *Obras completas*, vol. 9, 105.

25. "Resumen documentado de la causa criminal seguida y sentenciada en el tribunal de la comisión militar de esta capital contra los reos Carlos Roberts, Juan Lagresse, Agustín Dragumette, Narciso Parchappe, y Marcos Mercher, por el delito de conspiración contra las supremas autoridades de las Provincias-Unidas, y de Chile en Sud América." Moreno Martín, *Archivo del General José Miguel Carrera*, vol. 22, 122, 125, and 133–38.

26. Vicuña Mackenna, *El ostracismo de los Carreras*, 105.

27. The confessions of Luis and Juan José Carrera are reprinted in Moreno Martín, *Archivo del General José Miguel Carrera*, vol. 19, 283, 287–89 and 295–97. See also Barros Arana, *Historia jeneral de Chile*, vol. 11, 223–40.

28. Letter dated December 26, 1817, in Moreno Martín, *Archivo del General José Miguel Carrera*, vol. 22, 207.

29. Barros Arana, *Historia jeneral de Chile*, vol. 11, 487–95.

30. Letter dated March 8, 1818, ANHCh, FV, vol. 237, pza. 4691.

31. Letter dated October 11, 1818, ANHCh, FV, vol. 237, pza. 4693. For notes dated April 11, 1818 (three days after the execution) from San Martín and O'Higgins requesting that no action be taken yet against Juan José and Luis Carrera, see ANHCh, FV, vol. 238-B, pza. 4186. Partisans of the Carreras charge that they knew it was too late to make any difference.

32. Luis simply asked that his surviving family members pay off his debts from his inheritance. Juan José asked that his share go to restore his wife's dowry and asked that an honest patriot write up the history of the Carreras; ANHCh, FV, vol. 238-B, pza. 4184.

33. Barros Arana, *Historia jeneral de Chile*, vol. 11, 496–510. On the trial and an account that asserts that officials in Mendoza had already received but suppressed news of the Maipú victory on the day of the execution, Bragoni, *José Miguel Carrera*, 159–207.

34. José Miguel Carrera, "A los chilenos," http://www.memoriachilena.cl/temas /documento_detalle.asp?id=MC0003656 (accessed May 15, 2013).

35. Letters dated June 19 and July 6, 1818, ANHCh, FV, vol. 237, pza. 4696 and 4697.

36. Letter dated October 11, 1818, ANHCh, FV, vol. 237, pza. 4694.

37. There are no letters between October 11, 1818, and August 23, 1819, in ANHCh, FV, vol. 237.

38. Reprinted in *RCHG*, no. 29 (1918): 253.

39. Statement of Fiscal Argomedo dated January 16, 1819, *RCHG*, no. 31 (1918): 142.

40. *RCHG*, no. 31 (1918): 145.

41. *RCHG*, no. 31 (1918): 150–51.

42. Quoted in Ondarza O., *Javiera Carrera*, 76.

43. His will can be found in ANHCh, FV, vol. 238-B, pza. 4193, reprinted in Moreno Martín, *Archivo del General José Miguel Carrera*, vol. 22, 192–94.

44. Letter dated October 26, 1820, ANHCh, FV, vol. 237, pza. 4703.

45. The Chilean representative in Buenos Aires informed O'Higgins of Javiera Carrera's disappearance on January 26, 1821; *Archivo de don Bernardo O'Higgins*, vol. 6, 192–93.

46. Letter dated May 20, 1821, ANHCh, FV, vol. 237, pza. 4708.

47. For a sympathetic account of Carrera's final campaigns by an Irishman, Mr. Yates, who fought under him, see the appendix to Graham, *Journal of a Residence in Chile*, 373–471.

48. Anonymous letter dated September 12, 1821, ANHCh, FV, vol. 238-B, pza. 4203.

49. Moreno Martín, *Archivo del General José Miguel Carrera*, vol. 22, 188, and *Archivo de don Bernardo O'Higgins*, vol. 6, 268–70.

50. For the correspondence between Javiera and her husband and son Pío during this period, see ANHCh, FV, vol. 237, pza. 4706–31.

51. Letter dated October 21, 1822, ANHCh, FV, vol. 237, pza. 4723.

52. Letter dated January 27, 1824, ANHCh, FV, vol. 237, pza. 4731.

53. Letter dated June 27 [1818] and included in the trial transcripts reprinted in *RCHG*, no. 29 (1918): 253.

54. Undated letter; *RCHG*, no. 12 (1914): 434. See also "Mi Javiera, siempre te seré una eterna reconocida por el cariño y cuidado con que a atiendes a mi pobre Juan." Undated letter; *RCHG*, no. 11 (1913): 220.

55. Letter of Tomasa Alonso Gamero de Muñoz to Javeria Carrera, September 9, 1817, ANHCh, FV, vol. 237, pza. 4673; also *RCHG*, no. 15 (1914): 57–59.

56. Letter dated November 23, 1817, ANHCh, FV, vol. 237, pza. 4678; *RCHG*, no. 15 (1914): 64–65.

57. Letter dated November 3, 1817, ANHCh, FV, vol. 237, pza. 4676; *RCHG*, no. 15 (1914): 61–62.

58. Letter dated October 8, 1817, ANHCh, FV, vol. 237, pza. 4675; *RCHG*, no. 15 (1914): 61; see pp. 57–67 for all of Alonso Gamero's letters to Javiera Carrera. Similarly after José Miguel's death, Javiera wrote to Juana Pino de Rivadavia to ask that she intercede on her behalf with her husband, Bernardino Rivadavia, in Argentina; letter from Pino de Rivadavia dated December 12, 1821, in Vergara Quiroz, *Cartas de mujeres en Chile*, 112.

59. Letters dated November 3 and 23, 1817, ANHCh, FV, vol. 237, pza. 4676 and 4678; *RCHG*, no. 15 (1914): 61–62 and 64–65.

60. Letter dated December 18, 1817, ANHCh, FV, vol. 237, pza. 4679; *RCHG*, no. 15 (1914): 66–67.

61. Two published versions of her appeals are undated, but one mentions the recent transfer of Juan José from San Luis to Mendoza and so likely was written in November, and another refers to assurances she had received thirty days earlier; *CHDI*, vol. 7, 128–30, and Moreno Martín, *Archivo del General José Miguel Carrera*, vol. 19, 154. For petitions dated November 15 and 20, 1817, to Director Pueyrredón in which Javiera Carrera requests that their asylum in the United Provinces be respected and that they not be sent to Chile, see Moreno Martín, *Archivo del General José Miguel Carrera*, vol. 19, 159–62.

62. Draft letter dated December 17, 1817, ANHCh, FV, vol. 237, pza. 4686; *RCHG*, no. 17 (1915): 240–41.

63. *CHDI*, vol. 7, 131–34; quote on 131.

64. Letter dated April 16, 1818, ANHCh, FV, vol. 237, pza. 4692.

65. Letter dated October 10, 1817, ANHCh, FV, vol. 237, pza. 4680; *RCHG*, no. 16 (1914): 407–9.

66. Letter dated November 14, 1817, ANHCh, FV, vol. 237, pza. 4681; *RCHG*, no. 16 (1914): 409–11.

67. Letter dated November 24, 1817, ANHCh, FV, vol. 237, pza. 4682; *RCHG*, no. 16 (1914): 411–14.

68. Letter dated March 8, 1818, ANHCh, FV, vol. 237, pza. 4691.

69. *CHDI*, vol. 7, 148–55; quote on 148–49.

70. Vicuña Mackenna, *El ostracismo de los Carreras*, 211.

71. Letter dated November 14, 1817, published in Moreno Martín, *Archivo del General José Miguel Carrera*, vol. 19, 157.

72. Letter dated November 24, 1817, ANHCh, FV, vol. 237, pza. 4682.

73. Letter dated November 14, 1817, ANHCh, FV, vol. 237, pza. 4681; *RCHG*, no. 16 (1914): 409–11; quote on 411.

74. Graham, *Journal of a Residence in Chile*, 249.

75. Letter dated October 11, 1818, ANHCh, FV, vol. 237, pza. 4694.

76. Letter dated June 1, 1817, ANHCh, FV, vol. 237, pza. 4662.

77. Italics indicate passages translated from code. Letter dated June 1, 1817, Moreno Martín, *Archivo del General José Miguel Carrera*, vol. 18, 219–21; section in code on p. 220 and deciphered by José Miguel Barros.

78. ANHCh, FV, vol. 237, pza. 4662.

79. Entry dated July 9, 1817, in the copybook of José Miguel Carrera, published in Moreno Martín, *Archivo del General José Miguel Carrera*, vol. 18, 270. For references to a plan to seek refuge in the United States, see letter from Javiera Carrera to Pedro Díaz de Valdés dated July 1, 1817, FV, vol. 237, pza. 4663; *RCHG*, no. 11 (1913): 220; letter from José

Miguel Carrera to Javiera Carrera, *RCHG*, no. 12 (1913): 423–25; letter from Ana María Cotapos to Javiera Carrera, undated but from Mendoza so likely May 1817, ANHCh, FV, vol. 237, pza. 4659; *RCHG* , no. 12 (1913): 434–35; letter from José Miguel Carrera to Javiera Carrera dated August 2, 1817, FV, vol. 237, pza. 4647; *RCHG*, no. 13 (1914): 454–56; and undated letter from Juan José Carrera to Javiera Carrera, FV, vol. 237, pza. 4669; *RCHG*, no. 13 (1914): 460–61.

80. Vicuña Mackenna, *El ostracismo de los Carreras*, 134; on his attempt to stay in Mendoza with his wife, see 33–34.

81. ANHCh, FV, vol. 237, pza. 4657; Moreno Martín, *Archivo del General José Miguel Carrera*, vol. 18, 149–52; quote on 151.

82. Undated letter in 1818, likely in August, from Juan José Carrera to Javiera Carrera, ANHCh, FV, vol. 237, pza. 4669.

83. Published in Moreno Martín, *Archivo del General José Miguel Carrera*, vol. 19, 84–86; quotes on 84 and 86.

84. Letter dated November 14, 1817, ANHCh, FV, vol. 237, pza. 4681; *RCHG* , no. 16 (1914): 409.

85. In a letter to Mercedes Fontecilla in April 1817, José Miguel approved of her returning to Chile, although he would miss her, and promised to try to raise funds for her journey; Moreno Martín, *Archivo del General José Miguel Carrera*, vol. 18, 156–57.

86. Quote from a letter dated October 26, 1820, from José Miguel Carrera to Javiera Carrera, ANHCh, FV, vol. 237, pza. 4703.

87. Letters dated February 6 and 20, 1821, ANHCh, FV, vol. 238-B, pza. 4201 and 4191; Vergara Quiroz, *Cartas de mujeres en Chile*, 106–9.

88. Moreno Martín, *Archivo del General José Miguel Carrera*, vol. 18, 157.

89. In the preface, he thanks his friend José Miguel Carrera Jr. for sharing these letters with him; Vicuña Mackenna, *El ostracismo de los Carrera*, 18 and 92.

90. Moreno Martín, *Archivo del General José Miguel Carrera*, vol. 18, 207.

91. Undated letter, probably late April 1817, ANHCh, FV, vol. 237, pza. 4643; *RCHG*, no. 11 (1913): 216.

92. Quoted in Ondarza O., *Javiera Carrera*, 102.

93. "Proceso por correspondencia subversiva contra doña Ana María Cotapos, doña Rosa Valdivieso, Pbro. don José de la Peña, don Tomás José de Urra y José Conde, 1817–1818," *RCHG*, no. 29 (1918): 272.

94. Moreno Martín, *Archivo del General José Miguel Carrera*, vol. 19, 295.

95. *RCHG*, no. 30 (1918): 114.

96. *RCHG*, no. 31 (1918): 150–51.

97. Moreno Martín, *Archivo del General José Miguel Carrera*, vol. 22, 88.

98. Moreno Martín, *Archivo del General José Miguel Carrera*, vol. 22, 88. There is no evidence, however, that Cotapos was forced to leave Santiago; Maria Graham, who stayed with the Cotapos family, said that Ana María spent five months in the convent where she met another widow, whose brother she would later marry; Graham, *Journal of a Residence in Chile*, 252.

99. *Archivo de don Bernardo O'Higgins*, vol. 6, 255.

100. *Archivo de don Bernardo O'Higgins*, vol. 5, 280.

101. *Archivo de don Bernardo O'Higgins*, vol. 6, 268–69. Javiera Carrera wrote that Fontecilla had complained that Zañartu was not fulfilling his promise to get her a

safe-conduct, which suggests that O'Higgins was slower to forgive; letter to Pedro Díaz de Valdés dated April 1, 1822, ANHCh, FV, vol. 237, pza. 4717; Vergara Quiroz, *Cartas de mujeres en Chile*, 128.

102. Graham, *Journal of a Residence in Chile*, 223.

103. She took her youngest child, Pedro, aged four, with her into exile, and her adult son from her first marriage accompanied her brothers.

104. Letters dated May 1, 20, and 31, 1810, in ANHCh, FV, vol. 237, pza. 4627, 4629, and 4630; Vergara Quiroz, *Cartas de mujeres en Chile*, 64–78.

105. Letters dated May 18 and 20, 1810, in ANHCh, FV, vol. 237, pza. 4628 and 4629.

106. Letters dated May 18, May 20, and June 25, 1810, in ANHCh, FV, vol. 237, pza. 4628, 4629, and 4631.

107. All the letters carry news of the children, the quote is from May 18, 1810, ANHCh, FV, vol. 237, pza. 4628.

108. Letters dated May 18, May 31, June 25, and July 2, 1810, ANHCh, FV, vol. 237, pza. 4628, 4630, 4631, and 4632.

109. Letter dated June 16, 1813, in Vergara Quiroz, *Cartas de mujeres en Chile*, 84–85. For correspondence about employment between patriot authorities and Díaz de Valdés, see Moreno Martín, *Archivo del General José Miguel Carrera*, vol. 2, 101 and 408–9.

110. ANHCh, FV, vol. 238-B, pza. 4237; Vergara Quiroz, *Cartas de mujeres en Chile*, 86.

111. Undated letter but with December 16 before signature, ANHCh, FV, vol. 238-B, pza. 4230; *RCHG*, no. 11 (1913): 202.

112. Letter dated October 5, [1814], ANHCh, FV, vol. 237, pza. 4633; *RCHG*, no. 11 (1913): 197.

113. Letter dated November 15, 1824, ANHCh, FV, vol. 238-B, pza. 4237; *RCHG*, no. 11 (1913): 198.

114. Undated letter but with December 16 before signature, ANHCh, FV, vol. 238-B, pza. 4230; *RCHG*, no. 11 (1913): 202.

115. Letter dated February 17, 1817, ANHCh, FV, vol. 237, pza. 4695; *RCHG*, no. 11 (1913): 205–8.

116. Letter dated July 1, 1817, ANHCh, FV, vol. 237, pza. 4663; *RCHG*, no. 11 (1913): 220.

117. Letter dated May 31, 1810, ANHCh, FV, vol. 237, pza. 4630.

118. Letter dated November 15, 1814, ANHCh, FV, vol. 238-B, pza. 4237; *RCHG*, no. 11 (1913): 199.

119. Letter dated June 4, 1817, ANHCh, FV, vol. 237, pza. 4667; *RCHG*, no. 1 (1911): 393.

120. ANHCh, FV, vol. 237, pza. 4700; Moreno Martín, *Archivo del General José Miguel Carrera*, vol. 22, 286–87.

121. Letter dated December 21, 1821, ANHCh, FV, vol. 237, pza. 4712.

122. Letter dated November 15, 1814, ANHCh, FV, vol. 238-B, pza. 4237; *RCHG*, no. 11 (1913): 202. See also letter dated October 5, 1814; *RCHG*, no. 11 (1913): 198.

123. Letter dated May 14, 1817, ANHCh, FV, vol. 237, pza. 4660; *RCHG*, no. 11 (1913): 219. She reported in a letter dated September 19, 1817, that Domitila was well but that her father would not let her come live with her; ANHCh, FV, vol. 237, pza. 4671; *RCHG*, no. 14 (1914): 338.

124. Letter dated December 12, 1816, ANHCh, FV, vol. 237, pza. 4636; *RCHG*, no. 11 (1913): 204.

125. Letter dated August 17, 1821, ANHCh, FV, vol. 237, pza. 4711; Vergara Quiroz, *Cartas de mujeres en Chile*, 111.

126. Letter dated February 8, 1822, ANHCh, FV, vol. 237, pza. 4715; Vergara Quiroz, *Cartas de mujeres en Chile*, 113.

127. Letter dated February 8, 1822, ANHCh, FV, vol. 237, pza. 4716; Vergara Quiroz, *Cartas de mujeres en Chile*, 126.

128. Undated letter, but he references the fall of O'Higgins, so likely from early 1823, ANHCh, FV, vol. 238-B, pza. 4195.

129. Quoted in Ondarza O., *Javiera Carrera*, 76.

130. Vicuña Mackenna, *Doña Javiera de Carrera*, 6, 19, and 41.

131. Vicuña Mackenna, *Doña Javiera de Carrera*, 21 and 36.

132. Vicente Grez, *Las mujeres de la independencia*, 23.

133. Adams, *Notable Latin American Women*, 123–32.

134. Letter dated July 30, 1817; ANHCh, FV, vol. 237, pza. 4666; *RCHG*, no. 1 (1911): 390–92. For a protest to the government for still holding onto one of the family's houses five months after his return from Juan Fernández, see ANHCh, FV, vol. 238-B, pza. 4178.

135. For example, letter dated April 1, 1817, to Mercedes Fontecilla, Moreno Martín, *Archivo del General José Miguel Carrera*, vol. 18, 156; letter dated December 26, 1817, to Ana María Cotapos; Moreno Martín, *Archivo del General José Miguel Carrera*, vol. 19, 207; and undated letter to Javiera Carrera, ANHCh, FV, vol. 237, pza 4643; *RCHG*, no. 11 (1913): 216.

136. Letter dated June 4, 1817, ANHCh, FV, vol. 237, pza. 4667; *RCHG*, no. 1 (1911): 393–94.

137. Letter dated September 19, 1817, ANHCh, FV, vol. 238-B, pza. 4181; *RCHG*, no. 1 (1911): 396.

138. Letter dated November 22, 1817, ANHCh, FV, vol. 237, pza. 4683; *RCHG*, no. 1 (1911): 396–98.

139. Letter dated February 28, 1818, ANHCh, FV, vol. 237, pza. 4690; *RCHG*, no. 1 (1911): 402–3.

140. Letter dated August 17, 1817, ANHCh, FV, vol. 237, pza. 4668; *RCHG*, no. 1 (1911): 395.

141. Letter dated June 4, 1817, ANHCh, FV, vol. 237, pza. 4667; *RCHG*, no. 1 (1911): 393–94.

142. Letter dated July 30, 1817, ANHCh, FV, vol. 237, pza. 4666; *RCHG*, no. 1 (1911): 390–92.

143. Moreno Martín, *Archivo del General José Miguel Carrera*, vol. 18, 259.

144. Letter dated November 22, 1817, ANHCh, FV, vol. 237, pza. 4683; *RCHG*, no. 1 (1911): 396–98.

145. Letter dated December 10, 1817, ANHCh, FV, vol. 237, pza. 4683; *RCHG*, no. 1 (1911): 398–400.

146. Letter dated September 7, 1817, Moreno Martín, *Archivo del General José Miguel Carrera*, vol. 19, 79.

147. Letter dated July 24, [1817], *RCHG*, no. 12 (1913): 434.

148. *CHDI*, vol. 7, 315–30.

149. Moreno Martín, *Archivo del General José Miguel Carrera*, vol. 22, 234–35.

150. Documents reproduced in the appendix to Vicuña Mackenna, El ostracismo de los Carrera, 489–90.

151. Moreno Martín, *Archivo del General José Miguel Carrera*, vol. 22, 246–48.

152. Letter from Javiera Carrera to Pedro Díaz de Valdés dated June 16, 1813, Vergara Quiroz, *Cartas de mujeres en Chile*, 84–85.

153. Letter dated February 17, 1817, ANHCh, FV, vol. 237, pza. 4695; *RCHG*, no. 11 (1913): 208.

154. ANHCh, FV, vol. 816, f. 41; Moreno Martín, *Archivo del General José Miguel Carrera*, vol. 22, 249.

155. Moreno Martín, *Archivo del General José Miguel Carrera*, vol. 22, 249–54.

156. See, for example, letters dated January 30, March 15, and May 14, 1822, ANHCh, FV, vol. 237, pza. 4714, 4718, and 4721.

157. Letter dated July 3, [1821], ANHCh, FV, vol. 237, pza. 4699.

158. For discussions of Domitila's care, see letter from Javiera Carrera to Pedro Díaz de Valdes, dated November 15, 1814, ANHCh, FV, vol. 238-B, pza. 4237; Vergara Quiroz, *Cartas de mujeres en Chile*, 87; undated letter from Díaz de Valdés to Javiera Carrera, FV, vol. 238-B, pza. 4230; *RCHG*, no. 11 (1913): 203; letters from Díaz de Valdés to Javiera Carrera dated February 8, 1820, and April 2, 1821, ANHCh, FV, vol. 237, pza. 4702 and 4706. The quote is from a letter from Díaz de Valdés to Javiera Carrera dated October 3, 1818, ANHCh, FV, vol. 237, pza. 4699; although in the same letter, Díaz de Valdés did write that he had asked permission from the government to send their son Santos to Javiera, but it was not granted.

159. Letter dated October 3, 1818, ANHCh, FV, vol. 237, pza. 4709.

160. Letter dated October 3, 1818, ANHCh, FV, vol. 237, pza. 4699. See also his letter dated February 8, 1820; ANHCh, FV, vol. 237, pza. 4702. In his testament, José Miguel Carrera stipulated that his son be educated in the United States, but his wish was not carried out; Moreno Martín, *Archivo del General José Miguel Carrera*, vol. 22, 193.

161. Letter dated August 24, 1819, ANHCh, FV, vol. 237, pza. 4701.

162. Letters from Javiera Carrera to Pío Díaz de Valdés y Carrera dated August 17, 1821, and February 8, 1822, ANHCh, FV, vol. 237, pza. 4711 and 4715; Vergara Quiroz, *Cartas de mujeres en Chile*, 111 and 113. Ignacio de la Carrera also assured his daughter that Díaz de Valdés was doing a good job of educating Pío; letter dated June 4, 1817, ANHCh, FV, vol. 237, pza. 4667.

163. *RCHG*, no. 30 (1918): 100.

164. Letter dated September 7, 1817, in Moreno Martín, *Archivo del General José Miguel Carrera*, vol. 19, 77–78.

165. Undated letter likely from April 1817, ANHCh, FV, vol. 237, pza. 4658; Moreno Martín, *Archivo del General José Miguel Carrera*, vol. 18, 158.

166. Quoted in Ondarza O., *Javiera Carrera*, 69.

167. For depictions of these and other women of the independence era, see Grez, *Las mujeres de la independencia*; Adams, *Notable Latin American Women*, 123–32; Chambers, " 'Drying Their Tears.' "

1. Diary of Manuel de Salas, *Archivo de don Bernardo O'Higgins*, vol. 19, 455.

2. Moreno Martín, *Archivo del General José Miguel Carrera*, vol. 22, 212–14 and 219.

3. *Archivo de don Bernardo O'Higgins*, vol. 19, 367–69.

4. *CHDI*, vol. 23, 192.

5. Urrejola Montenegro, *Los Urrejola de Concepción*, especially 91–95, 102–51, and 410–52.

6. Egaña, "El Chileno consolado en los presidios" [1825], *Archivo de don Bernardo O'Higgins*, vol. 20, 13.

7. Petition from Eyzaguirre dated February 15, 1815, AHNCh, FAJE, vol. 5, f. 76.

8. AHNCh, FAJE, vol. 5, f. 96.

9. For copies of petitions from the prisoners to the Spanish governors in 1815 and 1816, see AHNCh, FAJE, vol. 5, ff. 74–75, 96–99, and 100–103; and *Archivo de don Bernardo O'Higgins*, vol. 19, 254–75, 292–95, and 363.

10. *Archivo de don Bernardo O'Higgins*, vol. 19, 276.

11. Egaña, "El Chileno consolado en los presidios," 29 and 31. According to witness testimony presented by María Mercedes Salas, by the time her husband José Antonio Rojas was allowed to return to the mainland for medical treatment in October 1815, he was unable to walk, was incontinent, and could not follow normal conversation; *Archivo de don Bernardo O'Higgins*, vol. 19, 167–73.

12. *Archivo de don Bernardo O'Higgins*, vol. 19, 270.

13. AHNCh, FAJE, vol. 5, ff. 100–100v.

14. Egaña, "El Chileno consolado en los presidios," 11.

15. Egaña, "El Chileno consolado en los presidios," 5.

16. Egaña, "El Chileno consolado en los presidios," 25. For more on the tribulations of Egaña's family, see 71–75.

17. AHNCh, FAJE, vol. 5, ff. 71 and 73 (quote).

18. Egaña, "El Chileno consolado en los presidios," 25.

19. Egaña, "El Chileno consolado en los presidios," 250–56; quotes on 253.

20. AHNCh, FAJE, vol. 5, f. 51; also reprinted in Eyzaguirre, *Archivo de la familia Eyzaguirre*, 261.

21. AHNCh, FAJE, vol. 5, ff. 53–59; and Eyzaguirre, *Archivo de la familia Eyzaguirre*, 261–65.

22. AHNCh, FAJE, vol. 5, ff. 88–89. For an example of the prisoners themselves casting blame on José Miguel Carrera, see AHNCh, FAJE, vol. 5, f. 74.

23. AHNCh, FAJE, vol. 5, f. 66; and Eyzaguirre, *Archivo de la familia Eyzaguirre*, 266.

24. AHNCh, FAJE, vol. 5, f. 72.

25. Egaña, "El Chileno consolado en los presidios," 63. His wife and daughters were refused an audience with the captain general, but "by the force of tears" were able to meet with his secretary; Egaña, "El Chileno consolado en los presidios," 26.

26. *Archivo de don Bernardo O'Higgins*, vol. 19, 107.

27. *Archivo de don Bernardo O'Higgins*, vol. 19, 475–76. Eyzaguirre also sent detailed instructions to his wife on steps to be taken for his own defense; AHNCh, FAJE, vol. 5, ff. 80–81; and *Archivo de don Bernardo O'Higgins*, vol. 19, 304–7.

28. Vol. 1, no. 19 (March 23, 1815) in *Viva El Rey*, vol. 1, 125.

29. *Archivo de don Bernardo O'Higgins*, vol. 19, 194.

30. AHNCh, FAJE, vol. 5, ff. 100–103.

31. Underlined in the original; *Archivo de don Bernardo O'Higgins*, vol. 19, 395–96.

32. *Archivo de don Bernardo O'Higgins*, vol. 19, 398.

33. *Archivo de don Bernardo O'Higgins*, vol. 19, 400–410.

34. *Archivo de don Bernardo O'Higgins*, vol. 19, 178–80.

35. *Archivo de don Bernardo O'Higgins*, vol. 19, 85–91; quote on 87.

36. AHNCh, JS-Civ, leg. 374, pza. 1, Divorcio entre Doña Mercedes Fontecilla y Don Felipe Calderón (1814), f. 3.

37. AHNCh, JS-Civ, leg. 374, pza. 1, f. 38.

38. AHNCh, JS-Civ, leg. 374, pza. 1, f. 82v and 114; see also f. 38.

39. See, for example, decisions in AHNCh, JS-Civ, leg. 374, pza. 1, ff. 46, 49v, 69–70, and 79.

40. AHNCh, JS-Civ, leg. 374, pza. 1, f. 309.

41. AHNCh, JS-Civ, leg. 374, pza. 1, f. 310.

42. ANHCh, JS-Civ, leg. 192, pza. 1, Don Felipe Calderón contra su Mujer Doña Mercedes Fontecilla sobre perjuicios, ff. 5–6 and 12.

43. ANHCh, JS-Civ, leg. 192, pza. 1, 112v. Prisoner Manuel de Salas noted the arrival on Juan Fernández of Calderón along with thirty-three others on January 27, 1817, and Calderón is on the list of passengers picked up by a patriot ship on March 25, 1817; *Archivo de don Bernardo O'Higgins*, vol. 19, 426 and 474.

44. ANHCh, JS-Civ, leg. 192, pza. 1, ff. 17v and 18v.

45. ANHCh, JS-Civ, leg. 192, pza. 1, f. 31.

46. ANHCh, JS-Civ, leg. 192, pza. 1, f. 26.

47. ANHCh, JS-Civ, leg. 192, pza. 1, f. 59; the case was appended to the one already begun in 1817 but with a new cover sheet (f. 58) titled Causa de infidencia seguida por Don Felipe Calderón de la Barca contra Doña Mersedes Fuentesilla.

48. ANHCh, JS-Civ, leg. 192, pza. 1, ff. 60–67.

49. ANHCh, JS-Civ, leg. 192, pza. 1, ff. 72v–73. The position of fiscal had multiple duties in the Spanish and Spanish American judicial system; it will be translated as either prosecutor or state attorney.

50. ANHCh, JS-Civ, leg. 192, pza. 1, ff. 127–30.

51. ANHCh, JS-Civ, leg. 192, pza. 1, f. 142.

52. ANHCh, JS-Civ, leg. 192, pza. 1, f. 163.

53. ANHCh, JS-Civ, leg. 192, pza. 1, ff. 125v–126v.

54. ANHCh, JS-Civ, leg. 192, pza. 1, ff. 170–71.

55. ANHCh, JS-Civ, leg. 192, pza. 1, ff. 176v–177.

56. AHNCh, JS-Civ, leg. 374, pza. 1, Divorcio entre Doña Mercedes Fontecilla y Don Felipe Calderón (1814), f. 328v.

57. *Archivo de don Bernardo O'Higgins*, vol. 12, 211.

58. *Archivo de don Bernardo O'Higgins*, vol. 12, 210.

59. ANHCh, JS-Civ, leg. 192, pza. 1, f. 144.

60. *Archivo de don Bernardo O'Higgins*, vol. 18, 155–56.

61. *Archivo de don Bernardo O'Higgins*, vol. 7, 269. Similar warnings were issued about José Ignacio Plaza whose mother was a known royalist; *Archivo de don Bernardo O'Higgins*, vol. 8, 355.

62. From an edict quoted in Barros Arana, *Historia jeneral de Chile*, vol. 11, 325. A census of the diocese of Concepción in 1791 counted 105,114 inhabitants, though it probably reflected an undercount; Collier, *Ideas and Politics of Chilean Independence*, 4, note 2.

63. Barros Arana, *Historia jeneral de Chile*, vol. 12, 88–109.

64. AHNCh, MG, vol. 101, f. 26.

65. Arroyo Alvarado, *Historia de Chile*.

66. Barros Arana, *Historia jeneral de Chile*, vol. 12, 485–502; see also León Solís, *Ni patriotas, ni realistas*.

67. AHNCh, MG, vol. 49, Reclamos de Jefes en la Campaña del Sur, f. 10; Arroyo Alvarado, *Historia de Chile*, 59–60.

68. Ramón Arriagada, memorandum dated July 8, 1817, AHNCh, MG, vol. 23, IC (1817–1834), f. 192.

69. Letter dated December 4, 1819, from Freire to O'Higgins, ANHCh, MG, vol. 48, IC, Ejército del Sur (1817–1819), f. 341.

70. ANHCh, MG, vol. 6, Sumarios y Procesos, July 4, 1817, Causa Criminal seguida contra Feliz Bello acusado de llevarle víveres y correspondencia al enemigo.

71. ANHCh, MG, vol. 88, Sumarios y Procesos, pza. 1, January 16, 1819, Sumario seguido contra Martin Orrego y Tomás Encalada por protejer una partida enemiga, ff. 6–7. A guard sent Agustina Alarcón to his superior officer in August 1817 along with a report that every day women went to Talcahuano with food for their husbands and sons; letter from Pascual José Tenorio to Sargento Mayor Enrique Martínez dated August 3, 1817, *Archivo de don Bernardo O'Higgins*, vol. 28, 66.

72. ANHCh, MG, vol. 6, Sumarios y Procesos, October 14, 1817, Causa criminal contra el platero Juan José Caro por haber ocultado en su casa dos ocasiones a su hijo Antonio espia del enemigo de Talcaguano [sic], f. IV.

73. ANHCh, MG, vol. 6, Causa criminal contra Juan José Caro, f. 4–4v.

74. ANHCh, MG, vol. 6, Causa criminal contra Juan José Caro, ff. 2–2v.

75. ANHCh, MG, vol. 6, Causa criminal contra Juan José Caro, ff. 3–4.

76. ANHCh, MG, vol. 6, Causa criminal contra Juan José Caro, ff. 5–10.

77. ANHCh, MG, vol. 6, Causa criminal contra Juan José Caro, ff. 10v–11.

78. ANHCh, MG, vol. 6, Causa criminal contra Juan José Caro, f. 12v.

79. ANHCh, MG, vol. 6, Causa criminal contra Juan José Caro, ff. 16–17.

80. ANHCh, MG, vol. 6, Causa criminal contra Juan José Caro, ff. 19–19v.

81. Although I have not located trials by Spanish authorities of insurgent couriers, royal officials did prohibit such correspondence; see orders published in the royal gazette of Santiago on January 23 and February 19, 1816, in *Viva El Rey*, vol. 2, 51 and 83.

82. ANHCh, MG, vol. 6, Sumarios y Procesos, June 29, 1817, Causa criminal seguida contra las Garcias y demas comprendidos por la correspondencia que se les ha descubierto con los Enemigos de Talcaguano. I have left the original spellings, punctuation, and capitalizations or lack thereof in quotes from all these letters.

83. For the quote, ANHCh, MG, vol. 101, f. 91.

84. ANHCh, MG, vol. 101, f. 54v.

85. ANHCh, MG, vol. 101, f. 46.

86. ANHCh, MG, vol. 101, ff. 66–66v.

87. ANHCh, MG, vol. 101, ff. 29–29v. The recipient of the letter was presumably the merchant Manuel Pantoja who fled Concepción for Lima in 1817 but returned some

time before the end of 1822; ANHCh, JC-Civ, leg. 20, pza. 1, Autos sucitados por Don Manuel Pantoja sobre reclamar sus bienes en el ramo de secuestros de esta Provincia (1822). From the southern town of Los Angeles in 1820, María Rosa Mier, possibly a relation of Manuel de Mier, petitioned to have a sequester order on her inheritance from father José Mier lifted but no decision was recorded; ANHCh, JC-Civ, leg. 14, pza. 9, Doña Rosa Mier sobre que cese el embargo a una casa y demás propiedades.

88. ANHCh, MG, vol. 101, f. 2.

89. ANHCh, MG, vol. 101, f. 24.

90. ANHCh, MG, vol. 101, f. 34v.

91. ANHCh, MG, vol. 101, f. 29.

92. ANHCh, MG, vol. 101, f. 79v.

93. ANHCh, MG, vol. 101, f. 91v.

94. ANHCh, MG, vol. 101, f. 2.

95. ANHCh, MG, vol. 101, ff. 91v–92.

96. ANHCh, MG, vol. 7, August 19, 1817, Criminal contra Carmen Vernal [sic], Maria Gajardo i otras por mantener correspondencia con el enemigo, ff. 106–7.

97. For example, ANHCh, MG, vol. 101, f. 11, 13, 22, 26, and 27v.

98. Letter dated October 21, 1820, ANHCh, MG, vol. 101, f. 33.

99. Letter dated November 21, 1820, ANHCh, MG, vol. 101, f. 52.

100. Letter dated October 21, 1820, ANHCh, MG, vol. 101, f. 33.

101. Letter dated October 21, 1820, ANHCh, MG, vol. 101, f. 33.

102. Letter dated October 21, 1820, ANHCh, MG, vol. 101, f. 33v.

103. ANHCh, MG, vol. 6, Sumarios y Procesos, July 3, 1817, Causa criminal seguida contra Antonia Andariena por tener correspondencia con los Enemigos de Talcahuano.

104. ANHCh, MG, vol. 101, f. 17.

105. ANHCh, MG, vol. 101, f. 35.

106. ANHCh, MG, vol. 101, f. 91v.

107. ANHCh, MG, vol. 101, f. 50.

108. ANHCh, MG, vol. 101, f. 50v–51.

109. Memorandum dated August 16, 1821, ANHCh, MG, vol. 123, Sumarios y Procesos, pza. 3, Proceso formado contra Josefa Garrido por infidencia i espionaje.

110. ANHCh, MG, vol. 7, Criminal contra Carmen Vernal [sic], Maria Gajardo i otras, f. 110v.

111. ANHCh, MG, vol. 7, Criminal contra Carmen Vernal [sic], Maria Gajardo i otras, f. 106.

112. ANHCh, MG, vol. 7, Criminal contra Carmen Vernal [sic], Maria Gajardo i otras, f. 118.

113. ANHCh, MG, vol. 7, Criminal contra Carmen Vernal [sic], Maria Gajardo i otras, ff. 119v–20.

114. ANHCh, MG, vol. 7, Criminal contra Carmen Vernal [sic], Maria Gajardo i otras, f. 121.

115. ANHCh, MG, vol. 109, Sumarios y Procesos, pza. 11, 1820, Causa criminal seguida de oficio contra los Indibiduos de esta Plaza [Valdivia] que mantienen correspondencia con el faccioso Andrés Palacios, f. 52.

116. ANHCh, MG, vol. 109, pza. 11, ff. 7–8.

117. ANHCh, MG, vol. 109, pza. 11, ff. 4v–6v.

118. ANHCh, MG, vol. 109, pza. 11, ff. 8–10v and 15–16.

119. ANHCh, MG, vol. 109, pza. 11, f. 58.

120. ANHCh, MG, vol. 109, pza. 11, f. 47.

121. ANHCh, MG, vol. 109, pza. 11, f. 46.

122. ANHCh, MG, Sumarios y Procesos, vol. 123, pza. 3, Proceso formado contra Josefa Garrido por infidencia i espionaje.

123. ANHCh, MG, vol. 123, pza. 3.

124. *Archivo de don Bernardo O'Higgins*, vol. 7, 227–28 and 245–47. Enrique Larenas similarly requested a leave from La Serena in the north to check on his children in Concepción who were staying with a relative he feared might influence them to support the crown; *Archivo de don Bernardo O'Higgins*, vol. 8, 249.

125. *Archivo de don Bernardo O'Higgins*, vol. 8, 264.

126. *Archivo de don Bernardo O'Higgins*, vol. 8, 292. Pedro de Elgueta similarly inquired whether O'Higgins had any word of his father-in-law who had been imprisoned on the island of Quiriquina in the bay of Concepción; *Archivo de don Bernardo O'Higgins*, vol. 8, 276.

127. *Archivo de don Bernardo O'Higgins*, vol. 1, 261 and 274–79; *Archivo de don Bernardo O'Higgins*, vol. 21, 76–81.

128. Grez, *Las mujeres de la independencia*, 43–46, 71–73, and 93–94.

129. *Archivo de don Bernardo O'Higgins*, vol. 10, 312–13.

130. Article dated August 2, 1817, *Gazeta de Santiago de Chile*, *Archivo de don Bernardo O'Higgins*, vol. 10, 61–63.

131. ANHCh, MG, vol. 6, 1817, Causa criminal seguida contra Gabriela Velasques, por tener armas ocultas en su casa.

132. ANHCh, MH, vol. 56, Autos contra Manuel Donoso y Melchor Roxas, ff. 34–55; quote on f. 440v.

Chapter 3: *Émigrés, Refugees, and Property Seizures*

1. Vol. 2, no. 11, *Viva El Rey: Gazeta del Gobierno de Chile*, vol. 2, 48.

2. *Archivo de don Bernardo O'Higgins*, vol. 19, 203–4.

3. *Archivo de don Bernardo O'Higgins*, vol. 19, 200–207; on San Miguel, see 202–3.

4. Letter dated July 30, 1817, ANHCh, FV, vol. 237, pza. 4666; also *RCHG*, no. 1 (1911): 390–92.

5. Memorandum dated July 30, 1819, Moreno Martín, *Archivo del General José Miguel Carrera*, 215.

6. ANHCh, FV, vol. 237, pza. 4470.

7. Opinion dated June 19, 1817, ANHCh, FV, vol. 237, pza. 4470.

8. ANHCh, FV, vol. 237, pza. 4470.

9. On measures taken to provide for dependents affected by sequestration who might otherwise burden local communities during the American Revolution, see Brown, "The Confiscation and Disposition of Loyalists' Estates in Suffolk County Massachusetts." For claims of loyalist women for compensation by Britain, see Norton, "Eighteenth-Century American Women in Peace and War." In an analysis of James Martin's lawsuit to recover his mother's dowry property, Linda Kerber demonstrates

that the postrevolutionary government of the United States exempted women from both treason laws and loyalty oaths, hence allowing for reconciliation with loyalist children but the exclusion of women from the rights of citizenship; Kerber, *No Constitutional Right to Be Ladies*, 3–33. For a comparative case of two loyalist women attempting to reclaim property, see Chambers and Norling, "Choosing to Be a Subject." Women were successful in recovering confiscated property under the Rosas regime in early-nineteenth-century Argentina; Hingson, " 'Savages' into Supplicants."

10. For an overview of ecclesiastical divorce under Spanish law, see Arrom, *The Women of Mexico City, 1790–1857*, 206–58.

11. *Novísima Recopilación*, libro 12, título 7 on treason; libro 11, título 25 "de los sequestros y la administración de los bienes litigosos"; libro 11, título 13 "de la restitución in integrum." Also Partida VII, Title II, Laws I and IV; Burns, *Las Siete Partidas*, vol. 5, 1318. For other works on property seizures during Chilean independence, see Sergio Fernández Larraín, "Prólogo," *Archivo de don Bernardo O'Higgins*, vol. 24, ix–xxix; Cárdenas Gueudinot, "Secuestro de bienes de prófugos en el gobierno de O'Higgins"; Cárdenas Gueudinot, "O'Higgins y la Junta de Secuestros de Valparaíso." The Spanish Crown authorized the sale of sequestered property in Venezuela in late 1814; Stoan, *Pablo Morillo and Venezuela, 1815–1820*, 81–85 and 123–27.

12. *CHDI*, vol. 26, 33–34.

13. Guerrero Lira, *La contrarrevolución de la independencia en Chile*, 261–62.

14. For the list pertaining to Concepción, see *Archivo de don Bernardo O'Higgins*, vol. 19, 219–20.

15. *Archivo de don Bernardo O'Higgins*, vol. 19, 229.

16. For announcements of rentals of houses and estates, see *Archivo de don Bernardo O'Higgins*, vol. 19, 200–204 and 235–36. For cases in which this principle is articulated, see *CHDI*, vol. 35, 207, 280, 283–84, and 364.

17. Guerrero Lira, *La contrarrevolución de la independencia en Chile*, 266–67.

18. *Archivo de don Bernardo O'Higgins*, vol. 24, 43.

19. *Archivo de don Bernardo O'Higgins*, vol. 19, 207–8.

20. *Archivo de don Bernardo O'Higgins*, vol. 19, 208–11, quote on 209.

21. Fernández Larraín, "Prólogo," *Archivo de don Bernardo O'Higgins*, vol. 24, x.

22. ANHCh, CM, primera serie, Ejército Real (1813–1817), f. 470v.

23. *Boletín de las leyes i decretos del gobierno*, vol. 1, 14–16.

24. *Boletín de las leyes i decretos del gobierno*, vol. 1, 28–30.

25. *Archivo de don Bernardo O'Higgins*, vol. 24, 95–148.

26. *Archivo de don Bernardo O'Higgins*, vol. 7, 238.

27. *Archivo de don Bernardo O'Higgins*, vol. 8, 259–60.

28. Data taken from Molina A., *Bosquejo de la Hacienda Pública de Chile desde la Independencia hasta la fecha*, 56–57.

29. The broad charge does not indicate whether the commission could sell real estate as well as moveable items, a matter that would later become highly contentious; *Archivo de don Bernardo O'Higgins*, vol. 24, 13.

30. *Boletín de las leyes i decretos del gobierno*, vol. 1, 114–16.

31. *Boletín de las leyes i decretos del gobierno*, vol. 1, 300–303; see also 364–71.

32. ANHCh, MH, vol. 2, f. 224.

33. Report dated April 21, 1819, ANHCh, MH, vol. 56, f. 548v.

34. Report dated April 21, 1819, ANHCh, MH, vol. 56, ff. 548–48v.

35. *Archivo de don Bernardo O'Higgins*, vol. 19, 196.

36. *Archivo de don Bernardo O'Higgins*, vol. 19, 216–18.

37. *CHDI*, vol. 35, 173, 176, 178, 213, 227, 245, and 306.

38. Ley 78 de Toro; *Archivo de don Bernardo O'Higgins*, vol. 19, 234, 221–22, and 230–31.

39. *Archivo de don Bernardo O'Higgins*, vol. 19, 221–22, 224–28 and 235.

40. *Archivo de don Bernardo O'Higgins*, vol. 26, 130–31.

41. *Archivo de don Bernardo O'Higgins*, vol. 24, 45.

42. *Archivo de don Bernardo O'Higgins*, vol. 24, 48.

43. Letter dated April 30, 1817, *Archivo de don Bernardo O'Higgins*, vol. 24, 48.

44. *Archivo de don Bernardo O'Higgins*, vol. 24, 42.

45. ANHCh, MH, vol. 21, ff. 301–3. Mónica Zamora was unsuccessful in reclaiming a house whose buyers had fled the country before paying all they owed her; ANHCh, MH, vol. 57, ff. 227–28.

46. *Archivo de don Bernardo O'Higgins*, vol. 24, 149–50. Villota's brothers were patriots according to Lamar, "The Merchants of Chile, 1795–1823," 40–41.

47. ANHCh, MH, vol. 24, leg. 3, no. 62; ANHCh, JS-Civ, leg. 296, pza. 3, Chopitea contra Alvano sobre devolución de una casa.

48. ANHCh, MH, vol. 21, ff. 206–8. Catalina Castro was given a one-time payment of 250 pesos out of her husband's property to cover alimentos; *Archivo de don Bernardo O'Higgins*, vol. 26, 184–85. In a reversal of the gender pattern, Pedro Díaz de Valdés was granted 90 pesos a month from the estate of Ignacio de la Carrera; ANHCh, FV, vol. 816, Secuestro de los bienes del difunto Ignacio de la Carrera.

49. ANHCh, MH, vol. 21, ff. 161–66v. Perhaps a similar lack of influence accounts for the case of Margarita Pozo, who was given only ten days to find another place to live with her children; *Archivo de don Bernardo O'Higgins*, vol. 26, 76; ANHCh, CM, primera serie, tomo 1151, Secuestros (1815–1837), f. 98.

50. ANHCh, MH, vol. 56, ff. 191–92v.

51. Patriots often referred to Chilean-born royalists as "de-naturalized." ANHCh, MH, vol. 56, ff. 445–446v.

52. ANHCh, JS-Civ, leg. 833, pza 10, Sobre el secuestro de bienes del prófugo Don Melchor Rojas (1818).

53. *Archivo de don Bernardo O'Higgins*, vol. 26, 165.

54. Reprinted in *Archivo de don Bernardo O'Higgins*, vol. 26, 167. For similar cases, see *Archivo de don Bernardo O'Higgins*, vol. 26, 184–85.

55. *Archivo de don Bernardo O'Higgins*, vol. 24, 81.

56. ANHCh, MH, vol. 21, ff. 528–31v.

57. ANHCh, MG, vol. 34, Correspondencia del Gobierno Delegado con el Director Supremo (1817–1818), ff. 58–59.

58. ANHCh, CM, primera serie, tomo 1157, Secuestros (1819–1822), f. 130.

59. ANHCh, CM, primera serie, tomo 1152, Comisión de Secuestros (1816–1820), 171–72v. For the other case, see ANHCh, MH, vol. 21, ff. 455–59v.

60. For a comparative case of redistributing confiscated assets to build support for revolution, see Pashman, "The People's Property Law."

61. ANHCh, CM, primera serie, tomo 1154, Secuestros (1817–1819); MH, vol. 21, ff. 80–81, and MH, vol. 56, ff. 1–4.

62. ANHCh, JS-Civ, leg. 836, pza. 10, Dominga Romero y otros sobre la devolución de efectos secuestrados por el gobierno realista (1817).

63. ANHCh, MH, vol. 22, f. 243.

64. ANHCh, AFL, vol. 38, pza. 51. A similar request from Pedro Barnachea is missing a final determination; AFL, vol. 38, pza. 66.

65. ANHCh, RA, vol. 2263, pza. 1, María Cornelia Olivares sobre cumplimiento de la donación hecha por el Gobierno de una estancia que fue del realista fugado Juan Antonio Olate, situada en el título de Quilmo y Larquén, Chillán (1831). For an idealized description of Olivares, see Grez, Las mujeres de la independencia, 69–72.

66. Barros Arana, Historia jeneral de Chile, vol. 13, 689–90 and 779, note 15.

67. ANHCh, JS-Civ, leg. 1235, pza. 6, Don Vicente García con el Fisco sobre devolución de bienes secuestrados (1829), f. 3.

68. ANHCh, JS-Civ, leg. 1235, pza. 6, f. 4.

69. ANHCh, JS-Civ, leg. 1235, pza. 6, f. 8.

70. ANHCh, JS-Civ, leg. 1235, pza. 6, f. 13v.

71. ANHCh, CM, primera serie, tomo 1156, ff. 26–27.

72. ANHCh, CM, primera serie, tomo 1150, f. 281.

73. For twenty manuscript notations of amounts granted by O'Higgins in the wake of Chacabuco to women and disabled soldiers, see ANHCh, AFL, vol. 38, pza. 26.

74. Quoted in Barros Arana, Historia jeneral de Chile, vol. 11, 325.

75. Beauchef, Memorias militares para servir a la historia de la independencia de Chile, 111.

76. Archivo de don Bernardo O'Higgins, vol. 10, 403.

77. Memoranda and miscellaneous accounts about supporting the refugees can be found in ANHCh, CM, primera serie, tomo 1150, Secuestros (1814–1828), tomo 1152, Comisión de Secuestros (1816–1820), and tomo 1248, Solicitudes y decretos supremos (1817–1820).

78. ANHCh, CM, primera serie, tomo 1150, Secuestros (1814–1828), Reglamento sobre la emigración de Concepción, ff. 265–66.

79. ANHCh, MH, vol. 20, ff. 41–42v.

80. Letter dated June 28, 1818, ANHCh, CM, primera serie, tomo 1150, f. 263; MH, vol. 56, f. 42.

81. At the rate of one half real for every four pounds of meat; ANHCh, MH, vol. 56, f. 43.

82. ANHCh, CM, primera serie, tomo 1152, ff. 50–60.

83. ANHCh, CM, primera serie, tomo 1152, f. 60v.

84. ANHCh, MH, vol. 56, f. 46.

85. ANHCh, MH, vol. 56, f. 519.

86. Letter dated Dec. 16, 1818, ANHCh, CM, primera serie, tomo 1150, Secuestros (1814–1828), ff. 190v–191.

87. Letter dated June 28, 1819, ANHCh, CM, primera serie, tomo 1150, f. 263; MH, vol. 56, f. 42.

88. ANHCh, CM, primera serie, tomo 1152, f. 38.

89. ANHCh, CM, primera serie, tomo 1150, Secuestros (1814–1828), f. 274.

90. ANHCh, CM, primera serie, tomo 1152, f. 49.

91. ANHCh, JS-Civ, leg. 313, pza. 6, Doña Josefa Dumont sobre que se declare un mayorazgo a favor de Doña Nicolasa Toro su pupila (1818).

92. This is the last document I have been able to find on the case, but Nicolasa did become the next countess, so one can presume the family recovered the estate; ANHCh, MH, vol. 56, ff. 60–67. On the family, see Amunátegui y Solar, *La sociedad chilena del siglo XVIII*, vol. 3, 2 and 31–40.

93. The month and day are illegible; ANHCh, MH, vol. 56, f. 504.

94. Decree dated February 8, 1819, *Archivo de don Bernardo O'Higgins*, vol. 12, 67.

95. ANHCh, MH, vol. 56, f. 521.

96. ANHCh, MH, vol. 56, f. 522.

97. ANHCh, CM, primera serie, tomo 1149, ff. 191–92.

98. *Archivo de don Bernardo O'Higgins*, vol. 12, 127–28. By late 1819, both the new head of the Sequestration Commission, Rafael Bascuñán, and the treasury officials reported that the funds available to support refugees, in either cash or kind from sequestered property, had simply run out; ANHCh, MH, vol. 40, legajo 9, letra F, no. 83.

99. *SCL*, vol. 4, 353.

100. *SCL*, vol. 4, 353–54.

101. *SCL*, vol. 4, 354.

102. *SCL*, vol. 4, 355.

103. *SCL*, vol. 4, 358–59.

104. ANHCh, JS-Civ, leg. 140, pza. 7, Don Rafael Beltrán con Don Vicente Ovalle (hoy con su testamentaria) sobre reivindicación de la Hacienda del Parral enajenada por el Fisco.

105. *CHDI*, vol. 35, 531–32.

106. *SCL*, vol. 6, 160.

107. *CHDI*, vol. 35, 563.

108. ANHCh, CM, primera serie, vol. 1156, and Expediente iniciado por Doña Petrona Mantega sobre la entrega de la Hacienda del Manzano.

109. ANHCh, CM, vol. 1156, f. 67.

110. ANHCh, Expediente iniciado por doña Petrona Mantega , f. 4.

111. ANHCh, Expediente iniciado por doña Petrona Mantega , f. 9.

112. ANHCh, Expediente iniciado por doña Petrona Mantega, f. iv.

113. ANHCh, Expediente iniciado por doña Petrona Mantega, f. 16.

114. AHNCh, CM, primera serie, tomo 1149, Secuestros (1814–1828), ff. 237 and 241.

115. AHNCh, CM, primera serie, tomo 1149, f. 232.

116. AHNCh, CM, primera serie, tomo 1149, f. 234.

117. AHNCh, CM, primera serie, tomo 1149, f. 243v.

118. For his actions in Congress, see *SCL*, vol. 10, 150–54; *SCL*, vol. 11, 18–19; *SCL*, vol. 17, 271–73.

119. ANHCh, AFL, vol. 38, pza. 68.

120. Opinion dated June 18, 1822, ANHCh, AFL, vol. 38, pza. 68.

121. ANHCh, JS-Civ, leg. 764, pza. 23, Toribio Plaza con el Fisco sobre cobro de pesos por secuestro de bienes (1822), f. 10.

122. ANHCh, JS-Civ, leg. 764, pza. 23, f. 10v.

123. ANHCh, JS-Civ, leg. 764, pza. 23, f. 10v.

124. ANHCh, JC-Civ, leg. 48, pza. 5, Juan Bernardo Ruiz sobre reclamo de una casa (1821); ANHCh, JC-Civ, leg. 6, pza. 1, Autos sucitados por la Comisión de Secuestros sobre derecho a la casa de Don Juan Bernardo Ruiz (1822).

125. ANHCh, JC-Civ, leg. 20, pza. 1, Autos sucitados por Don Manuel Pantoja sobre reclamar sus bienes en el ramo de secuestros de esta Provincia (1822), f. 1.

126. ANHCh, MH, vol. 28, f. 17.

127. ANHCh, MH, vol. 28, ff. 21–22. For more on Fresno, his enterprises and family, see Salazar and Pinto, *Historia contemporánea de Chile*, vol. 4, 24–36.

Chapter 4: Constituting the Greater Chilean Family

1. Emphasis in the original; petition is undated, but followed by a marginal note dated September 23, 1823; Moreno Martín, *Archivo del General José Miguel Carrera*, vol. 22, 258–59.

2. Moreno Martín, *Archivo del General José Miguel Carrera*, vol. 22, 260–68 (treasury), 269 (sentence), and 272 (appeal of Barros).

3. She then proceeded to repeat language from the earlier writs filed by Aráoz; ANHCh, FV, vol. 237, pza. 4521.

4. *SCL*, vol. 7, 145.

5. *SCL*, vol. 7, 193–94.

6. *SCL*, vol. 7, 282–83.

7. *SCL*, vol. 7, 278–89.

8. *SCL*, vol. 7, 305.

9. *SCL*, vol. 11, 9, 18–19, 127, and 121; and AHNCh, MI, vol. 71, f. 171.

10. *SCL*, vol. 10, 407–8.

11. *SCL*, vol. 13, 37 and 116–17. For Mena's earlier involvement with sequestration, see the report published in *SCL*, vol. 4, 179–80.

12. *SCL*, vol. 17, 103.

13. *SCL*, vol. 17, 156–57.

14. *SCL*, vol. 17, 231.

15. *SCL*, vol. 17, 243.

16. *SCL*, vol. 17, 243.

17. *SCL*, vol. 17, 243.

18. *SCL*, vol. 17, 272.

19. *SCL*, vol. 17, 433.

20. *SCL*, vol. 17, 460–61.

21. Barros Arana, *Historia jeneral de Chile*, vol. 13, 730.

22. ANHCh, JC-Civ, leg. 119, pza. 9, Doña María Juana Maturana sobre secuestro de una casa y terrenos (1824), f. 1.

23. ANHCh, JC-Civ, leg. 106, pza. 1, Lujardo Elgueta con el Fisco sobre devolución de casa secuestrada (1825), f. 1.

24. ANHCh, JC-Civ, leg. 106, pza. 1, f. 2.

25. ANHCh, JC-Civ, leg. 35, pza. 4, Esteban Fonseca sobre vindicación y desembargo de su casa y tierras (1825), f. 3 (Fonseca) and f. 7 (Sierra).

26. ANHCh, JC-Civ, leg. 35, pza. 2, f. 8v, and MI, vol. 71, Oficios del Congreso (1824–1829), ff. 171–71v.

27. ANHCh, JC-Civ, leg. 5, pza. 6, Antonio Fernández sobre devolución de una hacienda secuestrada (1825). It is not clear whether the court was unaware of the 1820

decree retroactively legalizing sales or whether that applied only to the jurisdiction of Santiago.

28. ANHCh, JC-Civ, leg. 22, pza. 8, Autos sucitados por Doña Carmen Rojas sobre vindicación y desecuestro de dos ranchos que tiene en Talcahuano (1826); quote on f. 11. For another case of confusion, see ANHCh, JC-Civ, leg. 50, pza. 6, Marcela Sepúlveda y otras sobre devolución de casa y sitio secuestrados (1826).

29. ANHCh, JC-Civ, leg. 28, pza. 3, Doña María Jesús Arregui sobre devolución de casa y sitio secuestrados, f. 1.

30. ANHCh, JC-Civ, leg. 28, pza. 3, ff. 2v–3.

31. ANHCh, JC-Civ, leg. 28, pza. 3, f. 1.

32. ANHCh, JC-Civ, leg. 28, pza. 3, f. 3.

33. Entry dated December 19, 1826; ANHCh, IC, vol. 31, Correspondencia de la Municipalidad con los Colejios Electorales (1820–1828).

34. Entry dated December 19, 1826; ANHCh, IC, vol. 31.

35. Copy of a memorandum dated September 19, 1828; ANHCh, IC, vol. 31.

36. September 19, 1828; ANHCh, IC, vol. 31.

37. ANHCh, JC-Civ, leg. 85, pza. 7, Juana Navajete y compartes contra los Ministros de la Tesorería sobre entrega de un sitio secuestrado (1846), ff. 27 and 40–41.

38. ANHCh, RA, vol. 2263, pza. 1, María Cornelia Olivares sobre cumplimiento de la donación hecha por el Gobierno de una estancia que fue del realista fugado Juan Antonio Olate, situada en el título de Quilmo y Larquén, Chillán (1831), ff. 12v–13.

39. ANHCh, RA, vol. 2263, pza. 1, ff. 4–4v.

40. ANHCh, RA, vol. 2263, pza. 1, ff. 40–41.

41. AHNCh, JS-Civ, leg. 687, pza. 14, Modesto Novajas sobre devolución de una casa secuestrada en Valparaiso (1823), f. 19.

42. AHNCh, JS-Civ, leg. 687, pza. 14, ff. 77v–78.

43. AHNCh, JS-Civ, leg. 687, pza. 14, f. 47.

44. AHNCh, JS-Civ, leg. 687, pza. 14, f. 48.

45. AHNCh, JS-Civ, leg. 687, pza. 14, f. 58.

46. AHNCh, JS-Civ, leg. 687, pza. 14, ff. 75–76.

47. AHNCh, JS-Civ, leg. 687, pza. 14, ff. 75–76.

48. AHNCh, JS-Civ, leg. 687, pza. 14, ff. 59v–60.

49. AHNCh, JS-Civ, leg. 687, pza. 14, ff. 148v–49.

50. AHNCh, JS-Civ, leg. 693, pza. 13, Isidro Olave protesta cobro de pesos por secuestro de bienes (1820); quote on f. 39.

51. *Archivo de don Bernardo O'Higgins*, vol. 24, 130, 149, and 152–53.

52. Barros Arana, *Historia jeneral de Chile*, vol. 11, 13–16, footnote 4.

53. *Archivo de don Bernardo O'Higgins*, vol. 24, 184–85; *SCL*, vol. 5, 404–6.

54. ANHCh, RA, vol. 2114, pza. 1 y 3, Andrés Carlos de Vildósola sobre justificar su conducta política y que se le devuelvan los bienes secuestrados.

55. ANHCh, RA, vol. 2114, pza. 1 y 3, pza. 3, f. 15/37.

56. ANHCh, JS-Civ, leg. 945, pza. 1, Don Juan Bautista Uría con Don Pedro Chacón Morales sobre una casa (1828), quote on f. 87.

57. ANHCh, JS-Civ, leg. 945, pza. 1, f. 118v.

58. ANHCh, JS-Civ, leg. 945, pza. 1, f. 28.

59. ANHCh, JS-Civ, leg. 945, pza. 1, ff. 34–35.

60. For Chacón's arguments, see ANHCh, JS-Civ, leg. 945, pza. 1, ff. 94–113.

61. ANHCh, JS-Civ, leg. 945, pza. 1, f. 126.

62. For an example of multiple and contradictory orders on the same piece of property, see AHNCh, CM, primera serie, tomo 1154, Secuestros (1817–1819).

63. ANHCh, CM, primera serie, tomo 1157, Secuestros (1819–22), ff. 98–120.

64. ANHCh, JS-Civ, leg. 140, pza. 3, Expediente seguido por Don Rafael Beltrán con el Fisco sobre devolución de sus vienes, agregado a la causa que sigue el primero con Don [Paulino] Mackencie sobre devolución de un fundo (1827), 30v–31.

65. ANHCh, CM, primera serie, tomo 1157, Secuestros (1819–1822), ff. 116–17

66. ANHCh, JS-Civ, leg. 945, pza. 1, f.14v.

67. ANHCh, JS-Civ, leg. 378, pza. 2, Sobre la devolución de la hacienda Cucha-Cucha entregada a Ramón Freire, ff. 67v–68v.

68. SCL, vol. 19, 434. Returned émigré Manuel Antonio Figueroa petitioned Congress when the Prieto administration declined to take action on his petition for "incorporation in the greater [Chilean] family" under the terms of the 1821 act; SCL, vol. 20, 92 and 140–42.

69. SCL, vol. 21, 440.

70. SCL, vol. 21, 604 and SCL, vol. 22, 104.

71. SCL, vol. 23, 26.

72. Documentos parlamentarios, vol. 1, 238.

73. SCL, vol. 23, 333–35.

74. For the Senate discussions, see SCL, vol. 23, 350–440, and for the House of Representatives, see SCL, vol. 24, 165–202.

75. Anguita, Leyes promulgadas en Chile, vol. 1, 256–58, 281–82, and 318.

76. SCL, vol. 27, 155 and 315; SCL, vol. 28, 243.

77. The text of the 1844 treaty with Spain is available at: http://www.historia.uchile. cl/CDA/fh_article/0,1389,SCID%253D15698%2526ISID%253D563%2526PRT%253D15695 %2526JNID%253D12,00.html [accessed July 7, 2008].

78. Documentos parlamentarios, vol. 4, 283–306.

79. Letter dated June 30, 1853, in Documentos parlamentarios, vol. 4, 303.

80. Anguita, Leyes promulgadas en Chile, vol. 1, 616–17.

81. ANHCh, JS-Civ, leg. 378, pza. 2, f. 58.

82. ANHCh, JS-Civ, leg. 378, pza. 2, f. 3.

83. Letter dated September 2, 1824, from Freire to Juan de Dios Rivera; ANHCh, JS-Civ, vol. 378, pza. 2, Sobre la devolución de la hacienda Cucha-Cucha entregada a Ramón Freire, f. 1. For a history of the family and this estate, see Urrejola Montenegro, Los Urrejola de Concepción.

84. ANHCh, JS-Civ, leg. 378, pza. 2, f. 55.

85. ANHCh, JS-Civ, leg. 378, pza. 2, ff. 67v–68v.

86. For the questions the lawyer prepared for witnesses regarding the actions of these siblings, ANHCh, JS-Civ, leg. 378, pza. 2, f. 89.

87. ANHCh, JS-Civ, leg. 378, pza. 2, f. 72.

88. ANHCh, JS-Civ, leg. 378, pza. 2, f. 121.

89. The various measures related to the administration of the estate can be found in ANHCh, JC-Civ, leg. 90, pza. 11, Don Ramón Freire con el apoderado de los herederos de Don Alejandro Urrejola sobre posesión de hacienda secuestrada "Cucha-Cucha."

90. ANHCh, JC-Civ, leg. 134, pza. 2, Los herederos de don Alejandro Urrejola con los Ministros de la Tesorería principal sobre devolución de los bienes del finado Obispo don Agustín Urrejola.

91. Anguita, *Leyes promulgadas en Chile*, vol. 1, 465.

92. Cárdenas Gueudinot, "O'Higgins y la Junta de Secuestros de Valparaíso," 79–80. Marti Lamar identifies him as the Santiago merchant with the tenth greatest volume of trade; Lamar, "Doing Business in the Age of Revolution," 91.

93. AHNCh, MH, vol. 21, ff. 206–10.

94. Letter from San Martín to José Ignacio de Zenteno; *Archivo de don Bernardo O'Higgins*, vol. 9, 151–57.

95. The amount of 10,000 pesos is recorded in the trial record, but Gueudinot says the total was 40,000 pesos. ANHCh, MG, vol. 75, no. 14, Sumario criminal contra el Español Rafael Beltrán por obstinado en el Sistema Real (1818); Cárdenas Gueudinot, "Secuestro de bienes de prófugos en el gobierno de O'Higgins," 109–16; Cárdenas Gueudinot, "O'Higgins y la Junta de Secuestros de Valparaíso," 77–86.

96. ANHCh, MG, vol. 75, no. 14; ANHCh, JS-Civ, leg. 140, pza. 4, Causa promovida por Don Rafael Beltrán contra el Señor Albacea de Doña Ignacia Valdés sobre nulidad del Remate de la Hacienda de las Balzas.

97. ANHCh, JS-Civ, leg. 140, pza. 7, Don Rafael Beltrán con Don Vicente Ovalle (hoy con su testamentaria) sobre reivindicación de la Hacienda del Parral enajenada por el Fisco, f. 10.

98. ANHCh, JS-Civ, leg. 140, pza. 7, f. 143.

99. Even former business partners had little positive to say about Beltrán; ANHCh, AFL, vol. 77, Secuestro de Bucalemu (1817–1823), especially ff. 93–95 and 98–99.

100. For a brief overview of Chopitea's life and political adventures, see Amunátegui y Solar, "Una víctima de la Patria Vieja," 368–72. Lamar lists him as the Santiago merchant with the greatest volume of commerce in the late colonial period; Lamar, "Doing Business in the Age of Revolution," 91.

101. *Archivo de don Bernardo O'Higgins*, vol. 19, 215.

102. *Archivo de don Bernardo O'Higgins*, vol. 24, 109–10, 115, 120, 127–28, 141, and 148–49.

103. *Archivo de don Bernardo O'Higgins*, vol. 24, 148–49; ANHCh, MH, vol. 22, leg. 3, no. 62.

104. *Archivo de don Bernardo O'Higgins*, vol. 26, 128–41.

105. Cárdenas Gueudinot, "O'Higgins y la Junta de Secuestros de Valparaíso," 79–80.

106. ANHCh, MH, vol. 22, leg. 3, no. 62; ANHCh, JS-Civ, leg. 296, pza. 3, Chopitea contra Alvano sobre devolución de una casa.

107. ANHCh, JS-Civ, leg. 1550, pza. 1, Don Pedro Nicolás de Chopitea con el Fisco sobre que se declare por alzado cualesquiera secuestro que se hubiese hecho en sus bienes por lo respectivo a dependencias activas, ff. 3–4.

108. ANHCh, JS-Civ, leg. 1550, pza. 1, f. 13.

109. ANHCh, JS-Civ, leg. 1550, pza. 1, f. 3v.

110. ANHCh, JS-Civ, leg. 1550, pza. 1, ff. 16–17.

111. ANHCh, JS-Civ, leg. 1550, pza. 1, f. 42.

112. ANHCh, JS-Civ, leg. 1550, pza. 1, ff. 23–26; *Archivo de don Bernardo O'Higgins*, vol. 26, 138.

113. ANHCh, JS-Civ, leg. 1550, pza. 1, f. 43 and 51v; for the text of the law passed on Nov. 17, 1835 and specifically Article 2, Number 9, see Anguita, *Leyes promulgadas en Chile*, vol. 1, 256–58.

114. ANHCh, JS-Civ, leg. 296, pza 3, f. 117v.

115. ANHCh, JS-Civ, leg. 296, pza 3, ff. 118v–21v. For the case of the Castro family, whose lawsuit was also unsuccessful in the 1840s, see *Gaceta de los Tribunales* [vol. 1], no. 67 (April 22, 1843), 1; *SCL*, vol. 33, 300.

116. *Gaceta de los Tribunales*, vol. 13, no. 644 (December 16, 1855), 5545; vol. 13, no. 657 (March 17, 1855), 5743; vol. 15, no. 700 (January 12, 1856), 6411; vol. 15, no. 707 (March 1, 1856), 6510; and vol. 15, no. 749 (December 20, 1856), 7182. On Ascasivar in Spain, see Archivo General de Indias (Sevilla), CHILE 427 (1811–1836) expedientes e instancias de parte sobre Real Hacienda, unnumbered document from December 1823, CHILE 407, Exp. 44, and Archivo Histórico Nacional (Madrid), ESTADO 6317, Orden de Isabel la Católica, Exp. 93. An initial sentence in favor of Pedro Félix Vicuña was overturned only on the grounds that one of the documents showed evidence of tampering; AHNCh, JS-Civ., leg. 1521, pza. 2, Pedro Félix Vicuña solicita que el Fisco le indemnice el valor de los bienes secuestrados a su tío (1855); *Gaceta de los Tribunales*, vol. 15, no. 734 (September 6, 1856), 6941.

117. *Gaceta de los Tribunales*, vol. 15, no. 741 (October 25, 1856), 7053–54.

118. *Gaceta de los Tribunales*, vol. 15, no. 722 (June 14, 1856), 6751; *Gaceta de los Tribunales*, vol. 15, no. 731 (August 16, 1856), 6894.

119. *Documentos parlamentarios*, vol. 9, 417.

Chapter 5: Protecting Soldiers' Patrimony

1. Letter dated April 12, 1828, ANHCh, FV, vol. 238, pza. 4199; Moreno Martín, *Archivo del General José Miguel Carrera*, vol. 27, 248.

2. Letter dated May 1, 1828; Moreno Martín, *Archivo del General José Miguel Carrera*, vol. 27, 250.

3. Moreno Martín, *Archivo del General José Miguel Carrera*, vol. 27, 250.

4. ANHCh, MG, vol. 150, Doña Mercedes Fuentecilla [sic], viuda del Brigadier Don José Miguel Carrera (1828), ff. 248–49.

5. As shorthand throughout this chapter, military pension and montepío will be used interchangeably to refer to pensions for widows and orphans rather than those for retired military personnel. Under Spanish and Spanish American law, children whose father was deceased were considered "orphans" even though their mother might still be living. The 1796 montepío regulations were reprinted in Varas, *Recopilación de leyes*, vol. 3, 309–51. For historical analyses of the montepío, see Vergara Quiroz, *Historia social del ejército de Chile*; Chandler, *Social Assistance and Bureaucratic Politics*; Miller, "Bourbon Social Engineering." For disability benefits claimed by career soldiers in early nineteenth-century Chile, see Pinto Vallejos and Valdivia Ortiz de Zárate, *¿Chilenos todos?*, 264–79.

6. The primary sources for this chapter are the 354 applications for montepío pensions between 1819 and 1855, seven civil lawsuits contesting rejected applications, and legislative debates.

7. Anderson, *Imagined Communities*; Viroli, *For Love of Country*.

8. ANHCh, MG, vol. 150, Doña María Luisa Benavente, madre del Capitán Don José Ignacio Ibieta (1826), f. 124v.

9. ANHCh, MG, vol. 150, Benavente, f. 127.

10. Dependents of an officer even below the rank of captain qualified if he died in battle; chapter 8, article 6 of the 1796 regulations; Varas, *Recopilación de leyes*, vol. 3, 322.

11. ANHCh, MG, vol. 212, Doña María del Tránsito Montenegro, madre del Subteniente Don Juan José Figueroa (1834), f. 9.

12. ANHCh, MG, vol. 179, Doña [María del] Rosario Fernández Valdivieso, madre del Teniente Coronel Don Manuel Jordán (1830), f. 3.

13. ANHCh, MG, vol. 212, Doña Josefa Claverías, madre del Teniente Don Nicolás Gorigoitía (1834), f. 171.

14. ANHCh, MG, vol. 92, Doña Rafaela Barba, viuda del Capitán Don Pedro López (1823).

15. ANHCh, MG, vol. 302, Doña Martina Gómez, viuda del Subteniente Don José Santos Muñoz (1840), ff. 22v–23.

16. ANHCh, MG, vol. 179, Doña Dolores Maturano, viuda del Capitán Don José Aguila (1829), f. 11.

17. ANHCh, MG, vol. 179, Maturano, f. 6.

18. *Archivo de don Bernardo O'Higgins*, vol. 10, 271.

19. ANHCh, MG, vol. 212, Doña Quiteria Varas y Recabarren, viuda del General Don José María Benavente (1834).

20. Decree dated March 28, 1817; Anguita, *Leyes promulgadas en Chile*, vol. 1, 46. The pension for beneficiaries of captains under the official montepío was approximately fifteen pesos monthly.

21. ANHCh, JS-Civ, leg. 105, pza. 3, Expediente seguido por Doña Juana de Dios Baeza con su hermana Doña María sobre derecho al Montepío de su padre Don José Baeza, f. 8.

22. ANHCh, JS-Civ, leg. 105, pza. 3, f. 8.

23. ANHCh, JS-Civ, leg. 105, pza. 3, 13; Anguita, *Leyes promulgadas*, vol. 1, 124.

24. Many royal officers had switched to the patriot side by 1820, so Vergara Quiroz attributes the law to their political influence; *Historia social del ejército de Chile*, vol. 1, 162. The daughters of other royal officers quickly applied for and received the resumption of pensions granted to their mothers; see the files of Doña Teodora Contreras, hija del Capitán Don José Contreras (1824); Doña Mercedes y Doña Nieves Palacios, hijas del Teniente Coronel graduado Don Alonzo Pérez de Palacios (1824); Doña Lucía y Doña Josefa Molina, hijas del Teniente Coronel Don Lúcas Ambrosio Molina (1827); Doña Leocadia y Juana Mena, hijas del Capitán Don Francisco Mena (1828); Doña Benigna y Doña Mercedes Calderón, hijas del Capitán Don Pedro Nolasco Calderón (1828); Doña Rosa Cárcamo, viuda del Teniente Don Francisco Javier Velásquez (1828), all in ANHCh, MG, vol. 150; Doña Gertrudis y Doña Antonia Benavente, hijas del Teniente Coronel Don Juan Benavente (1830); and Doña María Josefa Santa María, hija del Teniente Coronel Don Antonio Narciso de Santa María (1831), in ANHCh, MG, vol. 179.

25. Letter dated September 2, 1823, ANHCh, MG, vol. 73, Correspondencia con el poder legislativo (1818–1828).

26. ANHCh, JS-Civ, leg. 435, pza. 5, María del Rosario Gómez solicita pensión de gracia por viudez de Gregorio Henríquez (1824), f. 15. For another denial owing to having married before being promoted to captain, see ANHCh, MG, vol. 92, Doña Micaela Calderón, viuda del Capitán Don Justo Polloni (1823).

27. ANHCh, MG, vol. 150, Doña Josefa Gómez, viuda del Capitán Don Justo Quinteros (1826).

28. Varas, Recopilación de leyes, vol. 1, 219–21.

29. Varas, Recopilación de leyes, vol. 1, 220.

30. Letter dated August 22, 1826, ANHCh, MG, vol. 73.

31. ANHCh, MG, vol. 150, Doña Josefa Gómez, viuda del Capitán Don Justo Quinteros (1826).

32. ANHCh, MG, vol. 150, Doña María del Rosario Gómez, viuda del Capitán Don Gregorio Enrriquez [sic] (1828).

33. ANHCh, MG, vol. 179, Doña Dolores Maturano, viuda del Capitán Don José Aguila (1829), f. 11.

34. For another reapplication and approval, see ANHCh, MG, vol. 179, Doña Dolores Silva, viuda del Ayudante Mayor Don José Guzmán (1831).

35. Varas, Recopilación de leyes, vol. 1, 338.

36. ANHCh, MG, vol. 179, Doña María Sambuesa, viuda del Capitán Don José María Iñíquez (1829).

37. ANHCh, MG, vol. 212, Doña Josefa Obando viuda del Sarjento Mayor Don José Antonio Henríquez (1833).

38. ANHCh, MG, vol. 273, Doña Dolores López, viuda, del Subteniente Don Manuel Romero (1838).

39. ANHCh, MG, vol. 273, López, ff. 7v-8.

40. ANHCh, MG, vol. 273, López, f. 11.

41. ANHCh, JS-Civ, leg. 765, pza. 9, Doña María Rita Polloni con el Fisco sobre cobro de pesos por un montepío (1833).

42. ANHCh, MG, vol. 302, Doña María Antonia García, viuda del Capitán Don Santiago Lincongur (1840).

43. ANHCh, MG, vol. 302, Doña Juana Inostrosa, viuda del Capitán Don Rudesindo Granadino (1840).

44. ANHCh, MG, vol. 302, Doña Isabel Herbert, viuda del Teniente Coronel Don Miguel María Occarol (1840); Varas, Recopilación de leyes, vol. 2, 38.

45. Anguita, Leyes promulgadas en Chile, vol. 1, 318.

46. For the case that set this precedent, see ANHCh, MG, vol. 347, Doña Mercedes Pérez, viuda del Ayudante Mayor Don Félix López (1847).

47. Opinion dated October 24, 1849; ANHCh, MG, vol. 371, Doña Emilia Gacitúa, viuda del Capitán Don José Manuel Molina (1849).

48. ANHCh, MG, vol. 371, Gacitúa.

49. Opinion dated October 31, 1849, ANHCh, MG, vol. 371, Gacitúa.

50. "Montepío militar: servicios prestados como individuos de tropa" (July 9, 1853); Varas, Recopilación de leyes, vol. 2, 384.

51. Vergara Quiroz, Historia social del ejército de Chile, vol. 1, 156.

52. ANHCh, MG, vol. 179, Doña Antonia Mateluna, viuda del Capitán Don Patricio Ferreira (1831), f. 5.

53. ANHCh, MG, vol. 302, Doña Tomasa Henríquez, viuda del Capitán Don José Plaza (1840).

54. ANHCh, MG, vol. 302, Doña Norberta Chaparro, viuda del Capitán Don Justo Urra (1840), f. 7.

55. ANHCh, MG, vol. 212, Doña Luisa Arriagada, viuda del Teniente Don José María Rios (1834).

56. ANHCh, MG, vol. 316, Doña Carmen Molina, viuda del Capitán Don Juan de Dios Ugarte (1842).

57. Loveman and Lira, *Las suaves cenizas del olvido*.

58. Collier, *Chile: The Making of a Republic*, 49. On the campaign for reconciliation in this period, see Loveman and Lira, *Las suaves cenizas del olvido*, 121–39.

59. For a list of officers cashiered in 1830 and subsequently reincorporated into service, see Varas, *Recopilación de leyes*, vol. 2, 726–29. On press coverage of the war, which increasingly emphasized the unity of Chileans, see Stuven, "La palabra en armas."

60. The president approved these requests under the special faculties granted to the president by Congress on January 31, 1837, for the duration of the state of war; Anguita, *Leyes promulgadas en Chile*, vol. 1, 270.

61. ANHCh, MG, vol. 325, Doña Carmen Mújica, viuda del Teniente Coronel Don Ramón Picarte (1843), f. 1. Another widow indicated that she had tried to apply for a pension as early as 1831; ANHCh, MG, vol. 273, Doña Loreto Villagrán, viuda del ex-Capitán Don Manuel José Gutiérrez (1838).

62. ANHCh, MG, vol. 325, Mújica.

63. ANHCh, MG, vol. 309, Doña Francisca Fuenzalida, viuda del Coronel graduado Don Manuel Urquizo (1842), f. 1.

64. ANHCh, MG, vol. 309, Hijos del Capitán Don José Domingo Meneses (1841), f. 1.

65. Varas, *Recopilación de leyes*, vol. 2, 5–6.

66. ANHCh, MG, vol. 302, Doña Josefa Demetria Ureta, viuda del Sargento Mayor Don Juan de Dios Solís (1840).

67. ANHCh, MG, vol. 309, Fuenzalida, ff. 20v–21.

68. ANHCh, MG, vol. 316, Doña Teresa Lazo, viuda del ex-Teniente Coronel Don José Castillo (1842), f. 4. The same case applied in ANHCh, MG, vol. 330, Doña Mercedes Mardones, viuda del Sargento Mayor Don Pedro Antonio Gacitúa (1844).

69. ANHCh, MG, vol. 330, Doña Dolores Ross, viuda del Teniente Coronel Don Bartolomé Asagra (1844).

70. Varas, *Recopilación de leyes*, vol. 2, 67.

71. ANHCh, MG, vol. 334, Doña Rosa Muñoz, madre del Subteniente Don José Soto Aguilar (1846).

72. ANHCh, JS-Civ, leg. 1170, pza. 1, Don Jorge Huneeus como tutor de los hijos de don Guillermo De Vic Tupper, con el Fisco, sobre montepío (1843).

73. ANHCh, MG, vol. 406, no. 303, Doña María García, viuda del Teniente Don Manuel Enrique (1853); Varas, *Recopilación de leyes*, vol. 2, 384.

74. ANHCh, MG, vol. 391, Doña Pastora Zapata, viuda [*sic*] del Teniente Don José Luis Poblete (1852).

75. ANHCh, MG, vol. 406, Doña Josefa Ojeda, viuda del Capitán Don Manuel Rodríguez (1853).

76. *Sesiones del congreso nacional de 1853*, 235.

77. ANHCh, JS-Civ, leg. 899, pza. 1, Doña Micaela Solís, viuda del Ayudante Mayor Don Gaspar Calderón, con el Fisco sobre montepío (1844).

78. ANHCh, MG, vol. 406, Doña María del Rosario Campos, viuda del Sargento Mayor Don Domingo Binimelis (1853); *Sesiones del congreso nacional de 1853*, 236; Varas, *Recopilación de leyes*, vol. 2, 393.

79. ANHCh, MG, vol. 406, Doña Carmen Marín, viuda del Capitán Don José Silva Barceló (1853); ANHCh, MG, vol. 414, Doña Mercedes Luján, viuda del Ayudante Mayor Don Juan Félix Vargas (1854).

80. ANHCh, MG, vol. 391, Doña Manuela Caldera, viuda del Capitán General Don Ramón Freire (1852).

81. ANHCh, MG, vol. 414, Doña Manuela Warnes, viuda del General Don Joaquín Prieto (1855). Several other prominent Chilean veterans of independence also died in these years. Coronel Francisco Bulnes, the brother of President and General Manuel Bulnes, died in 1846; his widow received a montepío pension until her death in 1852 when it passed to his mother, Carmen Prieto; ANHCh, MG, vol. 347, Doña Ana María Rosas, viuda del Coronel Don Francisco Bulnes (1848), and vol. 391, Doña Carmen Prieto, madre del Coronel Don Francisco Bulnes (1852). When coronel and former minister of war Pedro Nolasco Vidal died in 1856, his daughters were awarded a montepío pension; ANHCh, MG, vol. 447, Las hijas del Coronel Don Pedro Nolasco Vidal (1856). General Francisco de la Lastra, brother of Javiera Carrera's first husband, died in 1851; ANHCh, MG, vol. 391, Doña Carmen Izquierdo, viuda del General Don Francisco de la Lastra (1852).

82. ANHCh, MG, vol. 414, Doña Juana Pedro Bueno, viuda del Coronel Don Clemente Lantaño (1854).

83. ANHCh, MG, vol. 406, Doña María Vivanco, viuda del Sargento Mayor Don José Antonio Zúñiga (1853).

84. ANHCh, MG, vol. 406, Doña Mercedes León, viuda del Capitán Don Francisco Gómez (1853), and vol. 414, Doña Dolores Rivas, viuda del Teniente Coronel Don Juan de Dios Ancieta (1854).

85. ANHCh, MG, vol. 414, Doña Mercedes Labarca, viuda del Teniente Coronel Don Juan Torres (1855). José Antonio Andrade also began as a private in 1817 and, although it took him thirteen years to become a commissioned officer at the rank of second lieutenant, he died at the rank of sergeant major; ANHCh, MG, vol. 447, Doña Benigna, Liborio y José María, hijos del Sargento Mayor Don José Antonio Andrade (1856). Buenaventura Pizarro began as a private in 1805 and retired in 1850 as a major; ANHCh, MG, vol. 447, Doña María Campusano, viuda del Ayudante Mayor Don Buenaventura Pizarro (1856).

86. ANHCh, MG, vol. 447, Doña María Dolores Pérez, viuda del Subteniente Don Inocencio Ponce (1856).

87. Jaksić, *Andrés Bello*.

88. Minutes of the debate, July 7 and 26, 1854; *Sesiones del congreso nacional de 1854*, 71–73 and 108–11; quote on 109.

89. *Sesiones del congreso nacional de 1854*, 72–73.

90. *Sesiones del congreso nacional de 1854*, 110–11.
91. *Sesiones del congreso nacional de 1855*, 39.
92. *Sesiones del congreso nacional de 1855*, 36.
93. *Sesiones del congreso nacional de 1855*, 45.
94. Varas, *Recopilación de leyes*, vol. 2, 434.
95. Varas, *Recopilación de leyes*, vol. 2, 434–35.
96. Varas, *Recopilación de leyes*, vol. 2, 480–81.

Chapter 6: Enforcing Paternal Responsibilities

1. ANHCh, JS-Civ, leg. 1059, pza. 15, Don Domingo Aldunate y Lastra con Doña Javiera de la Carrera sobre alimentos (1855), ff. 1–3.

2. Moreno Martín, *Archivo del General José Miguel Carrera*, vol. 22, 249–54.

3. Letter dated December 12, 1816, ANHCh, FV, vol. 237, pza. 4636; and *RCHG*, no. 11 (1913), 204.

4. ANHCh, JS-Civ, leg. 1059, pza. 15, ff. 86v–88.

5. ANHCh, JS-Civ, leg. 1059, pza. 15, f. 1.

6. ANHCh, JS-Civ, leg. 1059, pza. 15, f. 16.

7. ANHCh, JS-Civ, leg. 1059, pza. 15, ff. 36–37.

8. ANHCh, JS-Civ, leg. 1059, pza. 15, ff. 19v and 105v.

9. ANHCh, JS-Civ, leg. 1059, pza. 15, ff. 28–31.

10. ANHCh, JS-Civ, leg. 1059, pza. 15, f. 1.

11. ANHCh, JS-Civ, leg. 1059, pza. 15, ff. 43–61

12. ANHCh, JS-Civ, leg. 1059, pza. 15, ff. 106–8v.

13. ANHCh, JS-Civ, leg. 1059, pza. 15, f. 118–18v.

14. I compiled a list of all lawsuits over alimentos and custody from both the Real Audiencia and Judiciales de Santiago sections of the national archive; although the former were principally cases under Spanish rule and the latter under the republic, there was some overlap in cataloging. I also consulted sentences published in the *Gaceta de los Tribunales* between 1841 (the first year of that publication) and 1855; some corresponded to full case files but for others, no case file was located, suggesting that not all lawsuits were archived or at least not archived in the correct section. Therefore, any quantitative analysis cannot be precise. Rather, I calculated numbers of cases by quinquennium in order to trace general trends. Qualitative analysis of maintenance suits is drawn from all cases before 1830 and a sample from every five years between 1830 and 1855 (e.g., 1830, 1835).

15. In her research into requests for royal legitimation of children born out of wedlock, Ann Twinam notes that about half the cases included evidence that fathers had fulfilled their duty to provide for their offspring and that those who did not often faced criticism from their peers; Twinam, *Public Lives, Private Secrets*.

16. Partida IV covered family law, of which Title XV covered out-of-wedlock children and Title XIX covered the responsibilities of raising and supporting children (as well as the duty of offspring to support parents); Burns, *Las Siete Partidas*, vol. 4, 952–55 and 972–74. For an overview of Spanish family law as well as its application in colonial Chile, see Dougnac Rodríguez, *Esquema del derecho de familia indiano*. For

a study of the application of Portuguese law on illegitimacy in Brazil, see Lewin, *Surprise Heirs*.

17. For an overview of scholarship on the status of illegitimates, see Milanich, "Historical Perspectives on Illegitimacy and Illegitimates in Latin America."

18. Twinam, *Public Lives, Private Secrets*, 118–22; Premo, *Children of the Father King*, 155 and 202–5; García Peña, "Madres solteras, pobres y abandonadas," 647–91. In seventeenth-century Galicia, women sued for breach of promise but often settled for child support; Poska, *Women and Authority in Early Modern Spain*, 88–97. For seventeenth-century Lima, María Emma Mannarelli cites numerous lawsuits over establishing paternity in order to sue for a share of inheritance, but few over alimentos; Mannarelli, *Private Passions and Public Sins*.

19. The decree was subsequently incorporated into the *Novísima recopilación de las leyes de España*, 208.

20. Nara Milanich analyzed lawsuits brought by or on behalf of illegitimate children for either support or a share of inheritance; Milanich, *Children of Fate*, especially 41–69. For an overview of the laws on alimentos in Mexico, see Pérez Duarte y Noroña, "Los alimentos en la historia de México independiente." García Peña, "Madres Solteras," is the only study I have found specifically on alimentos suits, and she analyzes only those brought by unwed mothers, who seem to have been successful until paternity searches were outlawed in 1857. In a review of 240 lawsuits involving women in Caracas from 1835 to 1840, Arlene Díaz found twenty support disputes; of these all nine for children born out of wedlock were either settled or sentenced in favor of plaintiffs, as were seven of the eleven cases filed on behalf of wives and legitimate children; Díaz, *Female Citizens, Patriarchs, and the Law in Venezuela, 1786–1904*, 74–75. Christine Hünefeldt briefly discusses the tactics of husbands trying to delay payment of alimony to wives who had filed for divorce; Hünefeldt, *Liberalism in the Bedroom*, 84, 150, 166, 173, 253. Elizabeth Dore found a local court in Nicaragua that continued to pressure fathers to provide for out-of-wedlock children (generally the offspring of elite men and poor women) if the mothers agreed to give up custody; Dore, "Unidades familiares, propiedad y política en la Nicaragua rural."

21. For disputes between spouses, see ANHCh, RA, vol. 2560, pza. 2, Doña Francisca Xaviera Goycolea con Don Pedro Nolasco Valdés sobre contribución de alimentos para su persona y la de su hija (1793); vol. 2463, pza. 7, Juana Ramírez con José Antonio Frías, su marido, sobre alimentos (1797); ANHCh, JS-Civ, leg. 352, pza. 5, Doña María Josefa Fernández con su marido Don José Velazques sobre alimentos (1788); leg. 81, pza. 5, Doña Andrea Arredondo con su esposo Don Josef Salguedo sobre divorcio y alimentos (1800); leg. 945, pza. 4, Causa que sigue Doña Dominga de Urízar con su marido don Francisco Formas sobre alimentos, litis expensas y la dote (1805); leg. 882, pza. 11, Doña María del Rosario Serrano con Don Pedro José de Castro sobre alimentos (1805); leg. 919, pza. 8, Doña María del Rosario Toro demanda pensión alimenticia de su marido Don Manuel Astaburuaga (1807). Dougnac Rodríguez, who reviewed cases under the jurisdiction of the Captaincy General of Chile throughout the colonial period, found additional alimentos lawsuits between spouses; Dougnac Rodríguez, *Esquema del derecho de familia indiano*, 193–206, 322.

22. ANHCh, JS-Civ, leg. 1265, pza. 6, Don Ramón Gutierres con su madre Doña Mercedes Ríos sobre alimentos (1805); ANHCh, RA, vol. 2836, pza. 3, Autos de Don

Juan Manuel Espinosa contra la testamentaria del Coronel Don Juachin Espinosa sobre alimentos (1787); ANHCh, JS-Civ, leg. 745, pza. 6, Expediente seguido por Doña Dolores Peres contra Don Francisco Antonio de la Carrera sobre alimentos (1803); leg. 882, pza. 11, Doña María del Rosario Serrano con Don Pedro José de Castro sobre alimentos (1805).

23. ANHCh, RA, vol. 2632, pza. 6, Diego Martel sobre alimentos de sus hijos y de su mujer Catalina Clavería Murúa (1788); vol. 3152, pza. 12, Pedro Ponce, marido de María de la Concepción Olivera en autos por cobro de alimentos a Pascuala Olivera (1802); ANHCh, JS-Civ, leg. 687, pza. 6, Expediente promovido por el Procurador de Pobres a nombre de María Josefa Noriega contra Don Jorge Ureta por cobranza de pesos (1789); leg. 275, pza. 13, doña María Covarrubias demanda pensión alimenticia de su hermano don Antonio Covarrubias (1792); leg. 949, pza. 1, Don José María de Urmeneta con Don Ignacio Tomás de Urmeneta sobre remoción de tutela y demanda en alimentos (1803); leg. 1534, pza. 8, Doña Josefa Zañartu con acreedores á la testamentaría de su marido Don Juan Ignacio Goicolea, sobre contribución de alimentos de los bienes concursados (1791).

24. Maintenance lawsuits recorded in the judicial district of Santiago averaged almost five per year in the 1830s, twelve per year in the 1840s, and more than fourteen per year from 1850 to 1855. During the 1830s, the percentage of cases brought by offspring almost doubled compared to the pattern between 1785 and 1810. According to sentences printed in the official *Gaceta de los Tribunales* from 1841 to 1855, only 16 percent of alimentos lawsuits in Santiago were filed by spouses, 23 percent by legitimate offspring, and 43 percent on behalf of children born out of wedlock.

25. There may also have been an increase in informal relationships in Santiago between relatively well-off men and women of lower status who fled warfare or economic hardship in rural areas, resulting in an increase in out-of-wedlock births; see Salazar, *Labradores, peones y proletarios*, 260–90.

26. ANHCh, JS-Civ, leg. 220, pza. 2, Doña Carmen Carrasco con Don Ignacio Salvatierra sobre pensión alimenticia (1845), quotes on ff. 4 and 15v.

27. For postindependence Venezuela, Reuben Zahler found that wives suing for support sometimes did have to establish their good reputations; Zahler, *Ambitious Rebels*, 170–74.

28. ANHCh, JS-Civ, leg. 7, pza. 7, Tadea Aguila con Gerónimo Freire por pensión alimenticia (1813).

29. ANHCh, JS-Civ, leg. 243, pza. 4, Doña Rosa de la Cerda con Don Silvestre Valdivieso sobre alimentos (1830).

30. ANHCh, JS-Civ, leg. 429, pza. 1, Doña Carmen Goycolea con su esposo Don Manuel Rosales sobre alimentos y otras materias (7 cuadernos) (1833–1856).

31. ANHCh, JS-Civ, leg. 1247, pza. 1, Don Domingo Asenjo, en representación de su esposa Doña Manuela Rosales, con doña Carmen Goycolea, madre de esta, sobre alimentos (1843); leg. 1442, pza. 2, Doña Agustina Rosales con su padre Don Manuel por cobro de mesadas alimenticias juzgadas (1845); leg. 1442, pza. 3, Doña Agustina Rosales con Don Juan Antonio Guerrero sobre alimentos (1853); leg. 1442, pza. 3, Doña Catalina Rosales con Don Manuel Rosales sobre alimentos (1854); leg. 1443, pza. 12, Don Manuel Rosales el segundo con su Señora madre Doña Carmen Goycolea sobre alimentos (1854).

32. ANHCh, JS-Civ, leg. 1247, pza. 1, Don Domingo Asenjo, en representación de su esposa Doña Manuela Rosales, con Doña Carmen Goycolea, madre de esta, sobre alimentos (1843), ff. 41, 52. In the case of their adult son, however, the superior court decided that since he had been at boarding school at his father's expense at the time of the separation and settlement, Manuel Rosales would have to pay an additional amount directly to him when he filed suit against his mother in 1854; *Gaceta de los Tribunales* 14, no. 672 (1855): 5958.

33. Approximately 10 percent of maintenance suits were filed by adult legitimate offspring before 1820, rising to 20 percent in the 1830s, and 30 percent by 1850.

34. ANHCh, JS-Civ, leg. 781, pza. 2, Don Ricardo Price con su padre Don Ricardo Evans Price sobre alimentos (1845), quotes on ff. 4v, 7v, 19, 72v.

35. ANHCh, JS-Civ, leg. 1108, pza. 8, Mercedes Bascuñán con José María Bascuñán sobre alimentos (1835), ff. 5 and 7.

36. Partida IV, Title XIX, Law VI absolved parents of supporting "ungrateful" children but set a high bar: "This would be the case where one accuses the other, or attempts to fix a crime upon him for which he would deserve death, dishonor, or loss of property." Partida IV, Title XVIII, Law XIX held that a child who behaved ungratefully as an adult, "who, instead of serving those from whom they receive favors and showing gratitude for them, maliciously commit offenses against them, subjecting them to many annoyances by word and deed," should be resubjected to patriarchal authority. See Burns, *Las Siete Partidas*, vol. 4, 971, 974; Dougnac Rodríguez, *Esquema del derecho familia indiano*, 320. Studies from colonial Spanish America show that parents were rarely able to prevent marriages by filing charges of *rapto* (kidnaping and seduction); what is striking in this case is a father being forced to support financially a couple who married without his consent.

37. Claims on behalf of out-of-wedlock children averaged about 40 percent of the total between 1820 and 1855, up from about 15 percent prior to 1820.

38. These same criteria and patterns of judicial activism were true of the colonial period; Dougnac Rodríguez, *Esquema del derecho familia indiano*, 328–31. On the related filiation lawsuits, see Milanich, *Children of Fate*, 41–100.

39. AHNCh, JS-Civ, leg. 123, pza. 11, Doña Juana Barra contra Don Narciso Cotapos por alimentos (1833).

40. ANHCh, JS-Civ, leg. 453, pza. 3, Doña Isidora Grandón con Don Isidro Garcés sobre filiación de sus hijos y alimentos (1835), quotes on ff. 3, 30, 37v–38.

41. ANHCh, JS-Civ, leg. 201, pza. 5, Mercedes Canales contra Don Lázaro Tomás Ramos sobre filiación y alimentos para su hijo José Santos (1845).

42. ANHCh, JS-Civ, leg. 833, pza. 11, El Coronel Don Francisco Ibáñez con Doña Mercedes Rojas sobre unas mesadas (1822), f. 6.

43. This despite Partida IV, Title XIX, Law III: "But where the mother has control of them for some reason . . . and marries, she should not then have the care of them, nor is the father bound to give her any property for this purpose, but he should take charge of the children and rear them if he has the means;" Burns, *Las Siete Partidas*, vol. 4, 973.

44. ANHCh, JS-Civ, leg. 626, pza. 13, Doña Lorenza Mazuela con Don Bernardo Cadiz sobre alimentos (1845), quote on f. 41v.

45. ANHCh, JS-Civ, leg. 1091, pza. 3, Doña Mercedes Ayala contra Don Juan Manuel Palacios por alimentos (1855), quotes on ff. 13 and 92.

46. ANHCh, JS-Civ, leg. 626, pza. 13, Doña Lorenza Mazuela con Don Bernardo Cadiz sobre alimentos (1845).

47. During the colonial period, the titles of "don" and "doña" had been reserved for those who could claim a superior social status, but almost all the litigants in these nineteenth-century cases used the terms in their petitions. Although Torreblanca did not use the term, it was inserted on the title of the lawsuit.

48. ANHCh, JS-Civ, leg. 659, pza. 11, Doña Venancia Torreblanca demanda a José Moraga pensión alimenticia por hija natural (1835).

49. ANHCh, JS-Civ, leg. 1566, pza. 6, José del C. Letelier con Mateo Mesa sobre filiación y alimentos (1845).

50. ANHCh, JS-Civ, leg. 511, pza. 11, Juana Icarte con Mateo Icarte, sobre filiación y alimentos (1850).

51. ANHCh, JS-Civ, leg. 321, pza. 4, Manuela Echevers contra la testamentaria de su finado padre Don Rudecindo Echevers sobre alimentos (1850).

52. There were, however, also cases in which adult illegitimate offspring were granted inheritance rights; see ANHCh, JS-Civ, leg. 39, pza. 9, Autos que sigue Doña María del Rosario Alvares sobre alimentos de unos menores naturales (1817); leg. 206, pza. 5, Don Antonio del Canto con Doña Rufina del Campo, como albacea de Don Rafael del Canto sobre filiación y alimentos (1850); leg. 591, pza. 2, Doña Cecilia Loyola demanda a Don Miguel Martínez por mensualidades alimenticias (1850).

53. ANHCh, JS-Civ, leg. 190, pza. 5, Don Pedro Calancha con su madre Doña Alfonsa de la Rosa sobre administración de sus bienes y alimentos (1819), f. 9.

54. ANHCh, JS-Civ, leg. 1255, pza. 8, Don Alejo Grez con su Padre Don Bartolomé Grez sobre alimentos (1855), f. 15v.

55. ANHCh, JS-Civ, leg. 287, pza. 1, Doña María de los Dolores Cubé con Raimundo Molina por pensión alimenticia (1816–1824), quotes on ff. 1, 3, 7v.

56. For the full text, see Partida IV, Title XIX, Law IV; Burns, Las Siete Partidas, vol. 4, 973.

57. For fathers of legitimate children, see Partida IV, Title XIX, Law III; Burns, Las Siete Partidas, vol. 4, 973; and for fathers of children born out of wedlock, Partida VII, Title XVII, Law II; Burns, Las Siete Partidas, vol. 4, 960.

58. Both parents also implied that the other had some degree of responsibility in the death of the other two children; ANHCh, JS-Civ, leg. 166, pza. 3, Don Manuel Bravo con Doña Rosario Luco sobre minoración de una cuota alimenticia (1845), quotes on ff. 10, 18v, and 28v.

59. Given Solar's concern about the woman living in his wife's house and the vague discussion of his charges, it seems possible that she was the alleged lover; ANHCh, JS-Civ, leg. 209, pza. 1, Don Ignacio Solar con su esposa Doña Carmen Cañas, sobre entrega de sus hijos y que les suministra los alimentos (1844), cuaderno 2, ff. 146–47.

60. ANHCh, JS-Civ, leg. 209, pza. 1, Doña Carmen Cañas con su esposo Don Ignacio del Solar sobre reconocimiento de un documento (1848).

61. ANHCh, JS-Civ, leg. 886, pza. 2, Doña Josefa Sierralta con el Señor Don Antonio Gundián sobre entrega de los hijos del matrimonio (1849), quote in cuaderno 1, f. 12; for the prior case in which she won alimony just for herself, see leg. 886, pza. 1, Doña Josefa Sierralta con su esposo el Señor Don Antonio Gundián sobre alimentos (1848).

62. ANHCh, JS-Civ, leg. 886, pza. 2, cuaderno 2, f. 12.

63. ANHCh, JS-Civ, leg. 886, pza. 2, cuaderno 2, f. 30.

64. ANHCh, JS-Civ, leg. 1375, pza. 19, Don José Santos Nuñes contra Doña Pascuala Rojas sobre entrega de un niño (1852), ff. 8v, 11, 17v, and 19.

65. ANHCh, JS-Civ, leg. 665, pza. 12, José Santos Moreno con Doña Carmen Rodrigues sobre entrega de una hija (1824). In a similar case in which the mother retained custody; ANHCh, JS-Civ, leg. 679, pza. 9, Doña Carmen Navarrete con Don José Vicente Cornejo sobre entrega de una hija (1855).

66. ANHCh, JS-Civ, leg. 1053, pza. 12, Doña Nicolasa Aguila con Don Agustín Ramírez sobre entrega de una hija de ambos (1855), quotes on ff. 2 and 30.

67. ANHCh, JS-Civ, leg. 310, pza. 6, Espediente promovido por Don Pablo Donnay con Doña Petronila Muños sobre entrega de un hijo (1839), quote on f. 3v.

68. ANHCh, JS-Civ, leg. 623, pza. 10, Doña María Marín con Don Manuel Portales sobre filiación para sus dos hijos (1844).

69. Susana and Carlota Cifuentes, however, did exercise their right once they reached the age of twelve to request a different guardian. ANHCh, JS-Civ, leg. 92, pza. 5, Doña Carmen Astorga con la testimentaria de Don Manuel Cifuentes sobre filiación de y alimentos para sus hijas naturales (1845), quote in f. 20.

70. The last entry is a request from Gacitúa in 1860 for a copy of the baptismal certificate to present to the executor of the now deceased Cerda's estate; whether she got the executor to recognize her son's right to partial inheritance is unknown. ANHCh, JS-Civ, leg. 1560, pza. 1, Doña Antonia Gacitúa contra Don Francisco Cerda sobre alimentos y entrega de su hijo natural de ambos dos y cumplir la palabra de casamiento (1847). The superior court similarly gave a natural father the choice between paying child support or taking custody in ANHCh, JS-Civ, leg. 1247, pza. 2, Doña Carmen Goicolea contra Don Juan José Ugarte sobre alimentos (1850).

71. ANHCh, JS-Civ, leg. 1091, pza. 3, Doña Mercedes Ayala contra Don Juan Manuel Palacios por alimentos (1855), quote on ff. 60–61.

72. ANHCh, JS-Civ, leg. 1550, pza. 18, Don Napoleon Charpín con Doña Elvira Jiménez sobre entrega de un niño (1853), f. 12. For the initial child support lawsuit, see ANHCh, JS-Civ, leg. 1290, pza. 12, Doña Alvina Jimenes con Don Napoleon Charpín sobre alimentos (1853).

73. Partida IV, Title XV, Law IV; Burns, *Las Siete Partidas*, vol. 4, 953; Twinam, *Public Lives, Private Secrets*; Milanich, *Children of Fate*, 261, n.59.

74. ANHCh, JS-Civ, leg. 1094, pza. 6, Don Tadeo Baeza con Doña Rosario Ortíz sobre entrega de una niña (1851).

75. ANHCh, JS-Civ, leg. 1383, pza. 12, Doña Rosario Ortiz con Don Tadeo Baeza sobre entrega de una hija (1853), ff. 137–38v. In another case, the court ordered that a girl should not be in the custody of either of her natural parents, but the father successfully held onto her until he was arrested on theft charges in a separate incident; ANHCh, JS-Civ, leg. 1544, pza. 12, Manuela Calderón con Justo Pastor Peña sobre entrega de hija (1840).

76. ANHCh, JS-Civ, leg. 626, pza. 13, Doña Lorenza Mazuela con Don Bernardo Cadiz sobre alimentos (1845), f. 1.

77. See Partida IV, Title XX, Law III; Burns, *Las Siete Partidas*, vol. 4, 975–76; Article 239, *Código Civil de la República de Chile*, 61. In a study of child circulation in northern Mexico, Laura Shelton argues that judges there also favored the custody claims of

those who paid the costs of child rearing and required the few fathers who successfully reclaimed children to reimburse them; Shelton, "Like a Servant or Like a Son?" On the circulation of children in Chile between 1850 and 1930, see Milanich, *Children of Fate*, 157–215.

78. ANHCh, JS-Civ, leg. 310, pza. 5, Don José Rosa Donaire con Don José Ayala sobre entrega de sus hijos (1848). For a similar case and outcome, see ANHCh, JS-Civ, leg. 240, pza. 7, Expediente promovido por Don José Santos Cebreros con Doña Carmen Gusman sobre la entrega de una hija del primero (1841).

79. ANHCh, JS-Civ, leg. 965, pza. 15, Expediente que sigue Don Esteban Valles con Don Ventura Santana sobre retirar el primero a su hija del lado del segundo (1824).

80. *El Centinela*, vol. 1, no. 14 (Santiago, March 18, 1829), p. 55, included in the transcripts of ANHCh, JS-Civ, leg. 1159, pza. 3, José Cruz con Carlos Correa sobre entrega de hijo (1829).

81. The Correa de Saa surname was associated with prominent families; ANHCh, JS-Civ, leg. 1159, pza. 3, f. 8v.

82. ANHCh, JS-Civ, leg. 1159, pza. 3, f. 11.

83. ANHCh, JS-Civ, leg. 1544, pza. 12, Manuela Calderón con Justo Pastor Peña sobre entrega de hija (1840); leg. 1059, pza. 3, Seguido de oficio sobre el nombramiento de tutor de la menor Josefa Alcalde (1853).

84. ANHCh, JS-Civ, leg. 1193, pza. 7, Doña Dolores Escobar con Doña Dolores Romo sobre entrega de una nieta (1853), quote on f. 12. See also ANHCh, JS-Civ, leg. 936, pza. 12, El apoderado de Doña Petronila Urbina con Doña María Forsali sobre entrega de nieta (1835); leg. 998, pza. 6, Melchora Viera con Don Manuel Magallanes sobre entrega de un hijo (1840); leg. 1079, pza. 11, Doña Pascuala Armijo contra Don Pedro Méndez sobre entrega de una hija (1852).

85. ANHCh, JS-Civ, leg. 690, pza. 10, Doña Juana Núñez con el Presbítero Mariano Muñoz sobre entrega de menores (1845).

86. ANHCh, JS-Civ, leg. 760, pza. 5, Don Inocencio María Pizarro con Doña Cruz Morán sobre que se le entregue una hija (1844), ff. IV, 2, 10, 21.

87. Between 1850 and 1856, the superior court overturned twelve sentences from judges of first instance that had found in favor of such offspring; Milanich, *Children of Fate*, 46–66 and 263 n.77. Similar fears were raised in Brazil during the late 1830s; Lewin, *Surprise Heirs*, vol. 2, 233–63.

88. Milanich, *Children of Fate*, 54–60; Article 274, *Código Civil de la República de Chile*, 69.

89. See Milanich, *Children of Fate*, 56–65, and *Código Civil de la República de Chile*, 52–76.

90. Articles 219 (quoted) to 221, *Código Civil de la República de Chile*, 56–57. In addition, Article 240 explicitly excluded mothers from the exercise of patria potestad.

91. *SCL*, vol. 4, 264–65.

92. Saether, "Bourbon Absolutism and Marriage Reform;" Socolow, "Acceptable Partners."

93. *SCL*, vol. 4, 340.

94. *SCL*, vol. 4, 340.

95. For the text of the new law, see *SCL*, vol. 4, 340–42. For an interpretation that sees the 1820 law as *more* conservative than the 1776 pragmatic, see Andreucci Aguilera, "La Prágmatica de Carlos III sobre el matrimonio de los hijos de familia y su pervivencia en el derecho chileno."

1. Anguita, *Leyes promulgadas en Chile*, vol. 2, 168.

2. She also congratulated her nephew Francisco de Paula Figueroa Aráoz on his engagement to the niece of Dolores Larraín; letter dated May 2, 1856, ANHCh, FV, vol. 237, pza. 4614.

3. Varas, *Recopilación de leyes*, vol. 2, 67 and 135–36.

4. Varas, *Recopilación de leyes*, vol. 2, 135–36.

5. McEvoy, "El regreso del héroe"; see also Stuven, "Guerreros y sabios al Panteón Republicano."

6. Varas, *Recopilación de leyes*, vol. 2, 149 and 163; Anguita, *Leyes promulgadas en Chile*, vol. 1, 599.

7. Varas, *Recopilación de leyes*, vol. 2, 297–98.

8. Anguita, *Leyes promulgadas en Chile*, vol. 1, 484–85.

9. Desmadryl, *Galería nacional*, vol. 1, ix.

10. In Desmadryl, *Galería nacional*, vol. 1, 138.

11. The sole female author in the collection, poet Mercedes Marín de Solar, wrote the biography of her father José Gaspar Marín; Desmadryl, *Galería nacional*, vol. 1, 193–207.

12. On various commemorations, see Collier, *Chile: The Making of a Republic, 1830–1865*, 153–61.

13. Retamal Favereau, Celis Atria, and Muñoz Correa, *Familias fundadoras de Chile, 1540–1600*, 757–90.

14. Vicuña, *La belle époque chilena*.

15. Salazar, *Labradores, peones y proletarios*.

16. Milanich, *Children of Fate*.

17. Milanich, *Children of Fate*, 129–31; Méndez Notari, *Desierto de esperanzas*.

18. Klubock, *Contested Communities*; Rosemblatt, *Gendered Compromises*; Hutchison, *Labors Appropriate to Their Sex*; Tinsman, *Partners in Conflict*.

19. Power, *Right-Wing Women in Chile*; Baldez, "Nonpartisanship as a Political Strategy"; Mooney, *The Politics of Motherhood*; Stern, *Reckoning with Pinochet*; Thomas, *Contesting Legitimacy in Chile*. Chile also had a feminist movement; Kirkwood, *Ser política en Chile*.

20. Pérez Duarte y Noroña, "Los alimentos en la historia de México independiente;" García Peña, "Madres solteras, pobres y abandonadas;" Díaz, *Female Citizens, Patriarchs, and the Law in Venezuela*, 74–75; Dore, "Unidades familiares, propiedad y política en la Nicaragua rural."

21. Hingson, "Savages into Citizens."

22. Although family was not the focus of his research, Stephen K. Stoan uncovered debates over the rights of wives and heirs to sequestered property; Stoan, *Pablo Morillo and Venezuela, 1815–1820*, 83–86 and 124–27. Howard Pashman argues that for New York, the activities of the Sequestration Committee contributed to the process of building a new legal order; Pashman, "The People's Property Law."

23. Posada-Carbó, *In Search of a New Order*, 5.

24. The case of pensions after the U.S. Civil War is a widely cited example; less well known perhaps is that limited benefits were also instituted after the Revolutionary

War; Skocpol, *Protecting Soldiers and Mothers*; McClintock, "Civil War Pensions and the Reconstruction of Union Families"; Collins, "Administering Marriage."

25. See, for example, Meisel, "Women's Petitions and Political Culture in Early Independence Argentina."

26. *Código Civil de la República de Chile*, 300.

27. Will of Francisca Javiera Carrera Verdugo dated August 14, 1862, in Moreno Martín, *Archivo del General José Miguel Carrera*, vol. 33, 365–67.

BIBLIOGRAPHY

Archival Sources

AHNCh   Archivo Histórico Nacional de Chile (Santiago)
AFL   Archivo Fernández Larraín
CM   Contaduría Mayor
FAJE   Fondo Archivo Jaime Eyzaguirre
FV   Fondos Varios
JC-Civ   Judiciales de Concepción—Causas Civiles
JS-Civ   Judiciales de Santiago—Causas Civiles
IC   Intendencia de Concepción
MG   Ministerio de Guerra
MI   Ministerio del Interior
MH   Ministerio de Hacienda
RA   Real Audiencia

Miscellaneous Documents

CHDI   *Colección de historiadores y de documentos relativos a la independencia de Chile*
RCHG   *Revista Chilena de Historia y Geografía*
SCL   *Sesiones de los cuerpos lejislativos de la República de Chile, 1811–1845*

Published Primary Sources

Anguita, Ricardo, ed. *Leyes promulgadas en Chile desde 1810 hasta el 1ro de junio de 1912.* 6 vols. Santiago: Imprenta Barcelona, 1912–1918.

Archivo de don Bernardo O'Higgins. 36 vols. Santiago: Academica Chilena de Historia, 1946–[2005].

Beauchef, Jorge. *Memorias militares para servir a la historia de la independencia de Chile.* Edited by Guillermo Feliú Cruz. Santiago: Editorial Andrés Bello, 1964.

Boletín de las leyes i decretos del gobierno. 4 vols. Santiago: Imprenta Nacional, 1898–1901.

Burns, Robert I., ed., and Samuel Parsons Scott, trans. *Las Siete Partidas.* 5 vols. Philadelphia: University of Pennsylvania Press, 2001.

Cacho, Fernando. "Reflexiones políticas sobre las provincias del Sur de la América meridonal." *Araucaria: Revista iberoamericana de filosofía, política y humanidades* 3, no. 8 (2002).

Carrera, José Miguel. *Diario de José Miguel Carrera*. Reprint. Santiago: Nacional Quimantu, 1973.

Código Civil de la República de Chile. Santiago: Imprenta Nacional, 1856.

Colección de historiadores y de documentos relativos a la independencia de Chile [CHDI]. 43 vols. Santiago: Imprenta Universitaria, 1900–1966.

Desmadryl, Narcisse, Hermojenes de Irisarri, and Miguel Luis Amunátegui. *Galería nacional, o, Colección de biografías i retratos de hombre célebres de Chile*. 2 vols. Santiago: Imprenta Chilena, 1854.

Documentos parlamentarios: Discursos de apertura en las sesiones del congreso, i memorias ministeriales. 9 vols. Santiago: Imprenta del Ferrocarril, 1858–1861.

Eyzaguirre, Jaime, ed. *Archivo de la familia Eyzaguirre, 1747–1854*. Buenos Aires: Compañía Impresora Argentina, 1960.

Graham, Maria Dundas (Lady Maria Calcott). *Journal of a Residence in Chile, during the Year 1822*. New York: Praeger Publishers, 1969.

Letelier, Valentín, ed. *Sesiones de los cuerpos lejislativos de la República de Chile, 1811–1845 [SCL]*. 37 vols. Santiago: Imprenta Cervantes, 1887–1908.

Moreno Martín, Armando, ed. *Archivo del General José Miguel Carrera*. 40 vols. Santiago: Sociedad Chilena de Historia y Geografía, 1992–2011.

Novísima recopilación de las leyes de España. Madrid, 1805.

Sesiones del congreso nacional. 26 vols. Santiago: Imprenta Nacional, 1846–1865.

Varas, José Antonio, ed. *Recopilación de leyes, decretos supremos i circulares concernientes al ejército*. 2nd ed. 7 vols. Santiago: Imprenta de "El Progreso," 1870–1888.

Vergara Quiroz, Sergio. *Cartas de mujeres en Chile, 1630–1885*. Benito Juárez, Mexico: Editorial Andres Bello, 1987.

Vicuña Mackenna, Benjamín. *Doña Javiera de Carrera: Rasgo biográfico leido en el círculo de amigos de las letras*. Biblioteca de Autores Chilenos, vol. 23. Santiago: Guillermo E. Miranda Editor, 1904.

Vicuña Mackenna, Benjamín. *Obras completas*. 16 vols. Santiago: Universidad de Santiago, 1936–1940.

Viva El Rey: Gazeta del Gobierno de Chile (1813–1817). 2 vols. Santiago: Imprenta Cultura, 1952.

Secondary Works

Adams, Jerome R. *Notable Latin American Women*. Jefferson, NC: McFarland and Company, 1995.

Amunátegui y Solar, Domingo. *La sociedad chilena del siglo XVIII: Mayorzagos y títulos de Castilla*. 3 vols. Santiago: Imprenta Barcelona, 1901–1904.

Amunátegui y Solar, Domingo. "Una víctima de la Patria Vieja." *Revista chilena de historia y geografía* 53, no. 57 (1927): 368–72.

Anderson, Benedict. *Imagined Communities: Reflections on the Origin and Spread of Nationalism*. London: Verso, 1983.

Andreucci Aguilera, Rodrigo. "La Prágmatica de Carlos III sobre el matrimonio de los hijos de familia y su pervivencia en el derecho chileno." *Revista de estudios histórico-jurídicos* 22 (2000): 213–23.

Arrom, Silvia Marina. *Containing the Poor: The Mexico City Poor House, 1774–1871*. Durham, NC: Duke University Press, 2000.

Arrom, Silvia Marina. *The Women of Mexico City, 1790–1857*. Stanford, CA: Stanford University Press, 1985.

Arroyo Alvarado, Guillermo. *Historia de Chile: Campaña de 1817–1818*. Santiago-Valparaiso: Sociedad Imprenta-Litografia "Barcelona," 1918.

Baldez, Lisa. "Nonpartisanship as a Political Strategy: Women Left, Right, and Center in Chile." In *Radical Women in Latin America: Left and Right*, edited by Victoria González and Karen Kampwirth, 273–97. University Park: Pennsylvania State University Press, 2001.

Balmori, Diana. "Family and Politics: Three Generations (1790–1890)." *Journal of Family History* 10, no. 3 (1985): 247–57.

Balmori, Diana, and Robert Oppenheimer. "Family Clusters: The Generational Nucleation of Families in Nineteenth-Century Argentina and Chile." *Comparative Studies in Society and History* 21, no. 2 (1979): 231–61.

Balmori, Diana, Stuart Voss, and Miles Wortman. *Notable Family Networks in Latin America*. Chicago: University of Chicago Press, 1984.

Barbier, Jacques A. "Elite and Cadres in Bourbon Chile." *Hispanic American Historical Review* 52, no. 3 (1972): 416–35.

Barragán, Rossanna. "The Spirit of Bolivian Law: Citizenship, Infamy, and Patriarchy." In Caulfield, Chambers, and Putnam, eds., *Honor, Status, and Law in Modern Latin America*, 66–86.

Barros Arana, Diego. *Historia jeneral de Chile*. 16 vols. Santiago: R. Jover, Editor, 1884–1902.

Bauer, Arnold J. *Chilean Rural Society from the Spanish Conquest to 1930*. Cambridge: Cambridge University Press, 1975.

Boccara, Guillaume. "Etnogénesis mapuche: Resistencia y restructuración entre los indígenas del centro-sur de Chile (siglos XVI–XVIII)." *Hispanic American Historical Review* 79, no. 3 (1999): 425–61.

Bragoni, Beatriz. *José Miguel Carrera: Un revolucionario chileno en el Río de la Plata*. Buenos Aires: Edhasa, 2012.

Bravo Lira, Bernardino. *El absolutismo ilustrado en Hispanoamérica, Chile (1760–1860): De Carlos III a Portales y Montt*. Santiago: Editorial Universitaria, 1992.

Brewster, Claire. "Women and the Spanish-American Wars of Independence: An Overview." *feminist review* 79, no. 1 (2005): 20–35.

Brown, Matthew. "Adventurers, Foreign Women and Masculinity in the Colombian Wars of Independence." *feminist review* 79, no. 1 (2005): 36–51.

Brown, Matthew. "Inca, Sailor, Soldier, King: Gregor MacGregor and the Early Nineteenth-Century Caribbean." *Bulletin of Latin American Research* 24, no. 1 (2005): 44–70.

Brown, Richard D. "The Confiscation and Disposition of Loyalists' Estates in Suffolk County Massachusetts." *William and Mary Quarterly*, 3rd ser., 21, no. 4 (1964): 534–550.

Cárdenas Gueudinot, Mario. "O'Higgins y la Junta de Secuestros de Valparaíso." *Revista Libertador O'Higgins* 13 (1996): 77–86.

Cárdenas Gueudinot, Mario. "Secuestro de bienes de prófugos en el gobierno de O'Higgins." *Revista Libertador O'Higgins* 12 (1995): 109–116.

Caulfield, Sueann, Sarah C. Chambers, and Lara Putnam, eds. *Honor, Status, and Law in Modern Latin America.* Durham, NC: Duke University Press, 2005.

Cavieres Figueroa, Eduardo. *El comercio chileno en la economía-mundo colonial.* Valparaíso: Ediciones Universitarias de Valparaíso de la Universidad Católica de Valparaíso, 1996.

Cavieres Figueroa, Eduardo. *Servir al soberano sin detrimento del vasallo.* Valparaíso: Ediciones Universitarias de Valparaíso de la Universidad Católica de Valparaíso, 2003.

Cavieres Figueroa, Eduardo. "Transformaciones económicas y sobrevivencia familiar: Elites en la transición hacia un capitalismo periférico; Chile, 1780–1840." In *Formas familiares, procesos históricos y cambio social en América Latina,* edited by Ricardo Cicerchia, 97–111. Quito: Ediciones Abya-Yala, 1998.

Centeno, Miguel A., and Agustín E. Ferraro, eds. *State and Nation Making in Latin America and Spain: Republics of the Possible.* Cambridge: Cambridge University Press, 2013.

Chambers, Sarah C. "'Drying Their Tears': Women's Petitions, National Reconciliation and Commemoration in Post-Independence Chile." In *Gender, War and Politics: Transatlantic Perspectives, 1775–1830,* edited by Karen Hagemann, Gisela Mettele, and Jane Rendall, 343–60. Basingstoke, UK: Palgrave Macmillan, 2010.

Chambers, Sarah C. *From Subjects to Citizens: Honor, Gender, and Politics in Arequipa, Peru, 1780–1854.* University Park: Penn State University Press, 1999.

Chambers, Sarah C. "Letters and Salons: Women Reading and Writing the Nation in the Nineteenth Century." In *Beyond Imagined Communities: Reading and Writing the Nation in Nineteenth-Century Latin America,* edited by John C. Chasteen and Sara Castro-Klaren, 54–83. Washington, DC: Woodrow Wilson Center Press; Baltimore: Johns Hopkins University Press, 2003.

Chambers, Sarah C. "Private Crimes, Public Order: Honor, Gender, and the Law in Early Republican Peru." In *Honor, Status, and Law in Modern Latin America,* ed. Sueann Caulfield, Sarah C. Chambers, and Lara Putnam, 29–49. Durham, NC: Duke University Press, 2005.

Chambers, Sarah C., and Lisa Norling. "Choosing to Be a Subject: Loyalist Women in the Revolutionary Atlantic World." *Journal of Women's History* 20, no. 1 (2008): 39–62.

Chandler, D. S. *Social Assistance and Bureaucratic Politics: The Montepíos of Colonial Mexico.* Albuquerque: University of New Mexico Press, 1991.

Cid, Gabriel, and Alejandro San Francisco, eds. *Nación y Nacionalismo en Chile: Siglo XIX.* 2 vols. Santiago: Centro de Estudios Bicentenario, 2009.

Collier, Simon. *Chile: The Making of a Republic, 1830–1865: Politics and Ideas.* Cambridge: Cambridge University Press, 2003.

Collier, Simon. *Ideas and Politics of Chilean Independence, 1808–1833.* Cambridge: Cambridge University Press, 1967.

Collins, Kristin A. "Administering Marriage: Marriage-Based Entitlements, Bureaucracy, and the Legal Construction of the Family." *Vanderbilt Law Review* 62, no. 4 (2009): 1085–1167.

Corrigan, Philip Richard D., and Derek Sayer. *The Great Arch: English State Formation as Cultural Revolution.* Oxford: Blackwell, 1985.

Cott, Nancy F. "Marriage and Women's Citizenship in the United States, 1830–1934." *American Historical Review* 103, no. 5 (December 1998): 1440–74.

Cox, Ricardo. *Carrera, O'Higgins y San Martín*. Santiago: Corporación de Estudios Contemporaneos, 1979.

Davies, Catherine. "Colonial Dependence and Sexual Difference: Reading for Gender in the Writings of Simón Bolívar." *feminist review* 79, no. 1 (2005): 5–19.

Davies, Catherine, Claire Brewster, and Hilary Owen. *South American Independence: Gender, Politics, Text*. Liverpool: Liverpool University Press, 2006.

Desan, Suzanne. *The Family on Trial in Revolutionary France*. Berkeley: University of California Press, 2004.

Díaz, Arlene J. *Female Citizens, Patriarchs, and the Law in Venezuela, 1786–1904*. Lincoln: University of Nebraska Press, 2004.

Dore, Elizabeth. "Unidades familiares, propiedad y política en la Nicaragua rural: Diriomo (1840–1880)." In *Entre silencios y voces: Género e historia en América Central (1750–1990)*, edited by Eugenia Rodríguez Sáenz, 21–36. San José: Editorial de la Universidad de Costa Rica, 2000.

Dougnac Rodríguez, Antonio. *Esquema del derecho de familia indiano*. Santiago: Instituto de Historia del Derecho Juan de Solórzano y Pereyra, 2003.

Earle, Rebecca. "Rape and the Anxious Republic: Revolutionary Colombia, 1810–1830." In *Hidden Histories of Gender and the State in Latin America*, edited by Elizabeth Dore and Maxine Molyneux, 127–46. Durham, NC: Duke University Press, 2000.

Felstiner, Mary Lowenthal. "Family Metaphors: The Language of an Independence Revolution." *Comparative Studies in Society and History* 25, no. 1 (1983): 154–80.

Felstiner, Mary Lowenthal. "Kinship Politics in the Chilean Independence Movement." *Hispanic American Historical Review* 56, no. 1 (1976): 58–80.

Felstiner, Mary Lowenthal. "The Larraín Family in the Independence of Chile, 1780–1830." Ph.D. dissertation, Department of History, Stanford University, 1970.

Fliegelman, Jay. *Prodigals and Pilgrims: The American Revolution against Patriarchal Authority, 1750–1800*. Cambridge: Cambridge University Press, 1982.

Fuchs, Rachel G. "Seduction, Paternity, and the Law in Fin de Siècle France." *Journal of Modern History* 72, no. 4 (2000): 944–89.

García Peña, Ana Lidia. "Madres solteras, pobres y abandonadas: ciudad de México, siglo XIX." *Historia Mexicana* 52, no. 3 (2004): 647–91.

González, Ondina E. "Consuming Interests: The Response to Abandoned Children in Colonial Havana." In González and Premo, eds., *Raising an Empire*, 137–62.

González, Ondina E., and Bianca Premo, eds. *Raising an Empire: Children in Early Modern Iberia and Colonial Latin America*. Albuquerque: University of New Mexico Press, 2007.

Grez, Vicente. *Las mujeres de la independencia*. Santiago: Imprenta Gutenberg, 1878.

Grossberg, Michael. *Governing the Hearth: Law and the Family in Nineteenth-Century America*. Chapel Hill: University of North Carolina Press, 1985.

Guardino, Peter. *Peasants, Politics, and the Formation of Mexico's National State: Guerrero, 1800–1857*. Stanford, CA: Stanford University Press, 1996.

Guardino, Peter. *The Time of Liberty: Popular Political Culture in Oaxaca, 1750–1850*. Durham, NC: Duke University Press, 2005.

Guerrero Lira, Cristián E. "Carácter de los primeros gobiernos nacionales, representación y mecanismos de legitimación, 1810–1814." In Rosenblitt, ed., *Las revoluciones americanas*, 251–73.

Guerrero Lira, Cristián E. *La contrarrevolución de la independencia en Chile*. Santiago: Editorial Universitaria y Centro de Investigaciones Diego Barros Arana, 2002.

Haney, Lynne, and Lisa Pollard, eds. *Families of a New World: Gender, Politics, and State Development in a Global Context*. New York: Routledge, 2003.

Heuer, Jennifer Ngaire. *The Family and the Nation: Gender and Citizenship in Revolutionary France, 1789–1830*. Ithaca, NY: Cornell University Press, 2005.

Hingson, Jesse. "Savages into Citizens: Families, Political Purge, and Reconciliation in Córdoba, Argentina, 1820–1862." Ph.D. dissertation, Florida International University, 2003.

Hingson, Jesse. "'Savages' into Supplicants: Subversive Women and Restitution Petitions in Córdoba, Argentina, during the Rosas Era." *The Americas* 64, no. 1 (2007): 59–85.

Hünefeldt, Christine. *Liberalism in the Bedroom: Quarreling Spouses in Nineteenth-Century Lima*. University Park: Pennsylvania State University Press, 2000.

Hunt, Lynn. *The Family Romance of the French Revolution*. Berkeley: University of California Press, 1992.

Hutchison, Elizabeth Quay. *Labors Appropriate to Their Sex: Gender, Labor, and Politics in Urban Chile, 1900–1930*. Chapel Hill: University of North Carolina Press, 2001.

Jaksić, Iván. *Andrés Bello: Scholarship and Nation-Building in Nineteenth-century Latin America*. Cambridge: Cambridge University Press, 2001.

Jocelyn-Holt Letelier, Alfredo. *La independencia de Chile: Tradición, modernización y mito*. Santiago: Planeta/Ariel, 1999.

Jocelyn-Holt Letelier, Alfredo. *El peso de la noche: Nuestra frágil fortaleza histórica*. Santiago: Planeta/Ariel, 1997.

Joseph, Gilbert M., and Daniel Nugent, eds. *Everyday Forms of State Formation: Revolution and the Negotiation of Rule in Modern Mexico*. Durham, NC: Duke University Press, 1994.

Kerber, Linda K. *No Constitutional Right to Be Ladies: Women and the Obligations of Citizenship*. New York: Hill and Wang, 1998.

Kinsbruner, Jay. *Bernardo O'Higgins*. New York: Twayne Publishers, 1968.

Kirkwood, Julieta. *Ser política en Chile: Las feministas y los partidos*. Santiago: FLACSO, 1986.

Klubock, Thomas M. *Contested Communities: Class, Gender, and Politics in Chile's El Teniente Copper Mine, 1904–1951*. Durham, NC: Duke University Press, 1998.

Lamar, Marti. "'Choosing' Partible Inheritance: Chilean Merchant Families." *Journal of Social History* 28, no. 1 (1994): 125–45.

Lamar, Marti. "Doing Business in the Age of Revolution: The Major Import-Export Merchants of Chile." In *State and Society in Spanish America during the Age of Revolution*, edited by Victor M. Uribe-Uran, 89–117. Wilmington, DE: Scholarly Resources, 2001.

Lamar, Marti. "The Merchants of Chile, 1795–1823: Family and Business in the Transition from Colony to Nation." Ph.D. dissertation, University of Texas at Austin, 1993.

Lasso, Marixa. *Myths of Harmony: Race and Republicanism during the Age of Revolution, Colombia 1795–1831*. Pittsburgh: University of Pittsburgh Press, 2007.

León Solís, Leonardo. *Maloqueros y conchavadores: En Araucanía y las Pampas, 1700–1800*. Temuco, Chile: Ediciones Universidad de la Frontera, 1990.

León Solís, Leonardo. "Monarquistas hasta el ocaso: Los 'indios' de Chile central en los preámbulos de 1810." In Rosenblitt, ed., Las revoluciones americanas, 275–331.

León Solís, Leonardo. Ni patriotas, ni realistas: El bajo pueblo durante la independencia de Chile, 1810–1822. Santiago: Centro de Investigaciones Diego Barros Arana, 2011.

Lewin, Linda. Politics and Parentela in Paraíba: A Case Study of Family-Based Oligarchy in Brazil. Princeton, NJ: Princeton University Press, 1987.

Lewin, Linda. Surprise Heirs. 2 vols. Stanford, CA: Stanford University Press, 2003.

Loveman, Brian. Chile: The Legacy of Hispanic Capitalism. 3rd ed. New York: Oxford University Press, 2001.

Loveman, Brian, and Elizabeth Lira. Las suaves cenizas del olvido: Vía chilena de reconciliación política 1814–1932. Santiago: LOM Ediciones, 1999.

Mannarelli, María Emma. Private Passions and Public Sins: Men and Women in Seventeenth-Century Lima. Albuquerque: University of New Mexico Press, 2007.

McClintock, Anne. "Family Feuds: Gender, Nationalism and the Family." Feminist Review 44, no. 1 (1993): 61–80.

McClintock, Megan J. "Civil War Pensions and the Reconstruction of Union Families." Journal of American History 83, no. 2 (1996): 456–80.

McEvoy, Carmen, ed. Funerales republicanos en América del Sur: Tradición, ritual y nación, 1832–1896. Santiago: Ediciones Centro de Estudios Bicentenario, 2006.

McEvoy, Carmen. "El regreso del héroe: Bernardo O'Higgins y su contribución en la construcción del imaginario nacional chileno, 1868–1869." In McEvoy, ed., Funerales republicanos en América del Sur, 125–55.

Meisel, Seth. "Women's Petitions and Political Culture in Early Independence Argentina." Paper presented at the annual meeting for the Consortium on the Revolutionary Era, 1750–1850, Charleston, South Carolina, February 25–27, 2010.

Méndez, Cecilia. The Plebeian Republic: The Huanta Rebellion and the Making of the Peruvian State, 1820–1850. Durham, NC: Duke University Press, 2005.

Méndez Beltrán, Luz María. "La organización de los parlamentos de indios en el siglo XVIII." In Relaciones fronterizas en la Araucanía, edited by Sergio Villalobos, 107–73. Santiago: Ediciones Universidad Católica de Chile, 1982.

Méndez Notari, Carlos. Desierto de esperanzas: De la gloria al abandono: Los veteranos chilenos y peruanos de la Guerra del 79. Santiago: Centro de Estudios Bicentenario, 2009.

Milanich, Nara B. Children of Fate: Childhood, Class, and the State in Chile, 1850–1930. Durham, NC: Duke University Press, 2009.

Milanich, Nara B. "Historical Perspectives on Illegitimacy and Illegitimates in Latin America." In Minor Omissions: Children in Latin American History and Society, edited by Tobias Hecht, 72–101. Madison: University of Wisconsin Press, 2002.

Milanich, Nara B. "Whither Family History? A Road Map from Latin America." American Historical Review 112, no. 2 (2007): 439–58.

Miller, Gary. "Bourbon Social Engineering: Women and Conditions of Marriage in Eighteenth-Century Venezuela." The Americas 46, no. 3 (1990): 261–90.

Milton, Cynthia E. The Many Meanings of Poverty: Colonialism, Social Compacts, and Assistance in Eighteenth-Century Ecuador. Stanford, CA: Stanford University Press, 2007.

Molina A., Evaristo. Bosquejo de la Hacienda Pública de Chile desde la Independencia hasta la fecha. Santiago: Imprenta Nacional, 1898.

Mooney, Jadwiga E. Pieper. *The Politics of Motherhood: Maternity and Women's Rights in Twentieth-Century Chile*. Pittsburgh: University of Pittsburgh Press, 2009.

Norton, Mary Beth. "Eighteenth-Century American Women in Peace and War: The Case of the Loyalists." *William and Mary Quarterly* 33, no. 3 (1976): 386–409.

Norton, Mary Beth. *Founding Mothers and Fathers: Gendered Power and the Forming of American Society*. New York: Knopf, 1996.

Ondarza O., Antonio S. *Doña Javiera Carrera: Heroina de la Patria Vieja*. Santiago: Editorial Neupert, 1967.

Pani, Erika. "'Ciudadana y muy ciudadana'? Women and the State in Independent Mexico, 1810–30." *Gender and History* 18, no. 1 (2006): 5–19.

Pashman, Howard. "The People's Property Law: A Step toward Building a New Legal Order in Revolutionary New York." *Law and History Review* 31, no. 3 (2013): 587–626.

Pérez Duarte y Noroña, Alicia E. "Los alimentos en la historia de México independiente." In *Memoria del IV Congreso de Historia del Derecho Mexicano (1986)*, 2 vols., edited by Beatriz Bernal, 2:871–93. Mexico City: Universidad Nacional Autónoma de México, 1988.

Pinto Rodríguez, Jorge. "La Araucanía, 1750–1850: Un mundo fronterizo en Chile a fines de la colonia y comienzos de la república." In *Modernización, inmigración y mundo indígena: Chile y la Araucanía en el siglo XIX*, edited by Jorge Pinto Rodríguez, 9–54. Temuco: Ediciones Universidad de la Frontera, 1998.

Pinto Vallejos, Julio. "El rostro plebeyo de la independencia chilena, 1810–1830." *Nuevo Mundo Mundos Nuevos*, consulted July 26, 2013, http://nuevomundo.revues.org/59660.

Pinto Vallejos, Julio, and Verónica Valdivia Ortiz de Zárate. *¿Chilenos todos? La construcción social de la nación (1810–1840)*. Santiago: LOM Ediciones, 2009.

Posada-Carbó, Eduardo, ed. *In Search of a New Order: Essays on the Politics and Society of Nineteenth-Century Latin America*. London: Institute of Latin American Studies, 1998.

Poska, Allyson M. *Women and Authority in Early Modern Spain: The Peasants of Galicia*. Oxford: Oxford University Press, 2005.

Power, Margaret. *Right-Wing Women in Chile: Feminine Power and the Struggle against Allende, 1964–1973*. University Park: Pennsylvania State University Press, 2002.

Premo, Bianca. *Children of the Father King: Youth, Authority, and Legal Minority in Colonial Lima*. Chapel Hill: University of North Carolina Press, 2005.

Premo, Bianca. "Familiar: Thinking beyond Lineage and across Race in Spanish Atlantic Family History." *William and Mary Quarterly* 70, no. 2 (2013): 295–316.

Retamal Favereau, Julio, Carlos Celis Atria, and Juan Guillermo Muñoz Correa. *Familias fundadoras de Chile, 1540–1600*. Santiago: Dirección de Bibliotecas, Archivos y Museos, 1992.

Rosemblatt, Karin A. "Forging Families: Gender, Reform, and the Popular Front State in Chile." In Haney and Pollard, eds., *Families of a New World*, 119–38.

Rosemblatt, Karin A. *Gendered Compromises: Political Cultures and the State in Chile, 1920–1950*. Chapel Hill: University of North Carolina Press, 2000.

Rosenblitt, Jaime, ed. *Las revoluciones americanas y la formación de los estados nacionales*. Santiago: Dirección de Bibliotecas, Archivos y Museos, 2013.

Sabato, Hilda. *The Many and the Few: Political Participation in Republican Buenos Aires*. Stanford, CA: Stanford University Press, 2001.

Saether, Steinar A. "Bourbon Absolutism and Marriage Reform in Late Colonial Spanish America." *The Americas* 59, no. 4 (2003): 475–509.

Salazar, Gabriel. *Construcción de estado en Chile (1800–1837): Democracia de los "pueblos," militarismo ciudadano, golpismo oligárquico.* Santiago: Editorial Sudamericana, 2005.

Salazar, Gabriel. *Labradores, peones y proletarios.* 3rd ed. Santiago: LOM Ediciones, 2000.

Salazar, Gabriel, and Julio Pinto. *Historia contemporánea de Chile.* 5 vols. Santiago: LOM Ediciones, 1999–2002.

Salinas Meza, René. *El ideario femenino chileno, entre la tradición y la modernidad: Siglos XVIII al XX.* São Paulo: Centro de Estudos de Demografia Histórica da América Latina, Univ. de São Paulo, Faculdade de Filosofia, Letras e Ciências Humanas, 1993.

Salinas Meza, René. "Orphans and Family Disintegration in Chile: The Mortality of Abandoned Children, 1750–1930." *Journal of Family History* 16, no. 3 (1991): 315–29.

Salinas Meza, René. "Las otras mujeres: Madres solteras, abandonadas y viudas en el Chile tradicional (siglos XVIII–XIX)." In *Historia de las mujeres en Chile,* 2 vols., edited by Ana María Stuven and Joaquín Fermandois, 1:159–212. Santiago: Taurus, 2010.

Salinas Meza, René, and Igor Goicovic Donoso. "Amor, violencia y pasión en el Chile tradicional, 1700–1850." *Historia y Cultura* 24 (1997): 237–68.

Salvatore, Ricardo D. *Wandering Paysanos: State Order and Subaltern Experience in Buenos Aires during the Rosas Era.* Durham, NC: Duke University Press, 2003.

Seed, Patricia. *To Love, Honor, and Obey in Colonial Mexico: Conflicts over Marriage Choice.* Stanford, CA: Stanford University Press, 1988.

Serrano, Sol, and Antonio Correa Gómez. "De patriota o sarracena a madre republicana: Las mujeres en la independencia de Chile." *Tiempos de América: Revista de historia, cultura y territorio* 17 (2010): 119–30.

Shelton, Laura. "Like a Servant or Like a Son? Circulating Children in Northwestern Mexico (1790–1850)." In González and Premo, eds., *Raising an Empire,* 219–37.

Sinha, Mrinalina. "Gender and Nation." In *Women's History in Global Perspective,* 3 vols., edited by Bonnie Smith, 1:229–74. Urbana: University of Illinois Press, 2004.

Skocpol, Theda. *Protecting Soldiers and Mothers: The Political Origins of Social Policy in the United States.* Cambridge, MA: Harvard University Press, 1992.

Socolow, Susan M. "Acceptable Partners: Marriage Choice in Colonial Argentina, 1778–1810." In *Sexuality and Marriage in Colonial Latin America,* edited by Asunción Lavrin, 209–46. Lincoln: University of Nebraska Press, 1989.

Sommer, Doris. *Foundational Fictions: The National Romances of Latin America.* Berkeley: University of California Press, 1991.

Soto Gutiérrez, Carmen Gloria. "Entre el discurso historiográfico y la escritura íntima: Otra Javiera Carrera que emerge, vive y siente." *Nomadías* no. 15 (2012): 107–37.

Stern, Steve J. *Reckoning with Pinochet: The Memory Question in Democratic Chile, 1989–2006.* Durham, NC: Duke University Press, 2010.

Stern, Steve J. *The Secret History of Gender: Women, Men, and Power in Late Colonial Mexico.* Chapel Hill: University of North Carolina Press, 1995.

Stoan, Stephen K. *Pablo Morillo and Venezuela, 1815–1820.* Columbus: Ohio State University Press, 1974.

Stuven, Ana María. "Guerreros y sabios al Panteón Republicano: Los funerales de José Miguel Infante y Andrés Bello." In McEvoy, ed., *Funerales republicanos en América del Sur,* 31–56.

Stuven, Ana María. "La palabra en armas: patria y nación en la prensa de la guerra entre Chile y la Confederación Perú-Boliviana, 1835–1839." In *La república peregrina: Hombres de armas y letras en América del Sur, 1800–1884*, edited by Carmen McEvoy and Ana María Stuven, 407–42. Lima: Instituto Francés de Estudios Andinos and Instituto de Estudios Peruanos, 2007.

Stuven, Ana María. *La seducción de un orden: Las elites y la construcción de Chile en las polémicas culturales y políticas del siglo XIX*. Santiago: Ediciones Universidad Católica de Chile, 2000.

Thomas, Gwynn. *Contesting Legitimacy in Chile: Familial Ideals, Citizenship, and Political Struggle, 1970–1990*. University Park: Pennsylvania State University Press, 2011.

Tinsman, Heidi. *Partners in Conflict: The Politics of Gender, Sexuality, and Labor in the Chilean Agrarian Reform, 1950–1973*. Durham, NC: Duke University Press, 2002.

Twinam, Ann. "The Church, the State, and the Abandoned: *Expósitos* in Late Eighteenth-Century Havana." In González and Premo, eds., *Raising an Empire*, 163–86.

Twinam, Ann. *Public Lives, Private Secrets: Gender, Honor, Sexuality, and Illegitimacy in Colonial Spanish America*. Stanford, CA: Stanford University Press, 1999.

Urrejola Montenegro, Eduardo. *Los Urrejola de Concepción: Vascos, realistas y emprendedores*. Santiago: Centro de Estudios Bicentenario Chile, 2010.

Vergara Quiroz, Sergio. *Historia social del ejército de Chile*. 2 vols. Santiago: Universidad de Chile, 1993.

Vicuña, Manuel. *La belle époque chilena: Alta sociedad y mujeres de elite en el cambio de siglo*. Santiago: Editorial Sudamericana, 2001.

Vidal, Virginia. *Javiera Carrera: Madre de la patria*. Santiago: Editorial Sudamericana, 2000.

Viroli, Maurizio. *For Love of Country: An Essay on Patriotism and Nationalism*. Oxford: Clarendon Press, 1995.

Warren, Richard A. *Vagrants and Citizens: Politics and the Masses in Mexico City from Colony to Republic*. Wilmington, DE: Scholarly Resources, 2001.

Woloch, Isser. "War-Widows Pensions: Social Policy in Revolutionary and Napoleonic France." *Societas* 4, no. 4 (1976): 235–51.

Wood, James A. "Guardias de la nación: Nacionalismo popular, prensa política y la guardia cívica en Santiago, 1828–1846." In Cid and San Francisco, eds., *Nación y nacionalismo en Chile: Siglo XIX*, 2:205–32.

Zahler, Reuben. *Ambitious Rebels: Remaking Honor, Law, and Liberalism in Venezuela, 1780–1850*. Tucson: University of Arizona Press, 2013.

INDEX

Page numbers followed by f indicate illustrations.

spondence with Javiera Carrera, 53–57; exile to Juan Fernández, 33, 53, 55, 58, 62–64; father, role as, 28, 38, 55–58, 62–63, 92; provider, role as, 42, 56–57; sequestration of assets, 55, 57, 91–92, 125; will and testament of, 62–63, 182

Carrera family, 2, 18, 27, 29, 33, 38, 44, 60–61, 63–64, 75, 89, 92, 146, 192, 217; blame placed on, 62, 68; correspondence of, 27, 38, 88; exile of, 17–18, 36, 155–56, 225; political actions of, 3, 6, 30, 32, 34, 40, 150, 225; reconciliation with members, 36, 50–51, 156; rivalries with other families, 6–8, 32–33; sequestration of assets, 2, 50, 54–58, 91, 125–26, 182. See also names of individual family members

Carrera Fontecilla, Javiera, 29, 48, 156

Carrera Fontecilla, José Miguel, 29, 48, 156, 173, 213, 236n89

Carrera Fontecilla, Luisa, 29, 156, 213

Carrera Fontecilla, María Josefa, 29, 156

Carrera Fontecilla, Rosa, 29, 156

Carrera Pinto, Ignacio José, 213

Carrera Pinto, José Miguel, 213

Carrera Ureta, Ignacio de la, 1, 29

Castellón, Juan, 117–18

Castro, Catalina, 139–40, 246n48

Cauquenes, 208

El Centinela, 208

centralism, 8

Chacabuco, Battle of (February 12, 1817), 8, 73, 89, 92, 96, 102, 119, 137, 139–40, 150–51, 161, 177, 225

child custody: in divorce cases, 189, 199–202; of foster children, 207–11, 218, 263n77; in law, 197–98, 203–4; lawsuits over, 19, 72–73, 181, 185–86, 198, 221; of out-of-wedlock offspring, 202–7; sources on, 258n14

children: crimes of fathers, punished for, 93, 102, 105, 130, 140; French revolutionary policy on, 12; as future citizens, 140, 160; in political rhetoric, 13, 19, 44, 67, 76, 93, 147, 219; in sequestration of property cases, 15, 92–94, 98–99,

103–6, 116–17, 126, 128–30, 136–39, 153, 220; of slaves, 108; sympathy toward, 93, 101, 103–5, 117–18, 120, 128–30, 137, 167, 170, 220; as victims of war, 96, 110, 113. See also alimentos; child support; custody; filial obligations; filiation; fosterage; guardianship; orphans; orphanage

child support, 3, 17, 93, 181, 185, 187, 190–94, 201–5, 207, 211, 219. See also alimentos

Chile, 6f; in comparison to other countries, 4, 11, 219–22; economy of, 4, period of "Traditional Chile," 1, 12; political culture in, 16; population of, 5

Chilean society: hierarchies in, 5, 107, 212, 218; patriarchal structure of, 15, 222

Chillán, 6f, 7, 64, 76, 107, 132–33, 136, 177

Chiloé, 6f, 73, 84, 147–48, 174; battles over, 8–9, 133, 166, 177, 214, 226

Chopitea, Pedro Nicolás de, 102, 150–52

citizenship, 14–15, 42, 45, 107, 119, 126, 137, 145, 197, 221. See also naturalization

Civil Code of Chile (1855), 11, 178, 185, 205, 207, 211, 217–19, 222–23, 227

Civil Code of France (1804), 12

Civil War, United States, 265n24

civil warfare, 4, 14, 16, 18, 75, 126, 157–58, 172, 176, 181, 212, 200; in 1829, 213; in 1830, 127, 132, 142–43, 170. See also Lircay

Civil War of 1851, Chile, 11, 173–74, 177, 213, 227. See also Loncomilla

class (social), 15, 107, 111, 126, 153, 182, 186, 193, 198, 204, 209, 218. See also Chilean society; elites; lower classes

Concepción, 6f, 9, 63, 67, 206–7; evacuation of by patriots, 76, 98, 108–10, 112, 162, 226; evacuation of by royalists, 64, 76, 118–19, 140, 146, 226; population of, 5; sequestration of property in, 114–20, 133, 135–36, 142, 148; Trinitarian convent of, 64, 76; warfare in, 7, 31–32, 76–77, 79–84, 87, 98, 225

Conde, José, 35, 55

Loveman, Brian, 16
lower classes, 14, 180, 193, 195, 212, 218, 222. *See also* Chilean society; servants

MacKenna, Juan, 7, 33–34
Magallanes, Manuel, 155
maintenance allowances, 17–19; broad range of, 188; laws on, 182–86, 211; lawsuits over, 187–88, 197–98, 210, 212, 221, 260n24, 261n33; policies on, 188, 217; and sequestration, 99. See also *alimentos*
Maipú, Battle of (April 1818), 8, 36–37, 118, 140–41, 149, 168, 177, 225; anniversary of, 50
Mapuche, 5; as military allies, 76, 120; territory controlled by, 5, 64, 82, 114, 153, 177, 226
Marcó del Pont, Casimiro, 27, 65, 67, 69–71, 73, 95–96, 120, 150, 225
Marín de Solar, Mercedes, 265n11
marriage: civil registries of, 218–19; laws on, 13, 187, 191, 198, 211–12; national identity ties to, 114, 119, 141, 150–51; parental consent for, 54, 178–79, 187, 190–91, 211–12, 261n36; promises of, 187, 192–93, 203; regulation of, in the military, 156–57, 160–61, 163–67, 169, 172, 175–76, 178–81, 217, 222, 227; regulation of, for royal officials, 4, 30, 70. *See also* divorce; elites; *montepío*; Royal Pragmatic
Martínez de Luco y Caldera, Ramón, 20f
masculinity, 135, 139; of fathers, 45, 59–60, 191–92; of providers, 15–16, 120, 135, 183, 186, 219; of public figures, 41, 44, 59–61, 214–15; of soldiers, 15, 159–60; of sons, 9, 59–60, 87; of workers, 219. *See also* gender; honor
Matta, Guillermo, 215
men. *See* dependents; family roles; fathers; husbands; masculinity; sons
Mena, Pedro, 129
Mendoza, 6f, 89, 155–56; Carrera brothers tried and executed in, 35, 40–41, 43, 45, 55–56, 213, 225–26; patriot émigrés in, 7–8, 33, 37, 47, 52, 65, 70, 168; postal routes through, 35, 37; Rosa Valdivieso,

detained in, 39. *See also* Andes; Andes, Army of the
merchants, 4, 9–10, 25–26, 63, 65, 71, 119, 127, 134, 149–50, 190, 193, 196, 210, 212; as émigrés, 99, 102–3, 113–14, 126, 139–40, 146, 152
migration, 14–15, 18, 80; forced, 76, 79, 88, 112–13, 115. *See also* refugees
Milanich, Nara, 218
military service, 3, 15, 28, 88, 158–59, 168, 188, 216; calculating years of, 168, 174; ordinances for, 166, 222; and social mobility, 166, 168–70, 174, 177, 180; wartime bonus for, 167. *See also* heroes; heroism; honor; marriage; *montepío*; nationalism
Molina, Ignacio, 129–31
montepío: and Battle of Chacabuco, 161, 169; death in battle as basis for, 158–61, 168–69, 173–76, 180; decree of 1826 on, 163–64, 168, 179; law of 1829 on, 164–70, 174–76, 180, 226; lawsuits over, 161–62, 166–67, 172–73, 174–76; and morale, 159–61; and postindependence regulations, 178–81, 217, 222, 227; and reconciliation, 158, 170–74, 181, 220; and Spanish regulations, 156–57, 160–61, 163, 165, 168, 174–76, 178–80; and state finances, 159, 168, 178, 180–81; and waivers for unlicensed marriages, 165–66, 172, 176; for widowed mothers of unmarried sons, 158–59, 161, 172; years of service as basis for, 163–65, 167, 174, 180. *See also* orphans; pensions; veterans; widows
Montevideo, 6f, 40, 151; exile of Javiera Carrera in, 39–40, 54, 155, 182, 226; exile of José Miguel Carrera in, 33, 37, 39, 44, 46, 49, 57, 225
Montt, José Santiago, 141–43, 147
Montt, Manuel, 11, 145, 173–76, 178, 205, 213, 215, 226–27
Motherhood, in political rhetoric, 39, 55, 90, 128, 135, 159
mothers, 15, 41, 219; *alimentos* held responsible for, 184, 187–89, 195–96;

and child custody, 196–207, 209–10; in the civil code, 211; unmarried, 186–87, 191–94, 198, 204–5, 207–10, 222. *See also* Carrera, Javiera; Fontecilla, Mercedes; *montepío*

Nacimiento, 80, 111
nation: defense of, 156, 171; and family metaphor, 11, 14, 15–16, 31, 90, 106, 109–10, 120, 126, 128, 153, 157, 160–61, 173, 175, 181, 214, 216; as independent, 11, 162; sacrifices for, 16, 19, 159, 161, 181; service to, 163, 214. *See also* fatherland; "greater Chilean family"; national identity; nationalism; nation-state formation; *patria*
national identity, 3, 14; in familial terms, 92, 120, 153, 157, 160. *See also* nationality; naturalization
nationalism: and familial terms, 150, 221; and military service, 158; and war, 170. *See also* heroes; national identity; patriotism
nationality, 12, 14, 114. *See also* naturalization
nation-state formation, 2–3, 11, 16, 18, 89, 121, 125, 127, 157, 214, 221–23
naturalization, 12, 14, 52, 57, 117, 119, 133, 141; during French Revolution, 12; symbolic loss of, 78, 103, 135, 246n51. *See also* nationality
Novísima Recopilación, 184
Novoa, Jovino, 153
nuns, 64, 69, 76, 81, 148, 206. *See also* convents

O'Higgins, Ambrosio, 7
O'Higgins, Bernardo, 7, 96f; abdication of, 9, 132, 226; and aid to refugees, 106–10; commemoration of, 214–16; and evacuation of Concepción, 76, 109, 112, 226; and exile, 9; independence, role in, 8, 32–36, 38, 65, 72, 76–77; pensions awarded by, 157, 161–62, 167; rivalry with Carreras, 17, 27, 32, 34–35, 38–40, 50–51, 53; sequestration orders

on, 92, 96–97, 101, 103, 111, 113–14, 117, 119–20, 125, 142, 189; as supreme director, 9–10, 17, 36, 38, 49–51, 55, 57–58, 75, 89, 128, 155, 193, 216, 225
Olivares, María Cornelia, 107, 136–37
Order of Isabel the Catholic, 152, 177
Ordóñez, José, 83
orphanage, 210, 218
orphanhood, as metaphor, 43, 47, 67, 164
orphans, 13, 118; and French Revolution, 12; of war, 9–10, 139. *See also montepío*; orphanage; pensions
Osorio, Mariano: as captain general, 7, 26–27, 52, 64–65, 69–70, 120, 225; expeditions commanded by, 32, 62, 140–42, 149–51, 225; sanctions against patriots ordered by, 53, 55, 65, 70; sequestration orders on, 70, 91, 94–95, 98–99, 101, 126

Palacios, Andrés, 86–87
Palazuelos, María, 70
pardons, 9, 14, 170, 173, 181, 220; of Chileans, by king, 53, 70, 95; of Freire loyalists, 11, 158; requests for, 50, 56, 69; in Senate Resolution of 1821, 143, 146, 222. *See also* amnesty; reconciliation
partisanship, 10, 28, 61, 126, 170, 215, 217, 222. *See also rival political factions*
paternal authority. *See* filiation; patriarchal authority
paternalism, 4, 6, 11, 15–18, 64, 71, 157, 162, 221; of postindependence government, 21, 93, 104, 107, 112, 120, 138, 170, 174, 179, 181, 197, 216, 220; of royal government, 13, 44, 68, 70, 74, 101, 221
paternal responsibility, 3, 16, 19, 45, 49, 59, 82, 89, 181–82, 185, 188, 191, 197, 200, 211, 217, 222; and obligation to provide, 16, 18, 21, 181, 185–96, 209–11, 214, 217, 219–20
paternity: determination of, 12, 15–16, 186–88, 190–92, 194–95, 197, 202–4, 206–7, 210–12, 217, 223. *See also* illegitimacy
patria: in political rhetoric, 26, 40, 77, 79, 85, 105, 137, 141. *See also* fatherland